WORKERS AND EMPLOYERS IN JAPAN

WORKERS AND EMPLOYERS IN JAPAN

The Japanese Employment Relations System

edited by
Kazuo OKOCHI
Bernard KARSH
Solomon B. LEVINE

PRINCETON UNIVERSITY PRESS
UNIVERSITY OF TOKYO PRESS
1974

Copublished by
Princeton University Press
and
University of Tokyo Press
Library of Congress Catalog Card Number: 73-2464
ISBN: 0-691-03097-9

Preface

Research is almost always the result of cooperative effort—either directly or otherwise. This study is most explicitly cooperative. It is the joint product of thirteen individuals who had known each other for varying periods long before they began planning this book. Subsequently, they were assisted by a good number of others.

The study began sometime in 1964 or 1965 when it became apparent to us that for most Westerners Japan was still a mysterious and puzzling, even exotic, place. The strategies and tactics by which workers were managed in that society seemed to be especially puzzling. Several members of our group had published in English various studies on Japanese industrial relations, but there existed no single volume in English that purported to describe and analyze what John Dunlop has called the "industrial relations system" of the country. This work, then, is intended to fill that gap. The various chapters and their relations to each other were designed to provide a detailed guide to understanding Japanese industrial relations as a major aspect of Japan's reemergence into the top ranks of world industrial powers.

If the project had a specific beginning it was the result of a meeting in Boulder, Colorado, while one of our collaborators, Taishiro Shirai, was visiting the United States. Karsh was then visiting at Stanford and Levine was at the University of Illinois. The idea for the study developed as the three of us spent a week-end renewing old friendships and discussing mutual interests. We agreed that it was time to examine carefully developments in Japanese industrial relations and to present the results to a Western audience which was increasingly interested and concerned but largely without comprehensive, up-to-date materials. Further, we decided that our study would be the product of Japan's best scholars in the field. Specifically, we hoped to provide interested scholars with the work of Japan's own experts rather than the views of foreign observers. We decided that we would put this idea to our friend and colleague Professor Kazuo Okochi, then newly elected president of the University of Tokyo and in our view Japan's leading institutional economist. If he saw merit in it, we would ask him to join us as a senior collaborator.

In 1966, shortly after arriving in Tokyo for the year, Karsh discussed the project with Professor Okochi, who suggested that Karsh block out an outline of the volume's sections, chapter headings, and content, a timetable, possible resources for funding the work, and the like. Further discussions of the outline convinced Professor Okochi that it was feasible, however difficult it would be for the two Americans to join eleven Japanese in what was sure to become an unprecedented international effort.

Names of possible collaborators were suggested and Professor Okochi accepted the task of approaching Professor Mikio Sumiya, then dean of the Faculty of Economics at the University of Tokyo, with the suggestion that he join us and help to identify the most appropriate persons for the group and recruit them for the project. Thus, in addition to the two Americans and Professors Okochi and Sumiya, the following joined to form what we called the Japan Industrial Relations Research Group: Professor Toru Ariizumi, then dean of the Institute of Social Science attached to the University of Tokyo; Professor Wakao Fujita, Institute of Social Science, University of Tokyo; Professor Naomichi Funahashi, Faculty of Economics, Hōsei University, Tokyo; Professor Hisashi Kawada, Faculty of Economics and Executive Director (now emeritus), Institute of Management and Labor Studies, Keiō University, Tokyo; Professor Hideaki Okamoto, Sociology Faculty, Hōsei University, and Research Officer, Japan Institute of Labor, Tokyo; Professor Taishiro Shirai, Faculty of Commerce,

Hōsei University, Tokyo, and former Chief Research Officer, Japan Institute of Labor, Tokyo; Mr. Takeshi Takahashi, Chief of Research, International Labour Office, Japan Branch, Tokyo; Professor Masumi Tsuda, Faculty of Economics, Hitotsubashi University, Tokyo; Professor Shojiro Ujihara, Institute of Social Science, University of Tokyo. Professor Kazutoshi Koshiro, Faculty of Economics, Yokohama National University joined us later and worked with Professor Ujihara. It was agreed that the Americans would act as organizers and conceptualizers of the study and would be responsible for translating the material into English and for synthesizing and editing. The Americans would also themselves contribute appropriate substantive materials.

At least once a week through the Tokyo winter and spring of 1966–67 the entire group met, except for Levine, who remained at Illinois. Our discussions aimed at working out the specifics of the project. We sought a common perspective which would guide everyone's work, agreement on the elements that constitute Japan's industrial relations system, the focus and direction each collaborator ought to take, and finally a working outline of the book we were determined to produce. From the beginning we were determined to avoid producing a set of relatively disconnected essays or a "reader" on Japan. Comprehensiveness, integration, and, insofar as possible, a single writing style were what we sought. Expenses at this stage were generously met by the Division of Research and Study of the Japan Institute of Labor, then under the direction of Shingo Kaite.

During the course of our weekly planning meetings, it became clear that our progress would be substantially accelerated if we could all spend some time together away from the distractions of Tokyo and our normal duties and thereby complete the necessary planning. The Asia Foundation, through James Stewart, then head of its Tokyo Office, provided us with a generous grant which permitted us all to move to the East-West Center at the University of Hawaii for ten days of intensive discussions. Expenses while in Hawaii were met in part by Ford Foundation funds made available through the Keiō-Illinois Research and Exchange Project in Industrial Relations. Levine joined us there. The center provided us with meeting space and other local logistic support. Our discussions at Hawaii produced a detailed working outline of the volume as a whole and detailed outlines of the contributions of each collaborator. We also agreed that, with the exception of Okamoto and Takahashi, who would write in English, all other participants would write in Japanese. Thus the initial drafts of each chapter were prepared.

All manuscript drafts were received by Karsh and Levine at Illinois and were translated with the help of Yoshihiro Mizuno and Makoto Ohtsu, then graduate students in labor and industrial relations at Illinois. The draft translations were edited and sent to the original writers for checking on the accuracy of the translation. During the spring and summer of 1968, Karsh and Levine met individually and on occasion together with each collaborator in Tokyo to review progress and offer suggestions for changes that might better integrate the separate chapters and minimize duplication and overlap, and proposed additions where gaps were apparent. Second drafts were subsequently prepared to incorporate changes now made by original writers and these drafts were again returned to Tokyo for checking and approval. Karsh met with each collaborator in Japan in the summer of 1970. At that time, each chapter was again reviewed in detail with each of our colleagues and all final changes were confirmed. Further, where appropriate and necessary, statistics were up-dated and the bibliography expanded. All in all, the project took five years from initial planning in Tokyo to the completion of a final manuscript.

We are, of course, very much indebted to Mr. Kazuo Ishii, Associate Director and Editor, University of Tokyo Press, and to Mr. Shigeo Minowa, Director of the Press. Mrs. Barbara Dennis, now at the Industrial Relations Center at the University of Wisconsin in Madison, was invaluable to us in permitting us to exploit her editorial skills. Mrs. Elizabeth Kodama at the University of Tokyo Press has incurred our debt for her assistance in copy editing the final manuscript. There have been still others who have helped, particularly Japanese students and Keiō University faculty members visiting the University of Illinois Institute of Labor and Industrial Relations. Some funds required for the completion of the project were provided directly by both the Institute of Labor and Industrial Relations and the Center for Asian Studies at the University of Illinois.

This, then, is our joint view of the system by which men are managed in Japan, with primary focus on the modern sector of the economy. It is a depiction of the essential institutional and structural elements that comprised Japan's industrial relations system as of the beginning of the 1970s. It is presented with the expectation that continuing observation of Japan's rapidly changing society will suggest insights into general processes and mechanisms of change and into the specifics that explain how changing values, norms, and institutions affect the management of workers in industrial societies.

Bernard Karsh

Champaign, Illinois
December, 1972

Contents

WORKERS AND EMPLOYERS IN JAPAN

1. The Concept of a National Industrial Relations System

The principal objective of this study is to bring into sharp focus the major features of industrial relations in Japan as they have evolved and unfolded, especially in the highly dynamic years since World War II. For more than half a century, Japan has ranked among the few industrialized nations of the world. Yet, while considerable attention has long been given to the leading industrial societies of Europe and North America, comparatively little analysis has focused on the Japanese experience with industrialization. In particular, there has been a paucity of careful studies in English or other Western languages of the evolution of industrial relations in Japan; far less is known about the Japanese case than about various European countries, the United States, and Canada. It has become generally recognized that knowledge of industrial relations is central to understanding the complexities of human behavior in industrial societies. As a result, organized study of industrial relations has grown rapidly in recent years in many parts of the world. With the growth of industrial relations as a field of inquiry with its own conceptual base and methodological approaches, there has been increasing recognition that the case of Japan provides still another important variant of industrial behavior, but it has continued to lack systematic and comprehensive treatment.

The materials contained in the chapters that follow hopefully will provide perspectives and insights concerning aspects of Japanese industrial relations hitherto unclarified. In addition, they should provide the basis both for comparing Japanese industrial relations experience with that of other industrially advanced nations and for helping to gauge the course of industrial relations in the newly emerging countries which look to the industrialized countries for appropriate patterns of development.

Our second objective is of broader theoretical import. To examine industrial relations in any setting raises a host of questions that rest on assumptions about what is worthwhile investigating. It is our contention that the study of industrial relations at a national level is a key approach to analyzing the nature, or distinguishing features, of the industrialized society. Thus, we begin from the point of view that in the process of industrialization a nation tends to undergo profound changes in authority and power relationships among its participants and institutions. Merely because of the technological and economic arrangements that must accompany the industrialization process, these relationships inevitably display characteristics that differ in significant degree from those that were obtained prior to the unfolding of the process. It is to be expected, moreover, that industrialization will bring in its wake substantial shifts in political configurations and significant modifications in ideological and value systems which affect these relationships. Such changes in all likelihood will generate continuing tensions among the members and institutions of the industrializing society. Thus, throughout this volume, we will emphasize the analysis of change, to the extent that change can be detected and evaluated. This approach contrasts with other studies, which tend to stress continuity and traditional forms of behavior and values.

The Analysis of Industrial Relations

The relationships that emerge in modern industry are most clearly delineated in settings where human work must be performed in order for the industrial apparatus to operate and undergo elaboration. It is these relationships that have been called a system, or set of systems, of industrial relations, since the imperatives of industrialization demand a relatively ordered arrangement of expected behavior among those who participate or act in organizing, operating, and changing the industrial apparatus. Central to the industrial relations system is the obvious fact that industrialization requires two principal sets of actors: the managers (or decision-makers), who direct the operations, and the "managed" (or order-takers), who carry out the operations according to directions received. These employer-employee (manager-worker) arrangements come to embody guiding rules in many forms, written and unwritten, explicit and implicit, which specify to a greater or lesser degree the behavior expected of members of each group. The rules may cover an almost infinite variety of subjects, although the most commonly recognized are those that deal with wages, hours, discipline, welfare, and physical conditions of work. Some rules, especially those pertaining to the exercise of authority, deal with the procedures for regulating relations between managers and managed or their representatives, such as unions; others bear upon relations among the managed themselves, or between the managed and the physical industrial apparatus.

In addition, a third set of actors inevitably becomes involved in rule making. This set consists of governmental agencies which either are directly concerned with setting the conditions and procedures for making rules or directly determine the rules that apply to industrial work. Depending upon the type of political and governmental system that emerges in a nation in the process of industrialization, such agencies may exercise greater or lesser control over the rules that come into force or over the procedural machinery developed to set up the rules. In turn, looking to the larger setting of political power distribution in the society, the governmental agencies themselves may be subject to sets of rules as to their operations and decision making bearing upon the world of industrial work.

Our focus on the definition of industrial work derives basically from the idea already mentioned that the process of industrialization is generated by and in turn further generates a new ordering of functions and rules without which industrialization would be impossible. New labor markets must be created, labor forces must be recruited or assembled, specialization of functions and division of labor must be set up, different inducements to work must be provided, altered work hierarchies must be established, to mention but a few of the more important processes necessary for industrialization. It is because of these requirements that industrial relations is often defined as the "web of rules" relating managers to workers (or the managed), workers to workers, and workers to work, and the context in which these relations arise and take their meaning. Further, as John Dunlop observes, the total set of rules affecting the behavior of the three actor groups in their relationship to one another in the industrial work place comprises a system, or actually a subsystem, of the socioeconomic system.[1] We accept this conceptualization, particularly in view of its usefulness for penetrating the inner meaning of human relationships in industrial societies.

This approach recognizes, however, that the analysis of an industrial relations system may be undertaken at various levels of abstraction. For example, at least three levels are immediately suggested as analytical foci: (1) the nation as a whole, in which the emphasis is placed upon that combination of rules, actors, and values which, taken together, structures or constrains the managed with respect to the managers (and vice versa) as general propositions valid for the society as a whole; or (2) within the national context, an industrial sector, say, a given industry or a given region, in which one focuses on the rules and actors specific to that sector; or (3) an industrial plant, or even the shop floor, in which the objects of analysis are the particularistic rules and actors at this level. In a comprehensive analysis, of course, all of these levels should be examined and understood. Problems of inclusiveness as against exclusiveness are always faced by researchers, and hard and fast choices have to be made regarding the unit under observation and analysis.

We have chosen here to focus on the national level. We are, of course, aware that by doing so we are forced to a level of general-

1. See John T. Dunlop, *Industrial Relations Systems* (New York: Holt, 1958).

ization and abstraction that may not permit the discussion of all relevant units and the diversity of relationships; where marked deviations exist we attempt to account for them. We have chosen to examine the Japanese industrial relations system as a national entity because we are interested in attempting to provide a basis for comparing that system, in its major features, with what has developed in industrially advanced countries of the West. In so doing we expect to throw light upon the nature of the chief hypothesis our study aims to investigate, as discussed below.

Thus, our study of Japan is intended, not only to delineate the characteristics of Japan's national industrial relations system itself, but also, in doing so, to contribute to the goal of comparing national industrial relations systems in a variety of distinctly different historical and cultural settings. As has often been stated, Japan is the only example of a nation outside the Western world (assuming the Soviet Union to be basically Western) that has reached an advanced stage of industrialization. There has been some question as to how much Japanese society differed from Western societies in its preindustrial era, yet there is little doubt that it did differ enough to call for a careful comparison of what has emerged in Japan since industrialization began about a century ago with what has come to characterize Western industrial societies.

This volume does not directly undertake these comparisons except by inference (and, as will be noted, by necessity, because of the difficulties of applying concepts derived from Western experience to the Japanese case). However, it is hoped that the materials provided in this study will eventually permit just such an undertaking in far greater detail than is possible in the chapters of this book. The details examined chapter by chapter become the basis for a set of general propositions taken up in the concluding chapter of the volume.

The Idea of Convergence

The key proposition underlying this study, borrowed in part from Marxian analysis and more recently argued in *Industrialism and Industrial Man*,[2] is that almost everywhere the world is in the grip of industrialization. Surely, although unevenly, this hypothesis suggests, virtually every nation is compelled to undertake industrial growth and, once the process gets started, growth continues indefinitely and ineluctably, at least until a postindustrial era emerges.

The world's experience to date has been that industrialism does not descend upon the preindustrial society in one fell swoop, although the rate at which industrialization occurs has not been uniform among nations or even among parts of a given nation. While we are not directly concerned here with the forces that set industrialization in motion, it appears likely that the original conditions do have an important bearing upon the pace and structure of a country's industrialization. There is considerable certainty, however, that, once the process gets underway, it continually advances to higher and higher degrees of industrialization, whatever the cultural or national setting in which it takes place. Eventually, each society becomes industrial—at least in the statistical sense of half or more of its working population being engaged in nonagricultural occupations, divided into secondary and tertiary production or service sectors.

Thus far, only a handful of all the nations of the world have reached this stage. Most countries are at best only at the threshold and, indeed, it may be questioned whether industrialization is the only possible path for them to follow. Nonetheless, it appears plausible that, given the enormous development of international communications and information, the recent emergence of many new nations from colonial status, the problems generated by rapid population growth, and other similarly potent factors, industrialization has become a pervasive national objective throughout the world.

If this is the case, then the implications of industrialization for human relationships require close scrutiny. Industrialization must rely heavily upon the application of science and the utilization of precise technologies, if in fact it is to succeed. Both science and technology, although constantly changing in response to new discoveries, imply a standardization throughout the industrializing

---

2. Clark Kerr, John T. Dunlop, Frederick Harbison, and Charles A. Myers, *Industrialism and Industrial Man* (Cambridge: Harvard University Press, 1960).

world far more universal than the technical arrangements that existed in preindustrial societies. The key question that follows from this is whether universalized technology must be accompanied by a given, perhaps relatively narrow, range of possible human relationships and institutional forms or whether instead it may be congenial to a much wider variety of particularistic relationships and forms.

In more general terms, a critical problem for social science research is whether the relationships that define industrial work tend inevitably to take on the same characteristics regardless of the cultural and historical setting and regardless of the pace and structure of industrialization along the way. Some have argued that the "logic of industrialism" surely leads to this result. This argument has been called the "convergence" hypothesis; it means that technology, politics, economics, sociology, and psychology in the industrializing society take on a common configuration that supports the continued spread of industrialization throughout the society and permits industrialization to increase in complexity.

In terms of the concept of work, the end results hypothesized are a commonality, wherever industrialization takes place, of such phenomena as:

1. Work specialization, for which scientific training and education are all-important
2. Occupational professionalism with strongly enforced merit-based requirements for entry and advancement
3. Complete flexibility and mobility of the labor force in its allocation to industrial activities and processes
4. A reward or compensation system geared to rationally calculated economic contributions
5. The proliferation of economic bargaining between occupational or professional groups on a collective basis
6. An all-pervasive ethic of the value of science and scientific applications and innovations
7. A diffusion of political power throughout the society
8. The release of the individual from personalized or subjective controls over his behavior both at work and outside work.

One way to characterize this predicted evolution might be as the transformation of the society from one based on endowed status or ranking relationships to one based on achievement, or from particularistic to universalistic relationships. Still another way, to use Weberian terminology, is the replacement of substantive with formal rationality.

The thesis of the Marxians, and for that matter of the authors of *Industrialism and Industrial Man,* is simply that convergence is inevitable. Their analyses conjure up the image of an approaching uniformity in values, institutions, and relationships whenever industrialization occurs, although they disagree about the nature of the uniformity. Our concern here is not the type of uniformity that is supposed to emerge but whether uniformity emerges at all. We do not take issue with the notion that social change follows in the wake of industrialization or that it gives rise to further industrialization. Rather, in this study of Japan's industrial relations, we are engaged more fundamentally in an attempt to establish whether the range of variability in the social outcomes that accompany or result from the process of industrialization is wide or narrow. Our final chapter returns to this question, comparing selected aspects of the Japanese experience with that of the West.

Examining the Proposition: The Japanese Case

In choosing to examine Japanese industrial relations, we have selected a national case which has not only been inadequately portrayed in non-Japanese languages but which also, we believe, furnishes perhaps the most exciting laboratory now available for testing the notion of convergence. This has been especially so since the mid-1950s, when Japan, having completed its economic reconstruction and recovery from World War II, began to grow at an unprecedented rate which has been maintained to the present. An annual increase averaging about 10 percent in real gross national product and at least 15 percent in the index of manufacturing output is bound to induce sudden and widespread changes in economic structure, distribution of income, levels of consumption, mode of life, and complexity of technology and organization. Accordingly, while the historical benchmarks from which the growth began receive some attention, the major concern of the data presented here is the contemporary product of the changes that have occurred in the past twenty-five years.

It has been alleged that Japanese industrial relations present a rather unique case of a nation that has maintained, throughout the industrialization process, a traditional set of rules for behavior at work, or that traditional behavior was fully "exploited" in the course of industrialization. Indeed, it has been argued that Japan's success in industrializing is due in large measure to the preservation of traditional work relations. For example, the neglect of job evaluation and job descriptions, at least in the detail found in advanced Western countries, in favor of preindustrial status criteria such as age, sex, and length of service for the purpose of distributing work rewards is referred to as a carry-over to the modern factory of the status-differentiating indexes found in "traditional" village life. Further, Japan's so-called lifetime employment system is often said to be representative of the transfer to modern industry of formal rules that characterized the social relations of feudal Japan. Also, a superficial examination of the quality of manager-worker interpersonal relations in the modern Japanese factory easily, and perhaps erroneously, leads to the conclusion that these relations represent a carry-over to modern industry of the "paternalistic" master-servant status relations of traditional Japanese society.

Whatever the case may be with respect to these kinds of issues, it is now contended that, given the readily observable changes that industrialization has wrought in Japan's labor and product markets, political system, ideology, and levels of technology, such "traditional" elements, regardless of how they have been accommodated in the past, are now incompatible with the imperatives of further industrialization. Thus, the lifetime employment system is increasingly under attack or at least subject to sustained debate among Japanese employers, scholars, and others.

For example, in the face of the 1965–66 drop in the Japanese economic growth rate, worker redundancy became a serious problem for a large number of firms. In this connection, there was considerable discussion of the advisability of introducing a "layoff" system and thereby further modifying or even abandoning altogether the lifetime employment system. Similarly, as a result of the mounting shortage throughout the 1960s of young workers entering the labor market, plus perhaps the increased standardization of task requirements resulting from the growing use of common technologies, it appears that the "traditional" system of wage payment based on age and length of employment, sex, and amount of formal education may be gradually abandoned in favor of so-called merit criteria which relate rewards to actual technical requirements and make distinctions between workers on the basis of skill or job-related attributes rather than personal attributes.

Nonetheless, it is also argued that these two long-established characteristics of Japanese work relations actually have tended to perpetuate traditional Japanese "localism" and "particularism" despite the existence of national markets and standardized technologies and the weakening of regional or local differences in other spheres of human activity. Thus, it is asserted, the practice of lifetime employment combined with a reward system based upon traditional notions of "age and grade" is not necessarily incompatible with the requirements of industrialization, since these systems do not seriously impede rational operation of the product and labor markets. Increasing industrialization and economic growth may have, in fact, permitted the traditional practices to persist and perhaps even flourish.

These issues are merely illustrative of a large number of questions that should be answered concerning the ways (i.e., the rules) by which the "managed" are actually managed in Japan. They also illustrate, however, that, as Japan continues to assert itself as one of the leading industrial nations of the world, its existing system of industrial relations exhibits tensions and conflicts over whether changes in the rules of industrial work must take place. Thus, a major concern in this volume is to examine carefully the structure of rules that has emerged in the light of accompanying tensions and conflicts.

While the attempt to identify such conflictual tendencies is essential to throwing light upon the convergence hypothesis, it does not necessarily imply agreement or disagreement with the allegation that tradition carried forward from the preindustrial period has always characterized Japanese industrial relations. Evidence has continuously accumulated, as we shall see throughout this study, that what have often been taken as premodern traditions actually were social innovations or new responses to the industrializing process itself. Like other peoples, the Japanese are not averse to inventing "traditions."

Key Questions and the Scope of Analysis

This work, then, is addressed to three basic questions:

1. Considering the Japanese industrial relations system as consisting of a structure of rules, actors (including institutions and organizations), and values which are differentiated and elaborated into major identifiable elements, what are the essential facts that describe each of these major elements as they exist in the early 1970s?
2. What factors or forces—social, economic, political, and technological—may account for these facts?
3. What tensions or tendencies toward change may be seen in each of the major elements and in the system as a whole, and what may account for such tensions or tendencies?

In dealing with these key questions, the chapters that follow may be divided into four broad categories:

I. *The context*, including the broad outlines of the cultural and historical base, particularly the economic, political, social, and legal arrangements from which industralization proceeded and in which the present industrial relations system is implicated (Chapters 2–5).

II. *The rule-makers and rule making*, the leading actors in the system (managers, workers, and government), and the processes by which their interactions get worked out, particularly in collective bargaining and the settlement of disputes (Chapters 6–10).

III. *The substantive rules themselves* and the ways in which they are administered at the plant and public agency levels, including rewards for work, employment opportunities, and livelihood security (Chapters 11–12).

IV. *An overview* of these individual elements taken as a system by which the "managed" are managed, compared with what we have loosely referred to as the Western system (Chapter 13).

In all of this, of course, we are looking for evidence that may throw light upon the relevance of the convergence proposition and, in so doing, we are concerned with tendencies toward change and the social tensions these tendencies have generated.

2. The Emergence of Modern Japan

The Mid-Nineteenth Century

Foreign Pressures

In the mid-nineteenth century, Japan and Korea were the only countries in the Far East that had no open economic relations with the Western world. Beginning in the sixteenth century, European countries advanced eastward, succeeding in opening the ports of China by the first half of the nineteenth century.[1] These events attracted the economic and political attention of the Western powers to the Far East. Soon afterward the United States established its frontier on the West Coast, and by the mid-1800s it had crossed the Pacific and at least made appearances in the Far East. As European and American traders came by steamship to the Orient, they found it necessary to locate bases that could supply coal and water. Thus, Japan became the focus of their attention.

At the same time the coal-mining industry was operating rather extensively in the northern Kyūshū area and around the Inland Sea, and Japan had developed a coal market along her coast to supply fuel for the salt industry. As China had not yet developed coal mining, it was not difficult for Japan to supply the ships of Western countries with the coal they needed for fuel. Thus, the benefits of trade with Japan became apparent to Western nations, which consequently began to make strong demands that Japan be

---

1. The ports were opened after the Treaty of Nanking was signed in August 1842. This was a direct outgrowth of the Opium War.

opened to foreign intercourse. Under this pressure, Japan ended more than two centuries of isolationism.

Portugal was the first Western country to come to the Far East, and in the sixteenth century it formed a close relationship with Japan. Spain soon followed. In 1635, however, the Tokugawa government decided on a policy of isolation out of fear that local *daimyō* (feudal lords) might become economically and politically strong through foreign trade and that the pressure of the advanced Western countries might mount with the rapid propagation of Christianity as a lever. Since Holland, by then the most influential country in the Far East, was interested in trade rather than the propagation of Christianity, the Tokugawa government did permit limited trade with the Dutch at Nagasaki, the only door left open to the West. However, around the middle of the nineteenth century, tension in the Far East increased with the arrival of Britain and France in addition to Holland.[2] Moreover, Russia, having conquered Siberia, penetrated from the north, and the United States crossed the Pacific from the east to secure a foothold in East Asia.

The opening of its ports greatly affected Japan's industrialization. The Western industrial nations brought to Japan not only cotton and wool textiles and metal products but also weapons (warships, guns, and so on) for the Tokugawa government and its feudal clans. Silk, tea, coal, and other products became Japan's main exports. One effect of this early trade was that feudal lords attempted to accumulate funds by monopolizing special export products in their own particular clans. Farmers and peasants also became involved in competing for the overseas markets. The silk industry in Japan, formerly confined by the limited domestic luxury market, made contacts with the European market and expanded rapidly in size and production technology; its productivity increased accordingly. The coal-mining industry experienced similar development in response to the increased demand of foreign vessels for fuel. These developments in the Japanese silk and coal markets, viewed in conjunction with the world market, suggest that Japan was developing into a "monoculture" economy.

2. Seiichi Iwao, "Sakoku" [Isolation] in *Nihon rekishi: Kinsei* [Japanese history: The modern period], vol. 2 (Tokyo: Iwanami Shoten, 1963).

Soon Japan began to import textiles, metal products, and machinery manufactured in the developed Western countries. However, with Japan's own primary industrial products becoming specialized export goods, the resulting tendency toward monoculture suggested the possibility that Japan might become more or less colonized. Furthermore, the Western powers increasingly competed militarily among themselves to win influence in Japan; thus, for a time, it appeared that Japan might follow China in falling under the domination of the West.

It has been alleged that Japan was able to fend off colonization because, among other reasons, she began relationships with Western nations all at once with the opening of her ports. One result of this was the maintenance of a balance of power among the competing countries, which enabled her to avoid becoming subordinate to any one Western nation. Since China and Korea were in a similar situation, however, this alone is not sufficient to explain why Japan was able to remain independent and to succeed in industrializing. Other reasons may be found in Japan's economic and political history.

Internal Economic Development

The Tokugawa government was based upon a static system of agricultural production isolated from outside economic pressures. The government's fundamental policy was to collect as much taxes as possible in order to "keep farmers neither alive nor dead." Within this system, however, three factors emerged which were to destroy the static social relationships.

The growth of cities was one such factor. Under the traditional system, each local lord kept his samurai retainers around his castle and provided them with payment in kind rather than land. Thus, most of the clan's tribute was collected from peasants and brought into the castle town. Merchants handling this tribute and craftsmen producing various products for the lord and his retainers came to live in the castle town, now a populated "feudal city." Edo (now Tokyo), the seat of the Tokugawa government, had a population of one million by the end of the eighteenth century,

making it one of the largest cities in the world at that time. Four
hundred thousand people lived in Osaka, the commercial city,
and 300,000 in Kyoto, the residence of the powerless emperor.
Major castle towns of powerful lords had populations ranging
from 50,000 to 60,000.[3]

Living in such an urbanized community, the lord and his retainers needed currency to buy commodities. The lord obtained
money by selling through merchants all the tax rice he could spare.
Since most farmers were taxed to an extent that resulted in a subsistence level existence, they were left virtually without any surplus
that could be converted into funds for purchasing consumer products. Therefore, a money economy could not develop extensively
among the farmers, and instead an economic system based upon
exchange of goods evolved from the economy of the feudal lords.

The development of a money economy, however, increased the
economic power of the merchants; and in this process, as the living
standards of the lords and their retainers became more and more
luxurious, their debts to the merchants increased. They continued
to borrow money from the merchants at rising interest rates, and
ultimately the lords and retainers themselves became impoverished.

Nevertheless, status distinctions among the samurai, farmers,
craftsmen, and merchants were clearly established under the feudal system. The merchant's status was the lowest, and his activities
were judged least important in terms of the value system of the
Tokugawa era. This value system had not broken down even at
the end of the period, when the merchant, because of his increased
economic power, had become more influential than the lord and
the samurai class. A merchant class thus formed and in turn developed a commercial network. This development may be one of
the most important reasons the Japanese economy was not dominated by foreign merchants such as the overseas Chinese, who
came to control the commercial networks of Southeast Asia. At
the same time, and unlike the compradors of China, the Japanese
merchants avoided subjection to Western capital.

Moreover, even under the relatively static economic system of

3. Takeshi Toyoda, *Nihon no hōkentoshi* [Feudal cities in Japan] (Tokyo: Iwanami
Shoten, 1951), esp. pp. 148–80.

this isolationist era, agricultural productivity gradually increased. The feudal lords, suffering from financial difficulties, collected as tribute almost all increments in agricultural production. However, a portion was retained by the rich farmers who often served as village officials. Through their hands a money economy penetrated into the villages, and the debt-ridden peasants gradually parted with their mortgaged lands which thereby came under the control of the rich farmers. These well-to-do farmers, by employing seasonal and daily workers under serflike conditions, also produced *sake* (rice wine) or *miso* (bean paste), which helped them accumulate capital. Such was the beginning of industrialization, which enabled Japan to expand her silk, tea, and coal-mining industries and to agree to open trade with Western countries.

Farmers and Workers

Because the economic basis of the feudal society was agricultural production, the lord needed to tie the farmer to the land and limit his mobility, as was done also in feudal Europe. Furthermore, in the static agricultural society, the rural population found it necessary to limit its own reproduction, as its capacity to support the total population was fixed. In fact, Japan's population remained rather stable at little more than thirty million during the entire two hundred and fifty years of the Tokugawa regime. Since there was neither a major war nor a serious problem of famine except at the end of the era, these possibilities cannot account for the population stability. Rather, it was the result of more direct means than even those suggested by Malthus for population control. This was the so-called *mabiki* (thinning out), whereby unwanted pregnancies were aborted and unwanted babies killed by their parents.

Though the agricultural population was controlled, it does not follow that the poor farmers were able to alleviate their burdens. The Tokugawa government prohibited peasants from leaving their clans. Yet, if reduced to destitution in the face of poor crops, they often violated the feudal restrictions by becoming vagabonds and escaping into the cities or mines. If they escaped and were captured, they were forced to work at penal labor for the government or were sent back to their clan. Toward the end of the Tokugawa era, however, the number of runaway serfs and vagabonds notably increased.

Some runaways were employed by rich farmers to work on farms or in other businesses, such as manufacturing or mining. At the end of the Tokugawa era, at least by 1850, there was a considerable number of these workers who were free labor in the sense that they were no longer bound to the land, although the framework of social relationships had not changed. While they were employed on a contractual basis, the social status of masters and servants remained unchanged. In this sense these workers cannot be compared with modern wage labor, but they were in fact daily wage earners and may have represented the beginnings of the development of wage labor.[4] On the whole, runaway workers existed outside the framework of the feudal society and were regarded as almost nonhuman.

Craftsmen had developed highly restrictive guild and indenture systems, but by the latter half of the eighteenth century several factors were contributing to their destruction. As the masters' class became hereditary, journeymen had little opportunity to become masters and thus remained employed wage earners. Also, the guild and apprenticeship systems, which had not been firmly established, began to break up. Craftsmen could be divided into two groups: those who served the ruling class, such as swordsmiths, gold lacquer craftsmen, and so forth; and those who served the common people—carpenters, plasterers, and the like. Many of the latter lived in rural areas where neither the training nor the regulations of the guild system covered their trades. With the impoverishment of agricultural villages at the end of the Tokugawa era, these craftsmen were forced to migrate to the cities where

4. Mikio Sumiya. *Nihon chinrōdōshiron* [History of Japanese wage workers] (Tokyo: University of Tokyo Press, 1955), pp. 9–15. See also Rekishigaku Kenkyūkai (historical Studies Research Society), ed., *Hōken shakai kaitaiki no koyō rōdō* [Employed labor during the breakdown stage of feudal society] (Tokyo: Aoki Shoten, 1961), especially the chapters by Takamasa Ichikawa, "Nōson kōgyō ni okeru koyō rōdō" [Employed labor in rural industry], and Toshio Furushima, "Bakumatsuki no nōgyō rōdōsha" [Farm-employed workers at the end of the Tokugawa era].

they upset the regulations of the city guild system by reducing the journeymen's wage rates.[5]

By the mid-nineteenth century such economic and social conditions were generating forces that were substantially undermining the feudal system and were the harbingers of a new order. A missionary who came to Japan just after the opening of her ports wrote:

> Even in this authoritarian state there is also public opinion that cannot be overlooked. The power of public opinion is increasing all the time. Voices of the merchant class people are more influential. Having become acquainted with foreign traders, they learned what kind of social status the merchant has in other countries. They have become aware of their rights and more demanding of their rights. Therefore, it can be expected that in the near future the third estate will develop and have considerable influence on voicing this opinion in the people's diet.[6]

Political and Social Chaos

By the 1850s, the government and clans were suffering from serious financial problems. The lords found it increasingly difficult to provide their retainers with reasonable rations and often cut down on the amount of stipends or postponed payment. As a result, the lower-ranking samurai were forced to earn their livelihood by producing such things as lanterns or umbrellas at home—a condition that embittered them and generated antiregime sentiments among them.

The feudal lords, faced with these financial difficulties, increased the tax burden on the farmers. This resulted, as a matter of course, in land exploitation and made the farmers particularly susceptible to natural disasters and frequent crop failures. Poor crops meant starvation and despair; not a small number of farmers and their families actually starved to death.

5. Sumiya, *Nihon chinrōdōshi-ron*, pp. 36–37. See also Motō Endō, *Shokunin no rekishi* [History of the craftsman] (1956), pp. 142–71, 186–212.
6. Sakunoshin Motoda, *Rōkantoku Uiriamasu* [Williams: Our old bishop], p. 72.

In addition, as the relative prices of gold and silver favored the latter at the time Japan opened her ports, a great deal of cheap Japanese gold flowed out to foreign countries. This outflow, coupled with an increased amount of bad currency minted by the Tokugawa government at the end of the period, created serious inflation which affected the samurai and farmer classes, driving them to the point of bankruptcy.

The farmers' first response to exploitation and despair was a direct (and, because it was direct, illegitimate) appeal to the Tokugawa government and other agents of authority for relief. This appeal, however, did not save them from even worse poverty at the end of the Tokugawa era. Finally, the peasants resorted to village or countryside riots, attacking official residences, burning merchant houses, and battling with the samurai. This disorder developed into *yonaoshi ikki* ("reform-the-world" riots) in the mid-1860s, as farmers ranged over the country trying to reform society.

At the same time, as described above, foreign pressures were at work, demanding that Japan open her ports and backing up their demands with demonstrative actions along the coast. In an attempt to cope with these threats, the Tokugawa government and various clans spent large amounts of money on the production, repair, and maintenance of weapons. They attempted to import foreign-made warships, to build fortresses, and to introduce advanced Western technology.

Clans in southwest Japan, which had fairly frequent contact with Western countries, notably Satsuma (Kagoshima), Chōshū (Yamaguchi), Hizen (Saga), and Tosa (Kochi), were especially enthusiastic about such efforts, as they were keenly aware of the need to introduce advanced technology, especially military weapons, as a result of their experiences both in battle and in trade with Western countries.

At that time, moreover, the power of the Tokugawa government was declining rapidly in the face of the increasing political and economic disorder. Major clans in the southwest, especially Satsuma and Chōshū, took advantage of the situation by attempting to escape from Tokugawa control. Their strategy for taking over affairs of state and political leadership was to advocate exclusive loyalty to the emperor. Thus, the imperial family, which for generations had been maintained only as a symbol of national integration, was suddenly highlighted.

The Traditional Value System

To understand the cultural context surrounding Japanese industrialization, the value system of the Japanese people at the end of the Tokugawa period should be examined. The articulation of the emperor system with the values of the Japanese people and with Shintoism and Confucianism deserves special attention.

Two separate value systems coexisted in the Tokugawa period. One was the value system of the samurai or ruling class; the other was that of the common people—the farmer, the artisan, and the merchant.

In the samurai system, Confucianism was central. The Tokugawa government adopted Confucianism as official doctrine and diffused Confucian principles among the people in order to establish an ethical base for government control. After its introduction from China, Confucianism had been transformed by the Japanese, and among its various schools the Chu Hsi school became the most influential because of its stress upon the natural order which interprets and legitimates the existing social order as the natural state of affairs. While Chinese Confucianism emphasized filial piety, the Japanese also taught loyalty to the ruler as a central value.

Among the doctrines of Confucianism, one that had a great impact on the Japanese way of thinking was worldly rationalism—the notion that all things can be understood by learning the basic or underlying principle. This was a pragmatic or quasi-scientific view, which stood in contrast to the Buddhist view of the world as subject only to ceaseless change. Since the confrontation with nature was considered harsh in Western societies, rationality was sought not so much in nature as in human conduct acting upon and changing nature rationally. In contrast, since natural conditions were viewed as mild in Japan, harmony between nature and human beings, or society, was easy to emphasize. Nature was regarded as having its own laws, while human society, such as the family or village, was considered a part of nature. Accordingly, it was thought that the rationality of nature carries over to human society.

Moreover, as Japanese Confucianism centered around the logic and ethics of person-to-person social relationships, it left room for rather free and rational thought and action in the relationship between man and nature. This behavior was reflected in the positive attitude of the Japanese toward introducing Western technology at the end of the Tokugawa era. The notion of "Oriental ethics and Western technology" has persisted in Japan's relationship with the West.

This type of Confucianism became the dominant ethical view of the samurai class but was almost entirely unknown among the common people. Although this ethic penetrated to the rich farmers and village officials, who were next in rank to the samurai class, it was incomprehensible to the ignorant common people, whose view of the world was based on a different set of ideas. Buddhism retained some influence as an ethical base for the commoners, even though government policy toward religion had reduced Buddhism to a mere shell. Although the government did not recognize Buddhist religious values, it utilized Buddhism as a major instrument for placating the ignorant. Since Confucian ethics were officially proclaimed as guiding principles, the government required denominational registration in order to take measures against Christianity, which, after spreading rapidly in the sixteenth and early seventeenth centuries, had been forbidden in 1612. Under this policy, every person had to register at one of the Buddhist temples distributed throughout the country. This registration system thereby provided the government with demographic data which might be useful for assuring public order. Buddhism thus came to function primarily as a registry system without spiritual activity except for a few denominations like the Shin sect.

What actually supported the value system of the common people was a secular philosophy based on the traditional *ie* (household) and on the village community as a group of such households.[7]

7. *Ie* is a kinship community relating to land and other means of livelihood, which is handed down from ancestors and must be passed on, in turn, to descendants. It differs from the family in Western societies.

To them anything superhuman was regarded as a "god." In each family and village there was a guardian deity to whom prayers were offered for survival and prosperity. Existence centered not on other-worldly interests but on the present and on how to continue living in the community of the *ie* and the village.

This faith in the community persisted among the common people for a long time and created a powerful continuing basis for the implicit influence of the imperial family. The ancestors of the imperial family, who worshiped at the Ise Shrine, were thought of as the guardian deities of all the people. As a result, the authority of the imperial family was maintained through this religious faith. During the social chaos at the end of the Tokugawa period, such relatively primitive religious ideas were organized and articulated in the idea of "reverence for the emperor" in the attempt to overthrow the shogunate. Thus, Shintoism became established.[8]

The Meiji Restoration

Reorganization of the Political System

Political and social disorder resulted in the Meiji Restoration of 1868. Opinions differ as to whether it was a revolution aimed at destroying the feudal system and building a modern state or an effort to reform and rebuild the worn-out system.[9] Since this question is relevant to an analysis of the Japanese industrial relations system, it should be considered in detail here.

First, as noted earlier, there were already the beginnings of industrialization in Japan by the end of the Tokugawa era. Thus, Japan was not entirely unprepared for the introduction of Western technology. A money economy had spread, and a new class of

8. For ideologies at the end of the Tokugawa era, see Masao Maruyama, *Nihon seiji shisō-shi kenkyū* [Study of the history of Japanese political thought] (Tokyo: University of Tokyo Press, 1952), and R. N. Bellah, *Tokugawa Religion: The Values of Pre-Industrial Japan* (Boston: Beacon Press, 1970 [reprint of 1957 edition]).

9. See *Meiji ishin-shi kenkyū* [Studies on the history of the Meiji Restoration], 6 vols. (Tokyo: Heibonsha, 1959), especially vol. 3; and E. H. Norman, *Japan's Emergence as a Modern State* (New York: Institute of Pacific Relations, 1940).

merchants and small manufacturers had appeared. However, the Restoration did not depend on these factors alone. The principal impetus came from the major clans in the southwest, such as Satsuma, Chōshū, Tosa, and Saga, and especially from the lower-class samurai in these clans. Because of the necessity of earning livelihoods, these samurai were engaged in small cottage industries. Yet, although they were samurai and thus members of an elite class, they were caught in the impotence of the old political system and oppressed by the new forces of economic change.

In order to maintain independence from outside pressures, the Meiji government introduced new administrative and legislative techniques as well as engineering and technology related to production. Such changes were necessary also for the development of military power. The new government enacted various reforms, which were welcomed by the emerging capitalist class, and it attempted to put them into practice in a way that would not only maintain the traditional political power and social relationships but also derive positive advantages from these traditional elements. The government did not attempt to establish new social relationships.

For example, the government eliminated the traditional status system which ranked samurai, farmer, artisan, and merchant in descending order by reorganizing the system into three strata: peers, samurai, and commoners. The samurai class lost its ruling privileges, and universal military conscription was imposed. Although conscription generated occasional revolts among dissatisfied samurai, it served to train the people in the discipline of modern large-scale organizations and to spread the consciousness of an integrated nation among them.

The guiding principle in the formation of an integrated state, however, was the emperor system. Government leaders were most concerned with enhancing the spiritual and political power of the emperor, not with establishing a democratic system. The military were the armed forces of the emperor, and overall political authority belonged to him, a policy enunciated in the Meiji Constitution and the Imperial Rescript on Education.

In the early 1880s a movement for democracy called the Jiyū-minken Undō (Civil Rights Movement) appeared among two groups—samurai who were unable to gain access to political power, and the rising merchant class in rural areas. In order to fend off this threat, the government promised a popular parliamentary system, although it proclaimed that the "emperor, descended from one lineage in all times," possessed supreme power and that the proposed parliament would be based on his benevolence as a part of his sovereignty over the people. Thus, the government succeeded in creating the emperor system by incorporating the demands of the new era within the major elements of the old tradition.

The spiritual and religious aspects of the emperor system were clearly evident in the Imperial Rescript on Education of 1890. The rescript, which emphasized the notion of Japanese Confucianism in a modern form, was notable for two points: (1) the Confucian ethics of filial piety and loyalty, formerly influential only among the samurai class, now became a nationwide ethical code; and (2) these values were imposed from above, supported by the spiritual authority of the emperor. Thus, the emperor was endowed not only with political power but also with moral authority.

The establishment of such absolute power without significant resistance from the people was possible because of the persistence of the community faith discussed earlier. At the same time, this faith functioned as a symbol of the integrated state which had been threatened by both internal and external pressures. In this sense, the Restoration of 1868 represented the reorganization and strengthening of the traditional value system.

Innovation in the Economic System

Reform of the economic system was one of the key problems confronting the new Meiji government. The economic basis of the Tokugawa feudal system had been the land taxes collected from the farmer. However, industrialization required a market mechanism in which the key product, rice, would circulate as a commercial good. Thus, it became necessary to shift the basis of national finances from commodities to currency. For this reason, in

1873 the Meiji government revised the land tax system, certifying landowners as modern private property owners and at the same time maintaining the tax revenues as before but now requiring that taxes be paid in money rather than in kind.

Government expenditures for social and political reform rose dramatically in order to strengthen the military forces and defense industries to cope with the threat of the Western powers, and to maintain social order by repressing the dissatisfied samurai class. New administrative organs were established; the social and economic institutions were reformed so as to be more adaptable to a market economy; and advanced Western technology was introduced. Accordingly, it proved impossible to lower land taxes, which amounted to 80 percent of the total tax revenues in the 1870s.

The introduction of Western technology required particularly large expenditures. As the government itself demanded advanced technology and since private capital was insufficient for such investment, the government built modern factories and employed foreign engineers and skilled workers at high pay. Thus, the development of the large-scale factory system in modern Japan started with government enterprises.

The government also encouraged the development of light industries through private enterprise. After the opening of the Japanese ports, imports of cotton goods increased rapidly, creating a serious balance-of-payments problem which was met by a decision to establish a domestic cotton-spinning industry. It was also necessary to establish an export industry in order to be able to import Western technology and other resources. For this purpose, it became most desirable to proceed with the industrialization of silk manufacturing. The government purchased machinery for cotton spinning from England and for silk spinning from Italy and France. Model plants were constructed to introduce and spread the new technologies.

Since the merchants and the rich farmers had accumulated some capital, they were ready to embrace the government's industrial encouragement policy and to establish and manage cotton-spinning and silk-manufacturing factories. Most of the new silk filature entrepreneurs had only limited resources, so the new technology was transformed and proceeded only at a pace and scale compatible with the available capital.

At the end of the Tokugawa period, tenanted land comprised one-fourth of the total cultivated acreage in the farming villages. Rent was still paid in kind to the landowners even after the land tax began to be paid in currency. Although the land tax was cut by one-sixth in 1877, the tenant farmer's rents-in-kind were not reduced but continued to be collected and stored by the landowner. Furthermore, during the period of inflation after 1877, the price of rice rose enormously. Again, the tenant farmer did not benefit because rice continued to be the staple food for his family, and after his family's needs were met very little was left over to be sold; however, the price rise was beneficial to the landowner, who sold rice, thereby greatly increasing his income. Since land was such a safe investment, more and more acreage became concentrated in the hands of landowners who leased it to tenants. As a result, by the 1890s about 40 percent of all cultivated land was tenanted, and about half of the farmers were tenants.

The fact that the tenant system was widespread meant that investment in land increased without relation to farm productivity. A considerable part of the income that the landowners received as rent flowed into cities and was invested in commerce and industry. Though agricultural productivity gradually increased after the Restoration, it remained relatively stagnant compared with the productivity increases in manufacturing and mining. In these circumstances, the living conditions of the tenant farmers remained very poor; the smallest misfortune often resulted in bankruptcy for the farmer.

Socially and economically, farming villages stagnated while industrialization proceeded in the cities. Thus, as the traditional social and economic relations remained, a dual structure formed. Investment funds left the farming villages for the cities, where industrialization was progressing under the impetus of modern technology and production methods.

Although the government took precautions against the economic encroachment of foreign countries, Japanese social and economic conditions were unstable. As a result, foreign investment remained quite limited until the end of the Meiji period

(1868–1912). Nevertheless, despite the creation of social and economic imbalances, Japan succeeded in industrializing.

Formation of Management

Although Japanese industrialization developed by introducing advanced Western technology and employing foreign manpower, industrial management was promoted by the Japanese themselves. This factor may be distinctively Japanese, compared with the development of management agencies in India and the situation in developing nations after World War II. The status of the industrial manager in Japan, however, was not high at the beginning. Even though the Restoration changed the political system drastically, it resulted in the development of an absolutist bureaucratic government. Economic activity was still regarded as the common man's business, and consequently the industrial manager was not considered to be among the social elite.

As described earlier, Japanese industrialization was initiated in government enterprises engaged primarily in defense production. Managers in these establishments were largely government bureaucrats who originated among the lower-class samurai and had acquired some knowledge of modern industry and technology. They were progressive bureaucrats but not business managers. Few were competent, and, as a result, many of the enterprises they managed failed due to the excessive bureaucratization of overall administration. This was especially the case in those government enterprises in which advanced Western technology was introduced.

Later the merchant class emerged as leaders of private industry. This was possible because production was still on a small scale and there was room for merchants to play important roles in bridging the gap between production and consumption. Furthermore, merchants had already accumulated considerable capital by the end of the Tokugawa era, since most economic activity at that time was concentrated in commerce because it was most profitable.

While the social status of the merchant improved after the end of the Tokugawa period, it remained far below that of the bureau-

crat.[10] Since commercial activity implied an element of specula-
tion, and since fraud and deception often increased profits, merchants were deprived of the prestige that would have altered their
low position in the traditional status system.

The route to becoming a manager also preserved the traditional merchant status. A young man would begin his career in
commerce by becoming an apprentice for several years, expecting
promotion to clerk in charge of the day-to-day business. When he
acquired a family, he might be helped by his master to establish a
branch of the parent company or even his own firm. In the large
commercial enterprises, the competent clerk became a real manager; sometimes, when he was adopted into the owner's family,
he was able to gain power in the enterprise. This may have been
the origin of zaibatsu management, to be discussed in detail later.
It was not until after the 1890s that the large commercial firms
began to employ for middle management and engineering positions personnel who were high school and university trained.

The farming village was another source of managers, particularly for the silk-manufacturing industry. As noted earlier, this
industry developed especially among rich farmers during the
1870s and 1880s and, as a result, became subordinate to the merchants who controlled the market. The farmers themselves did
not develop into industrial managers, for after 1890 they tended
to become landowners deriving income from tenants. Rather it
was their sons who went to school to learn how to become middle
managers in the large enterprises in the cities.[11]

Thus, the relatively low status of the managers persisted into
the Meiji period, while a wide status gap between the white-collar
employee and the manual laborer remained within the management organization, with the latter at the bottom of the structure.

10. For example, Eiichi Shibusawa, a leading Meiji industrial entrepreneur, who
left his government post as tax department head and entered private industry, re-
marked: "People engaged in trade and industry at that time were of extremely low
dignity, and they were not allowed to see a government official unless they stood at a
distance of more than six meters." *Shibusawa Eiichi Jijoden* [The autobiography of
Eiichi Shibusawa].

11. For a more detailed account, see Johannes Hirschmeier, *The Origins of Enter-
preneurship in Meiji Japan* (Cambridge: Harvard University Press, 1964).

Formation of the Working Class

The effects of the political and social changes of the Meiji Restoration were felt by each class. The samurai, for example, lost status. Under the new political and military systems imposed by the Meiji government, the professional warrior became obsolete and, as a class, its traditional loyalty to the former lords remained an obstacle to the formation of a united nation. Moreover, government support of about 400,000 households of former samurai, which absorbed 40 percent of the budget, became so great a burden that in 1875 the government canceled samurai stipends. Instead, some 80 percent were paid in bonds with 7 percent interest which produced annual incomes of less than ¥70 on the average—hardly enough to guarantee a living standard equal to that of even the lowest-paid workers, who then earned from 20 to 30 sen daily (100 sen equaled 1 yen). The inflation of 1877 further reduced the real value of samurai incomes, forcing them to pawn or sell their bonds.[12]

Part of the craftsman class suffered the same deprivation. The armorers, gold lacquerers, and lacquer craftsmen, who had depended upon the demand of the feudal ruling class for their products, also lost the basis of their livelihood. The blow was greatest for the craftsmen who, prior to the Restoration, had enjoyed high status and tight guild regulations. Guild regulations of other craftsmen, such as carpenters and plasterers, had already been weakened toward the end of the Tokugawa period, so they were unable to offer any serious resistance when between 1868 and 1872 the Meiji government dissolved the guilds.[13]

Since they possessed no skills adaptable to the new society, the samurai and those craftsmen whose skills were no longer in demand had no means of support other than to earn their livings as unskilled laborers, working at home, or as day laborers or rickshaw pullers. Thus, their new position reduced them to the lowest class.

The largest group to migrate to the cities comprised poor peas-

12. Sumiya, *Nihon chinrōdōshiron*, pp. 53–66.
13. Ibid., pp. 33–38.

ants. Since both sale of land and migration were permitted after the Restoration, marginal and destitute peasants sold their land and escaped to the city slums with their families. However, lacking the skills that modern industry requires, they too were ill-equipped to become industrial workers.

Manpower for Japanese industrialization came essentially from two groups. The first and major source was children of former samurai, craftsmen, and peasants who migrated to the cities. They were employed as apprentices and became modern factory workers after training. Since young women were in demand to work in cotton and other mills, during the latter half of the nineteenth century mills were usually built near the slums which, inhabited by families who had migrated from the countryside, were then the main source of labor.

Craftsmen themselves were the second source of factory labor. Since training of skilled workers was urgently needed for industrialization, the skills of traditional craftsmen were used whenever possible, while many were retrained to become skilled workers. For example, in the government-controlled Yokosuka Shipbuilding Yard, the policy was "to employ one hundred ironworkers and one hundred woodworkers who had mastered the traditional Japanese art of production, to have them trained by Frenchmen in Western skills, and to let those who had mastered the methods train those who had not."[14] It was common for a carpenter to become a woodworker and for a casting craftsman to become an iron or steel molder.

There are several points to be noted in the training of Japanese skilled workers. Although an apprentice system was developed in the skilled trades in the 1880s, as in the case of the traditional craftsmen there were few skilled workers who knew how to train others. Further, the content of training was not systematized. Therefore, the apprentice had no way of learning a skill other than by imitating his master or a senior workman. Actually apprentices were used as low-wage helpers. The term of training was not fixed, and the skill of the workman was rated by his expertise

14. *Yokosuka kaigun senshō shi* [History of Yokosuka naval shipbuilding], vol. 1, p. 7.

and the length of his experience. Wage rates by job were not established.

Since most of the new industrial workers came from the ranks of poor peasants or former traditional craftsmen and former samurai who had been downgraded, their social status was low in comparison with that of artisans, and this was clearly reflected in their pay. Even the skilled workers received wages considerably lower than the daily pay of the craftsmen. Table 2.1 shows the earnings of the new printing trade workers compared with those of traditional carpenters and plasterers and day laborers in this early period.

Table 1.2
Daily Wages of Craftsmen and Workers, 1885–1892
(Unit=sen)

	1885	1887	1892
Carpenter	22.7	22.3	27.0
Plasterer	23.3	22.6	27.0
Printing worker	19.8	21.9	22.0
Day laborer	15.7	16.0	18.4

SOURCE: *Teikoku tōkei nenkan* [Imperial statistical yearbook].

Disruption and Rebuilding of Employment Relationships

The collapse of the feudalistic Tokugawa system brought about the breakdown of Confucian values, the ethical code of the ruling class. Although the primitive and traditional communal life code that existed in the people's creed became the basis of the emperor system, it was never verbalized in any articulate and systematic fashion.

The collapse of traditional values and the social turmoil accompanying the Restoration facilitated the government's attempts to introduce and disseminate new ideas and codes of conduct. For example, in 1872, when the Meiji government abolished human traffic, it was ordered that:

> traffic in humans or disposition of humans at the discretion of a master and exploiting human beings for their entire

lives or for a certain period of service should always have been banned as inhumane. The traditional practice of lifetime service under the guise of apprenticeship is actually human traffic exploitation. Therefore, such practices are strictly prohibited from this time on.[15]

However, as a result of the new freedom to sell land, to migrate, and to make occupational choices, the communal regulations were relaxed, the family system became unsettled, and traditional social relationships as a whole were loosened. The relationship between artisan and apprentice is an example. Not only was the apprenticeship, which was similar to bondage, abolished, but also the system itself was no longer maintained. The master-apprentice relationship became loose compared with earlier periods. According to a government survey,

> the relationship between employer and employee completely changed after the Restoration and old practices were broken. The attitude of the employee to the employer, the apprentice to the master, became like the day laborer. The employee and the apprentice have come to believe that work is only for wages. They are no longer concerned with the interest of the employer or the master, they try to obtain higher wages, they are unsettled and in the habit of moving from job to job, and they have no time to master one job for a lifetime. Such practices exert a great influence upon industry in general.[16]

The fact that the traditional master-apprentice relationship was broken does not mean that a contract relationship between employer and employee was established. Since the existing status relationship remained, the sense of responsibility for carrying out terms of a contract did not develop. Rather, workers frequently left their employers and migrated from job to job (for a more detailed description of job mobility, see Chapter 4).

In large plants, such as arsenals, where turnover of skilled workers often interfered with operations, a fixed-term employment sys-

15. *Dajōkan tatsu* [Cabinet ordinance], No. 295.
16. *Kōgyō iken* [Proposals on encouraging industry] vol. 18 (Tokyo: Ministry of Agriculture and Commerce, 1883), p. 92

tem was introduced to meet this problem. Typically, an employment contract for five or seven years was concluded with certain workers to whom higher wages were paid under an agreement that they were "not to withdraw from the company for any reason." However, even this type of contract was not fully observed.

The disruption of social relationships and the breakdown of traditional values occurred not only in employment relationships but also in society as a whole. The Meiji government, whose goal was the formation of an integrated nation-state, regarded as urgent the stabilization of social relationships. It sought to establish a value system compatible with the political system which located the center of authority in the emperor. Such a system was based on the Meiji Constitution and the Imperial Rescript on Education, which, in substance, restored and legitimated a hierarchy of authority. The idea of hierarchical relationships between master and servant, teacher and student, husband and wife, parent and child, and so forth, was disseminated through school and military education. On the basis of such stabilized social relationships, industrialization began to develop at the beginning of the 1890s.

Industrialization and Its Social Effects

By about 1890, Japan had completed preparations for full-scale economic development, and industrialization quickly followed. The production index rose from 4.5 to close to 200 between 1880 and 1930, and the number of industrial workers increased from about 400,000 in 1895 to almost 3,000,000 in 1930. Because an industrializing society requires workers whose skills are commensurate with its technological level, the society creates institutions to train skilled workers and develops an administrative system to supervise their employment and production. Western technology, which was the base upon which Japan industrialized, produced many similarities between Japan and Western countries, often more apparent than real, in institutional and administrative arrangements. Not only the Western apprenticeship and foreman systems but even the idea of American craft unions was introduced.

Further analysis, however, reveals that the apprenticeship and foreman systems and the craft unions were all affected by the characteristics of Japanese industrialization, and each system developed along lines quite different from the Western pattern. Regarding the apprenticeship system, for example, many of the new skilled jobs had not previously existed in Japan. Since no norm had been established for skill, content, and term of apprenticeship, training was not clear. As a result, the length of a worker's experience rather than the content of his training became the principal determinant of his qualifications as a craftsman. Although daily wage rates were established for artisans, there were no set rates for industrial workers, so from the beginning the skill of each worker was evaluated and ranked on the basis of experience and dexterity. Because apprenticeship standards were not established, job categories were never created.

The lifetime employment and length-of-service wage systems, however, are to be regarded not as traditional social relations but rather as innovations that developed in response to new needs. These are among many aspects of contemporary Japanese industrial relations that were created during the process of industrialization.

Before examining this development process in detail, it is useful to point out a few of the problems that underlay Japan's economic growth. The rapid spread of education was seen very early as an important need, and at the beginning of Japan's industrialization, four years of education was made compulsory. The percentage of males enrolled in school exceeded 80 percent by the end of the 1890s; and at the beginning of the twentieth century the rate for males age 6–10 years reached 95 percent and that for females 90 percent.[17] In 1908 compulsory education was extended to six years.

One factor favorable to economic development was the existence of a single common language. The spread of education facilitated the ability of the people to understand the new culture

17. Ministry of Education, *Economic Development and Education in Japan.*

and to communicate their understanding. However, while education became a powerful means of conveying the will of the nation
or of the enterprise, it also generated new social problems by
awakening the workers' personal and social consciousness.

Another noteworthy factor was the employment of female factory workers, who until the 1930s comprised a majority, reflecting
the prominent position of the textile industry. Most of the young
women workers migrated from the villages to work for relatively
short periods in order to supplement family incomes. For these
workers, a special labor administration system was developed that
emphasized company dormitories.[18] In order to understand contemporary industrial relations, however, we should direct our attention to the male workers.

The Development of Unions

The first labor union similar in organization and function to
Western unions appeared in Japan subsequent to the onset of the
Sino-Japanese War in 1897. Its origins can be traced to the Japanese who had gone to California to work and there formed a group
to study the developing American labor movement. Some then
returned home with the outbreak of the war, and among them was
Fusataro Takano,[19] who had met President Samuel Gompers of
the American Federation of Labor (AFL) and had been appointed
the AFL organizer for Japan. Takano, by winning the cooperation
of the intellectuals and appealing to the workers, succeeded in
establishing a union among ironworkers. Shortly thereafter unions
were formed among railway engine drivers and printing workers.

These unions not only were American-type craft unions in organization, as Takano advocated, but also followed the AFL ex-

18. See *Nihon shihonshugi to rōdō-mondai* [Japanese capitalism and labor problems]
by Mikio Sumiya, Kenichi Kobayashi, and Tsutomu Hyōdō, 1967, esp. ch. 2, sec. 3.
(Tokyo: University of Tokyo Press, 1967).

19. Concerning the relations among Takano, the AFL, and Japanese labor movement, see "Takano Fusatarō to rōdō-undō" [Fusatarō Takano and the Labor Move-
ment] by Mikio Sumiya, in *Keizaigaku-ronshō*, April 1963, and *Nihon rōdō undōshi no
hitokoma* [A chapter in the Meiji labor movement] by Hyman Kublin, 1959.

ample; a major function of the ironworkers' union was "to relieve its members in case of accidents and misfortunes," and a portion of the union dues was allocated to a fund for assisting members in case of injury, illness, death, or fire. The establishment of these unions demonstrated not only the considerable increase in the number of industrial workers resulting from the growth of the factory production system but also the sense of unity that emerged among workers in the same craft or trade based on common interests shared and communicated as they moved from shop to shop.

These unions, however, had several unique characteristics related to the social conditions of the Japanese working class. Because of the status system that underlay employer-employee relationships, they were unable to influence the labor market by regulating apprenticeships or bargaining collectively with employers. Therefore, the unions could not perform, either directly or indirectly, the function of improving the working conditions of their members. As a result, the purpose of the union was merely to assist members through mutual-benefit and other self-help activities. For example, the rules of the ironworkers' union stated that its purpose was to maintain and increase the interest of the trade, to cultivate good practices, to eliminate old abuses, and to help its members in distress in order to elevate the social status of the trade. Thus, upgrading the social position of the workers was the most important objective. The main issue of the railway engine drivers' strike in 1898, the most important up to that time, was the union's demand for social status for engine drivers equal to that of the clerks. The drivers demanded an end to the requirement that when receiving instructions they kneel on the floor while an assistant station master, sitting on a chair, issued orders. Low social status of workers was characteristic of Japanese labor relations until the end of World War I.

The new unions, however, suffered not only from internal weaknesses but also from oppression by employers and the police, who considered the labor movement a threat to the stability of the social order. By the end of 1901 the first Japanese union movement had virtually ceased to exist.

Labor Market Changes

In the five or six years after the Russo-Japanese War (1904–05) a great change occurred in Japanese industrialization. The textile industries, of which cotton spinning was most important, by that time employed close to 60 percent of the labor force. However, the growth rate of the machinery and chemical industries was most significant. Moreover, industrial concentration developed rapidly during this period. In the cotton industry, the "Big Ten" spinning firms established their hegemony, and monopolies also developed in the sugar, beer, and pulp industries. A few large companies had already been established in shipbuilding, the core of heavy industry. Even in the light industry sector, which was the heart of the entire industrial complex, "big business" soon emerged (see Table 2.2).

Table 2.2
Number of Industrial Workers by Industry, 1900–1914
(unit: thousands)

	1900	1907	1914
Textile	234	501	584
Machinery	30	67	108
Chemical	38	87	106
Food	25	95	96
Miscellaneous	23	85	111
Special industry	37	5	12
Total	388	842	1,018

SOURCE: *Kōjō tōkei-hyō* [Factory statistical table].

The zaibatsu, one of the characteristic features of the Japanese industrial structure, were formed during this period. These were giant family enterprises that operated as holding companies in diversified fields, owning nearly all of the stock of the related firms. Mitsui, Iwasaki, and Sumitomo emerged as the most powerful zaibatsu. These holding companies developed around banks, trading firms, shipping, and mining, and at the beginning of the twentieth century they spread into such industries as sugar, beer, pulp, metal, and machinery. They emerged as the largest of the big businesses and exerted an enormous influence upon the Japanese economy. As a result, there were at one extreme a relatively small number of large established enterprises which introduced advanced Western technology, while at the other a great number of small businesses remained. According to government statistics for 1909, workers in firms employing from five to ten persons constituted 14 percent of the total labor force, and workers in businesses employing fewer than fifty constituted 45 percent of the total. What is important, however, is that, as labor turnover in big business, especially in firms employing more than 1,000, decreased, wage differentials between the large and small businesses widened (see Table 2.3). These differentials, together with the welfare facilities of the big firms, were to have a major influence on the emerging system of industrial relations.

Table 2.3

Index of Wage Differentials in Manufacturing Industries by Size of Firms, 1914 (5 to 9 employees=100)

Industry	Size of Firm by Number Employed					
	10–29	30–49	50–99	100–499	500–999	1000 or more
Machine and tool	115.4	121.2	123.1	130.8	1250	146.2
Metal Refining	1087	108.7	108.7	102.2	—	152.2

Source: Ministry of Agriculture and Commerce, *Kōjō tokei sōhyō* [All inclusive tables of factory statistics, 1914].

Industrialization also affected the agricultural sector. Since the living conditions of rural farm laborers were so poor, migration to the cities continued and large-scale farming suffered as a result. At the same time, technological developments, together with government protection of small-scale farming, served in some measure to stabilize the lives of those who owned and worked their own small farms. After the beginning of the twentieth century, both medium-sized (more than 2 hectares) and marginal (less than 0.5 hectares) farming declined, while small-scale farming tended to increase. As a consequence of this, the nucleus of the Japanese rural community was maintained and even strengthened, and fewer peasant families migrated to the cities. Instead, it became only the second and third sons and daughters who left the farms to seek jobs in the cities.

Since these young workers migrated alone, dormitories to house them became an indispensable employment condition. The dormitory system was established in the textile industry in the 1900s, and all female textile employees lived in dormitories where they were closely supervised and controlled. Since skill was required of male workers as a result of industrialization, it also became common in this period for employers to establish institutions for training young workers. By also providing places to live, the dormitories kept down the turnover of male workers trained at company expense. Further, workers did not find it advantageous to change jobs during the depression period that occurred around 1910. Thereafter, the rate of labor mobility began to decline.

Formation of the Japanese Industrial Relations System

In 1907 two sensational labor riots occurred one after another in the Ashio and Besshi copper mines. Although these riots were crushed by army units dispatched to the scene, they so shocked management that, on the heels of still other labor disputes, significant changes in labor relations were ushered in. In the background of these incidents was the notable spread of education; 70 percent of those who were workers in 1910 had had at least the minimum four-year elementary education. Commenting on this change, one journalist of the day reported:

> At the time of the Sino-Japanese War, in a glass plant or a printing plant, not to speak of metal works, the so-called artisan habit of "not keeping his earnings overnight" became so popular that, although the workers wore Western clothes with closed collars and deer-stalker caps which were entirely different from the clothing of artisans in the city, they did not lose the artisan spirit. Today, as is readily seen, the workers, especially those in the arsenals, have gradually acquired the student style. Today, perhaps more than half of the workers have elementary school educa-

tions. As the number of educated workers increases, they seem to become more aware of their own worth.[20]

Thus, industrial relations were greatly disrupted, as no new rules had been formulated to replace old ones which were becoming obsolete and were discarded with the appearance on the industrial scene of a new kind of self-conscious worker.

Especially in large-scale enterprises, where traditional employer-employee relations were most disrupted by the progress of industrialization, stabilization was a matter of great urgency. Managers believed that increasing the length of employment was a basic condition for stabilization since it would create close relationships between the employer and the workers. The dormitory and trainee systems contributed to this end, but welfare facilities, especially the mutual benefit system, were also emphasized. This view developed from a new realization by employers of the efforts of artisans and miners to band together for purposes of mutual aid in case of sickness, injury, or accident. This was also the basic function of the labor unions after the Sino-Japanese War. The industrial workers' efforts, however, had been unsuccessful, so no systematic mutual benefits were available to factory employees. Thus, employers sought to establish *within* the enterprise systems that would guarantee employee welfare benefits.

A system in which the employers assume the responsibility for taking care of their employees' needs for life necessarily leads to the formation of paternalistic industrial relations. Moreover, this was a period when the government was attempting to bolster the traditional family system which it thought was threatened by the development of industrialization, the spread of urbanization and education, and the heightened self-consciousness of individuals. The employers therefore advocated emphasis upon a family-system type of effective human relations, especially parental affection. Once this ideology was introduced into Japanese labor relations, since it was related to the basic national value system, it was accepted by the workers with little resistance.

The mutual benefits and the dormitory and trainee systems not

20. "Tōkyō no kōjō-chi narabini kōjō-seikatsu" [A panorama of the factory area and factory life in Tokyo] by Gennosuke Yokoyama, in *Shin koron*, September 1910.

only met social and economic needs of the time but also aided the formation of an acceptable type of labor relations. What materialized was a set of rules in labor relations that fulfilled the requirements of a paternalistic system based on the values of the family system transposed to the industrial setting.

Elaboration of the Rules of Labor Relations

The rapid expansion of product and labor markets resulting from World War I temporarily delayed progress toward the establishment of new industrial relations rules. The postwar depression resulted in unemployment and a decrease in voluntary labor mobility on the one hand and increased labor union activity on the other. Therefore, stabilization of industrial relations loomed as an even more important problem for employers. Within this context the major characteristics of the Japanese industrial relations system were elaborated. The lifetime employment system followed. Under this system workers were to become permanent regular employees of a company at the time of their graduation from school, or at the end of their terms of military conscription, and were to serve there until they reached retirement age.

As mentioned earlier, the traditional family or village communal relationship, though under stress, remained firmly established; and when around 1910 the enterprise came to be regarded as a pseudo-family, an employee was considered a member of the enterprise family. However, tradition decreed that parents had the right to treat children in any way they wished, so when an employee's performance was poor or when business was in a slump an employer was relatively free to discharge his workers. Therefore, the lifetime employment relationship really was no more than an ideal for employee relations.

A system of employing temporary workers was also formulated as a buttress to lifetime employment for the regular work force. By the beginning of the 1920s, employers began to employ temporary workers to meet variations in labor force requirements. Temporary workers were not considered members of the family and therefore were not eligible for the benefits of the enterprise family system.

Later in the 1920s, there emerged a system under which wage increases and promotions for permanent workers were determined on the basis of their length of service in the firm. Before World War I an employee's skill had been evaluated annually and his wage adjusted accordingly. The subjectivity of this evaluation, however, created a considerable amount of discontent and became a major cause of worker turnover. To deal with these problems, employers considered it necessary to rationalize skill evaluation and to regularize advancement. As a result, the length-of-service reward system was institutionalized, although some range was still allowed for recognition of merit.

Still another factor that contributed to the establishment of this system was that, since no apprenticeship rules had been established, skill continued to be evaluated on the basis of experience. Moreover, a length-of-service system in which wages increased as workers became older and their living costs were greater was particularly suitable for workers whose starting wage level was low.

This system of labor relations, resting upon lifetime employment and age-grade rewards, determined to a great extent the organization and function of labor unions. After World War I, two types of labor unions were organized, indicative of the two sides of Japanese industrial relations. The first type was the craft or industrial union (in some cases a mixed union), which was formed within a local labor market and in many cases was based on radical socialist ideologies. Contributing to the establishment of this type of union was the fact that in Japan, where labor relations were strongly influenced by traditional status relationships, the employer did not regard a union as an equal party in negotiations— a notion supported by the government. These unions, which in earlier times had tried to solve workers' problems through negotiations, tended to argue that the only way to improve working conditions was to change social relationships as a whole. Accordingly, they united with the socialist movement, whose aims were to revolutionize the economic and political system. Syndicalism which emphasized the liberation of the individual was the dominant ideology until the early 1920s. But in the middle of that decade communism, which was organizationally more effective and ideologically more systematic, took its place and began to exert a major influence upon the Japanese labor movement and industrial relations.

Under these circumstances, the government barely tolerated reformist unionism while moving against the revolutionists. Universal male suffrage was established in 1923 in an effort to meet the demand for democratic participation in politics. Thus, by adding a political aspect to the labor and tenant farmer movement, the government greatly influenced its development.

This radical movement soon split into three major factions—a left wing with strong Communist Party influence, a right wing advocating democratic socialism, and a middle group. Further, under the pressure of mass arrests and imprisonment of the leadership, the left wing itself split, with a labor-farmer group emerging to form its own party. This group sought to adapt Marxism to the historical and social conditions of Japanese society and managed to retain legal status by formally separating from the then underground communists. It is important to note that these ideological and organizational splits were to influence strongly the post-World War II labor movement.

The other type of union was the enterprise union organized by employees within a single enterprise and called in those days the "vertical" union. Such unions were established within companies where lifetime employment relations had emerged and where, therefore, no contact existed through the labor market between employees of different enterprises. Because working conditions in a given enterprise became the concern only of that enterprise and its employees, in a sense it was reasonable for the union to organize only within the single company and to carry on discussions of working conditions only between the employer and the enterprise union. In the 1920s half the union members in Japan belonged to organizations of this type.

Generally, enterprise unions were formed in large-scale firms. In very small businesses, where working and business conditions were poor, the authoritative family system (i.e., master-servant social relations) prevailed, and neither paternalistic industrial relations nor the lifetime employment or length-of-service systems existed. In these establishments, if any union was organized, it was of the first type.[21]

The War Economy
and Japanese Industrial Relations

After the Manchurian Incident in 1931, Japan quickly developed a war economy whose demands imposed a heavy strain upon Japanese industrialization but at the same time promoted its development. Under these circumstances, certain elements of the emerging labor relations system were quickly abandoned, while others were strengthened. The impact of the war economy destroyed the balance in existing social relationships; therefore, there was a need to create new rules.

The outcome was an emphasis upon authority relationships in order to facilitate changes. Loyalty to the community was stressed as an ideology in order to relieve social strains. Moreover, there was no room for unions in this revised system, and not only the radical unions but also the milder vertical unions were banned.

To replace the unions, in each plant the government sponsored a Sangyō Hōkokukai (Association for Service to the State through Industry), the purpose of which was to suppress any individual or class demand and to promote cooperation with the war effort. As a result, organizations composed of all the workers in each plant were formed, even in plants where no organization of any kind had existed previously.

Labor mobility also became difficult as a result of strengthened manpower controls. Young and key workers were conscripted into the army, although they retained nominal status as employees. Students, too, were drafted into the munitions industry. With many employers having to adjust or close down operations, the result was a breakdown in the permanent employment system.

Changing or closing a business resulted in a break in employment continuity and thus made it impossible to maintain the

21. On the problem of the formation of the Japanese industrial system, see Mikio Sumiya, "The Development of Japanese Labor Relations," *The Developing Economies*, vol. 4, no. 4.

length-of-service wage system. This system, operated in peace-time, could no longer be used to determine wages in a war economy. Age rather than length of service then became a basic criterion for wage determination.

In turn, an age-based wage system generated a related need to guarantee minimum standards of living for workers. This was not only an indispensable condition for carrying on the war but also an idea that had been basic to the traditional paternalistic family system. For the same reasons, family allowances, to be paid by the enterprise, were established by law in the late 1930s.

As the economic and social strains increased, the fundamental characteristics of Japanese industrial relations became clearer. Apart from variations in its form, the industrial relations system thus established continued to exist and function even through the great social and political upheaval after World War II.[22]

22. For a discussion of changes in industrial relations during the war, see Sumiya, et al., *Nihon shihonshugi to rōdō-mondai,* ch. 4, sec. 4.

3. Contemporary Arrangements: An Overview

Revolutionary Changes

Political and Social Changes

The Japanese government surrendered unconditionally on August 14, 1945, when it accepted the Potsdam Declaration. The basic policy of the United States as an occupying nation following the war was, first, to demilitarize Japan completely so that the influence of militarism would be "totally eliminated from her political, economic and social life" and, second, to encourage "respect for fundamental human rights, particularly the freedoms of religion, assembly, speech and the press" and "the formation of representative organizations."[1]

In accordance with this policy, Supreme Commander Douglas MacArthur, in October 1945, directed the newly organized Shidehara Cabinet to undertake the following major reforms: (1) emancipation of women; (2) encouragement of the formation of labor unions; (3) liberalization of education; (4) abolition of the secret police; and (5) democratization of the economic system. Drastic changes followed, one after another. In October 1945 communists and other radicals were released from jail. In December 1945 Shinto was deprived of both its status as the state religion and its financial support from the government. During the same month the very progressive Trade Union Law, based upon the Wagner Act, was enacted, and the zaibatsu were ordered dis-

---

1. "United States Initial Post-Surrender Policy for Japan, September 23, 1945," in Douglas G. Haring, ed., *Japan's Prospect* (Cambridge: Harvard University Press, 1946), pp. 379–88.

solved because they had been responsible for promoting the war. In January 1946 ultranationalist bodies were abolished and undesirable individuals were purged from public service.

During this early period the Americans greatly influenced the basic characteristics of the Occupation policies for political and social reform, which fundamentally altered the foundation of the Japanese political and social system. The traditional society of the nation offered little resistance, as the Japanese people again were obedient to authority.

This did not mean, however, that either the Occupation policies or their intent penetrated the core of Japanese institutions. First, the policies themselves were moderated by the Japanese government which was charged with enforcing them. Second, the Occupation leaders' lack of understanding of traditional Japanese social relations precluded alteration of the basis of the society by such radical reforms.

The nature of the Occupation policies was reflected in the problem of changing the emperor system. Occupation policies, especially those devised by the United States, required that sovereignty rest with the people, and therefore the ultranationalist elements of the emperor system had to be eradicated, although the emperor was to remain as a unifying symbol for the Japanese people.

In October 1945 MacArthur directed that the Constitution be amended to embody this policy, and in November the Japanese government published a draft of a new constitution which included the following provision: "There shall be no change as to the basic principle that the emperor retains sovereignty." In reaction to this provision, the Supreme Commander for the Allied Powers (SCAP) warned that if the sovereignty of the emperor meant denial of the sovereignty of the people, SCAP might have to make a grave decision about the emperor's status. The Occupation then prepared a draft constitution and gave it to the Japanese government. The emperor publicly denied his divinity in January 1946, and in November of that year the government had no choice but to enact a new constitution in line with the SCAP draft.

As one commentator has pointed out, "the leaders thought that the enactment of a democratic and peaceful constitution which would satisfy the intention of SCAP was a necessary evil and the only way to maintain peacefully the existence of the emperor and to retain the national structure."[2]

Thus the absolute sovereignty of the emperor was denied. Sovereignty was to rest with the people, and parliamentary democracy was established as an institution. However, as already mentioned, the social foundations of the emperor system lay in the traditional community, and unless these foundations were dissolved, the traditional social relationships, with the emperor as the nucleus, would persist.

Japan's postwar parliamentary politics differed from prewar politics in several respects. First, militaristic pressures ceased to exist. Although the potential power of the bureaucracy remained, the Diet gained control of national politics. Second, along with the conservative parties, the Socialist Party increased its strength; it was the leading party in the 1947 election and formed a coalition cabinet with the conservative Democratic Party. Further, the Communist Party, with its goal of social revolution, also grew stronger. The support for the Socialist and Communist parties came from labor unions, poor farmers, and intellectuals in the urban areas.

Table 3.1
Number of Members of the House of Representatives by Party, 1947–1953

	Conservatives	Socialists	Communists	Others
April 1947	261	144	4	57
January 1949	339	60	35	32
October 1952	331	120	0	15
April 1953	314	138	0	14

As shown in Table 3.1, however, the conservatives maintained a majority in the Diet. The Liberal Party Yoshida Cabinet remained in power for six years beginning in November 1948, although until the formation of the Liberal-Democratic Party in November 1955 there were constant internal conflicts among the conservatives. The same is true of the socialists, who split into

2. Yoshitake Oka, ed., *Gendai Nihon no seiji katei* [Political processes of contemporary Japan, 1964

right- and left-wing groups. Thus the political situation remained unstable.

Economic Changes

The Occupation saw the threat of a return of militarism in the structure of the Japanese economy. Accordingly, it adopted a policy designed "to dissolve the big industrial and financial combinations which controlled most of the Japanese commerce and industry."[3] By this it meant the dissolution of the zaibatsu. The reasons given by the Occupation were, first, to release the enormous profits which the zaibatsu had earned unfairly during the war, and, second, to crush the economic forces which help totalitarian monopolistic powers, thereby preventing the re-emergence of militarism.

In September 1945 SCAP issued an order freezing the properties of fifteen zaibatsu families, including Mitsui and Mitsubishi. However, the Japanese government reacted very slowly in carrying out this order, and the Commission for Liquidation of Holding Companies was not formed until August 1946. By the end of 1946 the commission had selected sixty-five companies, including subsidiaries of the zaibatsu, as the dominant holding companies and had taken charge of their dissolution.

It may also be alleged that another reason for the order to disband the zaibatsu was to limit the potential power of the Japanese economy and to deprive it of its ability to compete with American capital in the Far Eastern market. In January 1947, the Far Eastern Advisory Committee of SCAP recommended that the scale of industrial and agricultural production be that of 1930 to 1934.

There was still another justification for dissolving the zaibatsu —the principle of free competition or the demand for democracy in the economy. The Occupation, in its documents ordering the dissolution of the holding companies, referred to the abolition of private monopoly and unfair trade restrictions. In accordance

---

3. "United States Initial Post-Surrender Policy for Japan," *op.cit.*, p. 49.

Table 3.2
Applications of Anti-Economic Power Concentration Law, 1948–1949

Company	Industry	Content of Order Issued	Date of Notice
Dai-Nippon Beer (Japan Beer Co.)	Food	Dissolution of old company; division into 2 companies	April 15, 1949
Mitsubishi Jūkōgyō (Mitsubishi Heavy Industries)	Heavy machinery	Dissolution of old company; division into 3 companies	June 4, 1949
Nihon Seitetsu (Japan Iron and Steel)	Steel	Dissolution of old company; division into 2 companies	December 17, 1948
Oji Seishi (Oji Paper Co.)	Paper	Dissolution of old company; division into 3 companies	January 7, 1949

with this policy, the Diet enacted the Antimonopoly Law, which authorized the establishment of the Fair Trade Commission, in April 1947.

Another in the series of economic democratization policies was the enactment of the Anti-Economic Power Concentration Law. While the dissolution of the zaibatsu was carried out by liquidating the holding companies and the aim of the Antimonopoly Law was to protect consumers by prohibiting cartels, the purpose of the Anti-Economic Power Concentration Law was to break up the large monopolistic enterprises. The law had a drastic effect. Table 3.2 shows several examples of its application. Nihon Seitetsu (Japan Iron and Steel Works) was a giant steel trust, partially owned by the government, and Oji Seishi was a monopoly corporation with an 80 percent share of the market in the paper manufacturing industry; after these corporations were divided, the resulting smaller firms in each industry became highly competitive.

Banking, however, was not affected by the antimonopoly policies, and since bank control of manufacturing companies was widespread in Japan, the zaibatsu banks survived and provided the foothold for the eventual zaibatsu revival. Although the traditional family ties had disappeared, the reorganization of the old zaibatsu, such as Mitsui, Mitsubishi, Sumitomo, and Yasuda (Fuji), took place after 1950 through financial and personal relationships.

Agricultural reform was another stepping stone toward democratization of the economy. The SCAP memorandum of December 1945 on land reform instructed the government to " 'remove obstacles to the revival and strengthening of democratic tendencies in Japanese villages,' establish respect for the dignity of man, and destroy the economic bondage which has enslaved the Japanese farmer for centuries of feudal oppression."[4]

The government, which depended upon the owners of farmland as an important segment of Japan's social foundation, resisted this reform and approved landowning of up to five *chōbu* in an attempt to enable 70 percent of the tenant-worked farmland to be re-

4. Ronald P. Dore, *Land Reform in Japan* (London: Oxford University Press, 1959), p. 134.

Table 3.3
Farm Household Structure by Land and Tenant Status, 1946–1949 (unit: thousands)

	Land Status			Household Status				
	Owned Land	Tenant Land	Total	Owner-Farmer[a]	Owner-Tenant[b]	Tenant-Owner[c]	Tenant[d]	Total
August 1946	2,833	2,373	5,207	2,154	1,183	997	1,574	5,909
August 1947	3,031	1,981	5,012	3,564	1,735	458	689	6,247
March 1949	4,310	648	4,960	3,822	1,591	411	312	6,176

SOURCE: Ministry of Agriculture and Forestry, *Nōchi kaikaku tenmatsu gaiyō* [Summary of report on the farmland reform] (Tokyo: Nōchi Kaikaku Kiroku Iinkai, 1951).

a. Owned 90% or more of the land they cultivated.
b. Owned 50–90% of the land they cultivated.
c. Owned 10–50% of the land they cultivated.
d. Owned less than 10% of the land they cultivated.

tained by the owners.[5] This effort was countered by the Allied
Powers, who tried to eliminate the feudalistic relationships by
means of land reform. Eventually a second farmland reform proposal was agreed to, and independent farmers were permitted to
possess up to three *chōbu* for their own use and up to one *chōbu* for
tenant farming. Thus the landlord system was virtually abolished
(see Table 3.3). Because of the farmland reform, farmers' unions,
which had been organized rapidly after the war with tenants as
the driving force, abandoned their struggles and almost ceased to
exist. As a result, farmers became a strong conservative bulwark
against radical ideologies and have since supported the Japanese
conservative political parties.

The Emancipation of Workers

The postwar social reform that exerted the strongest influence
upon Japanese society was the emancipation of workers, or the
recognition and encouragement of the labor union movement. In
Japan's prewar days, because the government and employers
regarded the labor unions as undesirable organizations, the right
to organize was not recognized. Accordingly, unions had no right
to engage in disputes or to negotiate. Under the Occupation
administration, however, the labor union movement was expected
to contribute to the democratization of employer-employee relations within enterprises as well as labor-management relations
in society. This was in accord with the United States Policy Directive of September 22, 1945, issued from the White House, which
ordered that "encouragement shall be given and favor shown to
the development of organizations of labor, industry and agriculture, organized on a democratic basis."[6] SCAP moved directly to
implement this policy by ordering the Japanese government to
prepare legislation that would protect workers' rights. Three labor
laws were thus enacted: the Trade Union Law in December 1945;
the Labor Standards Law in February 1947 which stipulated a

5. 1 *chōbu* = 0.992 hectares.
6. Solomon B. Levine, *Industrial Relations in Postwar Japan* (Urbana: University of
Illinois Press, 1958), p. 24.

forty-eight-hour week; and the Employment Security Law which abolished such feudalistic remnants in employment relations as bondage.

Under these circumstances, labor unions organized one after another, beginning with the All-Japan Seamen's Union, or Kaiin, which was rebuilt in October 1945. The number of union members reached 381,000 by the end of 1945, matching the prewar maximum, and by 1948 the number had reached 6.5 million, representing a rate of organization of more than 50 percent of the labor force (see Table 3. 4).

Table 3.4
Growth of Labor Union Organizations and Membership, 1945–1949

	Dec. 1945	June 1946	June 1947	June 1948	June 1949
No. of unions	509	12,007	23,323	33,900	34,688
No. of union members (thousands)	381	3,680	5,692	6,534	6,655
Estimated rate of organization (%)	3.2	40.0	45.3	53.0	55.8

SOURCE: Ministry of Labor, *Rōdō-kumiai kihonchōsa* [Basic survey of labor unions] (Tokyo, published annually).

In the economic confusion caused by Japan's military defeat and the rapidly progressing inflation that followed, all workers faced difficulties in making a living; therefore, in an effort to protect their livelihood and to oppose employers who were unable or unwilling to conform to reconstruction policies, they organized labor unions.

The unions demanded large wage increases, democratization of management, and abolition of the status system for employees, and used group pressure to achieve their goals. With the destruction of the value system that supported the old social order and because of the critical living conditions—lack of food, clothing, and housing—most union members became sympathetic toward radical union policies, although it is questionable to what extent they agreed with the political ideologies of the union movement. Stormy labor disputes raged, led by the left-wing labor unions.

The postwar labor movement differed from the prewar movement in quality as well as in size and breadth of organization.

First, not only was the right to organize approved by law, but the right to bargain collectively was also recognized so that working conditions now came to be determined by negotiations between employer and union. As mentioned in the previous chapter, in prewar days working conditions were arbitrarily determined by the employer, and collective bargaining was rarely carried on. Reacting against this prewar situation, unions in many cases attempted to gain advantages in collective bargaining by means of group physical pressure. Although rules for negotiation were not yet determined, such pressures were included among the great changes in Japanese labor relations.

Second, backed by labor union power, the social status of the working class rose rapidly. On the enterprise level the status system favoring clerical employees over manual workers was abolished, and the difference between the two came to be regarded as only functional; they grew very close to one another in terms of both working conditions and welfare facilities. Politically and socially, hardly anything could be determined at the enterprise level without considering the position of the union, and the union fiercely opposed all decisions or positions it regarded as disadvantageous to workers. Thus, various institutional relations in the Japanese social structure were undergoing great change.

Changes in Social Classes

As mentioned above, with political and social reform the structure of social classes in Japan was transformed. First, not only was the class status system altered with the abolition of the peerage, but in addition the landlord class, which had been one of the ruling groups in Japan, and the wealthy capitalist class, including the zaibatsu, disappeared almost completely.

Second, although the farmland reform measure did not apply to forests and forest owners were therefore unaffected, the traditional landed class as a whole became powerless. On the other hand, as tenant peasants became independent farmers in possession of their own land, they gradually turned conservative. Because the conservative parties maintained high prices for rice, the principal farm product, in order to stimulate increased food production, agricultural villages provided a solid and dependable base for the conservatives. Just as landlord-tenant relations had contributed to the social unrest of the prewar days, the postwar farmland reform in a sense contributed considerably to the stabilization of social relations.

Furthermore, while in the prewar period the price of rice was held down to keep it in line with workers' low wages, after the war government price-fixing provided relative advantages for the farmers, and farm living became more stable than life in the confused and distressed urban areas. Thus the economic and social condition of the farmers greatly improved. In spite of these changes, as a matter of self-protection, farmers did not dissolve their traditional village community relations, and neither the Occupation nor the government interfered in this area. Traditionalism remained one of the important factors contributing to conservatism in the agricultural districts.

The class most affected by postwar social changes was white-collar employees. These workers, who had never before organized unions, assumed leadership of the union movement right after the war's end, and in industries such as manufacturing and banking and in the public sector almost all white-collar workers became union members. They now regarded themselves as "workers" and collaborated with manual workers in dealing with their employers.

During the war, while wage increases for white-collar workers had been limited by wage control regulations, the wages of blue-collar workers had been increased to stimulate production. Therefore, wage differentials between the two groups had narrowed by the end of the war. Furthermore, because of the controls over the necessities of life during and after the war, the standard of living of white-collar and manual workers equalized. In the drive for democratization, white-collar workers saw that it was to their advantage to protect their livelihood through the union movement rather than to try to regain privileges that no longer existed. This development forced the white-collar groups into a dilemma after 1948, when management recovered its stability. On the one hand, they were performing managerial functions; on the other, they negotiated with the employer as union members.

Finally, in connection with the rise in the social status of workers, some attention should be given to the changes in the educational system and the rise in the educational level that took place in Japan after the war. In the prewar era, more than 99 percent of school-age children had received six years of compulsory education, and the proportion that received secondary education or its equivalent reached 70 percent of the appropriate age group. Thus, eight to eleven years of education was already common. This situation was basic to the reorganization of the educational system into the American-style 6-3-3-4-year system and to the introduction of 9 years of compulsory education. Furthermore, while the rate of senior high school attendance rose, at the same time many senior high school graduates were hired as manual workers in the chemical plants and steel mills. Thus, the educational level of workers rose considerably, and this, in addition to the pressure of the labor movement and the relative rise in the income level, contributed to the rise in the social status of workers.

Reconstruction and Rearrangement

Continuity and Discontinuity

The more basic the changes in Japanese society after the war, the greater the social and political confusion. The decade from 1945 to 1955, and especially the year 1945, was a period of travail in the birth of a new political and economic system and the establishment of new rules for operating it. Although demilitarization and democratization were the basic premises of the new system, and although policies such as the dissolution of the zaibatsu, farmland reform, worker emancipation, and establishment of parliamentarism were carried out, it was not certain how each of these elements would stabilize by itself and in relation to the others. This uncertainty resulted in tension and disputes throughout the early postwar period.

The new social institutions, with all the tensions and conflicts they created in the society, had the potential to change and restructure the traditional society in one way or another, once the direction of change was determined. However, the new institutions could not build and stabilize social relationships entirely different from those of the traditional society in the absence of certain social preconditions.

For example, the parliamentary system replaced the emperor system as the supreme political decision-making mechanism. However, in contrast to the rivalry of the two major prewar conservative parties, postwar politics has taken the form of a confrontation between a majority conservative party and a minority socialist party which find it extremely difficult to find a common ground for discussion. Conservatives attempt to pass bills by majority rule and socialists try to stop them, often by physically obstructing Diet operations. The conflict is not only a clash of interests, which could be settled by compromise, but also a disagreement over the basic issue of whether to maintain or change the existing social system. The reason the parliamentary system seems to function at all is that the conservatives for the most part enjoy an absolute majority. However, even within the conservative party—and in the socialist party as well—factions formed by personal relations rather than by policy differences play a major role.[7]

In prewar Japan it was understood that the family took precedence over the individual, that individual life was possible only within the family, and that the nation took precedence over the family. Therefore, it followed that the individual ought to be subject to the family and to the nation. Various postwar emancipation measures reversed the relationships between the state, the family, and the individual and made it clear that the family was composed of family members, and that the nation was supported by the will of the people. However, the necessary economic and social preconditions for this had yet to be provided. For example,

7. Even in the case of the Japan Communist Party, Chairman Tokuda, who had assumed power after the war, was later criticized as being too "paternalistic."

farmers now owned land averaging about one *chōbu* per farm. If they divided the land among their children, none of them could make a living as a farmer. Instead, one of the children—in many cases the eldest son—succeeded not only to the land but also to the house and the land on which it stood, thus contributing to the persistence of the family system.

Emancipated individuals and families, even in present-day society, find it difficult to exist without belonging to groups. In Japan, a group does not mean a body that is formed by the will of and for the sake of individuals. Rather, the interest of the group takes precedence over the interest of its members, and as a result the individual's pattern of behavior remains group-centered, as in the prewar period.

Because individuals are included in groups without guaranteeing the dignity and rights of each individual, the function and status of individuals in society and in a group are not clearly distinguished. When those who give directions and those who receive them are functionally separated within a group, this is regarded not simply as a matter of functional differentiation but also as a question of status differentiation. Therefore, in many cases a demand to abolish status relationships results in a demand also to minimize functional authority relations—a problem considered in greater detail below.

Reorganization of Industrial Relations

After the war, when half of all Japanese employees were organized in unions, they constituted a strong social force, and working conditions came to be determined by union-management collective bargaining. However, 90 percent of the unions became *enterprise unions*, each composed only of employees of a single enterprise. Except for public employee unions, national unions, despite their names, are merely federations of enterprise unions.

Even in the prewar era, insofar as the workers in large enterprises were organized, they were organized into enterprise unions. The postwar unions were organized primarily in large-scale establishments. According to 1947–51 industrial establishment statistics, workers employed by large enterprises with 500 or more employees accounted for only 30 percent of the total number of employees, but they comprised the majority of union members. In contrast, although workers employed by establishments with fewer than 100 employees accounted for 50 percent of the total, they comprised only about 10 percent of the total number of union members.

The fact that unions were organized within enterprises mostly by the employees of the large firms necessitated collective bargaining between employers and the employees. Although employers regarded collective bargaining with their own employees as undesirable but inescapable, they strongly opposed negotiation with outsiders, such as national union leaders. In this sense, the closed employment relations pattern of prewar days was substantially carried over—one of the reasons why the postwar unions are called enterprise unions.

Postwar enterprise unions can be analyzed in the context of the lifetime employment system. Lifetime employment relationships, which had been developed in the middle 1920s, were greatly influenced by postwar democratization. However, rather than being destroyed, they were reinforced as a solid institution.

Because the postwar economic confusion produced a large amount of unemployment, and because the living conditions of workers were extremely strained, unions made it their primary goal to maintain employment of their members and have always fiercely opposed any kind of dismissals. Thus, unless employers were under extreme economic pressure, they did not fire employees because they were certain that they would be damaged in the disputes that would inevitably follow. With the labor movement supporting the lifetime employment system, it became firmly established and resulted in intensifying the identification of union members with their employers—although the latter was not among the unions' objectives.

The length-of-service reward system became similarly well established. Japanese wages are generally determined for the individual on the basis of factors such as educational background, age, length of service within the enterprise, and job experience. Even after the war, when wages came to be determined by collective bargaining, there was no change in these criteria of wage determination. Wages are determined not by a worker's job or function but by his personal attributes.

After the war, however, a change occurred in the emphasis given to the various criteria. In the prewar period, because loyalty to the enterprise was stressed, length of service in the enterprise was considered most important, but after the war unions denied loyalty to the enterprise and demanded instead the workers' right to a livelihood. Since living expenses are most often determined by age, age became an important criterion. This shift in emphasis somewhat modified the length-of-service reward system, but this did not mean a complete denial of it. Rather, the system has been reinforced in a different form.

In connection with the lifetime employment system and enterprise unionism, another factor of importance is enterprise welfare facilities. Welfare facilities were important in forming the prewar familistic relations between employer and employee, and after the war, although the unions criticized the paternalistic nature of the welfare facilities, they did not reject the facilities themselves. Rather, they sought their expansion. Enterprises have acceded to these workers' demands as much as possible on the assumption that, as a result of such a policy, union members' identification with the enterprise would be strengthened.

This pattern is also apparent in the social security system. In large enterprises, the health insurance association of the enterprise controls the health insurance fund and programs. Even though the national insurance rate is the same for employees at all enterprises, regardless of size, the insurance income of large enterprises is greater than that of the medium-sized and small companies because their wage levels are higher. Moreover, because the working conditions in the large enterprises are better, the rate of accidents and illness is lower. Therefore, while the government-controlled health insurance programs for workers in small and medium-sized enterprises and for day laborers suffer from deficits, association-operated health insurance programs in the large enterprises are rich and their benefits are better.

However, only regular workers can enjoy all these benefits. With the reestablishment of the lifetime employment system around 1950, the number of temporary workers again began to increase. As the labor unions limit their membership to regular workers and refuse to admit temporary workers,[8] discrimination against temporary workers is practiced not only by the employers but also by the unions.

The Labor Union Movement and the Socialist Movement

Both Sōdōmei, or the Japan General Federation of Trade Unions, formally reorganized in 1946, and Sanbetsu, or the All-Japan Congress of Industrial Unions, which was established in 1946 as a concentrated body of left-wing unions, adopted socialism as their political program. This decision was in the prewar tradition. The prewar labor movement and the proletarian party movement were two sides of the same coin and a split in the proletarian party immediately resulted in a split in the labor union.

One of the reasons for this relationship between the political party and the union is that the suppression of the labor movement by the state authority was so vigorous that it was inevitable for the labor movement to struggle against authority on the political front. A more important reason, however, was that the economic pressure to keep wages low was so strong in the Japanese industrial relations system that the leaders of the labor movement were convinced that improvement was impossible under the capitalistic system. Such an opinion was easy for union members to accept during the postwar period of economic confusion and distress.

In addition, the political slogan functioned as a device for unity rather than for division among the enterprise unions. Under the lifetime employment system the labor market was confined within enterprises, and working conditions varied from company to company. Therefore, when industrial federations or national unions tried to develop a unified movement, it was difficult to use improved working conditions as a common goal. However, politi-

8. As for postwar temporary workers, see Mikio Sumiya, *Gendankai niokeru Rinjiko mondai* [The present stage of the issue of temporary employees], in *Nihon rōdō kyōkai zasshi* [Journal of the Japan Institute of Labor], March 1963.

cal slogans could be used since they had no direct connection with any of the individual enterprises.

Public employees' unions such as the National Railway Workers' Union, or Kokurō, and the Japan Postal Workers' Union, or Zentei, played an important role in the postwar labor movement. As wage increases for members of these unions required Diet approval, their demands were necessarily a political problem. Furthermore, in postwar Japan, politics and the economy were so closely interwoven that political considerations were vital for economic reconstruction, particularly since political power was utilized to oppress the labor movement. In response, the labor movement not only mobilized to oppose such an effort by the dominant conservative political party but also sought the support of the socialist parties in the Diet.

On the other hand, the socialist parties tried to use the labor unions to mobilize the people. Among the Sōdōmei-affiliated unions, socialist attempts to control the union resulted in leaders of the party becoming leaders of the union. In the case of San-betsu-affiliated unions, communists used party "fractions" to gain control and assume leadership of the unions. The democratization movement became popular within the unions in 1948, and the release of the union movement from such political control was soon demanded. However, Sōhyō, or the General Council of Trade Unions of Japan, which was formed in 1950 in response to these demands, found it necessary to be allied with the Socialist Party (left wing). In this case, however, the relationship took a different form, as leaders of Sōhyō joined the party and became representatives in local legislative bodies and in the national Diet. Thus, today the federation is in a position to exert great influence upon the party.[9]

Reconstruction of the Economy

Production, which had declined enormously as a result of the

9. See the analysis in Mikio Sumiya's article "Rōdō undō ni okeru hiyaku to renzoku" [Leap and continuity in the labor movement], in Oka, *Gendai Nihon no seiji katei*.

war defeat, the destruction of the economic base, and the confusion accompanying economic and political changes, began to
show signs of recovery in 1948, stimulated in part by the change in
Occupation policies. With the intensification of the cold war between the United States and Russia, President Truman issued the
"Truman Doctrine" in March 1947, in which he declared it to be
United States policy to support the free forces of the world in their
efforts to cope with totalitarianism. The interpretation of this
doctrine as it affected Occupation policies for Japan was stated by
Secretary of the Army Kenneth C. Royal in January 1948:

> The basic objective of U.S. policy immediately following
> the surrender of Japan was the prevention of future Japa-
> nese invasions. Real stabilization of Japan, or the strength
> of Japan as a nation, was considered as a matter of second-
> ary importance.
>
> Since then, a new situation has developed in world poli-
> tics and economy and in various defense problems and
> humanitarian ideas.
>
> The United States is determined to prevent Japan from
> engaging in an aggressive war on the one hand, and, on the
> other hand, the U.S. has as an objective the establishment
> of a strong and stable democracy in Japan to enable her
> to support herself and assume the role of a protective
> barrier against possible unrest in East Asia in the future.[10]

After this change in Occupation policies, Japan's own efforts at
economic reconstruction progressed with the establishment of a
policy for priorities. As emphasis was placed on the production of
materials basic to the manufacture of almost every product, highest priority was given to coal and steel; through increases in their
production, indirect expansion of other industries was expected.
Recovery of the Japanese economy after 1948 was greatly en-
hanced by the success of this policy. Manufacturing production,
which had fallen to 35 percent of the prewar level, surpassed the
prewar level in 1951 and continued to increase thereafter.

10. Speech at the San Francisco Commonwealth Club, entitled "Japan as a Wall
against Totalitarianism," published in *Jiji-nenkan* [Yearbook of contemporary prob-
lems], 1949).

One of the corollaries of this growth was inflation, and because of inflation enterprises were able to lessen their burden of debts incurred during and after the war. With increases in commodity prices, the incomes of the enterprises increased. Furthermore, inflation diminished, to a considerable degree, the cost of wage increases granted under the pressure of the labor movement. Thus, enterprises were able to accumulate capital at the expense of workers. Taking commodity prices during 1934 to 1936 as 100, the price index reached 1,803 in 1946, 5,908 in 1947, 14,956 in 1948, and 24,336 in 1949. As such vicious inflation also functioned to hinder economic development, both the Occupation forces and the Japanese government tried to curb it. They were successful, and after 1950 the economy stabilized.

Economic development after that period was attained chiefly through the "special procurements" during the Korean War in 1950 as well as through financial investment, loans, and credit expansion by the Bank of Japan. While the development of the postwar economy had been checked by deficits in trade balances, the special procurements brought the balance into "the black," making it possible to import large amounts of raw materials and machinery which were necessary to reconstruct and expand the Japanese economy. Capital needed to expand production was provided by funds from the United States and a credit increase by the Bank of Japan.

Since such fiscal and monetary policies were carried out mostly in order to support large enterprises which were relatively low credit risks, the result was a strengthening of these enterprises, which had previously been weakened by organizational dissolutions and management purges. Also, with a favorable change in the Occupation policy, the large enterprises recovered confidence, and in the spring of 1948 they formed Nikkeiren, the Japan Federation of Employers' Associations, in an effort to oppose the labor movement and to reestablish management rights. In 1950 the federation initiated a movement to establish a new labor administration system within enterprises to counteract labor union pressure.

This period was also a turning point for the labor movement. The 1949 amendments to the Trade Union Law narrowed the legal scope of the union movement, and following the outbreak of the Korean War in June 1950 the expulsion of left-wing activists from their unions, or the so-called red purge, was carried out on a large scale under SCAP pressure. The result was a weakening of the left-wing unions, where the democratization movement had already begun. Sanbetsu, which had taken the initiative in the postwar labor movement, rapidly declined after 1950, and Sōhyō, which was born with the support of SCAP, assumed leadership (see Table 3.5).

Table 3.5
Number of Union Members by National Center, 1948–1952 (unit: thousands)

	June 1948	June 1949	June 1950	June 1951	June 1952
Sōdōmei	873	914	835	313	219
Sanbetsu	1,228	1,020	290	47	27
Sōhyō	—	—	(2,765)	2,912	3,102
Independent national unions	3,087	3,403	3,253	913	?
Other independent unions	1,488	1,318	1,461	1,675	?
Total	6,677	6,655	5,774	5,687	5,720

SOURCE: Ministry of Labor, *Rōdō-kumiai kihonchōsa* [Basic survey of labor unions]. Figures for Sōhyō in 1950 are for the preparatory convention.

With the Korean War as the turning point, the Japanese economy revived rapidly, but this recovery was accompanied by inflation. In addition, the union movement became stagnant, increases in real wages were small, and the distressed living conditions of the workers did not improve. Under such circumstances, the labor movement, with Sōhyō as its core, developed a new program based on four peace principles, including "anti-rearmament." The unions saw factors within a rearmament economy that were antithetical to the improvement of the living conditions of workers, and from this principle a highly political program evolved.

The egg that had been thought of as a chicken hatched into a duck. Thus, Sōhyō finally completed the restructuring of its labor movement and reopened the struggle against the employers in large enterprises who were trying to reestablish their leadership within those enterprises. Thus, in 1952 and through 1953, many fierce disputes occurred, each of which lasted for several months. The results of the strikes were by no means favorable for the unions, since the weakness of enterprise unionism became quite apparent as management recovered.

The Contemporary Situation

Establishment of an Oligopolistic System

The year 1955 marked a turning point for Japan's economy and society as well as for its politics. In 1954 the nation had begun to receive American economic and military aid, which was to be increased at an accelerated rate. The Self-Defense Agency was established, and Japan gradually began to rearm in 1955. By that time her economic recovery from the devastation of the Pacific War was virtually complete, and admission to the international General Agreement on Trade and Tariffs (GATT) marked her reentry into international trade. On the domestic front, as the pace of industrial reorganization increased, the former zaibatsu again emerged into a position of leadership. The merger of the four companies that had composed Mitsubishi Shoji (trading company) prior to the dissolution of the zaibatsu was approved in 1954; a year later the former Mitsui Bussan companies also merged. The Mitsui and Mitsubishi banks were the nerve centers for the rebuilding of their respective zaibatsu combines.

The improving economic situation both at home and in international trade had a great impact on domestic politics. The Socialist Party, which had split over the peace treaty issue, united once again in October 1955, and the conservative political sector, which had been divided since the end of World War II, merged into a single conservative party, the Liberal-Democratic Party, a move that led to the party's continuing control of the government. At the time of the formation of the Liberal-Democratic Party, its mission was described as follows:

The purpose of the occupation policies undertaken by the United States just after the war was mainly the weakening of Japan. The improper oppression of patriotism and of the concept of nationhood was the main concern in the revision of the constitution, the educational system, and other social institutions. In addition, national dignity was excessively diversified and weakened. This situation, associated with the recent changes in international relations, provided communists and a class-oriented socialist group with an opportunity to expand their power, and allowed the rapid emergence of these groups.

A new movement in both the economic and the political spheres aimed at the creation of a stable social order by amending the postwar reformation policies and "restoring" the old social relations and concepts. About the time this movement started, a major change took place within the Japan Communist Party, which had been one of the tension-producing factors in postwar society. Following the death of Stalin in 1953, the shift in emphasis in the international communist movement, centered in the Soviet Union, affected the Japan Communist Party, and at the sixth Japan Communist Party conference in 1955 it criticized its policy of ultra-leftist adventurism: "We recognize that imminent revolutionary situations do not exist in the present Japanese society." This analysis is evidence of the party's recognition that manufacturing production had been expanding and the economic cycle had been gradually stabilized as a result of the Korean War boom and the investment of American aid funds. In fact, the economic structure of postwar Japan had assumed a number of characteristics different from those of the prewar era.

First of all, the relative share of light industry, such as textiles, as a proportion of total industrial production declined, while heavy industry—iron and steel, shipbuilding, chemical, and others —increased its share. This shift was particularly notable in foreign trade, as exports of products of the chemical and the precision machinery industries expanded. Thus, the change in the industrial structure of Japan affected the structure of the labor force. Although the Japanese military industry had been completely de-

Table 3.6
Percentage of Total Output by Industry, 1954–1962

	Metal-working	Machinery	Chemicals	Ceramics	Textiles	Food	Wood-work	Misc.
1954	16.1	16.6	18.7	3.7	17.6	17.2	4.9	5.2
1956	19.7	18.1	18.4	3.3	16.8	16.5	4.4	4.8
1958	16.4	23.0	18.3	3.4	14.3	14.8	4.6	5.2
1960	19.1	26.1	17.8	3.5	12.3	12.0	4.3	4.9
1962	17.6	28.7	17.0	3.5	11.2	11.9	3.6	6.5

SOURCE: Ministry of International Trade and Industry, Research and Statistics Division, *Kōgyō tōkeihyō* [Census of manufacturers] (Tokyo, published annually).

stroyed, the proportion of male workers in the total labor force was still at the 65 percent level. The composition of the labor force, however, provided the labor movement with a broader base, as compared to the previous stage of industrial development.

Second, the economy, which had been dependent upon the military industries during the prewar and wartime periods, was now based on the production of consumer and capital goods. Private consumer expenditures, which until 1955 had been more than 60 percent of total national expenditures, had decreased, dropping by 1961 to the level of 51 percent. On the other hand, until 1955 private capital accumulation was less than 20 percent of the total capital invested. However, in the 1960s it increased to around 30 percent. The expansion of the machinery, metalworking, and chemical industries was supported by such changes in the demand structure (see Table 3.6).

Third, although the large corporations played the leading roles in the development process in the expanding industries, they had no monopolistic market control. Rather, oligopolistic competition was the significant feature. With the zaibatsu companies fragmented, the economy expanding, and technological change occurring, it was not hard for a new company to enter the market before 1955. In the iron and steel industry, one after another the old major open-hearth operations began continuous production of pig iron and steel, and they formed the Big Six of the industry. In the electric machinery industry, two large companies entered a market that had previously been confined to three major companies, touching off keen competition. In every other major industrial area, from five to ten large companies have been competing with each other since 1955. This competition was a basic feature of the Japanese economy in the 1960s, a market situation that can be called a competitive oligopolistic system.

Technological Changes and Economic Development

The very low average productivity of the Japanese economy as a whole in the postwar years was ascribed to the fact that, during World War II, investment in new production facilities had been ignored in order to give top priority to the production of war materials. When the war ended, production equipment and machinery were virtually in ruins. Productivity in the coal-mining industry at that time dropped to one-third the prewar level. In addition, during the wartime and early postwar years, when economic contact between Japan and the Western nations had been broken off, great technological changes had occurred in these countries and particularly in the United States. As a result, when Japan reentered the international economic market, the differences in productivity between these countries and Japan were surprisingly large.

Accordingly, these industries faced the problem of smoothing relations with the labor unions on the one hand and achieving rationalization of organization and technological change on the other. In 1951 the government established the Development Bank as a long-term financial agency to support this effort, and the Enterprise Rationalization Promotion Act was passed in 1952. In response to such government moves, industries developed programs to rationalize themselves. Before 1955 the emphasis of rationalization was upon the correction of the imbalances in the old production systems and on the curtailment of excessive production factors. Another goal was to upgrade the machinery and equipment in those sectors where productivity was especially low.

Rationalization entered a second stage after 1955. Under oligopolistic competition, the reduction of costs made possible by increased productivity, the improvement of the quality of products, and the production of new products were ascribed to the highly efficient machines and equipment rather than to workers' skill. Accordingly, a huge amount of equipment investment was assumed to be necessary, and this notion spread from the machinery industry to the iron and steel industry, a supplier of raw materials to the former, and to the sector supplying energy resources for various industries. As a result, the industrial structure improved remarkably. Thus, huge investment for new equipment and technological change has been the most important factor in the rapid growth of the Japanese economy since 1955.

Labor unions were strongly opposed to rationalization for fear that it would result in the discharge of workers. However, union resistance lacked effectiveness for two reasons. First, rationalization in the prewar days aimed at reducing the labor force in a time of depression and inevitably resulted in a large number of unemployed workers. In contrast, since technological changes after 1955 were introduced in the form of capital investment and in the process of rapid economic growth, the resulting rationalization did not require a reduction in the labor force except in such industries as coal mining, where the production expansion was relatively small. Although there were frequent problems caused by the transfer of workers within enterprises, conflict over the problem of discharge did not develop.

Second, there was no way for an enterprise to survive the oligopolistic competition unless it made technological changes. The relative market position of the enterprise was the key to gains by the enterprise union. If an enterprise maintained or increased its share of the product market, the union expected an improvement in working conditions. If the enterprise's share of the product market declined, the union modified its wage demands in an effort to assist the enterprise in regaining its market position. Thus, an enterprise union could not really object to technological changes, notwithstanding its antirationalization slogans.

As most of the newly introduced technologies were from the United States and European countries, they usually had the same effects with regard to quality and quantity of labor force as they had had in those countries. However, their acceptance by workers in Japanese industries took a somewhat different form. For example, in Japan a worker's job consciousness is weaker than his feeling of identification with the company, so he can adapt himself without much resistance to changes in job structures within the enterprise.

Technological change affected workers, and especially labor unions, in yet another way. The enterprise union usually was strongly rooted in the workshop, so that when a company tried to readjust its structure, a most important factor for the company was the establishment of management control. As a matter of course, such an attempt met the strong opposition of the union. However, the process of technological change can result in an adjustment favorable to management. Since the introduction of new technologies involves problems of manpower and determining work standards, problems that cannot be handled by the union because of lack of experience, the decisions are made almost entirely by management, and through this process it is able to regain a degree of control within the workshop.

In the course of economic growth and technological change in Japan, management recovered its confidence in negotiations with unions, and, conversely, the unions were placed in a situation where they found it increasingly difficult to engage in their activities within enterprises.

Establishment of Labor-Management Rules

The year 1955 also marked a turning point in the strategy of the labor movement. Among the leading national unions, criticism was voiced of Sōhyō's policy of attempting to reinforce enterprise unionism and to achieve economic and political emancipation by means of a joint union or people's struggle within a given region. This criticism was due to the fact that, even if an enterprise union tried to cooperate with unions of other industries in the same region, it found it difficult to conduct a strike and a wage-raise campaign without considering the relations among competing companies in an oligopolistic system.

For example, in the summer of 1953, when Zenji, or the National Automobile Workers' Union, went on strike, the enterprise union at the leading company, Nissan Jidōsha, continued to strike for several weeks after other Zenji unions had settled with their employers. While the Nissan strike continued, the other companies expanded their shares of the market, and Nissan Jidōsha was forced into a critical economic position. This situation endangered the economic well-being of the workers, many of whom blamed their union. Consequently, a union split developed and a second union was organized, which worked with the management to relaunch production at Nissan. Its membership increased very rapidly, and by the end of the year the first union had disappeared. In the end, this incident led to the dissolution of Zenji.

This problem was not unique to the automobile union but

occurred also in most other unions. Under the oligopolistic system, the main challenge for a labor movement based on enterprise unionism is to find ways to carry on the movement effectively. As a strategy to overcome this situation the labor movement developed a policy of promoting unified struggles by industry. Sōhyō's 1955 policy statement included the following: (1) a unified wage demand developed from the separate demands of affiliated unions which was designed as a minimum standard increase satisfying all affiliates plus an amount designated as "alpha" to be determined by the individual union; and (2) the union action to be staged at the workshop level but encompassing the entire national organization. Specifically, then, the policy emphasized that wage demands should be put on an industry basis and that the actual struggle for their unified realization should be conducted at each company. However, the power of individual industry unions was insufficient to implement this strategy and a united campaign among industry unions was necessary. Thus, in the spring of 1955 a joint struggle for a uniform minimum standard wage increase was staged by national unions in eight industries. This method of developing wage demands and acting for their realization was later called *Shuntō*, or Spring Labor Offensive, and it has since become a core activity of the labor movement.

With the adoption of this successful strategy, the former leaders were replaced at the Sōhyō meeting in the summer of 1955 by Kaoru Ohta of the Japanese Federation of Synthetic Chemical Workers' Unions, or Gōkarōren, and Akira Iwai of the National Railway Workers' Union, who were leading advocates of the industrywide joint struggle. It can be said that the Spring Labor Offensive, based on the joint struggle by industry unions, was a response of the labor movement to the developing Japanese economy based on oligopolistic competition.

Under the *Shuntō* system, and within the context of the existing Japanese economy, new rules of industrial relations have evolved. The following chapters will deal with these rules. Here only their principal characteristics will be pointed out.

First of all, the joint struggle by industry does not mean that the industry union at the national level gives the same wage goal and the same timetable to all its affiliated unions. The amount of the wage demand and the struggle schedule are determined according to the rank of each enterprise by size. The unions at the large oligopolistic enterprises become the pacesetters, and after they have conducted their struggles and won their wage increases the unions at the second-ranking companies enter into the process of collective bargaining, with the wage settlements at the large firms as their main target. In this way the struggle strategy corresponds to the dual structure of the economy in which the oligopolistic enterprises are the principal actors.

Second, although it is called a joint struggle by industry, only the amount of the wage demand and the schedule of action are arranged. The actual negotiations are carried out not at the industry level but at each enterprise, thus retaining the characteristics of enterprise unionism.

Third, when the union stages a strike for a wage increase, the date and duration of the strike are synchronized among competing enterprises. Thus, the strike is carried out without the serious tension experienced by both labor and management during the strikes just after the war.

Fourth, the Spring Labor Offensive starts with a series of demands—a wage increase, objections to rationalization, political objectives, and so on—but ends with an agreement on only a wage increase. This means that the fundamental nature of the Spring Labor Offensive is a movement for wage increases.

The Spring Labor Offensive has gradually expanded to embrace a wider range of unions; more than six million workers were involved by 1970. The fact that this movement, which was initiated by Sōhyō, the left-wing federation, and later joined by Chūritsurōren, or the Federation of Independent Unions, has turned into the one trade union struggle for the betterment of working conditions should be regarded as an expression of the basic characteristics of the Japanese labor movement since 1955.

It was a natural outcome of the *Shuntō* movement that the Workers' Fellowship, an organization of important Sōhyō leaders, proposed "Japanese-type trade unionism" in 1960. It emphasized, for the first time, the economic function of the Sōhyō movement. The term "Japanese-type" was used recognizing that, since "capital is closely associated with the power of the government and oppresses workers strictly," it was necessary "to establish, first of all, democratic rights and to break the political barriers at the same time" to achieve their economic goal. Also, one can see here the reason Japanese-type trade unionism is still flexible, as are the rules of industrial relations.

Changes in the Structure of the Population

Economic development since 1955 has brought about other changes in the structure of Japanese society. Among the most notable have been the result of rapid urbanization. According to the 1965 national census, the population has decreased since 1960 in 25 of the 46 prefectures; during the same period the population of Tokyo increased by 600,000, making it a megalopolis with an urban population of 8.9 million; in addition, the population of neighboring Yokohama increased by 400,000. Public investment has been unable to keep pace with the urban growth rate, and cities continue to expand with poor dwellings and grossly inadequate traffic, drainage, and park facilities.

The urban way of life has also penetrated farm villages by means of television, motorcycles, and automobiles. More than 90 percent of agricultural households have television sets, and over 50 percent of them have motor scooters or motorcycles. Thus, the difference in the mode of living between cities and villages has been greatly narrowed.

Associated with these changes in the mode of living are changes in family structure. The traditional Japanese family was an extended family composed of not only a couple and their children but also the husband's parents and occasionally his brothers and sisters. This family form broke down after the war. With the rise in their social position, women no longer repress their own wills as they used to do, and they no longer want to live with their husband's parents. Moreover, in the cities, housing conditions are so inadequate that it has become physically impossible for a large family to live together. This development has accelerated the breakdown of the traditional family structure and has strengthened the so-called nuclear family pattern.

Table 3.7

Birth and Death Rates and Size of Family, 1920–1965

	Birth Rate	Death Rate	Average Life Expectancy*		Persons per Household
			Male (years)	Female (years)	
1920	36.2%	25.4%	42.1	43.2	4.89
1930	32.4	18.2	44.8	46.5	4.98
1940	29.4	16.5	50.0	54.0	5.00
1950	28.1	10.9	58.0	61.5	4.96
1955	19.4	7.8	63.9	68.4	4.97
1960	17.2	7.6	65.3	70.2	4.54
1965	18.5%	7.1%	67.7	73.0	4.05

*Figures for 1920 are the average from 1920 to 1925; the figures for 1930 are the average from 1926 to 1930; the figures for 1940 are the figures for 1937.

Important to the change in family structure is the fact that the structure of the Japanese population has shifted from a pattern of high to low birth and death rates (see Table 3.7). The birth rate, which had remained around 30 percent during both the pre- and postwar periods, dropped to less than 20 percent in 1955. Accordingly, the average number of household members, which had been 5 until 1955, dropped to 4.5 in 1960 and 4.0 in 1965. The number of children per couple decreased to 2, less than enough even to reproduce the population. The trend is the same in both cities and villages. In villages, however, because it is still common for the parents to live with their son's family, the number of persons per household is larger than the number in urban households. But here, too, the average number of persons per agricultural household is declining; the figure was 5.9 in 1955 and only 5.3 in 1965. Thus, agricultural villages can no longer be the source of labor force supply.

Meanwhile, the tendency toward lower birth and death rates has caused a change in the status of children in the family; that is, the expectations surrounding children's achievement and expenditures on their education have become high—a kind of democratization of the family in the sense that parents have come to recognize each child's personality and to give each child a better educational opportunity. Indeed, the children's voice in a family has become considerably louder. However, another aspect of this tendency for increased expenditure on children's education is the traditional desire on the part of parents to depend upon their children when they reach retirement and old age. In Japanese society a good education guarantees an individual's future because education is open to every social class and those who are graduated from a good school can enter a higher social class. Thus, educational levels in postwar Japan have risen rapidly. More than 70 percent of junior high school graduates enter senior high schools, and 30 percent of senior high school graduates enter a junior college or university. Some of the senior high school graduates become blue-collar workers, and the universities, which used to be the place where the future social elite was educated, have become educational centers for white-collar workers. Thus, a gap has been created between reality and the desire of the parents to enable their children to enter a higher social class.

Changes in Life Styles

The changes in the household structure and character mentioned above have disrupted the traditional family system and destroyed the value system upon which the family system depended. Before the war Japan had to support large military expenditures, despite its low production capacity. Therefore, frugality and diligence were among the most important economic virtues. Each social class had its own pattern of consumption and mode of living. However, as mentioned above, the postwar era saw great changes in the social classes. The relationship between the landlord and tenant was broken and every farmer became independent, although differences remained in size of farms. The workers increased their social status with the help of the unions. Thus, the difference in the mode of consumption between blue- and white-collar workers has diminished, and, as a result, consumption patterns have become considerably standardized. Second, since the industries that took the initiative in the economic growth after 1955 were primarily those producing durable consumer goods such as electric appliances and automobiles, the Japanese economy itself has stimulated the expansion of consumer demand. Furthermore, the real wages of workers have increased as a result of annual wage increases, and farmers' incomes are also higher than they were as a result of the conservative government's high rice price policy by which it expected to ensure the continued political support of the farmers, and the farmers' supplementary income from wage-earning jobs. For this reason, living standards have risen rapidly, although a number of imbalances remain.

The rise in the standard of living has affected the social consciousness of workers. They no longer regard themselves as belonging to the lower class but instead think of themselves as middle class. According to a recent "Survey of Public Opinion concerning the Peoples' Living," conducted by the Cabinet Secretariat, more than 90 percent of the people regard their standard of living as above average, and according to a union survey the majority of workers regard themselves as living an above-average life. The 1967 Sōhyō annual report states that "among workers the so-called middle-class consciousness became crystallized."[11] Young workers in particular, who have no fear of unemployment in a tight labor market and who enjoy a high rate of wage increase, have become less critical of the existing political system, more positive with regard to present conditions, and more indifferent to politics. This is in sharp contrast with the situation immediately after the war when the young workers were more radical.

The general satisfaction described above does not mean, however, that the people have no complaints. Imbalances in living standards are most clearly seen in housing conditions. Urbanization was well under way before many of the houses destroyed in the war were reconstructed or replaced. As a result, the housing shortage in the cities is very serious and the average size of newly built houses, including privately owned homes, is only 36 square meters. In the Tokyo-Yokohama district, for example, 28 percent of the total households are in quarters judged substandard in terms of per capita space. As housing shortages cause a rise in the price of land, houses, and, accordingly, rent, it becomes too expensive, relative to income, to improve housing or to rent housing that is adequate. As a result, it is common for a family of four to live in a small apartment of 36 square meters which also contains a televi-

11. Sōhyō, Research Department, *Annual Report: Analysis of Japanese Politics, Economy and Labor* (Tokyo: Sōhyō, 1967), p. 122.

sion set, an electric refrigerator, and an electric washing machine. In such a situation the family is unable to enjoy a comfortable life, and they tend to seek pleasure outside—at the seaside, in the mountains, and in the amusement centers in the city. The higher incomes of people have made it possible for them to buy television sets or in some cases, automobiles, but they still do not have enough to obtain better housing.

Thus, although people generally accept the Japanese social system, nevertheless they complain about various contradictions derived from imbalances in living conditions. These complaints, together with inflation, provide the source of energy for the workers' annual Spring Labor Offensive and the rice price increase movement of farmers. Also, some people have developed strong feelings of alienation because the important economic and political decisions are made in places beyond their reach, and because conservative control of the system is becoming increasingly firm. Although urbanization caused some anxiety within the Liberal-Democratic Party, which had depended upon the agricultural districts for support, economic growth, by creating a middle class among the ranks of workers, has benefited the party by attracting a portion of this new middle class to it. As a result, the socialist parties, both left and right wing, have not been able to make gains much beyond one-third of the Diet seats. Most of the self-employed people and unorganized workers who are dissatisfied with both the conservative and the socialist parties have sought religious help from Sōka Gakkai and support the Kōmeitō (Clean Government Party) which was established in 1962 as Sōka Gakkai's political wing, but is now independent of the religious group. In spite of this, it is very likely that the Liberal-Democratic Party may enjoy an absolute majority and may be able to maintain itself under an arrangement by which its intraparty factions alternate in power. The reason for this is as follows: although the people's frustration over the social stabilization is seen in various forms such as the rapid growth of Sōka Gakkai and the widespread student movement, the government's economic policy has succeeded in maintaining a high economic growth rate and in raising the living standards of the people. The relationship between the business leaders who control economic activities and the major factions of the Liberal-Democratic Party is very close, and these business leaders strongly support the continuation of the conservative government.

The Labor Shortage and Industrial Relations

Just when it seemed that technological change, economic growth, and changes in social life would result in the establishment of rules of industrial relations at the workshop level, the industry level, and the national level, a serious problem arose which was to undermine those rules. The problem was a labor shortage caused by the rapid growth of the economy.

As mentioned above, since economic growth has been so rapid since 1955, the increase in productivity per worker has not been able to absorb the increase in the demand for labor, and a labor shortage has been apparent since 1960, in contrast with the earlier excess labor supply situation. In 1955, the total number of employed workers was estimated at 17,780,000. By 1960, the number had increased to 23,700,000, and in 1967 it was 30,710,000. The reason for this increase is that the large enterprises, which had previously restrained themselves in hiring new workers in order to provide jobs for those employees made redundant by technological changes, started to see a need for larger labor forces. In addition, the small and medium-sized businesses, which produce consumer goods and parts for the large firms, found it difficult to afford labor-saving machines and thus could keep up with increased production mainly by increasing their labor forces.

Labor shortages, especially of young workers, are most acute in the small and medium-sized firms where working conditions are inferior to those of the large enterprises. Although the *nenkō* (length-of-service) wage system does not operate fully in these companies, the young workers are poorly paid.

In a period of technological change, where jobs are simplified and repetitive even in the small and medium-sized plants, young unskilled workers are most in demand. At the same time, there is an excess of high-paid middle-aged and older workers. Once one of these workers loses his job, it is very difficult for him

Table 3.8
Number of Employed Persons, by Industry and Status, 1950–1965

	Agriculture and Forestry				Other			
	Total	Self-Employed	Unpaid Family Workers	Employees	Total	Self-Employed	Unpaid Family Workers	Employees
1950	16,532	5,449	10,372	711	19,135	3,835	1,875	13,425
1955	15,405	5,127	9,616	665	23,848	4,267	2,276	17,305
1960	13,699	5,044	8,112	513	30,001	4,643	2,396	22,972
1965	11,116	4,484	6,283	349	36,501	4,809	2,939	28,753

Source: Prime Minister's Office, Bureau of Statistics, *Kokusei chōsa* [National population census] (published every 5 years).

to find another position with desirable working conditions. Thus, at least until the late 1960s, the labor shortage in Japan had two aspects: the shortage of young workers and the excess supply of middle-aged and older workers.

At any rate, the imbalance of demand and supply of young workers has resulted in a rise in wage levels. Small and medium-sized firms have to pay wages at least as high as those paid by the large firms and in some cases they pay even more in order to retain or hire workers. Thus, for instance; in spite of the recession in 1962, wage levels rose and wage differentials by the size of firm for workers under age thirty had virtually disappeared by 1966.

These two factors—the imbalance of demand and supply of young workers, and rising wages—have drawn young workers from the rural areas, accounting in large part for the urbanization trend described above. Population flow from farming villages to towns has been very rapid, and even the oldest sons, who formerly stayed in the villages to succeed their fathers as farmers, have begun to leave for the cities. As a result, as shown in Table 3.8, the number of family workers engaged in agriculture and forestry decreased over the ten-year period from 1955 to 1965 by ore than 3,000,000, or one-third of the total number of persons so employed in 1955. Moreover, the plants which the industrial districts could no longer accommodate moved to agricultural districts and absorbed the local labor force. Therefore, while the number of persons engaged in agriculture and forestry decreased from 16.5 million to 11.1 million, or by one-third, during this period, the number engaged in nonagricultural occupations increased from 19.1 million to 36.5 million, an increase of almost 100 percent. As a result, the agricultural population as a proportion of the total population dropped to 23 percent, which was lower than the 24 percent share held by the manufacturing population.

In addition, since 1960, not only young workers but also middle-aged workers have increasingly begun to shift from firms providing inferior working conditions to those offering better ones. One result is a shortage of day laborers, construction workers, and stevedores, and adult workers have begun to come into the factories not only from the neighboring rural areas but also from remote areas. In the areas bordering on factory districts, farm labor commonly has been undertaken by farmers' wives and old people, and easily operable farm machinery has been introduced.

Under these circumstances, since price increases depress the living standards of workers, labor unions have demanded large wage increases in the Spring Labor Offensives since 1960. Their success in obtaining monthly wage increases of ¥3,000 to ¥5,000 every year between 1960 and 1968 is ascribed not to the power of the unions but to the fact that labor market conditions have favored them. Irrespective of union power, the starting salaries of new school graduates have increased sharply.

However, technological change and large wage increases have aggravated the tension between labor and management. As mentioned before, the *nenkō* wage system is based on length of service or experience, but the new technologies often make the "most experience" factor obsolete. The unions' demands for wage increases based on age have been modified to incorporate subsistence pay with the wage factor based on age. However, this wage system does not provide an incentive to increase production. Since 1956, Nikkeiren has advocated introduction of a new wage system based on ability and efficiency, and many firms are giving this proposal serious consideration.

The lifetime employment system, or *shūshin koyō*, has become a heavy burden on Japanese companies. As the average age level of workers in a company increases, the average wage level and costs also increase. This problem creates another—how to increase pay under the *nenkō* system (see Chapter 10 for a more detailed discussion). The sharp rise in wages cuts into the budget available for a company's welfare facilities, which would weaken paternalistic labor-management relations. If the trend toward merger of enterprises and monopolization in order to protect firms from the effects of the liberalization of capital continues, the present labor movement, particularly the pattern of unified strikes by vertical unions based on the oligopolistic economic system, will be affected.

In any case, Japanese industrial relations patterns, established so recently, are already being forced to change as a result of many new tensions.

4. The Legal Framework: Past and Present

Legal frameworks are embedded in social contexts and vary according to nation and to time. So it is with the legal framework of labor-management relations. For example, the legal framework in Great Britain, where modern labor-management relations were established prior to political democracy, is very different from that in other countries, where modern labor-management relations were established after democratic political institutions were achieved. In countries such as Britain, both labor and management (especially labor) attempt to minimize emphasis on the law, but where democratic political institutions preceded the development of modern industrial relations, laws are relied upon more heavily. Needless to say, Japan belongs in the latter category.

It is important to note here that the major impetus for Japan's modernization came *from above*. The emperor granted a constitution before the people were politically aware; they were given civil law codes before their consciousness as citizens had developed. Legally, the shift "from status to contract" was almost complete. However, status in terms of master-servant relationships continued to dominate the relations between employer and employee as well as between landlord and tenant. A relationship similar to that of parent and child continued to exist.

From the beginning of the development of the legal framework, in the early Meiji period, workers and tenants appeared to be dissatisfied with status-oriented practices and demanded equal rights. Employers and landlords opposed these demands with their own claims for legal freedoms of contract, especially the freedom to terminate workers. In practical terms, this meant freedom to discharge employees at the work place and the right to end tenancies. In other words, when workers and tenants became aware of their rights as citizens, employers and landlords also demanded their own rights. Due to the resulting organization and resistance of workers and tenants, labor and farm disputes occurred.

The government retaliated with oppressive laws and tighter administration from above. In order to remove this oppression and to achieve substantial equality between labor and management, the establishment of still other basic rights was necessary. This goal was not realized, however, until after the Pacific War, when workers were emancipated through enactment and enforcement of a new Japanese constitution and the establishment of various labor laws. Against this background, some of the reasons for the excessive legalism in Japanese labor-management relations may be understood.[1]

Individual Japanese almost instinctively dislike handling human relations through laws or in the courts. When a Japanese is sued in a civil case, for example, he suffers as if he were being prosecuted as a criminal. A victim of a traffic accident will usually settle the matter privately, even if this entails the loss of justified indemnity, rather than take the case to court. To cite another example of this attitude, when a newly employed worker automatically becomes a member of a union composed of the employees of his company, he does not object to the collection of union dues from his wages.

It is little wonder that union leaders, who are neither law- nor contract-conscious, believe that such practices need not be covered in collective labor-management agreements. They realize that to replace the individual worker-employer relationship with a collective relationship is to elevate the relationship to the level of laws and contracts, for only by so doing can workers be on an equal

1. At the initial stage of organization, it is likely that many unions went on strike mainly because they had been given the right to strike. Union leaders were generally eager to test the bounds of legality for hostile action and to extend them as far as possible.

footing with employers.[2] It is generally said that the "excessive" legalism in present-day Japanese labor-management relations stems from the "immaturity" of the parties, but actually the immaturity arises from the concepts about basic social relations described above.

Accordingly, under these circumstances, labor legislation plays a very important role in Japanese industrial relations. Furthermore, both the substance and the administration of labor legislation retain the character of a set of rights imposed from above. In this chapter we shall describe the initial labor legislation enacted under the aegis of the Occupation forces and try to trace the policies and activities of the government and public agencies with regard to industrial relations since the end of World War II.

Initial Labor Legislation under the Occupation

The emancipation and protection of workers were carried out by the enactment of laws under pressure from the Occupation forces. The process of emancipating the workers was somewhat different from the process used for the peasants. Whereas land reform depended on legal action for the purchase of land from the landlords, the emancipation of workers was realized only by abolishing former laws and regulations which had oppressed union activities.

To keep pace with the rapid organization of unions after the war, the Trade Union Law was enacted (December 22, 1945) and enforced (March 1, 1946), whereby workers' rights to organize, bargain collectively, and engage in labor disputes were formally guaranteed. It was after the adoption of the Trade Union Law that the new constitution was proclaimed on November 3, 1946, and made effective on May 3, 1947. A provision of the constitution guarantees "the rights of workers to organize, bargain collectively and carry on other collective actions." This provision declares the basic policy of collective industrial or union-manage-

2. Instead, while collective bargaining is under way, union leaders very often instruct their members to wear head or arm bands or to put a ribbon on their chests lettered with slogans such as "Unity" or "Victory." By wearing these signs workers feel that they are acting in combination on an equal footing with their employer.

ment relations, which had actually already been materialized in the Trade Union Law.

Another feature introduced to Japan by the Trade Union Law, in a clause patterned after the Wagner Act of the United States, was the concept of unfair labor practices. To administer this section, the law established tripartite labor relations commissions composed of labor, management, and public representatives. A Central Labor Relations Commission in Tokyo and local labor relations commissions in every urban and rural prefecture were to examine unfair labor practice cases.

Subsequently, in order to prevent or solve labor disputes, the Labor Relations Adjustment Law was enacted on September 27, 1946; it provided that the labor relations commissions should also adjust labor disputes, through conciliation, mediation, and arbitration. On the other hand, the law prohibited workers engaged in safety maintenance work from striking, and workers in public utilities were required to submit disputes to mediation thirty days prior to any strike (later shortened to ten days).

The basic policy concerning individual industrial or employer-employee relations rests upon the guarantee for all people of the right to maintain minimum standards of wholesome and cultured living—the so-called right to livelihood provided in Article 25 of the new constitution. Article 27, Section 1, declares that all people have the right and the obligation to work, while Article 27, Section 2, states that minimum standards of wages, working hours, rest, and other working conditions are to be fixed by statute. However, the constitution is not interpreted to mean that individual workers have a right to request the state or a particular employer to provide work, since the "right to work" article is to be regarded only as a declaration of policy. Also there are no standards given for setting minimum wages and working conditions. The "right to work" and the establishment of minimum working conditions depend entirely upon the enactment of statutes by the Diet.

Thus, the Labor Standards Law was enacted and came into force on September 1, 1947. This law stipulates protection for women and young people and sets minimum standards for terms and conditions of all individual and collective employment contracts. Minimum requirements cover prior notice in case of firing, fair standards for wages and working hours, safety and hygiene in plants and other places of business, and the employer's duty to provide workmen's compensation in labor accidents. Further, the law stipulates that working conditions must be agreed upon bilaterally, with both parties on an equal footing, and it prohibits discriminatory treatment of workers, forced labor, and exploitation by intermediaries. The act also calls for the guarantee of workers' civil rights in employment relations.

Together, the Trade Union Law, the Labor Relations Adjustment Law, and the Labor Standards Law—called the "three labor laws"—constitute the pillars of the legal framework for labor relations in present-day Japan. Initially, the emancipation and protection provided by the three laws were to cover all workers; with only the minor exceptions mentioned above, there was to be no substantial discrimination aginst public employees and workers in public utilities.

This principle, however, was abrogated beginning with the Occupation's prohibition of the attempted general strike on February 1, 1947, and then with the issuance of General MacArthur's letter to the Japanese government in July 1948, announcing his new policy of delineating the rights of public employees. Government Ordinance No. 201, issued soon after the MacArthur letter, prohibited strikes by public employees and other acts of protest against the employer and denied the principle of wage determination by collective bargaining in public employment. On December 20, 1948, furthermore, the railroads, the tobacco monopoly, and later the telephone and telegraph industries, all of which were government-operated, were designated public corporations and placed under the purview of the newly adopted Public Corporations Labor Relations Law. In 1952, labor-management relations in five additional government operations —the postal service, the forestry agency, the printing bureau, the mint, and the alcohol monopoly—which had been governed by the National Public Service Law, were transferred to the juris-diction of the new act, retitled the Public Corporation and

National Enterprise Labor Relations Law. Similar legal changes were enacted for employees of local governments and local public corporations.

Thus, workers in the public sector came to be covered by laws different from those applied to private industrial workers, and different laws were adopted covering different types of public workers. This situation not only has considerably hindered the development of solidarity among workers in the public and private sectors but also has prevented united action by workers within the public sector. This policy of division, under the conservative government, has continued to the present.

Public Policy Formation and Labor-Management Relations

Usually government is considered to mean primarily the administrative branch, rather than the legislature or judiciary, but in some cases it is taken as the entire governmental machinery of a nation in its broadest sense. As a rule maker in labor-management relations, government plays its most important role through administration, but the Diet as the legislative branch and the courts as the interpretative agency cannot be ignored in the Japanese case. While in this section we will discuss government in its broadest sense and deal in turn with each of the three governmental branches, because Japan employs a parliamentary cabinet system, and because the administration usually takes charge of the drafting of bills, a close relationship exists between the Diet and the administrative branch, and it is difficult to consider rule making in the Diet apart from the administration.

In a review of the mutual relationships among the three branches of government provided in the Japanese constitution, it should be noted first that, under the strong influence of the Occupation forces, sovereignty came to reside with the people, not with the emperor. The bicameral Diet, consisting of representatives of the people chosen by the people, is the supreme organ of national power. The prime minister, representing the majority party, is designated by the Diet and especially by the House of Representatives as the highest executive body of the administration. While the Cabinet has the duty to execute faithfully the laws enacted by the Diet, it may also issue Cabinet orders to carry out provisions of the constitution and the laws. Further, while the Cabinet has its basis in the Diet, it is vested with the right to dissolve the House of Representatives on its own judgment. In this way the road is open to seek the opinion of the people about important current problems.

As for the judiciary, the members of the Supreme Court are appointed by the Cabinet, while judges of the lower courts are appointed by the minister of justice from among persons nominated by the Supreme Court. All judges, however, are independent in the exercise of their consciences and are bound only by the constitution and the laws. Their status is guaranteed, and a judge may be removed only by an impeachment court consisting of members of both houses of the Diet. The Supreme Court has the power to determine the constitutionality of any law enacted by the Diet and of any order, regulation, or official action of the administration.

Thus, the three functions—legislative, judicial, and administrative—are formally separated from one another under a system of checks and balances. The government takes the role of rule maker in labor-management relations through the three separate functions based upon the policies declared in Articles 27 and 28 of the constitution. In practice, however, the relationship between the Diet and the Cabinet is very close.

The first step in the enactment of laws is for the administrative section of the relevant ministry to prepare a draft under the direction of its minister. In many cases, during the period of preparation, the opinion of an inquiry commission is taken into consideration; for example, in amending the Labor Standards Law, consultation takes place with the Central Labor Standards Council. Depending on the importance of the problem, the minister concerned may adjust a prepared draft, taking into account the opinion of the policy investigation commission of the ruling party. The bill is then submitted to the Cabinet for consultation and approval before going to the Diet. If both the House of Representatives and the House of Councilors pass the bill, it becomes a law.

In a few cases, members of the Diet submit bills directly to the Diet, but it is much more common for the government administration to offer bills. For this reason, the role of the administration in the legislative process is large. Also, since the Cabinet has the power to enact orders to execute the provisions of laws within the framework of the constitution and the laws, the importance of the administration becomes even greater. Nonetheless, the Diet, within the framework fixed by the constitution, has the power to legislate and does enact the most important rules or laws governing labor-management relations.

It was not only the majority party in the Diet that decided the content of labor legislation immediately after World War II. During the Occupation period, the Supreme Commander for the Allied Powers (SCAP) possessed supraconstitutional powers and exerted a strong influence over the administration and the Diet. For example, in regard to the right of public employees to engage in disputes, MacArthur issued orders to restrict such disputes, which materialized in Government Ordinance No. 201. Based upon this ordinance, the National Public Service Law was amended, and the Public Corporations Labor Relations Law was enacted. It may be said that contemporary changes in labor policy in the United States both directly and indirectly influenced Japanese legislation as the policy of SCAP changed.

Theoretically, Japanese labor legislation after the peace treaty in 1952 was free from the influence of the Occupation and directly tied to the constitution. The guarantee by Article 28 of the constitution of "the right of workers to organize and to bargain and act collectively" was and has remained the most important basic regulation. However, although the guarantee is expressed unconditionally, the Diet, in which the conservative party has continuously held a majority since the new constitution became effective, has always taken the position that this right may be restricted by considerations of "public welfare." This opinion is also regarded as the basis for various laws restricting the rights of workers in the public sector to engage in disputes and to bargain collectively. The courts, which are vested with the power to determine the constitutionality of the laws, have tentatively approved such an interpretation by other sections of government.

However, it must also be noted, with regard to restrictions on the right to engage in disputes and to bargain in the public sector, that conventions of the International Labor Organization (ILO) on standards for labor-management relations have considerable influence over the Japanese Diet. This has been clearly demonstrated by cases in which, partly because the "progressive" (i.e., socialist and communist) parties are always in the minority in the Diet, national unions such as the National Railway Workers' Union, or Kokurō, and the Japan Postal Workers' Union, or Zentei, as well as Sōhyō have appealed to the ILO on the grounds that labor's right to organize was violated. As a result, a special commission was sent to Japan by the ILO to investigate, and subsequently Japan ratified ILO Convention No. 87. Since the constitution provides that "treaties concluded by Japan and established laws of the nations shall be faithfully observed" and also requires Diet approval for conclusion of treaties, treaties are interpreted as having priority over laws.[3]

The progressive parties have never held a majority of seats in the Diet, nor are they likely to do so in the near future. Since the difference in numerical strength between the conservative party and the progressive parties is so wide and party control over members so strong, there is no hope for the labor movement to obtain favorable laws in the Diet by supporting the few sympathetic members within the conservative party. Also, as the formulation of the budget is left entirely to the Cabinet, the chance of legislation introduced by an individual Diet member being passed is quite small. Thus, legislation on labor policy is controlled by the conservative party, and, generally speaking, the role the progressive parties can play at present is limited to

3. The Diet ratified the convention on June 13, 1965, but made only tentative revisions in several clauses of the National Public Service Law, the Public Corporation and National Enterprise Labor Relations Law, and other acts where they were in conflict with the convention. Actually, the Diet left further investigation and adoption of the revisions to the Public Service System Investigation Council, which was required to conclude its work no later than June 13, 1966, in order to prevent the possibility that provisions in conflict with the convention would become null and void, thus causing confusion.

preventing the deterioration of existing labor legislation. Even this role results in their disturbing Diet deliberations, at times resorting to physical force.

Nonetheless, because debates and interpolations before the Diet budget committee are widely reported in the mass media, the Diet does play a considerable role in informing the people about what the government thinks about labor-management relations and how the progressive parties which claim to represent the interests of workers react to the government's policies.

Emancipation of workers by the Occupation was full and thorough, or at least was believed to be so by the Japanese workers. However, beginning with the issuance of the prohibition order against the February 1 General Strike (1947), public policy became increasingly restrictive. The restrictions can be broadly divided into two groups. One, as already noted, distinguishes between workers in the public and private sectors. Even though in later years these restrictions came into conflict with the rights to organize and to bargain collectively specified in ILO Conventions No. 87 and 98, successive Cabinets have continued the policy of discrimination against workers in the public sector. Since there seemed to be no possibility of revising the laws through parliamentary means, workers in the public sector came to rely upon force in the form of strikes in an effort to recover the right to strike.

The other restrictions called upon the labor movement to exercise moderation. For example, the tactic of "production control," which placed production activities of an enterprise in the hands of the union, was judged illegal by the Supreme Court in 1950, while the resort to general strikes was suspended by the above-mentioned Occupation order. By 1949, a proviso was added to the Trade Union Law to the effect that in no case was use of violence to be interpreted as a proper act of a labor union. Then, in 1952, a new provision on "emergency adjustments" was added to the Labor Relations Adjustment Law. This stated that when, "because of the case being related to a public welfare work, or being of a large scale, or being related to a work of special nature, suspension of the operation thereof arising from an act of dispute seriously threatens national economic activities or daily life of the nation and only when there exists such a threat," the prime minister had authority to decide upon an emergency adjustment. For fifty days after announcement of his decision, acts of dispute were to be prohibited. Also, in August 1953, the so-called Strike Restriction Law was enacted; this law prohibits "acts of interrupting directly the normal supply of electricity" and such "acts of suspending the normal operation of coal mine safety maintenance activities provided for in the Mine Safety Law as endanger human lives in mines, inflict ruinous or serious damage on mineral resources, destroy vital facilities in coal mines, or cause damage in coal mining."

Administration of Policy

Among the Japanese government agencies that have responsibility for labor-management relations is the Ministry of Labor. The ministry, however, does not take charge of every sphere of labor-management relations. For example, labor-management relations of seamen, including seamen employment exchanges, labor accidents, and unemployment insurance, fall under the jurisdiction of the Ministry of Transportation. Supervision of mine safety is under the jurisdiction of the Ministry of International Trade and Industry. Part of labor-management relations, in a broad sense, such as health insurance and retirement pensions, is the responsibility of the Ministry of Health and Welfare. In the treatment of national public employees, the National Personnel Authority performs important functions. In terms of the government functioning as an employer, moreover, every agency enters the scene. Among these, the Ministries of Finance, Postal Services, Agriculture and Forestry, and International Trade and Industry, which have field offices, play the most important roles.

Before turning to the nature and organization of the Ministry of Labor, we should point out several problems that face the Ministries of Transportation and of International Trade and Industry, among others, in handling labor-management relations in their respective fields. Since these ministries are concerned with the management of enterprises, such as in shipping or mining works, and because they have responsibility for industrial development, they can contribute to the stabilization of labor-management relations by using their influence in a fair manner. Indeed, in the sphere of labor-management relations related to seamen, for example, there has been no request to remove this function from the Ministry of Transportation. However, there is some danger that the ministries may place too much emphasis upon industrial development at the expense of the workers. Thus, in the area of mine safety maintenance, whenever a major accident occurs, there are repeated demands to shift responsibility to the Ministry of Labor. It is claimed that the Ministry of Labor can easily perform this duty, which requires only that it be fair to both labor and management according to principles of equality of labor and management and mutual noninterference of the parties, and because it does not have to look after the interests of any particular industry.[4] Because administration of labor-management relations is shared by several ministries within the Cabinet, either ministerial conferences must be called to settle common problems, or the Prime Minister's Office must make the necessary adjustments.

The Ministry of Labor

The Ministry of Labor originated in the prewar Social Bureau of the Home Affairs Ministry. It was this bureau that, in 1920, drew up Japan's first trade union bill; the Ministry of Agriculture and Commerce also drew up a bill, which was rather restrictive in nature. The Social Bureau's proposal was more progressive, an

4. The Ministry of Education is also deeply involved in labor-management relations. Virtually all teachers in elementary, junior high, and senior high schools but not at universities are local public service employees. Therefore, their treatment is left to negotiations between each local government and its corresponding branch of the Japan Teachers' Union (Nikkyōso) and the Japan High School Teachers' Union (Nikkōkyō). Although Nikkyōso insists on negotiations with the minister of education not only on working conditions of teachers but also on the problems of education, successive ministers have rejected these demands because of the left-wing orientation of Nikkyōso.

indication that among the bureaucrats in the Ministry of Home Affairs, which dealt mainly with police administration, there were top officials who were adaptable to world trends after World War I. Although the trade union bills were brought before the Diet several times before 1930, none became law. Rather, Japan began to turn toward the right, down the road to the Manchurian Incident and World War II. Just before the Pacific War broke out, the Social Bureau was made independent of the Ministry of Home Affairs, and in 1938 it became a part of the Ministry of Health and Welfare. On September 1, 1947, a separate Ministry of Labor was established which, under the guidance of the Labor Section of SCAP, was to be a more progressive agency in the field of labor-management relations than the former Social Bureau.

At the time of its inauguration, the staff of the Ministry of Labor was composed chiefly of the staff of the former ministries of Home Affairs and of Health and Welfare. However, as time went on, these staff people, who from the beginning had an interest in labor-management relations, were prepared to become specialists in the industrial relations field. Although they were at a disadvantage in specializing in a narrow field, their ability as skilled administrators overcame this drawback. Since 1953, for example, there have been labor attachés stationed at embassies and legations in foreign countries such as the United States, Great Britain, and West Germany, as well as at the ILO. This demonstrates Japan's increasing interest in labor situations abroad, and it is safe to say that, stimulated by information gathered through these antennae, the staff of the Ministry of Labor has reached international levels in ability and knowledge.

The Ministry of Labor, like other ministries, consists of several bureaus. At first there were only four—Labor Policy, Labor Standards, Women's and Minors', and Employment Security. Employment policy came to attract much attention around 1955, and as a result the Vocational Training Bureau, separate from the Employment Security Bureau, was set up in 1958. In order to put more stress upon the prevention of labor accidents, in 1967 the Department for Prevention of Labor Accidents was separated from the Labor Standards Bureau. These bureaus administer the laws in their respective fields, draw up government ordinances and orders, and frame bills when necessary.

Administration of union-management relations, such as the formation of labor unions, collective bargaining, acts of dispute, and mediation and arbitration, is the responsibility of the Labor Policy Bureau. Its main concerns are administration of the Trade Union Law and the Labor Relations Adjustment Law, matters within the authority of the minister of labor under the National Public Service Law and the Local Public Service Law, and procedures for appointing members of and enforcing the rules of the labor relations commissions and the Public Corporation and National Enterprise Labor Relations Commission.

Immediately after the war, when the workers were emancipated for the first time and were inspired to organize unions, they demanded that employers bargain collectively and relied upon strikes to enforce their demands. The Labor Policy Bureau and its counterpart, the labor policy section at the local government level, played a most important role in these activities. The primary functions of these agencies were to eliminate interference by employers and to protect and enhance the freedom of workers to organize. They faced the problem of preventing labor unions, especially those organized on the enterprise level, from receiving financial assistance from the employer, particularly when the Labor Section of SCAP criticized these practices. The unions, however, took as a matter of course the use of the employer's premises for offices, utilizing the employer's equipment, and having the employer pay the wages of those engaged in union work. The unions reasoned that such benefits were obtained as the result of their struggles, while employers considered that bearing such minor expenses would help maintain industrial peace.

However, because the SCAP Labor Section continued to insist that unions should not become company dominated, the Labor Policy Bureau proposed in 1949 a revision of the Trade Union Law which stated that "those who receive the employer's financial support in defraying the organization's operational expenditures" would no longer be approved as labor unions under the law. The unions at first resisted this proposal, but, since the practice of payment of wages by employers to full-time union officers had been gradually diminishing, their resistance has decreased over time. However, benefits such as the employer's furnishing of minimum office space, which is allowed by law, have remained general practice. Also, a certain proportion of the total number of employees in a company (the ratio differs according to the type and nature of the industry, but is usually one for every three to five hundred workers) were recognized as working full time for the union even though holding positions as company employees. Some even rose to offices in higher union organizations; Kaoru Ohta, for example, served as chairman of Sōhyō for a decade. If such full-time officers should wish to return to their work place, in principle they are guaranteed the position and wages that they would have had if they had not become union officers. Many collective agreements make this a clear stipulation.

Similar treatment of full-time union officers was permitted for unions in the public sector, but, following ratification of ILO Convention No. 87 in 1965, after considerable controversy, the government restricted these practices. It was finally decided that public sector employees who become full-time union officers may hold their employee positions for no more than three years.[4a] During the three-year period, they must decide whether to remain professional full-time union officers or to return to the work place as employees.[5]

One problem that always faces labor administration is union action in disputes. When an extreme act violates the criminal code, it may become the basis for an indictment as a criminal action; and when an extreme act damages the employer beyond rightful limits and the employer therefore sues the union or its leaders for damages, the case is dealt with in a civil action. Further, when the employer fires a person responsible for an

4a. Recently the term was lengthened to five years.

5. In this connection it is interesting to note an ambiguity raised by ILO Convention No. 98, which specifically exempts government employees from the protection of the freedoms of association guaranteed in Convention No. 87. In the French and English texts of the convention, government employees are strictly defined as those who are engaged in the administration of the state, i.e., civil servants. However, in the Japanese text ratified by the Diet this is translated simply as "government employees," leaving doubt as to whether Convention No. 98 applies to employees of public enterprises.

excessive act in a dispute and the discharged person asks for relief on the grounds of an unfair labor practice, the case can be judged either by a labor relations commission or by a court. Labor administrative agencies are expected to give advice or guidance so that such cases will not occur. Since the government, however, includes the public procurator's office, when acts of dispute appear to exceed lawful limits, the government warns that it will bring a criminal charge against the participants through this office. The union commonly sees this as intimidation. Also, since the government drafts legislation to deal with large-scale strikes in public welfare work and other industries, the Ministry of Labor, whose essential function is to protect the formation of unions and to encourage collective bargaining, sometimes gives the impression of intimidating the unions.

This dilemma first arose in the interpretation of the method of dispute known as "production control," frequently practiced between 1945 and 1949, whereby the union temporarily assumed control of the enterprise. In 1946, the prime minister's statement on maintaining social order and speeches of the minister of health and welfare (the Ministry of Labor had not yet been established) and of the director of the Labor Policy Bureau all declared the illegality of production control. The courts, however, varied in their decisions regarding its legality, and it was not until 1950 that the Supreme Court decided that production control was illegal in principle. By that time its use in labor disputes had virtually ceased.

By 1954 the accumulation of judgments and decisions of many lower courts had resulted in the establishment of certain limits on acts of dispute, except in special cases. At that time, the Ministry of Labor assembled the leading case theories and issued a vice-minister's notice entitled "On the Prevention of the Exercise of Illegal Acts in Labor Relations." Partly because the notice covered such crucial problems as the limits of picket lines and partly because it included areas where court-made law had not yet been established, the notice generated controversy among unions and among scholars concerned with industrial relations.

Soon after the war it became an important duty of the minister of labor to promote the formation of labor unions and to encourage employers and employees to conclude agreements through collective bargaining. Most agreements in those days were so simple that they merely declared basic policies such as "The company approves the union as the party for negotiation," or "The company shall be operated in a democratic way." Concerning the latter point, some agreements included clauses about the disposition of company property or personnel affairs whereby the company shall "make prior consultation with the union," "decide after consultation with the union," or, in extreme cases, "carry out after consent of the union." Furthermore, such agreements had clauses stating that, until a new agreement was concluded, the existing agreement would be extended automatically.

These agreements became a great hindrance to employers when they attempted to reconstruct their enterprises by curtailing personnel during the period of the Dodge Plan's anti-inflation policy.[6] It was for this reason that the provision on agreements in the Trade Union Law was twice revised in order to open the way for employers to terminate unilaterally agreements having automatic extension clauses.

After 1955 union-management relations entered a period of stability. By 1960, although there was no immediate need to revise the labor laws, the Ministry of Labor established a Commission for the Study of Labor Laws in order to investigate actual conditions and problems of labor-management relations. The commission, after seven years of study, issued a report dealing only with the private sector, the gist of which seemed to support the existing legal system as a whole, although it expressed disapproval of the political inclinations of unions. The report received a rather cool reception from trade union leaders, who were suspicious of the study.

Employment Stabilization and the Law

Stabilization of employment is important as a national policy.

6. This program, which aimed at dealing with the rampant postwar inflation, eliminated government deficit borrowing and inflationary note issues, ended government subsidies to private business, stabilized the rate of exchange, and placed controls on prices. It was very effective in ending the inflationary spiral.

Right after the war there were 4.0 million persons displaced from war industries, 2.3 million soldiers demobilized at home, 2.55 million soldiers demobilized abroad, and 1.2 million repatriated civilians. Added to the number of people already unemployed, this brought to 10 million the number of people seeking jobs. In order to cope with this rapid increase in unemployment, an antiunemployment policy committee was established in November 1945, the Cabinet issued its Principles of Antiunemployment Policy in February 1946, and employment preference in public works was given to unemployed persons. After establishment of the Ministry of Labor on September 1, 1947, and the passage of the Employment Security Law at the end of November of that year, there followed the Unemployment Allowance Law and the Unemployment Insurance Law. By the end of 1948, when the Occupation issued its nine principles for economic stability and thereby undertook a deflationary policy, many workers were displaced from enterprises that had retained them even though they were redundant. These measures spurred a movement for abrogation of provisions calling for preconsultation concerning personnel affairs in labor agreements. In order to meet this problem, not only were the Unemployment Insurance and Employment Security laws revised, but in addition the Unemployment Policy Law was enacted, which established a relief work program for the unemployed and required public works to employ the jobless, through public employment security offices, at a given rate.[7] Although these

7. Unemployment relief work must first satisfy the following five conditions: (1) employment of as many workers as possible; (2) selection of areas where unemployed are numerous; (3) sufficiency in meeting the needs of the unemployed; (4) establishment of wage rates above a specified level; and (5) flexibility in scale in order to meet changes in the employment situation. Then the minister of labor must proceed to establish plans for those areas designated as having high unemployment and set up a schedule for implementation of the plan. In addition, the unemployment relief work must absorb unemployed through arrangements with public employment security offices, but the wage rate decided by the minister of labor must be below that for equivalent work in private industries (in 1964 this provision was revised to allow determination on the basis of the content of work by regional groups).

The report of the Unemployment Policy Investigation Council in April 1956 emphasized the following measures for countering unemployment: (1) elimination of factors that hinder the growth of employment, such as the excessive extension of working hours and increase in nonregular, temporary workers; (2) enforcement of a minimum wage system and expansion of social insurance in order to increase stability of employment in medium, small, and petty establishments; (3) construction of

employment security measures were by no means complete, they appear to have achieved the effects intended, to a certain extent.

While the Korean War, which broke out in June 1950, revived the stagnant Japanese economy, several business recessions occurred prior to 1955. Most industries, to protect themselves against slump periods, followed a policy of not increasing the number of regular workers employed and of relying instead upon temporary workers and subcontract labor. After 1955, however, the Japanese economy regained its prewar level, and employment policy shifted from antiunemployment measures, which guaranteed minimum standards of living for the unemployed, to measures aimed at attaining full employment, which guaranteed every person equitable treatment according to the level of the national economy. This change is seen in the reports and opinions of the Unemployment Countermeasures Council. In April 1957, the Employment Deliberation Council Establishment Law was enacted, "in order to contribute to the operation of the government policy to attain full employment." Under this law the Employment Council was established as a subsidiary agency of the Prime Minister's Office.

Together with these developments, vocational training became an important policy aim, based on the assumption that improvement in the quality of the labor force would make it easier for workers to change jobs and would also increase the supply of skilled labor for industry.

Vocational training, based upon the Employment Security Law, and apprenticeship training, provided for in the Labor Standards Law, were integrated in a new Vocational Training Law enacted in 1958, which also covered skill certification. The first objective of the law was to train and certify skilled workers needed in manufacturing and other industries. The system was

---

houses for workers in order to facilitate labor mobility and relieve the geographical disparities in the demand for labor; (4) provision to retrain workers whose skills are in little demand; and (5) expansion of the social security system in order to prevent an increase of the rate of participation in the labor force. Also, the report stressed the need to integrate unemployment countermeasures and employment policies, set up an agency that would be responsible for their enforcement, and establish survey research and investigation machinery.

divided into public vocational training and enterprise vocational training. Public vocational training has been performed at (1) general vocational training centers established by the prefectures; (2) integrated vocational training centers and central vocational training centers established by the Labor Welfare Corporation (later called the Employment Promotion Corporation) as welfare facilities under unemployment insurance; and (3) vocational training centers for disabled persons, established by the central government or by the prefectures. The central government bears part of the cost of the first and third centers. Not only is training at these facilities available free of charge to workers, but in addition the central government or the prefecture in fact pays allowances to the trainees, according to their circumstances. In the case of enterprise vocational training, the prefectures provide assistance by supplying facilities, sending trainers, and furnishing materials. Those who finish either of the training courses take skill examinations conducted by the Ministry of Labor.

The payment of allowances for trainees augments the unemployment compensation system. Payment of vocational training allowances and extension of unemployment insurance benefits were adopted in the Displaced Coal Miners' Temporary Measures Law in 1959, in a partial amendment to the Unemployment Insurance Law in 1960, in the Employment Promotion Projects Corporation Law in 1961, and in amendments to the Employment Security Law and to the Emergency Unemployment Countermeasures Law in 1963. However, at present, workers who are under the jurisdiction of a given law are paid allowances only according to that law; there is as yet no coordination of the various laws.

In addition to vocational training, the government has been faced with the problem of developing measures for workers displaced because of changes in the industrial structure and in technology—especially notable in coal mining and at the American military bases in Japan. The Employment Promotion Corporation was set up to alleviate the situation, and in 1966 the Unemployment Countermeasures Law made it a government responsibility to formulate basic plans to prevent unemployment, to strengthen guidance for job seekers and employers seeking workers, to train and secure skilled workers, to establish a system of occupational change allowances, and to promote employment of old and middle-aged workers. Thus, the government has taken an active role in promoting employment.

The Labor Standards Law

The Labor Standards Law, enacted under the guidance of the Occupation, established standards for wages, hours, rest, and other working conditions, fulfilling the constitutional stipulation. The standards specified are, on the whole, up to international levels. However, a law of this nature cannot be made effective merely by promulgation. An enforcement system and a strong will to implement the law are also necessary.

As the system for enforcing the Labor Standards Law was inadequate in the beginning, only the most important provisions were implemented at first—the elimination of contract labor, especially for female workers, which had existed since prewar days, and the elimination of forced labor. Later, as additional enforcement officers were employed and trained, controls over the employment of minors and night work of females were enforced. In enterprises where unions were organized, the law was not blatantly violated because the union played a watchdog role.

In 1949, when industrial reconstruction became a problem during the period of deflation brought on by the Dodge Plan, the dual structure of Japan's industry became the object of widespread discussion, and the opinion was frequently expressed that the Labor Standards Law was too severe for small and medium-sized enterprises. While the enforcement ordinance of the law was revised, most of the changes only simplified the procedures; very few were substantive. In 1951, various employer organizations advocated revision, aided by an Occupation statement approving reexamination of the laws adopted since the end of the war. However, since there was little agreement among labor, management, and public agencies during the reexamination by the Central Labor Standards Council, the revisions of the law adopted in 1952 did not result in a decisive lowering of standards.[8]

In the years that followed, the employers demanded revision whenever an occasion arose. For example, in 1953 the Japanese Chamber of Commerce and Industry requested (1) revision of uniform application of the law and substitution of a simple and flexible statute for small and medium-sized enterprises; (2) correction of the "excessively" protective provisions; (3) abolition of "unreasonable" interference and control provisions; and (4) simplification of the procedures. In 1954, the Ministry of Labor responded to these demands by pointing out the technical need to adjust the legal system and to simplify administrative work, and it then requested the Central Labor Standards Council to submit a draft for a revision of the ministry's ordinances in these areas. The draft was accepted, and the ministry issued a new enforcement ordinance which, unlike the 1952 amendment, was not unanimously agreed upon by the three parties. Even then, the revisions did not constitute a substantive lowering of labor standards.[9]

In 1955, in response to further employer pressure, the government established another committee to examine the allegation that the Labor Standards Law was particularly unfair to small and medium-sized firms. However, during the several months of this committee's deliberations, circumstances changed so that by the end of 1956 the committee concluded that, at the present stage, the law should not be revised, and in May 1957, it sub-

8. The major revisions dealt with lessening employer control over intracompany savings systems, development of agreements with representatives of the majority of workers for deductions from wages, simplification of wage computation during paid vacations, special provisions for controlling overtime work and night work by females, and approval of employment of workers between sixteen and eighteen years old in night shifts expressly for conducting apprenticeship training.

9. The revisions were limited because they applied only to the enforcement ordinance and not to the law itself. The major revision included abolition of prohibiting by ordinance the control of overtime extending more than three months, simplification of procedures to eliminate the need for prior approval in addition to reporting, allowing several new exemptions on overtime previously stipulated by the ordinance. (For example, the nine-hour day which had been allowed only in commercial establishments employing fewer than ten employees was extended to those with up to thirty employees. Similarly, additional exceptions were made in the prohibition of night work by female workers.)

mitted a report to that effect to the minister of labor. Since that time there have been no visible efforts to revise or weaken the Labor Standards Law. Instead, the government has been concentrating on the employment problem.

Administration of the Labor Standards Law is the responsibility of the Labor Standards Inspection Office, which follows the principle of enforcing "the most important items first," through both inspection and guidance. Around 1955, the number of items covered by strict inspection began to increase, and inspectors concentrated on the eight-hour-day regulation in the miscellaneous manufacturing sector, and upon the weekly day of rest in retail enterprises. However, because the demand for new school graduates increased after 1957, establishments with poor working conditions found that it was no longer possible to employ these workers. A result was the ironic phenomenon that labor standards came to be observed because of efforts of the Employment Security Offices to induce these employers to commit themselves to observing the standards in order to recruit needed workers.

Thus, in time, the problems faced by the Labor Standards Inspection Office changed. One new problem was nonpayment of wages and retirement allowances in depressed industries such as coal mining. The government was obliged to assist workers with financial and other help. Another was an increased number of labor accidents in the construction and mining industries. The government attempted to control these accidents by revising safety rules and by enacting the Law on Labor Accident Prevention Organizations in 1964, by which the government encouraged employers in industries with high accident rates to form voluntary organizations to set reasonable safety standards in their respective industries.

A third problem that emerged was company control of employee savings. It has been a common practice for the employers to accept deposits from employees at a rate of interest higher than the commercial bank rate (the so-called intracompany savings system). The reaction of workers toward the system has not necessarily been antagonistic. However, when the Sanyo Special Steel Company went bankrupt and was unable to repay its depositors, the incident attracted public attention, and the Central Labor Standards Council took up the problem of whether intracompany savings systems should be abolished or, at least, amended. In the end, the system continued but with the restriction that savings would be taken out of wages only up to a limited amount and rate of interest, and that there should be reserves to assure repayment.

The Women's and Minors' Bureau is responsible for investigating and advising with respect to problems of women and minor workers; it also enforces the child labor prohibition and deals with the problems of family labor. Women and minors, unlike adult males, are extensively protected by the Labor Standards Law but are no different from ordinary workers in the application of trade union rights. The Employment Security Offices pay special attention to their employment, while the Labor Standards Inspection Office is charged with supervising their conditions of work. In addition, the Women's and Minors' Bureau also carries out surveys and proposes measures not directly connected with labor-management relations.

Since World War II, the status of women has risen remarkably, both legally and socially. However, their status as workers is still relatively low and most often temporary, and they are subject to discrimination in promotion, the age limit system, and so on. Not a small number of work rules include an article to the effect that female workers are to retire when they marry, especially if the husband is an employee of the same company. Very recently these kinds of regulations have been declared void by the courts, and there is an increasing tendency for married women to become regular full-time or part-time workers and to return to their work places after periods of absence. This tendency has become particularly strong in the past several years since labor shortages have become apparent. In the field of employment development and protection, the Women's and Minors' Bureau no doubt has contributed to the increase in importance and status of female workers.

The Minimum Wage Law, which provided a substructure for enforcing a uniform minimum wage system by ordinance, was linked with the Labor Standards Law. However, no such ordinances have been issued. Partly because of growing demands by unions and partly because of favorable economic conditions since 1956, the government has followed a policy of establishing minimum wages based on a separate Minimum Wage Law, enacted and enforced in 1959. At first this law gave legal sanction to agreements concluded among employers, but now no minimum wage regulation can be set up without worker participation.

The Judiciary

The Japanese constitution prohibits the establishment of extraordinary tribunals and specifies that the entire judicial power is to be vested in a Supreme Court and in such lower courts as are established by law. It is also legitimate for administrative bodies such as the Fair Trade Commission to make judicial decisions on specific cases. In the field of labor-management relations, the various labor relations commissions as well as the courts have jurisdiction over unfair labor practice cases. The labor relations commissions, however, do not administer justice as courts of last resort. Their orders, including fact-finding, are fully reviewable by the courts. The commissions, therefore, *can assume only an administrative role* strictly bound by provisions of law.

Trials are conducted by district courts and courts of appeals for hearings of fact and by the Supreme Court for hearings on law. The majority of judgeships are held by career judges, as a matter of principle. This seems to influence labor-management relations cases to some extent. In the early postwar period, when the Occupation took measures to emancipate the workers and the new constitution guaranteed fundamental labor rights, judges were faced with a new legal system as well as with new laws, such as the three primary labor acts. It appears that they were embarrassed by their conflicting interpretations. For example, there were considerable differences among the district courts in decisions on the appropriate limits to acts of dispute. However, a common tendency developed among judges to reach decisions that met the actual requirements of labor-management relations, a trend that was influenced in part by the argument, based on the sociology of law, that courts should discover "living law."[10] As a result, even in cases of productiont ontrol the lower courts did not necessarily find it illegal. This attitude of the court arose partly from momentary hesitation over stopping production in a situation where commodities were in very short supply and partly from the fact that strikes would not be effective in inflationary conditions, especially when employers had lost their self-confidence and were unwilling to produce while waiting for price increases. Many provisional dispositions of legality were decided upon which permitted the handing over of control of enterprises to committees made up of representatives of the employer, the union, and an independent third party (usually all representatives were lawyers). However, in 1950, as the economy stabilized, the Supreme Court decided that production control was illegal.

The attitude of judges that "living law" met the requirements of actual social living is common in most areas of the law. In the case of labor laws, the use of this doctrine constitutes one of the major reasons labor unions, despite their verbal denunciations of reactionary court attitudes, do not actually distrust the courts strongly, as has been the case in American and British history. Moreover, because it has been almost impossible in the Diet to revise or abolish laws that suppress the labor movement or to improve laws that protect and encourage organized labor, workers attempt to obtain from the courts as favorable interpretations as possible under the existing legal system.[11]

Still another point is that Japanese judges do not hesitate to step into any area of the people's lives when they think it necessary to do so to provide legal protection. Thus, they take up family problems, disciplinary problems in local assemblies, and in some cases the validity of student expulsions from schools or universities. Likewise, when there are controversies over sanctions ex-

10. Sociology of law was introduced into Japan around 1920. Scholars in this school insisted that Japanese jurisprudence had become overly conceptual or dogmatic and that law should be found not merely in written codes but also in the actual life of the people. Many lawyers were influenced to some extent by this school, and the influence escalated when Anglo-American jurisprudence entered Japan after World War II.

11. This is one of the reasons the Sōhyō Bengodan (Sōhyō Defense Council) was established.

acted by unions, such as suspension or expulsion of members, the cases may be tried in the courts. It is not rare for a person expelled from a union for disobeying a union decision regarding political action to appeal to a court to invalidate the expulsion.

Although the view that decisions should reflect actual requirements in labor-management relations is common among all the courts, there are some differences in degree between the lower and higher courts, especially the Supreme Court. Because lower courts deal with the actual facts of labor-management relations, they tend to mete out justice in concrete terms. Lower court judges are likely to consider whether a union leader, appearing in court as the accused, actually deserves punishment, even though he might have engaged in extreme action during a labor dispute. They even sympathize with the workers when the employer tries to suppress the union. Thus, the limits of appropriate action in disputes are interpreted loosely and, even in the case of an act that violates criminal law, in many cases stays of execution are granted. There have been almost no cases of imprisonment of those engaging in illegal acts of dispute. On the other hand, the Supreme Court tends to respect abstract justice from the viewpoint of social order as a whole. For example, it regarded production control under any circumstances as undermining the basis of the private ownership system and therefore illegal.

Although there are some differences between higher and lower courts, the role of the courts as the rule maker in labor-management relations has been very important. Rules for labor-management relations in Japan have not emerged out of voluntary negotiations between labor and management. Thus, the role of the court is seen not only in making decisions on problems outside the framework of negotiations but also in situations where negotiations between labor and management are insufficient. Since freedom and rights were endowed by legislation from above, neither labor nor management has had a clear understanding of the limits of its freedoms and rights. This is especially true of workers, due partly to lack of knowledge and partly to the efforts of unions to secure as much freedom and as many rights as possible. Despite these experiences, it is now safe to say that the situation has improved to some extent as a result of both court-established case law and the parties' increased familiarity with labor-management relationships, such as collective bargaining.

Labor Organization and the Law

The workers' right to organize is guaranteed by Article 28 of the Japanese constitution. There is disagreement over whether the article only declares that the state must not interfere with efforts of workers to bargain collectively or whether it guarantees the right of workers to organize vis-à-vis their employers. However, most interpretations of this article deny that the law guarantees the right of workers to refrain from joining a union. Since the Trade Union Law and other laws call for employers to respect the right of workers to organize and protect them from employer violations by means of an unfair labor practice system, this argument is not very meaningful. The predominant interpretation is that Article 28 guarantees the right to organize even to civil servants, and the Supreme Court has upheld this interpretation. However, the right of public employees to organize is not guaranteed in exactly the same way as it is for private sector workers. According to the Trade Union Law, whether a union is organized on a craft, industry, or enterprise basis is entirely up to the workers themselves. However, for the workers in the public sector, especially local government employees, the law is written in such a way as to make it more convenient for the workers to organize on an enterprise or establishment basis. If these workers had a common organization with outside workers, the union would have problems in acquiring legal recognition and in exercising its negotiating right.

In order for a workers' organization to enjoy the full privileges of a labor union, as accorded by the Trade Union Law, it must be free and independent from the employer (not admitting into the union those who represent the employer's interest and not relying on the employer for financial aid); it must not disqualify anyone because of race, religion, sex, social status, or family origin; its operation must be democratic (e.g., election of officers and decisions on strikes must be made by secret vote of the members); and it must not be an organization that engages primarily in mutual welfare or political action. It has been argued that workers' organizations which do not meet these conditions also enjoy the guarantee of the constitution, but the conditions of independence and democracy required by the Trade Union Law considerably influence the labor unions.

As a matter of fact, relatively few labor unions engage in welfare activities, although most carry on political action such as supporting candidates of the progressive parties (including financial support for campaigns) or peace movements. In the latter case, political funds generally are not collected separately, but there has been no action instituted by a member to stop unions from spending money for political purposes. Some unions also adopt sanctions such as suspending or expelling members for violating political decisions made by the union. There are opposing academic interpretations and judgments concerning the legal validity of these practices.

The guarantee of the right to organize is enforced primarily through the unfair labor practice system. First, when the employer controls or interferes with the formation or operation of a labor union, the party concerned can seek an injunction from a court or appeal to a labor relations commission for a stop order. Second, when an employer forbids workers from participating in union action—such as by concluding "yellow dog" contracts or by discharging or discriminating against workers for participation in union activities—the party concerned can appeal to the commission for reinstatement in his job and for the cessation of the employer's action. In such cases, it is understood that the party concerned can also appeal to a court for affirmation of the illegality of these acts. Unfair labor practices were subject to punishment as crimes in the original law, but the amendments of 1949 changed this to the principle of "restoration to original status."

The Trade Union Law further provides, in accordance with Article 28 of the constitution, that when the employer rejects collective negotiations with worker representatives without proper reason, this constitutes an unfair labor practice. Thus, employers are under a legal obligation to negotiate, and if an employer refuses, a labor relations commission can order him "to comply with a demand of collective bargaining in good faith." Of course, this law and the procedures under it were influenced by the Wagner Act. However, because the law has no special provision for the determination of the appropriate bargaining unit and the designation of a bargaining agent by election, theoretically even representatives of a small group of workers may demand negotiations. Although introduction of the bargaining system as practiced in the United States was suggested in 1949, it was not adopted because of the opposition of both labor and management. Both groups may have feared that the introduction of the American system would again unsettle labor-management relationships which had by then been tolerably stabilized. Moreover, although the American system was adopted in the original Public Corporations Labor Relations Law, it was abandoned in 1956 because of a judgment that the system did not function well.

Employers cannot reject collective bargaining demands of another union or a group of workers who are not union members. However, many unions include in their collective agreements with employers a provision that the employer will regard the union as the sole party with whom to negotiate (exclusive bargaining rights) even though such provisions have no legal effect. While "closed shop" clauses are not found in collective agreements in Japan because there are few craft unions, "union shop" clauses are very popular and are found in nearly 80 percent of all collective agreements. In this connection, Article 28 of the constitution is not interpreted as a legal obstacle to the union shop (contrary to the case in some European countries, e.g., Ireland), and there are no signs of a drive for "right to work" acts such as has been seen in the United States. Even though the union shop is permitted by law while exclusive bargaining is not, union shop provisions may legally affect only new employees who must join the majority union while the minority union, if there is one, is guaranteed status quo protection including bargaining rights.

Along with union shop clauses, so-called reverse binding provisions are found in a considerable number of collective agreements. These in effect state that a member of the union must also be an employee of the company. Under conventional union shop arrangements an employer has to dismiss an employee who is excluded from union membership, but what happens in Japan if the exclusion is voided by a court after the dismissal by the employer takes place? The courts answer only that the dismissal is null and void, so the dismissed worker continues to hold his position as an employee; satisfactory reasoning for this judgment has never been offered.

In Japan, where most of the labor unions are organized at the enterprise level, it is presumed that union officers are (or used to be) employees of the enterprise, or "insiders." Employers accustomed to negotiating with such officers deeply disapprove of the enterprise union's joining a higher federation and resent any outsider sent from the higher organization to represent the enterprise union at the bargaining table. Therefore, a considerable number of collective agreements provide that future bargaining is to be carried out only by officers who are employees of the enterprise. However, the validity of such contract clauses is questionable, since the Trade Union Law provides that "representatives of the union, or those who are authorized by the union, have the power to negotiate with the employer or the employer's organization for conclusion of the collective agreement or about other matters." Most scholars who take the position that the enterprise union framework should be made more flexible conclude that such special stipulations are invalid, and that unions can delegate authority to negotiate to outside parties, especially to their affiliated higher organizations.

When a collective agreement is formulated and signed by a union and an employer, they are under legal obligation to "keep the peace" for the duration of the agreement, and provisions concerning the treatment of workers are legally binding. In other words, any individual labor contract that does not meet the standards set in the collective agreement is invalid.

Standards of treatment decided upon by the collective agreement become the standard to be applied in individual contracts of employment because the collective agreement is concluded at the enterprise or establishment level. In this sense, it is different from the practice in European countries where the collective agreement functions as the *minimum* standard in the sense that the actual conditions of employment are usually higher.

The Trade Union Law stipulates two kinds of provisions for extension of the collective agreement. One is the extension within the plant or work place, which means that, when more than three-quarters of the workers who are employed regularly and engaged in the same kind of work in the same plant or work place come under the collective agreement, the agreement automatically applies to the rest of the workers. The provision, however, poses the problem of whether the agreement must extend to temporary workers engaged in work similar to that of the regular workers.

The other type of extension is geographical; that is, when the majority of workers engaged in the same kind of work in a district come under the same collective agreement, then, if certain procedures are followed, the agreement can be extended to others engaged in the same kind of work in the district. This provision is similar to the extension of collective agreements in Germany and France. Because traditional categories of work or crafts have not been established in Japan, there are few cases where this second type of extension actually applies.

In the public sector, labor unions under the Public Corporation and National Enterprise Labor Relations Law can bargain collectively with their respective employers and conclude collective agreements regarding only wages, working hours, standards of promotion and demotion, safety, hygiene, compensation for accidents, and other working conditions. Wage increases are subject to budget limitations. Unions of public service employees can request negotiations concerning working conditions, but they do not have the right to conclude collective agreements. In all public sector cases, matters concerning administration and operation of corporations and offices are not subject to negotiations.[12]

The right of workers to engage in disputes, the core of which is the right to strike, is also guaranteed by Article 28 of the constitution under "the right to engage in other collective actions." The right is provided even more concretely in the Trade Union Law, which states that (1) proper acts of dispute do not incur criminal responsibility; (2) neither the labor union nor workers who engage

12. See Chapter 8 for a detailed discussion of these matters.

in acts of dispute are responsible for damages if incurred in the cause of a proper act of dispute; and (3) workers are not to be dismissed or treated unfavorably because of their participation in proper acts of dispute.

The first point is a principle that was established relatively early in most countries. The second is different from provisions found in most Western countries in that the Japanese law gives immunity not only to the labor union but also to individual workers. In other words, if individual workers take part in strikes or other acts of dispute without terminating their individual labor contracts, unless there are unusual circumstances, their acts are regarded as proper acts of dispute, and participating workers are not held responsible for such acts as a breach of contract or tort. That the relationship between employer and employee does not end because of a strike has a remarkable effect in connection with the third point; that is, the employer can discharge those who participate in illegal acts of dispute, but in all other cases workers automatically return to their work places when the strike ends. Procedures for reinstatement are not necessary. The same is the case when an employer hires workers to replace strikers. The legal principle that a strike does not end the labor relationship but only suspends it conforms with the special features of Japanese labor-management relations—lifetime employment and enterprise unionism. By this practice confusion following strikes is avoided, and difficulties concerning the operation of social insurance and company welfare facilities are minimized.

The foregoing is the legal structure surrounding the strike in Japan. One characteristic of the Japanese form is that the labor union strongly resists the entrance of third parties into their work places. Mass picketing and sit-down strikes are manifestations of such feelings. Japanese court decisions and academic theories do not regard these methods of dispute as unconditionally illegal, an opinion that is also influenced by the principles of lifetime employment and enterprise unionism.

Thus, the workers' right to strike is heavily protected in Japan. If an employer hires scabs in an attempt to continue operating, he incurs strong resistance. Therefore, if he considers the demands of the union unacceptable and the dispute is prolonged, instead of hiring scabs, more often than not he will try to split the union and to form a "second" union. If this happens, labor-management disputes are apt to end in a legal quagmire over rights to union assets.[13]

Although the courts seem to place negative interpretations on the appropriateness of political strikes and sympathy strikes which the employer is not in a position to stop, there have been no decisions dealing directly with this problem.

In the public sector, however, the right of dispute is considerably limited. National and local public service employees are prohibited from participating in acts of dispute, and violators are discharged or otherwise punished. Agitation and instigation of acts of dispute are also punishable as crimes against the people.

That employees of national and local public corporations do not have the right to strike is a source of complaint from these workers because this prohibition contrasts sharply with the heavily protected right to dispute of private workers and because immediately after the war the public workers themselves enjoyed the right to dispute as a matter of principle. Therefore, recovery of the right to strike has been a constant demand, and demonstration strikes have been carried out during the past several years in the form of work place meetings.

The employers' right to dispute is guaranteed neither by the constitution nor by the Trade Union Law. In contrast to the established rule in Britain, strikes and lockouts in Japan are not treated equally by the law, but it is generally understood that a lockout by an employer is legal when it is carried out as a defensive play against partial strikes or slowdowns by employees. However, it is very rarely used.[14]

Employment Contracts and the Law

The emphasis having shifted from "status to contract," in present-day Japan everything now hinges upon what is called the

13. For details, see Chapters 8 and 9.
14. See Chapter 9 for a discussion of disputes.

"contract of employment" or "labor contract." The general principles of the law of contract are found in the Civil Code, and the contract of employment is covered in the provisions dealing with obligations, contracts, and employment. However, contracts of employment in the field of industry are regulated by labor legislation, which includes the Labor Standards Law. In explaining the labor contract, we have to look into the details of that law. Formally, the law is a multiple code containing various kinds of provisions. In the first place, an individual labor contract falls under the "Bill of Rights" in the Labor Standards Law, which delineates the working conditions that guarantee to workers a life befitting human beings: equality of labor and management in making decisions about working conditions; prohibition of discriminatory treatment of workers with respect to wages, hours, and other conditions of labor by reason of nationality, creed, and social status; equal pay for men and women;[15] prohibition of forced labor; exclusion of exploitation by intermediaries; and employer obligation to permit workers leave for performing their rights and duties as citizens.

Second, there are various provisions in the law designed to modernize the master-servant relationship, which has been dogged by the premodern restriction of status, and to secure the freedom of workers to move. For example, an individual labor contract must not be concluded for longer than a year; its terms and conditions must be clearly explained to the worker; and the employee may not be required to promise in advance to pay for damages or to participate in the intracompany savings system.

Third, employers are prohibited from terminating an individual labor contract while workers are under medical treatment due to industrial injury or disease or while on maternity leave. Employers are required as a rule to give thirty days' notice of dismissal to workers so that they will not be bewildered as a result of a sudden discharge.

In connection with this prohibition, courts have established

---

15. Discriminatory treatment of workers by reason of sex, except in wages, is not prohibited by the law, but, as mentioned above, courts have been establishing case law that discriminatory treatment of female workers without appropriate reason is against public policy and void.

case law on discharge, which may be divided into two types. The first occurs when the reasons for discharge are specifically listed in the company work rules. In this situation, the employer cannot discharge workers for any reasons other than those stated. When a dispute breaks out over the discharge, an examination is undertaken to determine whether there has been a correct interpretation and application of the discharge clauses of the work rules. If the application is wrong, the discharge is regarded as invalid. The second arises from the rule that the right to discharge must not be abused. Here, there are no formal stipulations in any established rules that the employer cannot dismiss his employees without just cause. However, if, when the employer is questioned by the court as to the reason for discharge, he is unable to give one that is satisfactory, the court generally decides to invalidate the discharge as an abuse of the right to discharge. Also, in interpreting work rules, if the worker is discharged when his conduct merits only a reprimand or suspension, the discharge is held invalid for the same reason.

What should be noted in the above cases is that, in terms of court law, when the decision is made holding a discharge invalid, then the individual labor contract is judged to have remained in force and the employee, even if rejected by the employer, is entitled to his wages. In other words, the court, by nullifying the discharge, allows a discharged worker to collect wages as a company employee instead of recovering damages. Thus, job security has acquired considerable legal protection. In the background is the lifetime employment principle and the knowledge that, for workers, discharge is equal to the death penalty.

Fourth, employers must pay wages in currency and in full. Deductions from wages for other than legitimate purposes are prohibited; wages must be paid to the employee himself (they are practically nontransferable); and they must be paid at least once a month on a fixed date.

Fifth, hours of labor are regulated to conform to an eight-hour work day and a forty-eight-hour work week, although several exceptions are allowed. The exceptions arise from the nature of an industry (nonindustrial workers, such as in distributive trades or services and especially in agriculture and the fishing industry);

from the workers' position in an enterprise (e.g., manager); or from the nature of the work (watchmen or intermittent jobs). An employer may be released from the eight-hour-day regulation by written agreement with the union organized by a majority of his employees, or, if there is no such union, by agreement with the representative of a majority of his employees. Such agreements must be sent to the Labor Standards Inspection Office for approval. There are no limits to the amount of overtime except as noted in the case of women and minors.

Sixth, a worker is entitled to six paid holidays a year after one year of employment in which he has had more than 80 percent attendance. Also, the number of holidays for a worker increases by one for each year of employment up to a total of 20. It is notable that a considerable number of employers give their employees more paid holidays than required by law, but most workers take their holidays not in one stretch but piecemeal, mainly to avoid wage losses when they must be absent for reasons of illness or for personal reasons.

Finally, the law establishes only basic principles regarding safety and hygiene standards. Details are separately stipulated in the Labor Standards Bureau's safety and hygiene rules. The incidence of industrial accidents, however, is by no means low in Japan.

The Japanese Civil Law Code approves claims for damages by a worker or his surviving family when the worker is injured or dies owing to the negligence of the employer or other employees. (There has never been a legal "common employment" rule nor is the principle recognized that a personal suit for damages ends with the death of the person concerned.) However, under the Labor Standards Law, when a worker is injured or becomes ill due to occupational causes, the employer is responsible for compensation even if he is not at fault. The contents of the obligations are as follows: workers suffering from industrial accidents are entitled to medical care or expenses for medical care. When a physical handicap persists after termination of medical care, the worker is entitled to compensation in an amount computed by multiplying his average wage by a certain number of days, depending on the seriousness of the handicap. When a worker is killed, his bereaved family, or those who depended on his income for their livelihood prior to his death, are entitled to survivors' benefits, the amount of which is equivalent to one thousand days of the worker's wages. Those who provide the funeral are entitled to sixty days of the worker's wages. Such rights are neither transferable nor garnishable.

So that these rights may be exercised without fail or delay, the Workmen's Accident Compensation Insurance Law provides that the government supervise the employers' compensation and labor accident obligations through insurance plans which most employers are required to join. Thus, there are few cases in which workers have to call the employer to account. However, to claim damages by reason of tort and to claim compensation based upon the Labor Standards Law are not mutually exclusive, and the amount of compensation already received through one action is credited against the other. Recently, the law was amended so that in certain cases, as when survivors are infants or aged, benefits are paid in the form of an annuity.

Protection for females and young people generally follows standards set at the international level. Notable special protections in the law prohibit young people from being forced to work under unsatisfactory working conditions because of the undue influence of a person having parental authority, and claims on the wages of young workers by a person with such authority.

The Labor Standards Law imposes obligations on employers to make rules regarding the time of reporting for and leaving work, computation of wages, termination of labor contracts, and the like; to submit such rules to a competent government agency; and to post the rules at places in the plant. At the time of setting and changing work rules, an employer must ask the opinion of the representatives of the majority of his workers in advance, but he does not need the approval of the workers. Therefore, he is able to issue or alter rules almost unilaterally.

This stipulation is criticized in some academic circles as contradicting the basic policy of the law—that decisions on working conditions shall be made by the workers and the employer on an equal basis. However, as unions are organized on an enterprise basis, workers actually have no difficulty in placing their objections about work rules on the collective bargaining table. Work rules are regarded as fair labor standards at the given plant, and they play an important role when a collective agreement is not reached, or when the agreement does not cover all working conditions. Their meaning is even more important with regard to discipline and punishment within the plant, as regulations in this area are not necessarily spelled out in detail in the collective agreement. However, because reasons for discharge are listed in work rules, many cases of dismissal do not fall under them, making necessary the concept of "just cause."

The Labor Relations Commissions

Various types of labor relations commissions perform important rule-making functions, more or less independent of the government. The Central Labor Relations Commission and local labor relations commissions take charge of general labor-management relations. The latter are established in each prefecture and are responsible for local cases, while the former handles cases that extend over two or more prefectures or are national in scope. Also, the central commission reviews decisions of the local commissions, and has the right to make rules concerning procedures for all labor relations commissions.

A labor relations commission is composed of an equal number of labor, management, and public representatives. In the case of the central commission, each party has seven representatives; for the local commissions, the number of representatives varies from five to eleven, according to the case load. Labor and management representatives are appointed by the minister of labor or by the prefectural governor from among persons recommended by the respective organizations. The public representatives are also appointed by the minister of labor or by the prefectural governor with the consent of the labor and management representatives. The number of public representatives who belong to the same political party as the appointing official must not be a majority.

Each labor relations commission has its own independent secretariat.

A commission, as an independent administrative agency, is vested with decision-making and adjustment functions. Decision making is carried out only by the public representatives and includes examination of unfair labor practice cases, determination of the qualification of labor unions,[16] and prosecution of acts of dispute that violate the requirement of prior notice in public welfare industries. The adjustment function is roughly divided into conciliation, mediation, and arbitration; the general procedures for each are provided in the Labor Relations Adjustment Law. The Central Labor Relations Commission is different from the American National Labor Relations Board in the sense that the former has adjustment functions. So far, the commission has achieved notable results in this area. Most of its cases are controversies over wages and other working conditions, but there have been some that concern grievance handling. One reason the practice of labor arbitration, common in the United States, has not been established in Japan is that the labor relations commissions are so readily available to perform this function.

Because the appointment of both labor and management representatives is based upon recommendations of their respective organizations, local power relationships among the unions are reflected in the composition of the labor representation of the local commission. This apportionment sometimes gives rise to very delicate questions because it reflects the power relationships at the national level and, in the case of unions, it determines the allocation of the labor seats to such national organizations as Sōhyō, Dōmei, and Chūritsurōren. Also, at one time it was very difficult to find public representatives who could obtain the approval of both labor and management. Today, however, there are far fewer difficulties in this respect.

Since the labor relations commissions possess both judicial and adjustment functions, they have been criticized for making ad-

16. The major points of examination are independence from the employer and democratic union constitution, both of which are required by the Trade Union Law. Unless the union passes this examination, it is not eligible to participate in the formal procedures provided in the law or to avail itself of the law's remedies.

justments in cases in which they are supposed to make judgments. For example, in an unfair labor practice case involving discharge, when the commission is expected to issue a reinstatement order, it often instead approves the discharge and requires only that the employer pay an amount of money to the worker rather than reinstate him. It is also argued, however, that if, as the result of this decision, the discharged worker is satisfied and the labor-management relationship thereafter operates smoothly, then there is no reason to object to the procedure. In actuality, the move to separate the two functions clearly is not so strong that there is any likelihood of amending the law.

The labor relations commissions' decisions in unfair labor practice cases can be brought directly to the courts or to the central commission for review. Thus, depending on the parties, it is possible that an unfair labor practice case may undergo five examinations: local commission, central commission, district court, court of appeal, and Supreme Court. This procedure causes delays in solution, and the possibility of a case review by the courts often has the effect of influencing the local commissions to be less flexible in their decisions. Thus, there are many cases of unfair labor practices which unions take directly to court. The courts have issued such provisional orders as "Comply with collective bargaining!" or "Don't unjustly interfere with the general meeting of the union which is to discuss whether or not to join the upper organization!"—a type of order that is usually issued only by the labor relations commissions. In this sense, the labor relations commissions and the courts compete with each other.

However, the procedures of the labor relations commissions are much simpler and less expensive than those of the courts. As workers in small and medium-sized enterprises have become organized since 1955, increasing numbers of unfair labor practice cases (mostly discharge cases) have been presented to the labor relations commissions. As a result, the number of representatives of each party was increased to eleven in the Tokyo Metropolitan Labor Relations Commission and to nine in the Osaka Prefectural Labor Relations Commission. In the large enterprises, however, there are apparently no unfair labor practice cases, although some unionists contend that there are "hidden" unfair labor practices connected with changes in work systems brought about by technological change.

In addition to the ordinary labor relations commissions, there are two special commissions. One is the Seamen's Labor Relations Commission, which is also divided into central and local commissions. Their organization and functions are similar to those of the regular commissions and require no further explanation.

The other is the Public Corporation Labor Relations Commission, which has jurisdiction over labor-management relations in the public corporations and national enterprises. Although the Public Corporation Labor Relations Commission is tripartite, the members representing the public corporations and their employees each number three, while the number of public members is five. The procedure for appointing members is almost the same as for the regular labor relations commissions except that it is the prime minister who makes the appointments and, in the case of the public members, merely consultation with rather than the consent of the labor and management members is required. Moreover, both houses of the Diet must approve the appointments. The reason for this is that under certain circumstances arbitration is compulsory. Decisions of the Public Corporation Arbitration Committee, which is composed of only the public members, are binding on both the labor and management parties and give the responsibility to the government "to make as much effort as possible to enforce its decisions."

The Public Corporation Labor Relations Commission is also vested with both adjustment and judicial functions, and its procedures are almost the same as those of the regular labor relations commissions. One major difference, however, is that the employees of public corporations do not have the right to engage in disputes but instead their working conditions are determined by third-party arbitration. Disputes not settled through voluntary negotiations between labor and management or through mediation by the tripartite commission are submitted to arbitration either upon the decision of the commission or at the request of the appropriate minister without the consent of labor and management.

Very few disputes have been settled by voluntary negotiations;

in most cases they are mediated and finally settled by arbitration. Arbitration by the Public Corporation Labor Relations Commission has strongly influenced working conditions in private industries as well as in the public enterprises. In other words, the decisions of this commission have played a significant role in determining the general trend of wage increases in Japan.

Thus, there has been no period in the past in which the government has been indifferent to industrial relations. However, the role of government has changed greatly as industrialization has progressed. As in other countries, in the early stages of industrialization legislative bodies, courts, and administrative agencies had little understanding of and sympathy toward workers. For example, judges who had been trained to understand and administer the common law were not likely to be sympathetic to the labor movement. Under common law all common action by workers —not only strikes and picketing but also any kind of agreement among them on minimum wages—was generally regarded as illegal. As in other advanced countries, Japanese workers approached the government to remedy their position. And, again, like the governments in other industrializing countries, the Japanese government and the judiciary were lacking in sensitivity to the situation. As in other countries, Japanese workers bore the brunt of the costs of the transition to industrialization.

However, as industrialization proceeded, the rights of workers to protection from the hazards of machines and factories and the insecurities of the status of employee began to be recognized with the enactment of more and more comprehensive legislation designed to regulate industry and protect workers. While in Western countries this general development of government involvement proceeded rather continuously, in Japan in some ways it was arrested in the 1930s with the onset of the Pacific War. Yet, the spread of government control and involvement in industrial relations was very rapid after 1945. In general, the Japanese developments ushered in by the enactment of the Trade Union Law, the Labor Relations Adjustment Law and the Labor Standards Law, all in rapid succession between December 1945 and April 1947, was not unlike the New Deal period in the United States which in the mid-1930s saw a virtually complete revamping of the entire structure of workers' rights as guaranteed by law. And as in other countries, it is to be expected that the role of government in industrial relations will continue to unfold as new and increasingly complex industrial relations problems continue to develop.

5. The Labor Market

Prior to 1955, the Japanese labor force had three major characteristics. First, the number of workers employed in primary industry was large both in absolute terms and as a proportion of total employment. From 1920, when the first population census was taken, until 1940, the number of workers employed in primary industry remained almost constant, fluctuating between 14.2 and 14.5 million. As a percentage of total employment, however, agricultural employment continuously decreased, from 53.6 percent in 1920 to 49.4 percent in 1930, and to 44.0 percent in 1940.

A reverse trend appeared in the post-World War II period with agricultural employment increasing to 17.2 million, or 48.3 percent, by 1950 as a result of the movement of city dwellers back to rural areas during the war. These people remained in agriculture after the war because of the virtual absence of employment opportunities in urban areas due to war damage and demobilization. If this segment of the population is excluded, however, the number employed in agriculture after the war remained at the level of 14.5 million. Of the estimated 800,000 young members of farm families (14 and 15 years old) who annually entered the labor force for the first time, half remained in agriculture, thus maintaining employment in primary industry at a constant level.[1]

1. Tatsuo Honda, "Nihon jinkō mondai no shiteki tenkai" [Historical Development of the Population Problem in Japan], *Nōson jinkōmondai kenkyū* [Studies on rural population problems] (Tokyo: Norin Tokei Kyokai, 1952), vol. 2.

A second pre-1955 characteristic was the relatively small proportion of wage and salary earners (or employees) in the total labor force and the relatively large proportion of self-employed and family workers. According to the estimates of Tadao Ishizaki, the employee ratio increased only from 29.5 percent in 1920 to 32.3 percent in 1930.[2] While it rose to 41.9 percent in 1940, by 1950 it had fallen to 34.6 percent. A partial explanation for the small employee ratio is the domination of agriculture by small farmers, who employed labor exclusively from their own households and engaged in labor-intensive farming. Another reason was that many enterprises in secondary and tertiary industries consisted of only household members. For example, the population census of 1950 showed that 30 percent of those employed in the building and construction industry were self-employed or family workers. These groups also accounted for 20 percent of the employment in manufacturing and 55 percent in wholesale and retail trade. With numerous petty household enterprises consisting of many family workers and few hired employees, the labor force participation rates of married women and older people tended to increase.

A third characteristic was that medium and small-sized enterprises predominated in private industries until 1955. Large firms were limited to such secondary industries as mining, cotton spinning, iron and steel, and machinery, and such tertiary industries as communications, railways, foreign trade, and department stores. Government enterprises and zaibatsu companies were dominant in these industries.

There are no complete statistics on the employment structure in the prewar period; however, according to the 1943 census of establishments, total employment in secondary and tertiary industries was 14.39 million. The distribution was as follows: 37 percent in very small-sized establishments (1 to 9 workers); 30 percent in small-sized establishments (10–99 workers); 15 percent in medium-sized enterprises (100–499 workers); and 18 percent in large firms (500 or more workers). In the smallest size group, the majority of the workers were self-employed and family workers.

2. Shōwa Dōjinkai, *Tōkei kara mita koyō to shitsugyō* [Employment and unemployment: A statistical analysis] (Tokyo: Showa Dojinkai, 1957), p. 40.

Extremely small enterprises characterized the Japanese employment structure in urban industries as well as in agriculture. The managers of these enterprises themselves were not full-time managers in a strict sense but rather were master craftsmen working with their families and other workers. Separation of the family budget from the enterprise accounts had not been achieved, nor did these firms have modern accounting systems. The workers were mostly young apprentices or unskilled common laborers. Since apprentices lived in their master's house, were supplied with food, clothing, board, and room, and received no cash except small amounts of pocket money, they were not particularly conscious of or concerned about "wages." Some of them later became masters of their own petty firms or were employed by larger companies as wage earners. The small enterprises constituted the "premodern" industrial sector, which developed simultaneously with the modern sector rather than diminishing as a result of industrialization. This development has been described as "the dual structure of the Japanese economy," the key concept explaining the characteristics of employment and industrial relations in the modern and the premodern sectors.

However, remarkable changes have appeared since about 1955, when Japan's economic growth began to accelerate after ten years of postwar reform and demilitarization. In the pages that follow, I shall deal with the causes and consequences of these changes.

Changes in the Demand for Labor

According to the population censuses, while total employment rose from 39.26 million to 47.63 million between 1955 and 1965, an increase of more than 8 million, the number of wage and salary earners rose more than 11 million during the same period (see Table 5.1). Thus, the employee ratio climbed from 45.8 percent to 61.7 percent of the labor force during this decade. The number employed in primary industry dropped by more than 4 million between 1955 and 1965, falling from 41.0 to 24.7 percent of total

Table 5.1

Employment by Industry, 1955 and 1965
          (unit: thousands)

Industry	1955	1965	Change
Total employment	39,261	47,629	8,369
Primary industry	16,111	11,747	−4,364
Secondary industry	9,220	15,201	5,981
Mining	535	342	− 194
Construction	1,783	2,674	891
Manufacturing	6,902	11,511	4,609
Metal, machinery, and chemical			
industry	2,428	5,098	2,670
Clothing and apparel	1,543	2,041	498
Other	2,932	4,371	1,439
Tertiary industry	13,928	20,662	6,734
Trade	5,473	8,586	3,113
Finance and insurance	623	1,161	638
Transportation and communications	1,819	2,866	1,047
Public utilities	230	274	44
Services	4,423	6,285	1,862
Service industries for individuals			
and amusement industry	1,829	2,182	353
Service industries for business			
establishments and repair industry	481	998	517
Other	2,114	2,425	311
Government	1,361	1,491	130

SOURCE: Prime Minister's Office, Bureau of Statistics, *Kokusei chōsa* [National
    Population Census] (Tokyo, published annually).

employment. In secondary industry, employment increased by
almost 6 million, from 23.5 to 31.9 percent, and in tertiary industry by almost 7 million, from 35.5 to 43.4 percent. In both the
secondary and tertiary sectors, with the exception of mining
which suffered a decline of 200,000, every industrial group gained
in numbers of employees, especially heavy industries such as
metals, machinery, and chemicals, which together had a remarkable increase of 2,670,000. Among them, the machinery and apparatus manufacturing industry, which is highly labor-intensive,
jumped most notably. In tertiary industry, trade, transportation
and communications, and services showed sizable increases in
terms of absolute numbers—3,110,000, 1,050,000, and 1,860,000,
respectively. In terms of the rate of increase, such industries as
wholesale trade, finance and insurance, passenger and freight
transportation, services for business establishments, and repairing

Table 5.2
National Income Percentages and Distribution of Employment by Economic
Sector, 1955 and 1965

Sector	Percentage of National Income		Percentage of Employment	
	1955	1965	1955	1965
Primary	22.7	12.5	41.0	24.7
Secondary	30.2	39.5	23.5	31.9
Tertiary	47.1	48.0	35.5	43.4

SOURCES: Percentage figures of produced incomes by industry: Economic
Planning Agency, Economic Research Institute, *Kokumin-shotoku
tōkei* [National Income Statistics] (Tokyo, published annually).
Percentage figures for persons employed by industry: *Kokusei
chōsa* [National population census].

made large gains. These changes in the number of employees by
industry reflect fairly the changes in industrial activity within
the national economy.

Table 5.2 shows the percentage of national income derived from
each sector of the economy. In 1955, primary industry accounted
for 23 percent of total national income, secondary industry for 29
percent, and tertiary industry for 47 percent. By 1964, their shares
had changed to 13 percent, 39 percent, and 48 percent, respectively. The increased weight of secondary industry is beyond
question, especially in view of the conspicuous transformation of
manufacturing. According to the census of manufacturers, the
heavy and chemical industries increased their proportion of value
added in manufacturing from 55.7 percent in 1955 to 66.3 percent
in 1964.

Quantitative changes were not the only effect of economic
growth upon the demand for labor. Qualitative changes in labor
demand also occurred, first in the heavy and chemical industries
and soon after in the light industries, construction, transportation
and communication, and even in trade and agriculture. Technological change resulting from the introduction of new equipment
required a labor force of a different quality. Generally speaking,
shifts in methods of production replaced manual work with mechanical work, rendered obsolete traditional skills that required
long experience or training, and made it possible for firms to train

workers rather quickly on the job or to employ them at simple jobs requiring little experience. While work could be simplified, the overall technical process was not.

It has become increasingly necessary for workers to be able to understand the mechanical structure of equipment, to judge and accommodate themselves quickly to changes, and to be able to view their own work within the context of the entire technical process. More and more they are required to have a greater degree of adaptability to accommodate continuously to large-scale and rapid technological changes. Thus, though jobs may be increasingly simplified and less manual, new and different kinds of skills and knowledge are required of workers.

Still another problem to be stressed is the social impact of high economic growth; that is, the increasing concentration and centralization of workers in large firms. This is a consequence of the concentration and centralization of capital accumulation which accompanies the growth of capital relative to labor. It results from "economies of size" and is especially apparent in Japan, where many small and medium-sized establishments exist. If we look at the percentage of employment by size of private establishments, according to the census of establishments, the proportion of the labor force in firms with fewer than 10 workers each for all industries decreased from 41.6 percent in 1957 to 33.5 percent in 1963. In manufacturing alone, it fell from 20.2 percent to 15.5 percent; and in commercial trade, where small businesses have been traditionally numerous, it diminished from 70.8 percent to 59.0 percent.

The 1956 and 1965 Employment Statistics Surveys show that the percentage of employees in establishments with fewer than 10 workers each decreased from 16.0 percent in 1956 to 8.6 percent in 1965 in manufacturing and from 44.6 percent in 1956 to 21.6 percent in 1965 in trade (see Table 5.3). In absolute numbers, employment in firms of this size fell in manufacturing and remained at the same level in commercial trade during this period.

Traditionally, in Japan, there have been many petty firms operated by family workers and a few employees. Most depended upon parent factories or commission merchants through con-

Table 5.3
Percentage of Employees by Size of Establishment, 1956 and 1965

Size of Establishment	Nonagricultural Industries		Manufacturing	
	1956	1965	1956	1965
1–9	21.0	13.8	15.9	8.6
10–29	14.3	15.3	19.3	15.7
30–99	11.7	14.8	17.9	17.8
100–299	6.6	9.9	11.3	13.9
300–499	2.3	4.0	4.1	6.0
500 and over	20.2	27.5	30.2	37.4
Public service	23.9	14.7	1.0	0.6

SOURCE: Prime Minister's Office, Bureau of Statistics, *Shūgyō-kōzō kihon chōsa* [Employment Statistics Survey] (Tokyo, published every three years).

signment or subcontracting systems, although some remained independent within small local markets. It is probable that the masters or petty owners worked along with members of their families or employees rather than performing solely managerial and administrative functions; in this sense, they were more like wage earners than managers. On the other hand, their workers were apprentices, trainees, or poorly paid employees unable to find better employment because of their low efficiency; few were skilled journeymen. Not a small number of these workers succeeded in becoming owners of such petty firms after acquiring enough skill and experience to be journeymen, while others moved into larger companies with better working conditions. Yet, it is appropriate to define this group largely as small producers rather than bona fide journeymen. Thus, Japan's working class was dominated by a large mass of workers who were partly employers and partly wage earners.[3]

Recent economic growth has resulted in an increase in the relative weight of the permanent wage-earner class and a decrease in that of the part-employer, part-worker group because of the decline of the petty firms. The population censuses show that the proportion of wage and salary earners in total employment climbed from 45.8 percent in 1955 to 61.1 percent in 1965. In secondary industry alone 87 percent of the males and 82 percent

3. See Shōjirō Ujihara, "Japan's Laboring Class: Changes in the Post-War Period," *Journal of Social and Political Ideas in Japan*, 3, no. 3 (Dec. 1965).

of the females were wage and salary employees, while in tertiary industry the proportions were 80 percent of the males and 82 percent of the females. Self-employed and family workers increased very little in absolute numbers and declined sharply relative to the total number of employed workers.

Table 5.4

Changes in the Number of Employed by Occupation, 1955 to 1965 (unit: thousands)

	1955	1965	Change	Percent Change
Professional, technical and allied workers	1,885	2,679	794	42.1
Managers, officials and proprietors (nonfarm)	841	1,415	574	68.3
Clerical workers	3,228	6,182	2,954	91.5
Sales workers	4,182	5,587	1,405	33.6
Farmers and fishery workers	15,874	11,676	−4,198	−26.4
Mining and quarrying workers	349	228	− 121	−34.7
Transportation and communication workers	1,078	2,076	997	92.5
Skilled and semiskilled workers and common laborers	9,442	14,327	4,884	51.7
Security service employees	430	575	145	33.7
Service workers	1,953	2,886	933	45.2
Total employed	39,261	47,629	8,368	21.3

SOURCE: *Kokusei chōsa* [National population census].

A final consequence of economic growth for labor demand was a distinctly changed occupational structure. According to a recent population census, the increase in the number of employed by occupation from 1955 to 1965 was greatest for production workers in secondary and tertiary industries. The number of skilled and semiskilled workers increased from 9,442,000 to 14,327,000 (see Table 5.4). Though this was an increase of about 50 percent, it was far less than the 92.5 percent increase for transportation and communication workers and the 91.5 percent increase for clerical workers. Though the total for these two categories was far less than that for production workers, these gains represented a remarkable increase in terms of both absolute and relative numbers. The number of professional and technical workers and managerial and administrative personnel increased also, although the increment was not so large. In other words, the white-collar occupations expanded alongside blue-collar work in secondary and tertiary industries.

The increase in the number of white-collar workers is attributable in part to technological change and in part to the expanded size of managements. The introduction of mass-production techniques, standardization, and continuous processes requires more maintenance and indirect workers but fewer direct production workers. A considerable portion of these indirect workers can be classified as white-collar. Moreover, enlarged corporate systems involve greater managerial complexes of white-collar workers. Furthermore, the numbers of professional white-collar workers employed in medical service, education, social welfare, and cultural activities and by government, financial, and banking agencies have been increasing with the urbanization of the working population and the introduction of new products into the daily lives of the great mass of people.

These tendencies have brought about changes in the quality as well as the number of white-collar jobs. There has been an increase in the relative number of salaried professionals who, being highly educated, have considerable independence in their jobs. Also, from the rationalization of office work through mechanization and computerization has emerged a new division of labor, the two new categories being routine work and intellectual brain work requiring complicated judgments. Accordingly, there is a clear distinction between clerical and technical workers and those in charge of administration.

Adjusting the Labor Supply to the Increased Demand

To adjust the labor supply to the changes in quality and quantity of labor demand without delay or friction requires either the acquisition and training of fresh hands or the retraining of workers who had become redundant in other industries or occupations.

There are several categories of new workers, the largest being new school graduates seeking jobs, housewives, and retired workers who wish to be employed again. Less important groups are adult males and unmarried youths who have finished their education but have never been employed. The most adaptable, of course, are the new school graduates. They are also relatively easily moved from one locality to another. Thus, for the most part, the occupational and geographical flexibility of workers depends upon the supply of new school graduates.

In this respect, the Japanese economy has had two advantages since 1955. First, the years since the mid-1950s have been a transitional period in which the demographic structure was being transformed from the high birth and death rates of the prewar period to the current low rates. The birth rate was as high as 30 to 35 per 1,000 in the 1930s but fell to 28.1 per 1,000 by 1950 and 17 per 1,000 after 1957. At the same time, the death rate, which was as high as 20 per 1,000 before World War II, declined to 10.9 per 1,000 by 1950 and to close to 7 per 1,000 between 1955 and 1964. Thus, there was a period between 1955 and 1966 when the children born in a time of high birth rates grew up in a time of low death rates, graduated from school, and became employed. According to the Basic School Survey of the Ministry of Education, the average number of new graduates from junior high schools each year was about 1,600,000 between 1950 and 1954, 1,900,000 between 1955 and 1959, and 2,400,000 between 1960 and 1964. The number of new graduates from junior and senior high schools and colleges and universities who obtained employment each year averaged about 1,100,000 from 1950 to 1954, 1,300,000 from 1955 and 1959, and over 1,400,000 from 1960 to 1964. In the 14 years from 1950 to 1964, new graduates totaled 15 million. Furthermore, since a substantial number were unable to find suitable jobs immediately upon graduation but were employed later, the total labor supply of new school leavers each year was even greater than these figures indicate.

Second, in addition to the rapid increase in the supply of new graduates, another reservoir of labor was made available for the secondary and tertiary industries because technological changes in agriculture produced redundant farm labor. Technological change swept agriculture as well as secondary industry after the war. Improved species of crops were developed and agricultural chemicals and machinery were introduced, all of which improved labor productivity and saved labor on the farms. Technological progress in agriculture in particular created a large amount of redundant labor from the traditional petty farms supported by the family system. On the other hand, because of the small average acreage per household, the effect of capital investment in the new agricultural technology was not highly productive but rather increased farming expenses and depressed the farm economy. Moreover, traditional side occupations of farmers such as straw goods processing and silk raising or sericulture were destroyed by the development and introduction of new products in secondary industry, while no alternative business was successfully exploited on their behalf.

According to the Survey of the Agricultural Economy in 1964, average annual farm income was ¥670,000, of which only ¥320,000, or less than half, was derived from farming itself. The remainder came from nonfarm businesses, mainly wages and salaries. In contrast, the Family Budget Survey of the Prime Minister's Office conducted in 1964 showed that the average total income of city worker households was ¥780,000 for salaried personnel,[4] ¥630,000 for permanent blue-collar workers, and ¥350,000 for casual workers and day laborers.

Only farm households operating more than two hectares of land had as much income as the salaried personnel. Such farms, however, accounted for only 7 percent of all farm households. Farmers who earned as much income as the permanent blue-collar workers operated between 1.5 and 2.0 hectares and comprised only 14 percent of the total. The income level of farmers with 1 to 1.5 hectares merely equaled that of casual and day laborers. Compared to the average for all industrial sectors, income levels in primary industry have remained very low (see Table 5.2) despite the technological advances in agriculture. The share of farm income has not advanced as much as the urban workers' share, thereby generating a redundant population in rural areas and

4. The total earnings include those received by all members of a family, excluding cash balances from previous months.

movement to the cities. This was especially true of new graduates with high mobility who entered urban jobs looking forward to better opportunities in industry than in agriculture. The number of farm children who graduated from school and remained on farms averaged about 400,000 per year in the years before and immediately after World War II. This number decreased to 290,000 in 1955, 140,000 in 1960, and only 70,000 in 1965.

The increase of new graduates and their shift to secondary and tertiary industry contributed greatly to adjusting labor supply to the change in labor demand. In particular, junior and senior high school graduates constituted a reservoir of production workers for manufacturing. College graduates and female senior high school graduates were candidates for salaried jobs.

In contrast, the migrant rural population was absorbed in such work as road transportation and construction, where job opportunities were open to them, whereas in other industries vacancies were filled only by new graduates. Since wages for such work were not paid on the basis of the length of service, even those who worked for only a short time were able to earn high pay strictly in proportion to their efficiency. It is noteworthy that, along with the increased number of farmers who were forced to obtain side jobs as wage earners, their eldest sons, or heirs, also began to leave the farms and work outside at full-time jobs in the vicinity of their homes, going back and forth each day, often as day laborers, in order to compensate for inadequate earnings in farming. Part-time farmers with subsidiary occupations amounted to 65.2 percent of all farmers in 1955 but rose to 78.5 percent in 1965. If farmers are classified as primary and secondary part-time farmers,[5] we find that the latter increased from 27.5 percent of the total in 1955 to 51.8 percent by 1965, with as much as 80 percent of their subsidiary employment being as wage earners.

Migration of the rural population took place first among the petty farmers and young people and later extended to the larger farmers and older people. Capital investment in agriculture was not worthwhile for petty farmers because of their limited acreage;

5. Primary part-time farmers are defined as those whose farming income constitutes more than 50 percent of their total income. Secondary part-time farmers are those whose farming income is less than 50 percent.

yet the rising cost of living forced them to earn more money from outside employment. Moreover, since seasonal fluctuations of labor demand are decreasing because technological change tends to require intensive work, continuous operation, and an increased degree of worker responsibility, the so-called half-farmer-half-worker type of part-time farmer who used to engage in seasonal work outside agriculture has tended increasingly to become a full-time wage earner. The reason these people cannot leave the farms and transform themselves into bona fide wage earners is simply that they own assets as small landowners. This is seen clearly in the Survey of the Agricultural Economy, which found that only 23 percent of the total income of very small farm owners operating less than 0.5 hectares consists of farming income. This differentiation of the peasantry had a great influence on the labor market between 1955 and 1965 by making available to secondary and tertiary industries an abundant supply of young workers.

Employers gained three advantages as a result. First, the new labor force was made up of single young workers whose costs of living were low, making it possible for employers to pay them low wages. Although from 1956 to 1960 starting rates for middle school graduates jumped from ¥4,150 to ¥6,020 per month and for high school graduates from ¥6,550 to ¥8,220, nevertheless, they were low compared to rates for adult workers.

Second, because the young workers were single, their migration costs were low, even though they moved from all over the nation into industrial centers such as the Keihin (Tokyo-Yokohama), Hanshin (Osaka-Kobe), and Chūkyō (Nagoya) areas. Employers did not find it necessary to spend large amounts for dormitories or other housing and welfare facilities.

Third, these workers proved highly adaptable to both the new technologies and the new environments. As growing percentages of them had attended upper grades of school, their efficiency was higher. The ratio of middle school graduates going on to high schools, including part-time education, rapidly swung upward from 44 percent in 1951 to 67 percent in 1965. At the same time, the percentage of high school graduates entering universities and junior colleges climbed from 17 percent to 25 percent during the same period. Thus, there was a shift in the composition of new school graduates obtaining employment. In 1955, middle school graduates numbered 700,000, high school graduates 340,000, and college graduates 85,000. In 1965, the totals were 620,000, 700,000 and 170,000, respectively. A particularly strong demand for female middle school graduates grew not only in traditional sectors such as the textile industry but also in new mass-production industries such as electrical appliances. A considerable portion of the male recruits from high school now also filled production jobs newly created by innovations in industries such as iron and steel, chemicals, and electric power. In 1965, about 40 percent of employed high school graduates were production workers—about the same percentage as those who held white-collar jobs.

From 1955 to 1964 Japanese industry met no serious difficulties in recruiting and training new workers to keep pace with technological change, although there were discrepancies between the content of their education and the actual skills and knowledge needed. In sum, the rather abundant supply of cheap labor with high efficiency may be cited as a major cause for the enormous capital accumulation and technological innovation during that period.

National income statistics indicate that personal consumption expenditures as a proportion of the gross national product fell from 60 percent in 1955 to 50 percent in 1964, although there were some fluctuations. On the other hand, private investment in plants and equipment grew from 9.5 percent to 18.8 percent, while capital formation by the government rose from 8.8 percent to 11.4 percent. This huge investment lowered labor's relative share in manufacturing from 36 percent in 1955 to 33 percent in 1965.

Differentiation among the farmers created a supply of cheap labor but in turn paved the way for higher wages. For example, between 1955 and 1964, the highest rate of increase in relative wages was obtained by outdoor workers in building and construction. According to the Monthly Labor Statistics Surveys, the wage level in building and construction stood at an index of 79.6 percent in 1955, compared with the average wage level for all industries, but climbed to 98.8 percent by 1966. The unfavorable wage differential for these workers in the earlier period was usually ascribed to the fact that traditionally there had been many seasonal migratory half-farmer-half-workers from rural areas employed in these industries. In more recent years, on the other hand, the lower differential has usually been attributed to labor shortages. Also, however, building and construction workers were increasingly becoming full-time workers even though seemingly employed as seasonal migrants, for the relative decline in farming income had forced them to rely more and more upon wages. At the same time, even the employers in these labor-intensive industries began to seek a more stable supply of highly efficient full-time workers because, with the larger amounts of fixed capital per worker, it became more profitable to operate continuously. Thus, increased productivity through mechanization resulted in greater ability of the employers to pay higher wages.

Significant changes in labor conditions are attributable to labor mobility on a nationwide basis. Most notable has been a general rise and equalization of wages by industry, size of establishment, locality, and the like. The new school graduates, especially from middle schools, and the day laborers—both highly mobile groups —became the first beneficiaries. The demand for production workers was concentrated on middle school graduates because of (1) the traditional employment system (under which recruitment of younger workers with low levels of education was preferred, so that they could be trained on the job within the establishment and employed for life); and (2) low starting wage rates. With the rising rate of high school attendance, the number of employed middle school graduates has dropped proportionately. An undersupply of these workers had already become apparent in the late 1950s. This trend increased competition among employers and accelerated a nationwide consolidation of labor markets for the new graduates. It should be recalled that prior to that time there had existed long-established local labor markets, even for new graduates, compartmentalized by industry and size of firm. Recruitment had been regulated by territorial and kinship relationships. For example, employers in the cotton spinning industry had drawn workers mostly from rural communities in the northeast and southwest. This hiring pattern had contributed to the development of a unique type of personnel administration based on the boardingin system. In the new electric appliance and machinery industries, however, employers depended mainly on workers already living in urban communities and willing to commute. Wages had to be higher because of housing and transportation costs.

The employers in the small and medium-sized industries usually relied on territorial ties which necessarily tended to compartmentalize labor markets and resulted in wide wage differentials even for young workers in the same industry or region. A similar situation prevailed in construction, where day laborers were recruited among migratory farm workers. These traditional labor market systems, therefore, began to break down during the late 1950s.

In light of these developments, in 1953 the government adopted a new employment exchange policy based on widened area service, especially for new graduates and seasonal migratory workers. It appeared very likely that the basic function of the employment exchanges was to aid in equalizing wages and working conditions.

Also, in response to these changes, organized labor launched a drive to unionize unorganized workers in small and medium-sized industries and to establish a national minimum wage system. Sōhyō, as far back as 1952, had made public a draft wage policy that contained basic wage goals for all workers as well as short-run targets. One demand was for a guaranteed minimum wage of ¥8,000 a month for all workers, or, in other words, for the establishment of a uniform minimum wage law. The policy was pursued through both legislative activities and wage disputes. Furthermore, the program presented at Sōhyō's annual convention in 1955 outlined a plan to launch "united action to raise minimum wages for the purpose of pushing up the general wage level for the mass of workers" and to establish "minimum wages, whether they be regional, occupational, or industrial." The program also declared at the same time the initiation of "struggles at the shop level, with each union demanding more than ¥8,000 in order to establish a minimum wage of ¥8,000 and to enact a nationwide uniform minimum wage law, culminating in a joint struggle both in and outside the Diet." Finally, "to strengthen the struggle position," Sōhyō proceeded to act on the following slogans: "Activate struggles at the shop level and concentrate them at the top among all the shops," "More emphasis on struggles by industrial unions," "Vitalize the regional organizations in order to promote joint actions at the regional level," "Try to strengthen the district councils," and "Organize the unorganized workers in the small and medium-sized firms by utilizing the regional organizations."

These activities, aimed at establishing minimum wages, helped to standardize wages by industry and region. It was realized in due course that minimum wages meant the starting rates for the middle school graduates, although that was to be made explicit later.

Employers reacted to the unions by attempting to keep the wage level stable through introduction of a periodic wage increment system that could annually revise base rates of individual workers as of a certain date each year. This system had two notable characteristics. First, although individual base rates were to be raised each year, the standard schedule which set the rates by age and length of service theoretically was not changed; that is, rates for workers of a given age and length of service were supposed to remain unchanged as stipulated in the existing standard schedule. Thus, if the retirement age was set at a certain age and all newly recruited workers were limited to new school graduates, the minimum and maximum wage rates presumably were fixed in advance.

Second, actual application of the system involved differential rather than uniform increases in rates each year according to various other factors such as education and job performance. In other words, the increases were payments by result. Under the system as actually applied, if the average age of the employees declined in a firm, the average rate of wage increases also would go down; if the average age went up, the average rate of wage increases also would go up. However, the system was less expensive and more predictable for employers than one utilizing uniform flat rate increases, called "base-ups," even if the average wage rates went up as a result of the periodic increments. This wage system also reflected job values and job performance and was geared to productivity to about the same extent as an incentive wage system. Therefore, it may be said that the proposal to introduce this system was intended in effect to prevent the establishment of minimum wages and a consequent rise in the general level of wages.

Employers in small and medium-sized firms undertook to combat the rising starting rates that resulted from the cutthroat competition for younger workers by making cartel-like agreements among themselves which set minimum wages within an industry or area. The first such agreement was signed by the Packing House Operators' Association of Shizuoka Prefecture in 1956 and later became the model for other industries when popularized by the Ministry of Labor through administrative persuasion. The Minimum Wage Law of 1959,[6] despite its stipulation of several ways for setting minimum wages, virtually revolves around employer agreements by industry.

The positions of the unions and management vis-à-vis the wage problem were quite opposite with regard to wage levels but led to the same result—pressure from the outside to standardize wages, especially starting rates.[7]

Labor Markets Since 1960

Rapid economic growth was reflected in the labor markets in a number of ways beginning in the early 1960s. The most important effect was the intensified labor shortage. Demand for new graduates, particularly for middle school graduates, soared rapidly because of both expanding business activities and fear of further shortages. The number of new middle school graduates per year fell from 750,000 or 800,000 between 1954 and 1960 and reached about 600,000 in the 1960s.

6. For details on this law, see Chapter 10.
7. One word, however, should be added about employee wage agreements for construction workers. The wages of these workers formerly were controlled indirectly by "prevailing wage" criteria announced by the Ministry of Labor as a budgetary base for public works. The construction workers' unions successfully fought this system, which was abolished in 1962. Then they consolidated the so-called agreed-upon wages, previously regulated separately by local unions, into a nationwide standard schedule. Agreed-upon wages are now stipulated uniformly in occupational schedules decided by the construction workers' unions.

The labor shortage further accelerated the migration of new graduates out of rural communities. While the number of middle and high school graduates employed in agriculture remained at 150,000 through the late 1950s, it diminished to less than 100,000 in the 1960s. The difference was employed mostly in secondary industry. Construction and transportation, which as a rule sought workers over twenty years of age and formerly recruited among the young workers who had remained in agriculture, had by the 1960s changed their policy and were recruiting among those employed in secondary industry. This policy change accelerated labor turnover among young workers.

Also, managements began to substitute high school graduates for middle school graduates in order to meet the labor shortage, because, as stated earlier, one reason for the insufficient supply of middle school graduates was their increased rate of entry into higher grades of school, resulting in a relative oversupply of high school graduates by the late 1950s. The substitution pattern already was appearing by the early 1950s in industries such as chemicals, iron and steel, and electric power, in which innovative equipment had been introduced. There were several factors that promoted substitution: (1) new technology requiring highly educated workers with sufficient technological knowledge; (2) the greater expense of training middle school graduates on the job to master the new technology; and (3) the prohibition, under the Labor Standards Law, of employment of minors under eighteen years of age during night shifts. Although high school graduates at first were not welcomed as production workers except in the industries mentioned above, the aggravated shortage of middle school graduates forced other industries to follow suit. These developments substantially dissolved the traditional employment hierarchy in which production workers were recruited exclusively from among elementary school graduates.

The demand for salaried personnel also expanded during this period. A considerable portion of the demand was met by an increased supply of female high school graduates, for, according to the Basic Survey on Schools, 80 percent of the employed female high school graduates were in white-collar jobs. Nevertheless, growing demand for labor at all levels resulted in an overall shortage, including new graduates from high schools and colleges.

The intensified labor shortage brought about several changes in the wage structure, which, while analyzed fully in Chapter 10, may be summarized here as follows:

First, the shortage pushed up starting wage rates of middle and high school graduates substantially. Rates of male middle school graduates rose 45 percent from 1956 to 1960, then soared 110 percent between 1961 and 1965. Rates for male high school graduates increased by 23 percent and 101 percent during the same two periods, respectively. Starting wage rates for females increased similarly.

Second, as may be estimated from the above figures, differentials between the starting wage rates of middle and high school graduates diminished. It became common managerial practice to pay the same level of wages to the middle school graduates with three years of service and average performance *and* to new high school graduates. Thus, the educational barrier in the labor market began to dissolve, and these two groups of new school graduates became competitive in the same labor markets. As wage differentials by educational level were reduced, the relative importance of education, long used as a factor in wage determination, declined.

Third, diminishing differentials in starting wages by level of education also tended to narrow differentials in starting wages between manual and white-collar workers. Even if the tradition of differentiating wages by educational background had continued, high school graduates now were about equally divided between production and white-collar jobs; and technological change was replacing manual and heavy work with nonmanual and brain work or with simple, repetitive operations. Thus, white- and blue-collar work tended to resemble one another in terms of job difficulty, degree of responsibility, and the like. In some cases, in fact, new production jobs were more difficult and required more responsibility than white-collar work, thus influencing the trend toward reducing wage differentials between blue- and white-collar for starting rates among younger workers.

Fourth, differentials by sex were reduced. The increased demand for white-collar workers was met mostly by females and male college and high school graduates. The enlarged employment opportunities for women workers, especially young females, in white-collar jobs helped to improve their wages. While white-collar jobs have always been paid favorably compared with other employment for women, expanded employment in this field improved female wages relatively. In turn, this expansion aggravated the shortage of female workers in the traditionally low-wage light industries.

Fifth, the impact of the shortage of new school graduates went far beyond wages for young workers. It also affected the wages of adult workers already employed. Under the traditional wage system in large enterprises, a worker's base rate depends upon his starting rate fixed according to educational background and upon subsequent annual increments. Since an individual's rate of increment differs according to jobs done, positions held, performance, and merit, wage differentials among individuals have actually been large. Nevertheless, it has been a general rule to determine base rates according to length of service, so that under this "length-of-service wage system," if starting rates are raised for new employees, it is necessary to revise the base rates of all already employed lest the equitable balance be lost. This is because the hierarchy of wage rates is not only a wage question but also represents the status ladder in the workshop, or a device for managerial control over the workers. Were equitable adjustments not made, the employees would become dissatisfied and their morale would deteriorate. According to this logic, rapid and large increases in starting rates spurred a general rise of the entire wage structure.

Still another factor that led to wage increases for the older workers was innovations in producing and popularizing new consumer goods, particularly durable goods that, in turn, have remarkably changed the standard of living of Japanese workers. Moreover, the widespread practice of care for preschool children outside the home in the urban communities and the prolonged education resulting from rising rates of entrance into schools of higher grades raised not only the cost of nursing and education in a narrow sense but also the expense of rearing children in general. Such factors meant a rise in the cost of living for adult workers with dependents.

While the shortage of new graduates resulted in a rise in starting wage rates, this rise alone could not expand the supply of young labor. As a result, the labor force was deployed unevenly, flowing mainly to industries with higher wages and more favorable working conditions. Firms that could not afford to offer improved conditions continued to suffer from labor shortages and were compelled to substitute older workers for young labor.

In competing for new graduates in labor markets, big business has had advantages over small. In the first place, even if differences in starting wage rates have narrowed, working conditions as a whole—including hours, fringe benefits, prospects for future wage increases, and social status—have been more attractive in large companies. Second, the single advantage of small business for young workers, despite their low wages and overwork, was the opportunity to master skills while still young and eventually to become masters. These possibilities, however, were greatly narrowed by the concentration of capital and production and one consequence of this was the concentration of young workers in big business. According to statistics of the Employment Stabilization Service, from 1957 to 1964 the ratio of new school graduates in small and petty establishments in manufacturing dropped from 54.8 percent to 28.5 percent for middle school graduates and from 48.6 percent to 18.7 percent for high school graduates.

The concentration of workers in large enterprises was attributable not only to employment of new graduates but also to movement of workers from small to large firms. According to the Ministry of Labor's Survey of Employment Trends for 1965, of the newly employed workers in manufacturing firms with more than 500 employees (in which labor turnover was not unusually high), 70.7 percent were recruited from among those never previously employed; and 61.7 percent were new school graduates. On the other hand, of the 29.3 percent previously employed, 19.2 percent came from secondary industry, 2.2 percent from primary industry, and 7.0 percent from tertiary industry. It may be seen from these figures that labor turnover within secondary industry is indeed high.

The Economic Planning Agency's Survey of Labor Turnover and Conditions of Wage Determination for 1964 also indicates the distribution of mobile workers (experienced recruits) by size of establishment. As shown in Table 5.5, the percentage of workers who moved from small to large firms was larger than the percentage who moved in the opposite direction. Most of those who moved to big firms were younger workers.[8]

Table 5.5
Prior Employment Status of Experienced Recruits by Size of Enterprise (Regular Workers Only)

Size of Former Enterprise	Size of New Enterprise			
	1,000 or More Employees	100–999 Employees	30–99 Employees	Under 30
5,000 employees and Over	28.7%	32.7%	26.2%	12.4%
1,000–4,999	19.7	47.9	21.8	10.6
100–999	7.3	46.8	25.6	20.3
30–99	1.1	7.9	64.5	26.5

SOURCE: Economic Planning Agency, *Rōdōryoku ryūdo-to chingin-kettei jijō chōsa* [Survey on labor turnover and wage determination] (Tokyo, 1964).

The changed distribution of labor has greatly influenced the characteristics of the work forces in small and medium-sized enterprises. For one, the age profile of the workers within such enterprises has moved downward as workers have become concentrated in large-scale enterprises (see Table 5.6). These differences in age composition of the labor force between the two groups is one explanation of why the average wage had been lower in small business. As pointed out by Mikio Sumiya, most of the labor force in the small and medium-sized enterprises had been young workers whose costs of living were lower and who did not seek

8. *Chūtosaiyō-sha*, literally "midterm employee," is a term used to designate a regular employee who was hired away from another firm or was hired at a time other than immediately following his school graduation. See Chapter 11 for details.

Table 5.6

1964 Monthly Wages of Experienced Recruits by Age Group and Size of Enterprise in Manufacturing (Male Workers Only)

Age Group	Regular Wages		Number of Workers	
	Enterprises Employing 1,000 or more Employees	Enterprises Employing 30–99 Employees	Enterprises Employing 1,000 or more Employees	Enterprises Employing 30–99 Employees
17 and under	11.5**	12.5**	25	53
18–19	17.4	17.5	28	13
20–24	20.3	22.6	42	32
25–29	24.8	24.4	17	20
30–34	27.5	27.9	8	14
35–39	29.2	27.1	4	11
40–49	28.6	29.8	3	12
50–59	25.7	25.6	2	9
60 and over	19.2	23.4	0	5
Total	19.3	20.7	129	169

NOTE: Experienced workers are defined as those with primary or junior high school educations and with less than one year of employment.
* Unit: thousand yen
** Roughly equivalent to starting rates for new graduates.
SOURCE: Ministry of Labor, *Chingin-kōzō kihon tōkei chōsa* [Basic survey of wage structure] (Tokyo, published annually).

wages as high as those of adult workers.[9] As far as young workers were concerned, whether employed in large or small enterprises, there were no significant wage differentials by size of firm. Nevertheless, the large percentage of young workers in the labor force of small businesses resulted in lower average wages compared to large firms. Further, wages for adult workers were lower in small firms than in large firms. As explained earlier, the increased uniformity of labor force composition by age among enterprises of different sizes has deprived small firms of this competitive advantage.

Second, increasing turnover of workers already employed also tended to equalize the starting wage rates of experienced workers. As Table 5.6 shows, few differentials remain in hiring rates for experienced recruits in manufacturing by size of enterprise.

Third, the reservoir of low-wage labor for replacing young

9. Mikio Sumiya, *Nihon no rōdō mondai* [Labor problems in Japan] (Tokyo: University of Tokyo Press, 1964).

Table 5.7
Female Labor Force Participation Rates 1955–1965
(percent)

Years of Age	1955	1960	1965
15–19	50.1	49.7	37.6
20–24	68.2	69.4	69.7
25–29	51.8	50.1	46.4
30–39	51.3	53.1	52.9
40–49	55.0	56.7	62.3
50–54	51.3	51.7	57.3
55–59	45.7	46.7	50.1
60–64	38.4	39.1	39.3
65 and over	20.6	20.9	17.5
Total	50.6	50.9	49.8

SOURCE: *Kokusei chōsa* [National population census].

workers has been composed of housewives and older workers employed on a part-time basis or to work at home. The recent trend in small businesses has been to employ middle-aged and older female workers. As seen in Table 5.7, the labor force participation rate of young women between 15 and 19 years of age declined remarkably from 1955 to 1965. This was due largely to their increased entrance rate into schools of a higher grade. The participation rate of women between 25 and 29 years of age also declined in the same period because the number of wives of urban wage earners and salaried employees with children increased. However, the rate for women over 30 years of age and below 60 grew because the labor shortage induced older married women into employment for purposes of gaining additional income.

Conclusion

I have outlined the process by which the labor supply has adjusted to the changed quality and quantity of labor demand caused by the rapid economic growth in Japan since 1955. I have also examined the factors that made this adjustment possible. On the surface it seems that the adjustment proceeded smoothly, but actually it cannot be asserted with certainty that no friction oc-

Table 5.8
Employment Distribution of Workers between 15 and
24 by Industry, 1956, 1965

	1956[a]	1965[b]
Agriculture	9.4%	8.6%
Construction	2.7	6.3
Manufacturing	45.3	35.2
Wholesale and retail trade	16.0	21.6
Transportation and com-		
munications	4.6	6.4
Services	10.1	13.9

SOURCE: Ministry of Education, Gakkō Kihon Chosa
(*School Basic Survey*) (Tokyo, published
annually).
a. Estimated on the basis of young workers graduated
from junior high schools, senior high schools, and
colleges between 1956 and 1965.
b. Actual distribution of young workers in 1965.

curred during the adjustment process and that no problems remain
to be solved. Some of these areas of friction and problems are
discussed below.

In the first place, the rate of labor turnover of young workers
has risen with economic growth. As seen in Table 5.8, considerable
change took place in the distribution of young workers by industry
from 1956 to 1965. Manufacturing's share declined, while construction, wholesale and retail trade, transportation and communication, and services made notable gains. It may not be possible to conclude definitely that these figures demonstrate the
turnover of young workers, but it is highly probable that those
new graduates who are not employed immediately upon graduation come into the labor market later and have an effect upon
the distribution of young labor among the industries. Estimates
are that about 10 percent of the new middle school graduates
and 20 percent of the new high school graduates are unemployed.
This is not to say that turnover of young labor is undesirable,
since it is unavoidable for young workers who have no employment experience to use a trial-and-error method until they find
suitable jobs. Nevertheless, it may be asserted that the concomi-
tant existence of high rates of unemployment and of turnover
among young workers (see Table 5.9) *and* the influx of young

Table 5.9
Rate of Entrance and Separation by Age Group (1966)

				Age Group					
		Total	19–	20–24	25–29	30–34	35–39	40–49	50+
Entrance rate	Male	17.1	61.2	22.3	12.8	9.7	7.9	7.4	9.4
	Female	31.2	14.3	20.9	24.0	24.3	22.7	21.2	14.8
Separation rate	Male	15.9	31.3	22.1	15.1	11.5	9.1	8.7	16.7
	Female	29.4	27.1	36.5	39.5	24.7	21.2	20.5	18.1

SOURCE: Ministry of Labor, *Koyō dōkō chōsa* [Survey on employment trends] (Tokyo, 1967), pp. 30, 68.

NOTE:
$$\text{Entrance rate} = \frac{\text{Number of those who got a job}}{\text{Number of employees (as of January 1)}} \times 100$$

$$\text{Separation rate} = \frac{\text{Number of those who quit a job}}{\text{Number of employees (as of January 1)}} \times 100$$

labor into blind-alley jobs at the very moment when increasing attention was being paid to the shortage of young labor have created friction. It cannot be determined whether this is attributable to maladjustments in the employment service and vocational training or to an imbalance in working conditions which influence motives for occupational selection and turnover. Labor turnover has intensified since 1960, though this cannot be verified statistically.

Second, despite the labor shortage, there has been labor redundancy leading to discharge and unemployment or underemployment. While the rapid growth of the Japanese economy resulted in a remarkable increase in labor demand, it also changed the quality of the labor force. Employers have been induced to replace high-wage workers with low-wage workers as long as the latter were equally or even more productive than the former. In other words, employers substitute low-paid workers with high productivity for high-paid workers with low productivity. This had led to redundancy and discharge.

To illustrate, the traditional length-of-service wage system fostered in modern Japanese industry corresponded in a sense to the worker-skill hierarchy or individual-worker productivity. However, rapid changes in technology undermined this system.

Workers with the greatest degree of adaptability to the new technology were the low-paid young workers, while the highly paid middle-aged and old workers were inflexible. When such an acute contrast exists in an enterprise or workshop, the employer has a strong incentive to reorganize the length-of-service wage system into an efficiency wage system based on merit rating or into a job-oriented wage system based on job evaluation—or he may prefer to substitute less expensive and more productive workers for expensive labor. The only obstacle in his way is the possible damage he may suffer from worker or trade union opposition to rationalization. The mass discharge of coal miners and the subsequent labor disputes that took place in the late 1950s as a result of reorganization provide the best example of this kind of opposition.[10]

Even in the growing industries, some employers have dismissed workers. Opposition to such discharges was silenced mainly on the condition that a premium rate of severance pay be paid and that discharges be limited to workers who retired voluntarily. Usually, such volunteers have been recruited exclusively from among older workers. According to Employment Service statistics, the number of bankruptcies per month ranged between 200 and 300; the number of employees discharged as a result ranged from 7,000 to 15,000.

Discharge of redundant workers has taken place through still another process: the merger of some enterprises and the disappearance of others. Although product markets have expanded and production capacity as a whole has remained below effective demand, firms have attempted to improve or maintain their competitive positions by investing in new technologies in order to gain profits from production on a larger scale. However, as production capacity approached overproduction, price competition tended to become cutthroat, further stimulating "rationalization" to strengthen competitive positions through labor savings and merg-

10. As shown in Table 5.1, the number of persons employed in mining decreased by 200,000 from 1955 to 1965. Also, a Ministry of Labor survey in 1962 showed that the age distribution of redundant workers discharged from coal mines was as follows: below 30 years of age, 15.9 percent; 30 to 39 years of age, 32.0 percent; and 40 years of age and over, 50.1 percent.

ers. Such developments result in redundant workers both within enterprises and from the disappearance of the less efficient.[11]

Solution of the problem of redundant workers has beeen difficult. If these workers are reemployed within a short period under equivalent or better working conditions, it is not a serious matter; but between 1955 and 1965 the problem took the form of labor dilution by the replacement of highly paid middle-aged and older workers with low-paid young workers. Therefore, the reemployment of redundant workers was not easy, although several governmental measures were enacted in an effort to solve the problem. The first, in 1958, was an act providing for temporary measures for the relief of displaced workers connected with the Occupation forces. This was followed by the Temporary Measures for Displaced Miners Law in 1959—praised as progressive legislation for dealing with unemployment—under which the government assumed the obligation to provide coal miners with relief such as special employment services, funds for the promotion of reemployment, loans for housing through the Reemployment Promotion Fund, and employment bounty paid to employers, and vocational training allowances. Despite these measures, the number of unemployed engaged in public works under the Emergency Unemployment Countermeasures Law—deemed the last resort for the unemployed—rose from 260,000 in 1954 to 310,000 in 1955 and 350,000 by 1960. Only in 1964 did the number employed in public works fall below the 300,000 level, and this was the result of revisions in the Employment Security Law of 1963, which stipulated special measures to promote employment of the middle-aged and aged unemployed. Several other measures for promoting employment were adopted for fear the unemployed would return to dependency on public works. However, even in 1967, a paragraph in the Basic Program for Employment read as follows: "Employment of middle-aged and old unemployed has faced greater difficulties than in the case of young unemployed. In 1966 only

11. According to the Fair Trade Commission, mergers numbered less than 500 a year prior to 1960 but increased to 800–900 a year after 1961. A survey by the Tokyo Commercial Inquiry Agency (a private company that undertakes research on business conditions) also showed that the number of bankruptcies was a little more than 1,000 a year prior to 1960 but increased to more than 6,000 a year by 1965.

one job vacancy existed for every two job seekers over 35 years of age."

The last problem, but by no means the least, is that the work force is aging. In the past, large numbers of wage earners left their initial employment to become self-employed. More young workers came into the labor market but later left it, providing a highly flexible balance in the market. Now, however, the economic foundation of the petty firms has deteriorated at the same time that death rates have declined. The supply of new school graduates has also been diminishing as a result of lower birth rates since 1950 and especially since 1955. Although it is not appropriate here to predict whether an absolute shortage of labor will continue in the future, we cannot deny that the lower birth rate is a factor contributing to the higher average age of the work force.

The aging of the labor force will influence the labor force structure in two ways. First, the number of workers with dependents will undoubtedly increase, and this, in turn, will bring forth mounting pressures for wage increases, since the cost of living for workers will go up and since workers with dependents will require more housing and other living facilities. Second, aging will lessen labor mobility as the proportion of the young in the labor force declines.

6. Management and their Organizations

The Status and Role of Managers in Large Firms

One of the salient characteristics of postwar industrial relations in Japan is the development of control by professional management in many of the leading enterprises in major sectors of the economy. Indeed, it is more than management by professionals who are separated from ownership; rather it is control by management with the absence of large-scale owners.[1]

This system of control with relative autonomy for professional managers has been one of the key factors in Japan's rapid economic growth. The significance of this factor is revealed when one looks at the structure of Japan's prewar industrial management with its high capital concentrations in the form of the zaibatsu. Although the large government enterprises, half public, half private trusts (for example, the Japan Steel Company and the Japan Hydroelectric Company), and the textile industry were outside the direct influence of the zaibatsu, zaibatsu concerns were the major suppliers of capital to these trusts, and their financial empires were the major trading banks for the textile firms.

At a relatively early phase in Japan's industrialization, many professional managers were recruited within and outside the zaibatsu enterprises. As early as 1928, graduates of institutions of higher education comprised well over 50 percent of top management in large firms; immediately before World War II, the pro-

1. See, for example, Harumi Urabe, *Keieisha* [Management] (Tokyo: Diamond-sha, 1956).

portion was more than two-thirds. Many of these managers were zaibatsu employees who were rigidly controlled by the parent companies.[2]

The giant Mitsubishi firm is a case in point. The relationship between the head office of the parent company and the so-called affiliated companies was specified originally in 1918. The 1918 edict provided five ways to control affiliated firms. First, the authority to make important personnel decisions was reserved for the president of the parent company, who nominated directors and auditors and determined their salaries. Second, the approval of the parent company was required for any changes in major company rules, decisions on the annual budget, distribution of net profits, and personnel decisions relating to senior staff. Third, auditing on an ad hoc basis was conducted by the parent company. Fourth, the head office required the reporting of estimated money incomes and expenditures, estimated profits and losses, and personnel decisions regarding staff category employees. Fifth, the head office was the channel for obtaining capital funds.

Thus, in addition to control through stock ownership and the authority to make key personnel decisions, all zaibatsu parent companies also exercised some degree of control over the administrative processes. The decisions at zaibatsu headquarters, though often said to be dynamic, tended to be oriented more toward securing economic opportunities and commercial interests and avoiding entrepreneurial risks. It goes without saying that the functional autonomy of professional managers was very limited under such a system.

A drastic change occurred after World War II. SCAP policy on the dissolution of the zaibatsu was vigorously applied to Mitsui, Mitsubishi, Yasuda, and others; altogether ten clans, involving fifty-six families, were effectively removed as controlling agents. The leading firms in the major sectors of the Japanese economy suddenly ceased to be family properties, and managerial functions were delegated to professional managers. There is little doubt that

2. Examples of systematic surveys on social class origins and the management and job careers of managers of large enterprises include Yoshimatsu Aonuma, *Nihon no keieisha* [Japanese management], Nikkei Shinsho No. 12 (Tokyo: Nihon Keizai-shinbun-sha, Feb. 1965); Hiroshi Mannari, "Bizinisu Erito" [Business elite] *Chūō Kōron*, June 1965 (Tokyo: Chūōkōron-sha, June 1965).

the industrial dynamism of the postwar period was due to the new autonomy of the individual enterprises. The structure of Japan's postwar industry, in contrast to its prewar structure, may be characterized by the lack of powerful centers which organize and control interenterprise relationships among large firms. It is true that during the period of rapid economic growth, beginning in the mid 1950s, several enterprise groupings were formed, such as the ex-zaibatsu enterprise groups of Mitsui, Mitsubishi, and Sumitomo, groups linked by the influential city banks (Fuji, Daiichi, Sanwa, and others), and groups centering around large industrial firms such as the Nissan Automobile Company, Ltd. Many instances of consolidated action among these groups may be cited. Yet one should stress that these groups have no dominating center and a relatively low degree of dependence on member banks as suppliers of capital. In short, they represent the competitive component of the affiliated enterprises in their industries. Essentially, they are alliances to protect and extend the autonomy of individual enterprises in their respective functional areas. As we shall see later, this autonomy also has significant implications in the realm of industrial relations.

The new system of "control by management" appears to accompany some institutionally patterned motivational orientations, and attention to this characteristic may provide some clues to understanding the behavior of the postwar managers. Many of them seem to have become influenced at least in part by an ideology embodying the notion of social responsibility, derived in part from an "other-directed" social character overtly reactive to significant "others."[3] The 1957 manifesto of Keizai Dōyūkai, or the Committee for Economic Development (an employers' group, explained more fully below), exemplifies the trend, since it stresses the need for social responsibility based on a new managerial phylosophy: namely, avoidance of further expansion of direct control by government; stable growth of the nation's economy through cooperation among enterprises; and increasing rationality of industrial management through scientific management.[4]

3. David Riesman, *The Lonely Crowd* (New Haven: Yale University Press, 1961), especially Chapter 6.
4. Keizai Doyukai, Keieihosaku Tokubetsu Iinkai (Japan Committee for Economic

In stressing social responsibility, the Keizai Dōyūkai manifesto emphasized the importance of professional managers as compared with the interests of stockholders, workers, and consumers. Economic power had become substantially centralized in large enterprises by the mid-1950s, and the nation's economy depended to a great extent upon the decisions of large firms. To postwar Japanese management, therefore, competitors, government, and enterprise unions had become the chief focuses of attention and objects of concern. Since the long-term market prospects were favorable, companies continued to compete primarily by expanding their production capacity, an emphasis that agreed well with government economic policy, at least until the late 1950s. In fact, insofar as this orientation contributed to the expansion of employment opportunities and an increase in product supply, it also conformed to the public interest. However, toward the end of the 1950s, managerial zeal and optimism with regard to expanding production capacity began to lead many industries to overcompetition.[5]

In a mixed economy, where private industries are highly developed, government economic policy assumes a significant role in performing supplementary functions. Under this system there are inherent tensions between political leaders and managers of large firms because the former are inclined to try to expand the role of nationwide economic planning while the latter attempt to expand or maintain the role of the private economy. Managers come both to depend upon and to resist the role of government, and out of this process emerge the conflicting possibilities of an alliance with government and a power struggle against it. Despite warnings in the Keizai Dōyūkai manifesto against the interference of government bureaucrats, expectations for expanding the supplementary and protective role of government continued to be strong on the part of many top-ranking managers, supported by the prewar tradition of "sponsored capitalism." The traditional alliance between government and large-scale private enterprise,

---

Development, Special Committee for Management Policy), *Keieisha no shakaiteki sekinin no jikaku to jissen* [Self-consciousness and the practice of management's social responsibility] (Tokyo: Keizai Doyukai, 1957).

5. For an example of severe self-criticism by management, see Hajime Maeda "Antei seicho eno daiichinendo taru ninshikio" [Let's form an attitude toward the first year of stable growth], in *Keieisha* [Management] (Tokyo: Nikkeiren, Feb. 1964).

though weaker than previously, has been preserved because of the continuing dependence of Japan's economy on international trade, and hence a greater role for government in stabilizing the economy. The alliance and close coordination between the managers and the government planners have been fostered by the elite standing of both in terms of social status, education, and, quite frequently, their families. However, the alliance does not imply the existence of a single shadow cabinet. Instead, due in part to the heterogeneous interests within industry and the intense competition among autonomous enterprises, divisions have emerged which intensify strife within the political camps.[6]

After the 1957 recession, a call for "voluntary adjustment" in the rate of industrial expansion was voiced at the level of national employers' associations. The Keizai Dōyūkai, for example, promoted the development of cartels to eliminate old equipment and machinery, to regulate capital investment, to encourage product specialization, and to establish machinery for interfirm coordination at the industry level. However, attempts at "voluntary adjustment" failed except in the coal industry which had been declining rapidly. The individual enterprises jealously guarded their autonomy, and heated competition for investment capital continued. Cartel actions over prices exerted pressure for productivity competition and invited still more capital investment.

At this point it is appropriate to stress a unique feature of inter-enterprise relationships in Japan: the tendency of firms of approximately equal size to remain competitive while smaller firms within an industry develop dependent or satellite relationships with the larger ones. This tendency toward the development of vertical dependent relationships was strengthened during the period of rapid economic growth as small and medium-sized firms established ties with major firms in terms of capital, manpower, and functions.

The results of a survey of large firms with listed stocks, as of September 1961, revealed the extent of the vertical relationships then existing: every one of the 125 major firms responding had

6. See, for example, Yoshinori Katō, *Zaikai* [Economic circles] (Tokyo: Kawade Shobō Shinsha, Feb. 1966); and Giichi Miyazaki, *Big business* (Tokyo: Kawade Shobō Shinsha, Mar. 1965).

vertical relationships with smaller firms, the average number being approximately 13.[7] The parent company held more than 50 percent of the stock of 60 percent of these related firms. Officials of director rank in 84 percent of the related companies were personnel from the parent companies, and operational relationships of some kind existed in 84 percent of the related companies, most of which were subcontracting firms. It is not uncommon for these related companies, in turn, to have close vertical relations with still other medium-sized and small businesses. There is no evidence that any change has occurred in this situation since 1961. It is obvious that ties of this kind are based on superior and inferior economic power, but a feeling of community interests within the context of human relationships also binds the firms together.

Out of the intense competition the need for so-called industry reorganization, having as its goals the elimination of excessive competition and the development of more stable monopsonies, was strongly advocated by government and industrial leaders. It had progressed to some extent by 1969, but it remains to be fully realized, for many companies felt that the autonomy of their enterprises was being threatened. A rise in exports resulting from increased demands, however, provided an outlet for excessive capacity goods. The overcompetition problem, nevertheless, still remains.

National Employers' Associations

Four employers' associations are important in Japan as pressure groups: Keidanren, or the Federation of Economic Organizations; Keizai Dōyūkai, or the committee for Economic Development; Nissho, or the Japan Chamber of Commerce and Industry; and Nikkeiren, or the Japan Federation of Employers' Associations—known collectively as the *zaikai*, or the "financial power center." A brief historical account of the prewar political structure and organization of national employers' associations would be

7. For recent trends in control of affiliated companies, see Kigyō Kenkyūkai (Business Study Association), *Kankei kaisha* [The affiliated company], *Decision Making System*, 1961, Japan Management School, pp. 104–07.

helpful in providing background for their present roles and functions.

In the Meiji period there emerged within the constellation of political power a hierarchy of value rankings, based on the premises of a patrimonial state, which persisted throughout the prewar era.[8] Beginning with the emperor at the top, the hierarchy descended in the following order: the court entourage (consisting of elder statesmen, the lord keeper of the privy seal, and the privy council); the government bureaucracy (administrative and military); the political parties; and finally, the pressure groups. Under the prewar scale of values, the higher the rank, the more sacred the people in that rank and the less power conflict among them; therefore, the greater the nonpolitical aspect. The lower the rank, the stronger the reverse trends.

Throughout the Meiji period, political power by and large was not substantially integrated, and political parties and pressure groups were not very significant. Early in the Meiji era, the power position of the business elite in society was far inferior to that of the political elite. The Shōgyō Kaigisho, or Chamber of Commerce, the forerunner of the present Nissho, was founded at that time but was organized essentially from above, largely for administrative purposes. As the importance of the business elite increased later in the Meiji era, a circle within this group, centering around the top leadership of the Shōgyō Kaigisho, began to develop a relatively strong pressure group vis-à-vis the political elite, especially the government bureaucracy.

Following World War I, political power began to be decentralized, with the growth of so-called Taishō democracy. The charismatic authority of the emperor declined sharply after the death of the Meiji emperor and as heroes of the Meiji Restoration retreated from their offices in the court entourage. Power centers emerged within the government, and the political parties began to be much more influential, as did the business elite. During this

8. For a discussion of the hierarchy of political power, see Yonosuke Nagai, "Atsuryoku seiji no Nihonteki kōzō" [The structure of pressure politics in Japan], in Nihon Seijigakukai (Japan Political Science Academy), *Nihon no atsuryoku dantai* [Pressure groups in Japan] (Tokyo: Iwanami Shoten, 1960). Regarding Nikkeiren as a pressure group, see Naoki Kobayashi, "Sengo jūyō rippō katei kenkyū" [A study of the legislative process of major postwar laws], in *Shakai kagaku gaiyō* [Summary of social sciences] (Tokyo: Faculty of Liberal Arts, University of Tokyo, 1953).

period the *zaikai* became the meeting place of the zaibatsu representatives who occupied influential positions in the business elite. Thus the *zaikai*, through its influence with political parties, became one of the leading groups among the elites in Japanese society.

However, even then the *zaikai* sponsorship of the political parties was not strong enough to influence the actual political process. The imperial bureaucracy retained substantial power vis-à-vis the parties, and when a political party came to power, it had to assume a nonpartisan, nonpolitical, "representative" role. Accordingly, other channels, of a more formal sort, were needed to exert pressure over the government bureaucracy. The national employers' associations—the Zensanren, or National Federation of Industrial Organizations, and the Nihon Keizai Renmei, or Japan Federation of Economic Organizations, concerned with economic affairs—came to the fore. These organizations, each led by zaibatsu representatives, were powerful vocal groups that could initiate coordinated action among their affiliated enterprises.

The polarization of political power under Taishō democracy created a political deadlock and, following a series of recessions after World War I and the ensuing depression which began in about 1926, eventually led to submission to military dominance over the political process. The *zaikai* subordinated itself to the military elite and during the World War II years sought survival and prosperity by cooperating. The managers of zaibatsu firms frequently took government posts, including cabinet positions. The two national employers' associations, in fact, disbanded shortly after the outbreak of World War II.

Government economic policy was crucial for economic recovery in the immediate postwar years, and, although *zaikai* action was very much needed, top management of the former zaibatsu firms refrained from formal *zaikai* functioning until the mid-1950s, due in part to the purge of former *zaikai* leaders and in part to a preoccupation with the internal affairs of their own enterprises. Instead the pressure groups became significant through organization at industry levels and/or through individually established informal channels. *Zaikai* action at the national level was undertaken largely by top managers of former non-zaibatsu enterprises or lesser zaibatsu firms.[9] Through this process, various informal links between the political and business elites were created. Only in the 1950s, when large firms had completed their recovery and begun to grow, did the influence of former zaibatsu firms and several other large enterprises increase to any great extent, as their top managements began to appear again as the principal instigators of *zaikai* action at the national level.

Keidanren (the Federation of Economic Organizations) was established in May 1946, its chief constituency being employers' associations at the industry level.[10] Since the industry-level associations historically had been formed through cartel actions, Keidanren became virtually a national federation of large enterprises. Although its historical antecedent may be said to be Nihon Keizai Renmei, its role on behalf of the *zaikai* increased in importance compared to what it had been in prewar days because of the extinction of the zaibatsu as a controlling headquarters. In many instances in the postwar era, Keidanren has become the center for coordinated action among the four *zaikai* bodies.

Nissho (the Japan Chamber of Commerce and Industry), as it now exists, was formally established in 1953 as the national center for regional and local chambers of commerce and industry. While it also represents the interests of medium-sized and small enterprises, its leadership has been taken over by the large firms that are the leaders of the *zaikai*.

Keizai Dōyūkai (the Committee for Economic Development) is a voluntary organization of managers as individuals. It is organized on a regional basis, but its activities have been coordinated nationally, and the problems it has dealt with have been national in scope. Since its inception in 1946, Keizai Dōyūkai has issued a series of public pronouncements on "progressive" managerial

9. On the behavior of economic circles in the postwar period, see Akira Sakaguchi, *Keieisha* [Management] (Tokyo: Kawade Shobō, May 1964).

10. See the following on the organization and function of Keidanren: *Keidanren no jūnen* [Ten-year development of Keidanren] (Tokyo: Keidanren, Oct. 1956). *Keidanren nijūnen-shi* [Twenty-year history of Keidanren] (Tokyo: Keidanren, 1963). To understand the organization and function of Shōkō Kaigisho (Chamber of Commerce and Industry) see Tokyo Shōkō Kaigisho (Tokyo Chamber of Commerce and Industry), *Tokyo Shōkō Kaigisho hachijūnen no kaiko* [Reflections on the eighty-year development of the Tokyo Chamber of Commerce and Industry] (Tokyo: Tokyo Shōkō Kaigisho, Jan. 1961).

ideologies which appeal to the public or society in general. It, therefore, is distinctly a postwar product.

Nikkeiren (the Japan Federation of Employers' Associations) is the business federation specifically concerned with industrial relations. Founded in 1948 but having Zensanren as its predecessor, it has been the prime management agent dealing with labor problems.

The leadership of the four bodies frequently overlaps, an indication of the existence of a core group among the *zaikai* leaders. Their political activities became particularly notable after 1955. It is said, for example, that Keidanren and Nissho were active in bringing about the amalgamation of the conservative parties in the mid-1950s in order to cope with the relative advance of the "progressive" forces in the 1955 spring election. Also, it is alleged that the *zaikai* played a significant role in the three changes of the prime ministership in the 1960s.

Formal pressure group actions directed toward the governmental process began to be evident during the mid-1950s. A well-known journalist, Akira Sakaguchi, aptly describes the trend:

> By 1957–58, Keidanren began to establish itself as the most influential pressure group, though until about 1955 it had been regarded as a quiet organization, in sharp contrast to the conspicuous activities of Keizai Dōyūkai. About 1963 it began to have a direct influence on the governmental process of drafting the annual budget. In addition to the customary routes of intra-governmental dealings with the Ministry of Finance to revive proposed budgetary plans (from various ministries, to respective branches under the policy research committee of the Liberal-Democratic Party, to the Ministry of Finance), a new route (various ministries, to Keidanren, to the Ministry of Finance) had been added. The top management of the larger firms, as the core of the power elite in recent years, was reflected in the internal structure of Keidanren. Its regular policy committees, numbering more than thirty, cover a wide range of both domestic and foreign affairs of national importance.[11]

11. Sakaguchi, *Keieisha*, p. 177.

The changing power position of the business elite and its rise to the peak of the power elites is also reflected in the public pronouncements of Keizai Dōyūkai on the standing of employers in society. On November 6, 1967, Keizai Dōyūkai issued an interim statement entitled "Toward the Industrial Welfare Society—The Responsibility of Managers in the New Era," which included the following declaration:

> We have the responsibility to contribute to social progress and security as an adviser to and cooperator with society, in addition to the responsibility for improving management practices as the innovator of technological change. In this sense, today's managers must become the economic statesmen upon whose shoulders these two roles fall.[12]

This self-image of the business statesman as promoter of an industrial welfare society is highly significant when compared to the series of self-images found in previous public pronouncements. In the so-called Ōtsuka proposal issued in the autumn of 1947, for example, managers were depicted as co-workers with capital and labor; the enterprises were to be under the co-ownership and co-directorship of all three parties. In the 1956 Keizai Dōyūkai manifesto, the consumer joined "capital and labor" as a significant party, with managers standing above them as coordinators of the conflicting claims of these interest groups. Thus, in the 1967 pronouncement, the community and society in general came to the fore, in addition to the others, with managers as responsible economic statesmen and "members of a pluralistic society."

The Structure and Function of Nikkeiren

The employers' organization that has played the most significant role in labor-management relations has been Nikkeiren, and an analysis of its functions and structure provides still another clue

12. Keizai Dōyūkai, *Sangyō fukushi shakai o mezashite* [Toward the industrial welfare society] (Tokyo: Keizai Dōyūkai, Feb. 1967), p. 13.

to the character of managerial policies in Japanese industrial relations.

Since its inception Nikkeiren has been known for its highly militant posture toward the labor movement. Of the several contributing factors, three appear to be the most important. First, Nikkeiren was founded in the midst of the upsurge of the postwar labor movement, against a background of the shift in SCAP's economic and labor policies toward strengthening the managerial stand vis-à-vis organized labor. Second, Nikkeiren is historically continuous, at least to some extent, with prewar managerial conservatism. Third, since Nikkeiren has no direct influence over the collective bargaining process, it has never been forced to make concessions and thus has been able to maintain a militant posture.

Nikkeiren's activities may be divided roughly into four periods. The first, from its founding in 1948 until the spring of 1950, was characterized by militant activities in industrial relations at the national, industrial, and enterprise levels. The major objective at the time the organization was established was to regain and safeguard management prerogatives against the then left-wing revolutionary assaults of the labor movement. Nikkeiren opposed the production control strategy of the unions and strongly urged revision of the Trade Union Law and the Labor Relations Adjustment Law in order to curb union power.

About 1947, the labor policies of the political elites began to be directed toward the goals to which Nikkeiren aspired. When SCAP issued its order to avert the scheduled general strike of February 1947 and again when the government wage policy adopted in October 1948 prohibited wage increases beyond the ability of individual enterprises to pay, the employers' stand against labor wage offensives was strengthened. In May 1948, the Trade Union Law and the Labor Relations Adjustment Law were revised, regulating the extent of union membership by excluding white-collar workers with managerial functions, and prohibiting union meetings during working hours. Also the laws permitted abandonment of automatic extensions of labor-management contracts and prohibited violent job actions.

In 1949, in accordance with the Dodge Plan for economic reconstruction, a series of plant closures and layoffs was enforced, resulting in the discharge of a large number of workers. In the private sector alone, 370,000 workers were dismissed. At the same time that the labor movement was strongly resisting these actions and the Sanbetsu unions were organizing a massive "industrial defense struggle," Nikkeiren was actively involved in coordinating the process of discharges and plant closures.

During the second period, lasting through most of the 1950s, Nikkeiren and Sōhyō, or the General Council of Trade Unions of Japan, became sharply opposed at various levels of industrial relations, following the organization of the latter in 1950. Pressures exerted by the two parties became particularly intense during the process of amending the Trade Union Law, the Labor Relations Adjustment Law, and particularly the Subversive Activity Prevention Law.

Pressure group actions by both Nikkeiren and Sōhyō took diverse forms, reflecting the polarized political power structure in postwar Japan. Nikkeiren and other employers' associations organized conferences and meetings with the conservative parties and with government officials; directed resolutions, proposals, and petitions to the government and political parties; lobbied members of the Diet; and intensified public relations activities through formal and informal meetings with newspaper editorial writers and contacts with labor officers of foreign embassies and consulates. Sōhyō, in turn, organized frequent protest strikes; communicated direct pressure by visiting government officials; put pressure upon individual Socialist members of the Diet; organized mass meetings and signature campaigns; issued resolutions and communiqués; and appealed to overseas labor organizations.

Intra-enterprise labor relations had become substantially stabilized at many of the large firms by the 1950s. At the 1955 extraordinary general meeting of Nikkeiren, Hajime Maeda, the managing director, noted in his report on the labor situation that ten years of "runaway" trade union activity had ended and the next ten years should be a period for employers to take the lead in introducing technological innovations, as Japan's economy was on the verge of rapid growth. This was the start of the third period.

Yet the sharp confrontation between Nikkeiren and Sōhyō continued, and during the last half of the 1950s a series of economic and political issues provoked struggles between the two. In the autumn of 1958 Sōhyō mounted a fierce nationwide struggle against revision of the Police Duty Discharge laws; in 1960 it opposed revision of the Japan-United States Security Treaty; and during 1959–60 it supported the coal miners in their historic dispute at the Mitsui Miike colliery (see Chapter 9).

Meanwhile, a significant change had begun to take place in the area of economic dealings between labor and management. As the heavy and chemical industries increased their strength in the economy, the unions in industries such as steel, shipbuilding, and chemicals began to assume leading roles in the Spring Labor Offensive, and the employers in those industries, in return for wage concessions, began to seek union cooperation in the introduction of new management practices and new technologies. This was the fourth period, which continued until the mid-1960s.

Nikkeiren, however, continued to take a strong stand in opposition to union wage demands, and even after 1960, despite the increasingly tight labor market, it insisted that the rate of wage increases be kept to 4 or 5 percent, in general opposition to Sōhyō's substantially greater demands in the annual spring offensives. The wage increases granted were at the level of 8 to 10 percent, far above Nikkeiren's prescription, and Managing Director Maeda lamented that wage increases greater than productivity increases in manufacturing were "humiliatingly forced rates."

The gap between actual settlements and Nikkeiren's prescription invited questions concerning the federation's effectiveness in labor relations at the enterprise level. Although the federation continued to grow steadily, there were signs that its influence was not keeping pace. At its inception in 1948, following the prewar organization pattern of Zensanren, Nikkeiren consisted of eight regional associations and twenty-three industrial organizations, such as the Japan Iron and Steel Employers' Association and the Ammonium Sulphate Fertilizer Industry Employers' Association. Later, prefectural and district organizations joined, bringing the total of local or regional affiliates to forty-seven, and the number of affiliated industrial organizations increased to a total of forty-eight. In the spring of 1965, there were about 27,500 member firms, representing almost all major Japanese firms and regional bodies serving medium and small firms.

Nikkeiren's growth, however, cannot be explained in terms of its influence over the collective bargaining process, because the trend seems to have been the reverse. Nor is it understandable as a result of its posture as a "fighting" organization since, at the enterprise level industrial relations have become relatively calm. Rather, growth seems to reflect the increasing professionalism of the personnel relations function at the enterprise level. Following the pattern of the prewar Zensanren, Nikkeiren has emphasized the professionalization of personnel managers and hence conducts research and training activities on behalf of individual enterprises. Particularly since the early 1960s, the personnel relations aspect of its activities has grown almost in proportion to the relative moderation of its militant posture, and instead of continuing to be the "fighting Nikkeiren," the federation has come to regard trade unions as partners in the promotion of economic growth. This change was explicitly noted in a resolution at the general meeting in 1963.[13] Examples of its professional orientation can be identified in such tendencies as the establishment of an economic research institute, a talent-development center, a job analysis center, and a section dealing with personnel relations.[14] In the early 1960s a committee was organized to formulate new managerial ideals in an attempt to provide leadership to personnel management in enterprises.

At Nikkeiren's inception, its leadership was recruited largely from the cotton and coal industries, since it was there that prewar experience and expertise in labor problems had accumulated. This leadership has remained, almost unaltered to the present time. Yet, as already mentioned, the cotton and coal industries have lost their relative positions within the Japanese industrial structure, and in the expanding industries, such as heavy industry and

13. Nikkeiren, *Kongo rōshikankei to keieisha no kenkai* [Future industrial relations and the employers' view: Resolution at the general meeting] (Tokyo: Nikkeiren, 1963).

14. When Nikkeiren appealed for frank communications with labor unions, including Sōhyō unions, Kaoru Ohta, then president of Sōhyō, responded that they were ready to comply.

chemicals, the customary "unique to Japan" industrial relations patterns have tended to undergo substantial change. One can imagine that a wide range of management orientations tending toward "partnership" might emerge. An example of one pole can perhaps be found in the following statement by Nikkeiren's managing director in his quest for new managerial ideals.:

> These four islands, though narrow in their geographical expanse, are our territories. Inside these, the Japanese race alone, with an emperor as the nation's symbol, and with no mingling of other races, is making a living, the people's psychological base depending on the emperor as the nation's symbol. There is no other example of such a unique nationality. This nationality must, and will, be maintained. Since it is within this framework that the economy develops and enterprises are managed, the answer to the questions what ought to be the state of enterprises and what is the right attitude of managers will become self-evident. Our task, therefore, is to write down that answer.[15]

In the Nikkeiren statement, one guideline for personnel relations was the following:

> One should not fail to devise skillfully, to enliven within the modern sense, the tastes that are unique to Japan and that remain in today's institutions, such as enterprise unions, the length-of-service-oriented wage system, permanent employment, and so forth.

This statement reflects the values that guided prewar personnel policies and the traditional aspects of personnel policies found in most of the major firms. Thus, while the statement recognizes the need for change, it fails to indicate the future direction of industrial and personnel relations. As it now stands, it is quite clear that the ideological leadership for enterprises in the area of industrial relations has shifted from the Nikkeiren to the Keizai Dōyūkai managers.

15. "Antei seicho eno daiichinendo taru ninshikio," *op.cit.*, p. 166.

Management Organization

Throughout the postwar period, management has been subjected to pressures to "modernize" according to the American model, modified to retain characteristic Japanese patterns. As a result, the formal organization of top management today closely resembles that of an American company.

The reasons for this are several. First, the commerce law was amended so that boards of directors were legally required in place of "control by stockholders" which had already been only nominal. Thus, "control by trustees" was instituted. Second, auditing by certified public accountants was introduced to replace ritualized inspection of the books by internal auditors. Third, top management, in order to be accountable to trustees, assumed responsibility for detailed company operations and reported to the board of directors. Fourth, a controller system was gradually adopted. Fifth, management by committee was introduced, so that general managers' committees, directly in line with the board of directors, were formed. Finally, top management training programs, patterned on American models, were introduced.

However, the traditional method of recruiting management, developed under the zaibatsu system, continued, and this in effect made the new structure function differently from what was originally envisaged. Following this tradition, members of the boards of directors have been recruited from inside the enterprise and the senior ranks of management. As a result, the board members are the general and department managers, and inevitably the established superior-subordinate relationships within the company hierarchy are carried into the board meetings, thus reducing the board's function to a ritualized approval of the decisions of the general managers' committee. The idea of trusteeship, *i.e.* representing stockholders interests, thus tends to be nominal. Another consequence is that the general managers' committee has become a powerful centralized decision center. In essence, the organization of Japanese top management has an oligarchical structure in which the same persons assume the leadership in making policy, managing operations, and auditing results.

Nevertheless, to say that nothing has changed substantially would be an error. The controller system has been installed but is far from being completely accepted. The traditional *ringi* system, in which the lower echelon of managers or staff originate drafts of policy decisions and submit them to the top management, continues to be used extensively in decision making, yet some decentralization has been taking place. According to a survey conducted by Keizai Dōyūkai in 1964, 91.9 percent of the major enterprises surveyed continued to use the *ringi* system; only 3 percent had abolished it.[16] However, 42.6 percent of the companies had modified their *ringi* systems between 1955 and 1958 mainly in the direction of simplifying the process, an indication that some degree of decentralization has been taking place.

Although there have been some changes, top management functions nonetheless have been and still are performed according to the hierarchical chain of command—president, vice president, executive general manager, general manager, director, department head, section chief, i.e. those who have the centralized authority to make decisions—with the participatory mechanism of the *ringi* system, through which lower echelon nonmanagerial staff members may draft top management policy.

Again, it should be stressed that significant changes appear to have begun. As controllers have gradually introduced centralized information processing, some degree of decentralization has taken place. This move, together with the upgrading of the staff function in many major companies, eventually had a profound effect on middle managers. As is discussed later in this chapter, some middle management have been eliminated in several cases at least. On the whole, however, the structural operation of the top management organization has experienced only moderate change. At the same time, however, tensions have increased, for which explanations are in order.

Within the hierarchy of directors, there have been wide cleavages between senior directors above the general managers and the junior directors below them, on such important subjects as authority, rewards, and criteria for appointment. The senior directors

16. Keizai Dōyūkai, *Wagakuni kigyō no ishikettei no jittai* [Actual conditions of decision-making in Japanese corporations] (Tokyo: Keizai Dōyūkai, 1964).

(the board chairman, president, vice president, etc.) both have more centralized authority and receive far greater rewards than the junior directors, whose positions are often only nominal and whose rewards are almost identical with those of senior department heads. A demographic survey of these two strata shows several different characteristics. There is a significant difference between the two in social origin. The senior directors, who come from the upper stratum of business circles, and sometimes from high governmental and cultural circles, had far easier access to their high positions in the enterprises than did the lower directors. Among the latter, opportunities were open to some extent to people from the middle stratum of society and business. Also, the age composition of the two groups is different. The majority of the senior directors are in their sixties, while most of the junior directors are in their fifties—an age difference that is highly significant in a society such as Japan's where social change has been drastic. In the postwar modernization of management, it appears that the social structure of top management is at least one of the most important elements.

Top management seminars, which began to flourish in the 1950s, were sponsored and conducted largely by the junior rank directors, who provided both the lecturers and the participants. If the repeated appeals of the Keizai Dōyūkai to establish "responsible" top management indeed echo the voices of the rank-and-file members, they come from the stratum below the senior directors, which would suggest the existence of built-in tensions within the double-decked structure of top management.

It appears that a rearrangement of authority relationships has been steadily, though slowly, taking place. The rather definite trend toward decentralization appeared around 1960 when the so-called reorganization of the head offices was accomplished at many companies. In the meantime, some of the directors of the early 1950s had risen to the top.

Thus, the positions of top management in large Japanese firms belong to the elite of the society, and access to these positions usually has been limited to those who have graduated from the well-known institutions of higher education and who have had long experience in various occupations within the enterprises. This, added to the influential position of large firms in the business and social sectors of society, has led to the development of an acute elite consciousness among managers in large firms. Many of them were recruited from the white-collar stratum, and their posts tend to imply senior positions in occupational life. Their prestige within the enterprise has been generally high.

The White-Collar Stratum of Management

Today no one questions that the emergence of white-collar employees as the "new middle class" has added to the complexities of class relations in modern societies. However, there are considerable country-by-country variations in the character of the white-collar social stratum, and its role in industrial relations also has varied.[17]

The white-collar work force as a stratum in Japanese society has a particularly complex character, reflecting the double-tiered structure of Japan's economy. Thus, for example, the white-collar employees of large firms are substantially above the blue-collar workers in terms of income; yet white-collar workers in the more numerous small and medium-sized firms have lower average incomes than those of blue-collar workers at the large firms. Also, there are differences between the two sectors in terms of educational careers, lifetime opportunities, and life styles.

In the large firms, growth has taken place within quasipatrimonial bureaucracies; in the small and medium-sized firms, it has occurred within the context of family businesses with traditional characteristics. In both cases, however, the social prestige of white-collar workers has continued to be higher than that of the blue-collar, and their opportunities for promotion have been relatively

17. In the case of England, white-collar workers as a distinct social stratum are not clearly identifiable on a scale of social prestige. Historically lacking identity as a stratum and with less of a tradition of organized dealings with employers, white-collar workers follow the lead of the blue-collar workers within the labor movement. In Germany, however, where there has been a strong identity as a social stratum, white-collar workers have organized a separate labor movement. In France, moreover, social distance from the managerial class and the tradition of revulsion against authority have made white-collar workers, even though they are culturally different from the blue-collar, a leading core in the ideologically militant labor movement.

open, although the differentials associated with their working conditions have continued to narrow throughout the process of industrialization. Intellectually and socially, white-collar workers as a social stratum have developed a class consciousness that appears to be rather unique to Japan.

This class consciousness, and the industrial relations behavior associated with it, was strikingly revealed in an extensive survey of white-collar workers made in 1961. Whereas nearly half of those responding said that they presently were in the "working class," defined in terms of identification with radical reform political parties, many of this same group perceived their future class affiliations as middle class and capitalist class rather than working class.

This ambivalent class consciousness manifests itself in various phases of industrial relations. White-collar workers have been at the core of the reform-oriented, politically conscious labor movement at the national level, but at the same time they have been among the leaders of cooperative labor unions at the enterprise level. For example, when industrial relations at the enterprise level have reached a crisis, in many cases a second union has been formed and has reached agreement with the company; this second-union movement frequently has been initiated by some portion of the white-collar group (see Chapters 7 and 9).

In tracing the origins of Japan's white-collar stratum, it should be stressed that the economic enterprises of both the shogunate and *daimyō* (feudal lords) and the large business of the merchant class had characteristics similar to those of patrimonial bureaucracies, though the management techniques may have been different. There are indications that in the former the emphasis was more on disciplinary control by rank order, whereas in the latter it was on more paternal leadership. Here it is important to recognize that the prewar pattern of Japanese enterprises was based essentially on an inherited traditional social structure.

In this prewar pattern, which emerged at the end of the Meiji period (1868–1912), developed throughout the Taishō period (1912–26), and became fixed by the early Shōwa era (1926—), the hierarchy was composed of the following rigid rankings: *shain* (company member), *junshain* (semi-company member), *jōyōkōin* (regular production member), and *shagaiko* and *kumifu* (outside worker and contract worker). These ranks were correlated with educational levels—high education (i.e., college preparatory schools), middle grade education, upper primary education, and at the bottom, primary education. Although ranking by education itself represented a break with the past, it did maintain continuity with tradition in spirit and social function. Specifically, in the successive educational reforms of the Meiji government, the ethos of education developed under the feudal regime was passed on. "Honor and loyalty," which had been stressed at the *daimyō* schools for samurai children, were adopted as the guiding principle of the new institutions of higher education. In general, it can be said that the emphasis on "health and ideas" at the private schools for lower samurai and upper-class townsmen was inherited as the educational goal for the new public normal schools. Similarly, in general, the virtues of "obedience and patience" at the private schools for commoners were carried over as the educational ideals for the new public elementary schools.

The *shain* had the characteristics of patrimonial bureaucrats. Their attachment to the enterprise was considered permanent, and the salary and promotion systems applied to them were based on length of service as the overt indication of their loyalty. Their fixed salaries implied that they were in service twenty-four hours a day; company housing provided for them near the establishments was based on a similar conception. They were treated as an elite group and, particularly in the zaibatsu enterprises, their careers led them to the rank of top management at either the parent company or related companies.

Among the *shain*, the *shokuin* class, white-collar workers, also enjoyed special treatment and were regarded as an elite group, particularly in the early Meiji period, since the need for talented personnel was great in both public and private bureaucracies. Adding to the prestige of the *shokuin* was the fact that the major source of manpower for administrative work was the samurai class.

By the middle of the Meiji period, a set of hierarchical status rankings was established among government officials, reflecting distance from the imperial house: imperial appointee (*shokunin*), personal imperial appointee (*shinin*), imperial-approved appointee (*sonin*), and junior official (*hanin*). In the zaibatsu enterprises, within the *shokuin* rank, a somewhat similar hierarchy existed: general trustee (*kanji*), director or manager (*riji*), secretary or counselor (*sanji*), and chief functionary (*shuji*). These two hierarchies eventually constituted major pillars of Japan's prewar class structure, with the imperial appointees and general trustees as the core of the upper class and the imperial-approved appointees and secretaries as the core of the middle class. The two frequently were linked by informal arrangements—school friendships and/or family relationships. Opportunities for upward mobility were open to the graduates of appropriate schools, thus guaranteeing a rather extensive circulation of the elite.

The *shain*, with the prospect of upward mobility, were expected to perform administrative functions. Even if they were assigned specialized functions, they were expected to make decisions based on the perspectives and viewpoints of their managers and the president.

The *junshain* (semi-company members) were treated somewhat similarly to the *shain*, but their attachment to the enterprise and their expectations for advancement were far less. They were hired as *employees* of the establishment, in contrast to the *shain*, who were recruited as *members* of the enterprise. Their employment relations were limited to the establishment until late in their careers. However, long employment tenure assured them of reaching the *shuji* and *sanji* level, that is, middle-class status. Although the paternalistic treatment accorded them was less extensive than that accorded the *shain*, it was still greater than blue-collar workers could expect. They functioned as specialists within specific fields.

Some of the paternalistic practices applied to the *jōyōkōin* (regular production workers) were a further reduced version of those applied to the *junshain*. In principle, the *jōyōkōin* had a permanent employment relationship under length-of-service welfarism; the *shagaikō* and *kumifu*, however, were contract employees whose labor was bought and sold on an hourly basis.

A centralized authority structure existed in juxtaposition with these hierarchical arrangements. The so-called *bunkabunshō*, the principle of authority allocation, has several distinctive characteristics, particularly when contrasted with "delegation of authority" in the Anglo-American sense. The former emphasizes limitation of authority: that is, the superior ranks reserve authority for themselves while specifying the area of responsibility of their subordinates. This concept stresses status and functionally diffuse relations. "Delegation of authority," in contrast, focuses more on functionally specific reciprocity. Moreover, the Japanese term regards "groups" as the units to which functions are allocated, while the Western concept emphasizes individuals.

Bunkabunshō thus has unique features in the functional differentiation of Japanese bureaucracies. Conceptually, the process of functional differentiation may be summarized as progressing through the following four stages: (1) differentiated capital flows according to the function of purchasing, production, and sales; (2) division of elements within each type of capital flow such as finance, technology, and personnel; (3) emergence of a managing cycle including planning, organizing, and controlling; and (4) separation of decision making into research, policy, and information. Functional differentiation up to the second stage took place in the process of Japan's industrialization, as line-control functions were developed. Since decision-making authority with respect to finance, personnel, and material management was reserved at the top, a production department had to submit draft proposals each time a decision was required—in the process known as the *ringi system*. The management officials responsible for finance, personnel, and materials would then examine the proposal from the operating department, advise on the direction of the top-level decision, or make decisions on behalf of the top management. Thus, with these rule-making and supervisory responsibilities over the purchasing, production, and sales functionaries, staff departments acquired quasi-line roles. As a result a quasi-line hierarchy emerged in the line departments. An organization of this type, the so-called *shokunō bumonbetsu soshiki* (organization by divided functional control) has been, at least until recently, and probably is now the predominant structure of Japanese industrial management. It has resulted in a system with large numbers of administrative personnel and very little specialization. Since white-collar employees were ranked above production workers and had more security and greater prospects for promotion leading to the upper or middle social classes, they performed supervisory functions of a kind over the line. These *shokuin-kōin* (white-collar blue-collar) differentials were the distinctive feature of the prewar Japanese social structure.

At least two factors, however, have long threatened this stratification system: the increase in white-collar employment and the general rise in the level of education. In the 1920s white-collar employees comprised about 10 percent of the nonagricultural labor force. After 1930, however, the increase in the number of white-collar workers was greater than the increase in the number of blue-collar workers, so that by the mid-1940s the white-collar ratio was 20 percent of the nonfarm labor force. The increase was due primarily to wartime growth of the heavy and chemical industries and the proliferation of government bureaucracies.[18]

Similar changes occurred in education. In 1919, less than 15 percent of all persons attending school were in schools above the elementary level: 0.8 percent in high schools and 16.8 percent in middle schools. The remaining 85.4 percent were elementary school students. By 1941 the proportion shared by the middle schools and higher education had nearly doubled to abaut 30 percent (higher education, 1.7 percent; middle schools, 26.6 percent). The proportion in elementary school had declined to 71.7 percent.

During the war years the combination of these two factors considerably diluted the notion that white-collar workers were superior to blue-collar. Within the white-collar group, female workers increased about eightfold, from 8,600 in 1930 to 68,600 in 1940. Between 1940 and 1945 the figures again nearly doubled. The proportion of female white-collar workers rose from 6.8 percent in 1930 to 17.7 percent in 1940; it has continued to increase at an accelerated rate since that time. As wartime manpower mobilization resulted in a mix of educational backgrounds among blue-collar workers, the differences between the office and the workshop tended to be reduced.

18. For an analysis of changes in the status of the white-collar labor movement in Japan, see S. B. Levine, "Unionization of White-collar Employees in Japan," in *White-Collar Trade Unions*, ed. Adolf Sturmthal (Urbana: University of Illinois Press, 1966).

Several other factors facilitated this process. The decrease in real wages was much larger for white-collar workers than for blue, reflecting in part the favored position of the latter in the labor market. The wartime-controlled economy further reduced differences in life style between the two. Blue-collar workers, with their stronger position in the labor market, occasionally generated disputes by demanding treatment equal to that of the white-collar group. The government's wartime labor policy, based on the principle of enterprise familialism as an imperial way of life, also promoted equalization measures. Thus, in 1941 the Personnel Management Orders for Important Establishments regulated the working conditions of both strata with an identical set of rules. The same word, *jūgyōin* (employee), applied to both. The two strata joined in the patriotic Sampō movement and through that organization attempted to improve their general welfare. While the notion of sharp status distinctions has more or less continued since then, the material grounds for them have been increasingly reduced.

As discussed in detail in Chapter 7, combined enterprise unionism emerged after World War II and in the immediate postwar years disrupted the hierarchical status order in industrial enterprises. In attempting to reconstruct the social order within their companies, top managers found no alternative but to regress to prewar patterns. This time the former status rankings, based on education and length of service, could no longer be justified. Accordingly, "status ranking" was rephrased as "qualification ranking"; "educational career" was reinterpreted as "ability classification"; and "length of service" was reconceptualized as "experience." Thus, *shikaku seido* (qualification system) replaced *mibun seido* (status system), with characteristics approximating prewar patterns, and was adopted in many large firms during the late 1940s and early 1950s.

Though many of the white-collar workers remained within unions and continued to be loyal to the lofty ideals of the postwar labor movement, as they returned psychologically to "line" positions they became less active in the leading unions and quite ambivalent about their class consciousness. The "ability-centered" *shikaku seido* soon created several basic dilemmas.

During the period of rapid economic growth, as use was made of newer technologies and administrative methods, especially in the heavy and chemical industries, both the increase in the number of white-collar workers and the rise in the education level of the work force became significant. From 1955 to 1963, the number of white-collar workers increased by about 50 percent and blue-collar workers by 38 percent. White-collar workers in 1963 numbered 9.1 million, or about 27 percent of the total nonfarm labor force. At present more than one-quarter of all nonfarm workers are white-collar employees.

The general rise in the educational level is even more striking. Of all persons attending school in 1960, almost 44 percent were in junior high school or higher institutions: 3.1 percent in higher education and 40.8 percent in the junior and senior high schools. The remaining 56.1 percent were in elementary grades. This trend continues to accelerate. In 1956, 47.9 percent of the junior high school graduates advanced to senior high school; by 1965 this ratio had risen to 70.6 percent. Likewise, the percentage of those advancing from the high school to the university level increased from 23.2 percent in 1951 to 27.2 percent in 1965.

The changes in the composition of the work force brought about by increased education have been most conspicuous in the heavy and chemical industries—steel, shipbuilding, electronics, automobiles, and machinery. In administration, in addition to the already expanded number of university graduates in the 30–40-year-old group, there are now a large number in the under 30 group. And in the production field, along with the increase in automation and mechanization and the extension of the three-shift operation, the number of so-called "gray-collar" workers, with a senior high school education, has increased.

Both the elite treatment for university graduates and the privileged position of the *junshain* became impractical by 1965, when senior high school graduates in manufacturing industries were distributed evenly in the office and production fields. Also, the imperatives for further functional differentiation within management exerted pressure to reorganize, or at least to greatly modify, the line organization with its centralized authority structure and the length-of-service social order.[19] The long-established pattern of organization by divided functional control began to undergo changes, and by the mid-1950s several staff functions had been added, such as comptroller, quality control, cost control, industrial engineering, and industrial training. Formerly these had been handled largely by the control staff. This emphasis on internal controls corresponded to management's focus in this period upon "production equal to sales." As noted earlier, around the mid-1950s competition for shares of the market generally intensified, capital investment grew to enormous size, financial stability became rather uncertain, and, as a result, the need for long range planning and an integrated approach to rationalizing operations became urgent. Eventually these developments brought about reorganization of head offices, but further functional differentiation was necessary. Planning, market research, research and development, and information processing staffs were strengthened, and management and control staffs, such as managerial accounting, quality control, and industrial engineering, were expanded. By the end of the 1950s a sizable proportion of the major firms had such planning and control staffs, reflecting the increasing differentiation. In addition, the functions of various operating departments were enlarged, thus expanding also the functions of sales, coordination with related firms, and overseas dealings.

As planning functions at the top increased in importance, delegation of authority over operations became necessary. With the introduction of the American concept of industrial management, the division system began to be employed; according to a 1964 Keizai Dōyūkai survey, such divisions were used extensively in 12.8 percent of the large firms surveyed, and partially in 17.6 percent. Where delegation of authority was not in the form of a division system, many enterprises nevertheless subdivided and systematized their profit and cost accounting. With this accountability went a degree of delegation of authority. In turn, managerial needs for supervisory pressure on subordinates also increased. The trend noted in 1964 has accelerated since.

19. For changes in organizational functions within the enterprise, see Ryūkichi Kitagawa and Hideaki Okamoto, *Howaito karā* [White collar] (Tokyo: Kawade Shobō Shinsha, 1964).

Further, as adjustment of line and staff relations became important, the reciprocal rights and obligations of each were defined. Up to the 1950s strictly staff positions were avoided for the most part by workers of *shokuin* rank. Acceptance of these positions could mean the loss of personal relationships within the established web of relations which proliferated along the departmental promotion ladder. However, when the importance of staff functions had become indisputably clear, professional posts were created, with prestige specifically provided, including a title and the prospects of a career leading to the top, and talented white-collar workers began to be recruited for these posts. This development marked the beginning of continuing infringement on established line jurisdictions so that the traditional multiladdered line hierarchy of department (*bu*), section (*ka*), and unit (*kakari*) began to become weakened and in some cases disrupted. Many prominent firms introduced formal examinations as an aid to selecting their senior managers and professionals. Delegation of authority and functional differentiation, though still limited, tended to create many posts requiring more initiative but also granting more autonomy than the previous positions, although they have also created much routine administrative and clerical work. As some planned approach was needed to develop appropriate manpower for the posts of senior professionals and managers, the large chemical company Shōwa Denkō, for example, established career development programs, while companies such as Toshiba Electric and Ishikawajima-Harima, a major shipbuiliing and heavy construction firm, instituted executive understudy programs. Many other enterprises adopted so-called self-evaluation reporting systems to compile data on the potential ability, interests, and career aspirations of their employees.

Under such circumstances, the "ability-centered" qualification system mentioned earlier could not remain the basic social order within large companies since it was essentially a classification based on educational background and length of service. Eventually it was rejected in favor of a length-of-service qualification system, while the new system of qualification by occupational function came to prominence. Under the latter, employees were classified on the basis of occupational functions such as administrative and clerical, technical and engineering, production work, and special functions. Within these functional groupings, rankings of managerial, professional, supervisory, senior grade, junior grade, and routine work were established. In administering the promotion and wage programs, more emphasis began to be put on ability and performance, although length of service has remained an important criterion.

The new system is a significant departure from the prewar pattern. It is highly selective and reduces the importance of status derived from educational level. It also denies in principle the significance of length of service if not related to the functional requirements of the job. In relating positions, the lowest grades, administrative and clerical work and production work, became equivalent, as did the lower grades of white-collar and unskilled blue-collar work. All this signifies an important departure from the traditional hierarchical pattern. In fact, during the rapid economic growth of the mid-1950s, wage differentials by length of service continued to diminish, whereas interindividual differentials in many firms tended to increase (see Chapter 10.)

Since the mid-1960s there has been even greater emphasis on functional ability. A new system now being devised aims to subdivide further the functional groupings in management and to develop modified wage progression curves by job groupings. The shift then is in the direction of occupational requirements based on job analysis as the major criteria for ranking.

The effect of these changes on the attitude of white-collar workers toward industrial relations is difficult to generalize. Nevertheless, it should be noted that professionalism has become widespread among the more ambitious graduates of institutions of higher education. Interenterprise occupational mobility, although still limited, has become more important among the talented, and a new term, *yūnōsha* (able persons), was created to designate them. Yet those who find new employment in the midst of their working careers are still termed *chūtō sayōsha* (midterm entrants) and continue to be discriminated against in personnel matters.

Professional associations have proliferated. The trend has affected even the labor market behavior of new college and university graduates, and many of them tend to look for occupational opportunities rather than for prestige companies, as they formerly did. Since the late 1940s increased union participation has been observed among the lower rather than the higher ranks of white-collar workers. Rapid economic growth and the job opportunities brought by functional differentiation of management appear to have accelerated this trend.

Those who have been less adaptable and whose social position has been on the decline have suffered loss of status—especially the middle-aged white-collar workers of both higher and lower grades. Generally, companies have avoided discharging them, continuing to guarantee at least their job security. But there has been no organized protection against the loss of status, and the labor movement has, on the whole, taken no positive measures concerning the status of older workers at the workshop level. A-mong lower-grade white-collar workers, the younger generation has had a different orientation. Some of the most able have been selected for promotion; many others have found an increasing number of opportunities outside the enterprises. The relative improvement of working conditions for the young, due to their shortage in the labor market, has made this possible. And, as will be noted, many of them have embraced different values. Thus, the ideology of many of the lower-grade white-collar workers, together with many of the blue-collar and an increasing number of "gray-collar" workers, tends in the direction of middle-class consciousness in a mass society.[20]

One after another of the attitude surveys conducted in the mid-1960s reported these and other significant trends. Among young workers, a widespread and increasing political orientation toward reform was reported, as well as an emphasis on ability and performance in their occupational lives. An extensive survey by Sōhyō in 1966 reported similar trends.[21] Many other surveys indicated that a shift away from collectivism and toward individualistic values appeared to be in the making. These developments are

20. For examples of comprehensive surveys on worker consciousness, see Hitoshi Matsuo, "Soshiki rōdōsha no ishiki dōkō" [Trends of organized worker consciousness of metropolitan residents], *Nihon Rōdōkyōkai Zasshi* [Journal of the Japan Institute of Labor], Jan. 1967.

21. Part of the survey on workers' consciousness made by Sōhyō is reported in *Gekan Sōhyō* [Monthly Sōhyō], Feb. 1967.

an indication of the profound changes now taking place in the quality of middle-class consciousness which has characterized Japanese white-collar workers. The trend, however, does not mean that they have become more involve in labor unions. But their numerical significance within the unions and their changing consciousness are likely to make them a vital pillar of union movements much more than in past.

The Status and Role of Work Group Leaders[22]

In Japan, as in many of the developing countries, work group leaders (or first-line supervisors) have been in the working class ranks, and their formal authority in industrial relations has been very limited—in fact almost nonexistent. However, their informal role has been substantial, and historically they have been the central figures in Japanese industrial relations. Throughout the postwar period, workshop leaders in Japan have demonstrated an allegiance to both labor and management, and at the establishment level they have been the stabilizing force in industrial relations.

Several significant changes, however, now appear to be occurring, and a brief historical review will help point out the implications of these changes. During the Meiji period, as in other countries during the early phases of industrialization, subcontracting systems became widespread in many industries. Shipbuilding and mining are notable examples. Subcontractors were the central authority figures in control of work and labor and, according to traditional *oyakata-kokata* (patron-client) relationships, had a simulated father-and-son relationship with the workers. This relationship had developed in the pre-Meiji medieval artisan society and had become the formal social relationship of the apprenticeship system. Under that system, the apprentice lived in the master's house and shared his daily life while learning a skill. However, relationships of this traditional artisan type were unable to survive

22. For a study on the status and role of supervisors, see Hideaki Okamoto, "Kōgyō-ka to genbakantokusha" [Industrialization and field supervisors] (Tokyo: Japan Institute of Labor, 1965).

in large modern enterprises in the face of increasing mechanization and bureaucratization.

By the late Meiji period, the large enterprises had begun to make active efforts to retain their skilled workers as well as to train apprentices at the shop level, and subcontractors began to be excluded from the shop. A new system of supervision was created during the 1920s and early 1930s, as industry was faced both with the need for increasing rationalization following World War I and with a growing labor movement. A new and carefully planned supervisory system known as the *shokuchō seidō* was introduced, in which attention to both production and the management of labor increased. White-collar engineers were assigned to work in the shop, and the personnel staff was located close to the shop. The functions of former subcontractors were redistributed among the line management, personnel staff, and new supervisors, the *shokuchō*.

Under the new system, however, the *shokuchō*'s authority was severely limited. For example, according to a 1928 survey of the role of the *shokuchō* at large enterprises in the Osaka area, conducted by the Ministry of Commerce and Industry, the *shokuchō* did not have autonomy even in scheduling. Their authority was limited to checking the progress of work and coaching workers in the performance of their jobs. In the realm of personnel relations, the functions of hiring and discharge belonged to the personnel staff. Other functions were performed by the white-collar engineers. Yet, de facto authority to make decisions on individual wage increases, rewards, and punishment tended to be delegated to the new supervisors, the *shokuchō*. Management's expectations of the *shokuchō* with regard to industrial relations centered around informal relations rather than formally prescribed duties. Since the *shokuchō* were responsible for job instruction through apprenticeship and on-the-job training, a patron-client type relationship emerged. The new relationship differed from its predecessor in that relations were no longer formally institutionalized, extending horizontally beyond individual enterprises, but were personalized and confined to the primary group. Management expected the *shokuchō* to be "model" senior workers within the informal group. Therefore, in screening for *shokuchō*, attention focused mainly on personality characteristics considered desirable for informal lead-ers. The *shokuchō*, having no power to hire or fire, relied on some-thing akin to patriarchal leadership, using rewards and punish-ment on the one hand and considerate personal attention to the workers' lives on the other. Since employment policies at the large firms determined the members of the shop group, intrashop social relations tended to be very close. As a result, the promotion system based on length of service with distinguished honor rewards at the top made the *shokuchō* post the symbolic summit of the regular worker's career, the target for rank-and-file aspirations.

Many deviations from these typical patterns could be cited. Every year not a few labor disputes break out over the arbitrariness of supervisory personnel, including persons of the *shokuchō* rank. Yet many more cases could be cited to illustrate the efforts of these supervisors, in alliance with the white-collar workers, to improve conditions for the workers. In the immediate postwar years, the *shokuchō* were a major source of leadership in forming unions—as those who suffered longest from the white collar-blue collar status differentials often took the lead in demanding the abolition of that stratification system. Since *shokuchō* were involved in the union movement, their responsibilities for personnel relations were transferred to persons higher up in line management or in the personnel department. The white-collar engineers and the *shoku-chō*, though they had been on the whole active in the labor move-ment, were also enterprise conscious, and this dual allegiance, as might be expected, created some role conflicts.

From the late 1940s until the mid-1950s, that is, during the pe-riod of so-called shop-order recovery, enterprises tried to strength-en the position of work group leaders and, in an attempt to get them back into the line hierarchy, their wage scale was adjusted to put a higher value on their length of service, and the supervisory allowance also was revised or increased. In addition, "training-within-industry" programs were introduced. During the years from 1949 to 1954, job instruction training courses were given to 250,000 supervisors, job relations training to 183,000, and job methods training to 60,000. However, in general, supervisors have maintained their allegiance to both the enterprise and the union. It was during this period that union organization at the shop level also became systematized, as emphasis on action at the shop level increased within the labor movement.

Since the mid-1950s, rapid and large-scale technological change, and the social change that accompanied it, have had a great impact on shop organizations, especially in the heavy and chemical industries. On the technical side, the need for manual labor and machine operators has been markedly reduced, and groups with a hierarchy of skills acquired by experience have been diluted as skilled workers often became monitors or observers of automatic processes. Maintenance functions became even more important than they had been.

Because of these developments, one of the important aspects of the work group leader's position, that of top rank in the skill hierarchy, has been lost. However, his relationship as agent for the administrative staffs has increased in importance, as have standards of required technical knowledge. These changes have occurred not only in the chemical and automobile firms, where some degree of technical expertise is required for the position of workshop leader, but even in the steel and shipbuilding industries, where the length-of-service element has remained conspicuously strong.

Changes in administrative practices and in the composition of work groups at the shop level also affected the customary relationships. Outside the shop organization, the number of engineers and technicians greatly increased, and the functions of various staff personnel gained in operational importance. Internally, the proportion of younger workers increased notably with the employment of senior high school graduates. The social order based on length of service was threatened, since adaptability to the new technology tended to be inversely correlated with age. Customary social groupings and patterns of interaction tended to break down with frequent intra-enterprise transfers. The former pattern of promotion channels was disturbed, and new channels were not yet defined. A generation gap over the value structure added to the deep conflict, while shop autonomy based on secretive personalized skills rather than on management and staff expertise was threatened. All of these factors contributed to social tensions within shop organizations.

Under these circumstances, the large enterprises felt a need to strengthen personnel functions at the shop level. "Personnel management by line personnel" became the slogan, and the role of supervisors was critically reexamined. Retraining programs were introduced, and criteria for selecting supervisors were changed so as to put more emphasis on technical knowledge and leadership. Eventually, around 1960, supervision began to be reorganized in many large enterprises.

An idea of the direction of these supervisory changes may be drawn from a survey conducted at 176 major establishments in 1967 by the Japan Industrial Training Association (Nihon Sangyō Kunren Kyōkai). Although length-of-service considerations are still dominant in the supervisor's post, several changes have been or are taking place. In many enterprises a majority of the former *shokuchō* positions are now occupied by graduates of universities and other higher educational institutions, the proportion of persons over forty years of age is markedly lower than it was under the traditional system, and the proportion of senior high school graduates has increased significantly. In many companies length of service has disappeared from the list of criteria for appointment to supervisory positions, and in a sizable number of firms completion of the specified training course has become an important qualification.

The role of work group leaders in industrial relations also appears to be changing, as they usually perform autonomously such functions as scheduling, determining overtime assignments, vacation, or early leave, approving absences from work for personal reasons, conducting safety inspection and on-the-job training, and communicating welfare practices to the workers.

Several characteristics of supervisory authority in industrial relations can be identified from the Industrial Training Association survey. Generally speaking, the functions of hiring, firing, and grievance handling still are performed by senior line management, although there are variations by industry and enterprise. In the chemical industry, for example, although responsibility for technical relationships tends to be centralized at the senior management level, personnel relations are usually delegated to junior management, which means that in fact the participation of work group leaders is substantial. The reverse is true in the labor-intensive shipbuilding industry, where work group leaders have substantial technical responsibilities. The pattern in automobile manufacturing lies somewhere between these two cases. In general, however, the trend appears to be toward more active participation of work group leaders in personnel functions.

This tendency is reflected in the reorganization of the supervisory system. Around 1960 the new system began to be devised in the large heavy and chemical industries, with *sagyōchō seidō* (a term invented as the equivalent of "foremanship" in the United States) at Yawata Steel as a notable example. Although there are variations among enterprises, emphasis is commonly placed on the supervisor's role in information processing and participation in personnel relations. The new *sagyōchō*, or foremen, are designated the top managers in the shop. The criteria for selecting them became stricter, as training up to the level of middle-grade graduate engineers was required. Thus, long-range training courses were devised, combining on-the-job training, job rotation, and instruction at company training centers. Since about 1960, training centers with facilities for offering training above the senior high school or at the college level had been established at many companies; training centers at large companies such as Tokyo Electric Power, Hitachi Electric, and Nihon Transportation even offer university-level courses.

The status and role of the new foremen, although based on the Western model, nonetheless appear to retain unique Japanese characteristics. Their position is now located within the management rather than the working-class stratum, but they constitute a special category of personnel. Since the proportion of work group leaders among elected union officers at the establishment or plant level has been declining rapidly, their position is "doubly marginal." Nevertheless, with a few exceptions, they continue to perform their traditional role as informal leaders within the shop. Around 1960, it should be noted, spontaneous foremen's study clubs within and beyond the enterprises began to proliferate, and in July 1961, a national study meeting for such supervisors was held for the first time.

The enterprises, recognizing the need to intensify personnel functions at the shop level, began to establish upward communications, such as workshop conferences, self-evaluation reporting systems, and attitude surveys. Personnel counseling also was introduced. In some cases a different structure of informal leaders, such as a lead worker system or a "buddy" system was established as a model to follow within the informal group. As a result, personnel relations at the shop level have become increasingly multilinear. In some cases activity was stimulated through the grievance-handling procedure as specified in the labor contract but rarely used previously. By now the trend is rather evident, and it appears that a new shop culture is in the making. The series of changes at the workshop level reflects, and in turn conditions, the changing character of personnel relations policies and indirectly affects changes in management's industrial relations ideology. The workers in turn began to confront management more directly. Toward the end of the 60s, the workshop group began to be more vocal in their demands concerning personnel practices.

Industrial Relations Ideology and Personnel Policy

In the realm of managerial ideology and personnel policy, new trends of historical significance began to be discernible in the mid-1960s. In *Industrial Welfare Society*, published by Keizai Dōyūkai in February 1967, a portion dealing with labor relations reads as follows:

> We recognize labor unions as functional groups contributing to social progress. We now stand at the beginning of a period of final examination and establishment of a basis of cooperation with the labor unions as good partners. It may become possible to establish favorable industrial relations policies, wage decisions, and other working conditions within individual enterprises. In doing so, we should insist firmly on the social responsibility of the unions.

And in *New Managerial Ideals*, a pamphlet issued by Keizai Dōyūkai in February 1965, the following statement was made with regard to personnel relations:

> Concretely, for example in the management of enterprises hereafter, flexibility and creativeness of the highest order are required. Accordingly, proper placement and evaluation of performance based on ability and ability-centered wage and promotion administration are necessary. Enterprises are now making decisions to reorganize themselves on the basis of abilities, and the length-of-service status system must be improved.

These statements may seem rather commonplace, even trite, to those who are familiar with institutional facets of industrial life in contemporary societies. They are highly significant, however, when one examines the history of Japanese managerial ideology and its relationship to labor and personnel relations.

The ideology of the prewar managers of large Japanese firms was industrial familialism, and their personnel policies were oriented toward the length-of-service status system. Under this ideology labor and management shared a common destiny in which they were mutually dependent, inseparable parts of a whole. Although this ideology had been formulated at the end of the Meiji era and during the Taishō period, at the time of the rise of the labor movement, it was more than just a rationalization or a logical managerial defense against the assaults of organized labor.[23]

Japan in those days was a patrimonial state. Managers were the elite in a country that was permeated with nationalism, and they acted as patrimonial bureaucrats within the zaibatsu industrial empires. The historic legacies of familialism, as values unique to Japan, had very real consequences for many members of the managerial stratum. Although there were perhaps many who had been intellectually freed from traditional values and merely found them expedient in directing workers with predominantly agrarian backgrounds, there were many others in whom the traditional values, reinforced with nationalism, were internalized.

23. For an article on company paternalism, see Hiroshi Hazami, *Nihon rōmukanrishi kenkyū* [Research on the history of Japanese labor administration] (Tokyo: Diamond-sha, 1964).

Some of the latter had led the organized employer movement in the 1920s in protest against the government's attempt to promulgate a trade union law. They achieved their goal, and some of them subsequently led the movement of Zensanren, the National Federation of Industrial Organizations, to infuse the ideology with suitable personnel policies.

In reality, many of the personnel policies were merely partial and less vigorous applications of policies directed to the patrimonial bureaucrats. Nonetheless, they were value derived and, therefore, could claim legitimacy based on the ideology of industrial familialism. Under this structure, the personnel department's function was to represent the claims of enterprise members. Having this somewhat representative as well as supervisory role, the department occasionally became involved in conflicts with the finance department. These disputes were supposed to be settled by top management decisions, still another characteristic of patrimonial bureaucracy. Thus, tension between capital and labor was built-in *within* the administrative system itself, though the system favored the interests of the former. The organization of the two prewar national employer's associations, Nihon Keizai Renmei and Zensanren, with the former performing economic functions and the latter dealing with labor problems, may be understood as corresponding to these built-in intra-management tensions. The two organizations were coordinated and controlled by informal circles formed at the Kōgyō Club, or Industrial Club, the meeting place of top figures in the business elite. Needless to say, trade unionism had no place within the ideology and policies of those organizations.

The industrial familialism that characterized prewar managerial ideology weakened after World War II, as the growth of the labor movement and the trend toward democratization in the political and social arena negated the fundamental authoritarian values contained in that ideology. The search for a new managerial philosophy began, but it was difficult.

In the autumn of 1947, the first attempt of any significance appeared in a piece entitled "A Proposal on the Subject of Enterprise Democratization—A Portrait of Revised Capitalism," written by Banjo Ōtsuka, one of the leaders of the Keizai Dōyūkai managers. This proposal conceived of the enterprise as owned by three partners—capital, labor, and managers—and directed, insofar as basic policy was concerned, by an assembly of the three; therefore, it proposed that drastic changes should be made in the enterprise structure under the capitalistic economy.

Still another aspect of the proposal has often passed unnoticed. With respect to labor unions, it suggested an enterprise-wide organization with a primarily cooperative role, although the conflicting interests of labor and management were not by any means negated. In essence, it proposed an ideology of enterprise—wide communalism, thus maintaining continuity with one of the important aspects of the prewar industrial relations ideology. Although the proposal did not have enough of an impact to stimulate an organized movement of any significance, it was suggestive of the new ideological direction emerging among the postwar managers.

However, employers in the late 1940s needed more concrete guidelines to reconstruct the social order of the workshops within their enterprises, that is, a set of principles to justify action. Employers looked for these principles, ideologically, in functional rationalism and in the American notion of industrial democracy. Some personnel administration techniques used in the United States were introduced. In September 1949, Nikkeiren, at its extraordinary convention, adopted a statement entitled "Our Views on New Personnel Management," and a similar resolution was passed again in March 1950. The new philosophy of industrial relations was stressed in all of these statements and resolutions, and the aims of labor relations activities were defined as the establishment of relationships of mutual trust and confidence and the need to modernize, rationalize, and increase efficiency on the basis of a labor-management relationship in which the rights and obligations of each party were specified. The strategic areas for the activities of labor and personnel relations were defined as: labor agreements, machinery for labor-management cooperation, employee relations, specification of the extent of union membership, a job classification system, and education and training of employees.

Related techniques from American sources were introduced

rapidly. These techniques, by nature culturally specific, had a number of unforeseen consequences when used to reestablish order within Japanese enterprises. Job classification and the job-oriented wage administration system were used to reconstitute the differentials based on educational level and length of service. Performance rating techniques were used largely in determining individual wages, with minimal emphasis being placed on in the job hierarchy and education. Management and supervisory formulas served as an indication of "confidence" in the ability of the personnel rather than as recognition and reward for the acquisition of occupational skills (for a detailed discussion, see Chapter 10).

However, during the late 1940s and early 1950s, when the social order within the enterprises was stabilized from the managerial point of view, the intra-enterprise social structure regressed toward the prewar pattern, and since this process accompanied Japan's economic recovery employers began to have confidence in what was unique to the Japanese social system within the industrial enterprises. Thus, the idea of a "unique-to-Japan" management ideology began to emerge at the time of the peace treaty in 1952. Writers and scholars as well as the managers themselves began to stress the rationality of the system as it had developed within the historical, economic, social, and cultural milieu of Japan and its dissimilarity to systems in other countries.

In June 1953, Nikkeiren published an "opinion regarding fundamental labor policies," emphasizing the need for (1) a change from wage determination through bargaining over increases in base rates to a system of specified periodic wage increments; (2) a broader and more rapid apprenticeship system; (3) expanded housing and medical facilities for industrial workers and expanded intra-enterprise welfare facilities; and (4) strengthening of intra-enterprise labor-management cooperation. A few days after publication of the statement, the labor minister announced labor policies similar to the Nikkeiren proposals. Thus, employer attempts to promote "unique-to-Japan" labor and personnel relations policies were reinforced by the government's labor policy, and permanent employment and length-of-service rankings became even more closely tied in with enterprise unionism than they had been in prewar days.

Gradually, beginning in 1960 and becoming quite marked after the mid-1960s, the bases of the management structure began to crumble, as the system was threatened by a series of economic, technical, and social changes. Production expansion in the climate of intense competition exerted pressure for further rationalization on the part of individual enterprises and pointed up the need for "reorganizations of industries." Production expansion required long-term stability in union-management relations, and "reorganization of industries" required at least the understanding, if not the cooperation, of labor unions at the industry level. Although the structure of enterprise unionism persists, the Spring Labor Offensive formulas devised at the national level, along with the labor shortages, have contributed to increasing the influence of national unions over union-management relations at the enterprise level. However, the influence still may be limited. Internally, due to technological and social changes and rising manpower costs, an increased emphasis on the partner relationship at the plant level became necessary.

The ideology of partnership in union-management relations and the policy based on the ability principle had come to the fore in the Keizai Dōyūkai statement of 1967. Since about 1960, and more extensively after the mid-1960s, long-range planning in the major firms began to include long-range labor and personnel relations programs containing values opposed to some of those in the "unique-to-Japan" pattern, particularly the traditional emphasis on educational career and length-of-service rankings.

However, the new ideology poses certain dilemmas. While recognizing the influential role of labor unions in society, the overwhelming majority of top managers, as a practical matter, favor enterprise-wide organizations and work actively to maintain this structure. Also, there seems to be a tendency on the part of enterprise unions at large firms to preserve their functional autonomy at the enterprise level. As of now, not much can be expected from national unions regarding the "partnership" ideology, even though it is beginning to extend to unions at the industry level.

While the enterprise unions in theory seek the stable social structure of a "pluralistic society," they seem content with the compartmentalization of the labor movement at the establishment level.

The "ability principle" is in use rather extensively at some of the major firms, as we have already seen, but there are problems inherent in this new orientation. A great majority of managers, while emphasizing the ability principle, stress the need for maintaining the permanent employment policy. The problem has been solved in part by so-called unique-to-Japan layoffs at several major enterprises, a system under which senior employees leave the enterprises during recessions. Also, since the ability principle necessarily involves selection and evaluation and places increased pressure on managers and supervisors, it tends to conflict with another managerial goal: achieving harmonious human relations within the workshop and settling grievances through company channels. More generally, individualistic values inherent in the ability principle are in direct contradiction to the collectivistic values to which many employers and managers adhere. Long-range planning at many firms, therefore, aims to continue to compromise gradually, placing increasing emphasis upon the ability principle. However, intense competition in and the continued use of the ability principle by heavy industry and chemical companies serve to accelerate this trend.

We have, thus far, considered the characteristics of the managerial state, the intra-enterprise social structure, and the ideologies and policies of labor relations in the sector of large firms. The reason for focusing on that sector is, in part, that union-management relations have been largely concentrated there. Yet the picture has changed during the recent period of rapid economic growth. Changing phases of industrial relations in the sector of medium-sized and small firms now appear to have significant implications for the future of Japanese industrial relations as a whole. Thus, any generalization about management and industrial relations requires a review of the situation within the small and medium-sized businesses.

Medium and Small Employers and Industrial Relations

One characteristic of Japan's industrial structure, when compared with that of industrially advanced Western countries, has been the relatively unimportant position of the medium-sized firms, while the small and very small enterprises have, from the Meiji era until very recently, occupied a predominant position in terms of number of workers as a proportion of the total nonagricultural work force.

Under the feudal regime in Japan, the work force was next to the bottom in the social hierarchy of warriors, farmers, artisans, and merchants. Its social standing and influence have in fact been very low since the preindustrial era. The leading segment of the merchant class joined the ruling stratum during the Meiji period, but people in the "old middle class," with their low social standing, found themselves in the lower class of society, a situation that has continued in Japan's closed culture. Eventually, within the hierarchy of Japanese industrial society, the medium and small employers who came from this stratum acquired a rank equivalent only to that of lower-grade white-collar or blue-collar workers whose social status also remained relatively low. Moreover, with this social standing went a heritage of conservative cultural traditions which tended to prevent the sector from modernizing. Before I discuss the tremendous impact of the recent rapid economic and social change on the traditions and culture of this sector, a more detailed description of its social structure is desirable, based on various statistical research studies which have been made in recent years in the manufacturing industries.

The great majority of enterprises with fewer than ten employees are very small firms employing fewer than five workers. Typically, they are composed of an artisan-employer, his family members, and one or two young apprentices. Frequently added to this basic group are a few middle-aged and older persons who are better described as half-employed, in terms of their working conditions. Since such very small enterprises have been able to produce little more than a livelihood for the employer and his workers, capital accumulation has been extremely limited. It has been difficult to expand this type of operation, within the web of established sub-contracting relationships; when it tries to expand, the very small enterprise faces the obstacle of intense competition from other very small enterprises. Also, a culture of the petit bourgeois type—a mental set historically judging an independent artisan able to earn his own livelihood as being a success in life—has tended to discourage persons in this stratum from breaking with the status quo.

Clusters of very small firms, although they often were in intense competition, sometimes developed a sort of preindustrial community, linked by relationships of kinship and other social ties. Thus, a distinctive culture was preserved. This phenomenon, which is indisputably clear in the case of industrial estates, such as Tsubaki in the metal trades and Ashikaga in textiles, is also discernible, though to a lesser degree, in the clusters of shops in the large industrial metropolises of Tokyo, Osaka, and Nagoya. In these firms one often finds the truest form of industrial familialism since they exist materially to produce a livelihood for an employer and a limited number of workers. The relationship between employers and workers tends to lack the element of capital-labor conflict. The employers themselves often work in the production process, and the workers often live in the employer's home and share his life. It is this factor of familialism that explains the often reported relatively high degree of satisfaction with the job and employers on the part of workers in the very small enterprises, despite their relatively poor working conditions, against which, nevertheless, protests have been increasing.

In firms with more than ten but fewer than fifty workers, the work force typically consists of an owner-manager with meager patrimonial resources and several skilled adult key workers. This kind of enterprise often operates at a marginal level of solvency. Managers or owners usually engage in sales and other commercial functions while the production management is often performed by artisan-supervisors. Many of the workers are recruited through personal and family connections of supervisors and other workers in the shop. Inside the shop the tradition of master-servant relations survives, though less and less as industrialization progresses. Though the workers are mobile, social connections play an important part in shifting to another employer. Workers' wages tend to peak at late middle-age (late forties or early fifties) and then decrease as, presumably, their skills reach maturity and decline. Even at the peak, it is difficult to earn a livelihood without overtime work or additional income from other family members. The elderly have been protected in this sector, within the framework of the extended family system. Although wages are based on skill and are generally low, supplementary allowances and ad hoc assistance for living expenses have been important, and because the supervisors have been influential in administering this assistance, it has been a basis for the survival of master-servant relationships. Thus, a type of familialism at the shop level, which may be properly called shop familialism, is a distinguishing feature of small enterprises.

In the sector of small and very small enterprises, the rate of unionization historically has been so low as to be statistically negligible. In the very small enterprise there usually has been no room for workers' organization. If there is a union, it has tended to be a union amalgamated on a territorial basis. An enterprise-wide employee organization that performs welfare functions is often found in the small enterprises. Labor union organization in this sector has tended to move toward one of two extremes: either union-management cooperation or unionism protesting the total socioeconomic structure of society.

Rapid economic and social changes since the mid-1950s have had a tremendous impact on this sector of the economy. In manufacturing, during both the prewar and the postwar years, clusters of small and very small enterprises were found largely in consumer goods manufacturing, the metal and engineering trades, and the construction and civil engineering fields. In economic terms, these enterprises operated in a market where profit margins were low and where cheap labor was available. However, with technological progress and the accompanying increase in the purchasing power of consumers, and with the relative rise in manpower costs, market opportunities traditionally open to this sector began to be attractive to medium-sized and large enterprises, and the small employers themselves began to accumulate somewhat more capital than previously. In addition, the general rise in the educational level of both employers and workers in the small enterprise sector had the effect of changing their orientation toward industrial management and life in general.

Around 1960, the so-called dissolution of small enterprises became a social problem. The technological change and rationalization movement that swept the sector tended to have one of two results: either the growth and expansion of a small firm or its decline and reappearance. Sōhyō's guide for organizers in the medium and small sectors in 1964, entitled "The Open Economy: The Direction of the Monopoly Movement," stated the following:

> It can be said today that rationalization and modernization— from layout and production scheduling on the technical side to production planning, cost control, quality control, and clerical operation on the administrative side—eventually reached the bottom of the pyramidal industrial structure. . . . It can be said, perhaps, that 70 to 80 percent of the workers in manufacturing industries are now working under the same degree of modern-style management.

This statement perhaps exaggerates the extent of rationalization, but it has been particularly notable in the small enterprise sector; in the process, many of the small enterprises have grown to medium size, while many others have declined, remained stagnant or have been reorganized as a newer type of small business.

The medium-sized enterprises, with more than one hundred but fewer than three hundred employees, tend to have distinctive characteristics which place them in still another category in terms of social structure. The majority are family- or clan-owned, but they are managed by professionals with relatively high educational levels. The background of the workers also tends to be different, as the number of employees whose parents are urban in origin has increased markedly in recent years, in contrast with small and very small enterprises where workers are family members or apprentices with rural backgrounds. The enterprises themselves are of the specialized factory type, usually mass-producing a limited product. The key workers are recruited from the open labor market on the basis of their skill, and there is a strong tendency for their positions to be determined and graded by their performance and ability. The labor standards applied are product or industrywide standards, as enterprises of this type typically are companies related to large firms where the organizational code stresses efficiency. The firms enjoy comparatively continuous profits, although their profitability is markedly lower than that of the oligopolistic enterprises. Their organizational code is efficiency centered, the inducement usually being in terms of economic incentives. All of these organizational characteristics frequently give rise to rather extensive and serious tensions.

During the most recent period of economic growth, the proportion of enterprises of this type has increased. Provided that the dissolution of small enterprises continues, which is likely, the tendency toward growth of the specialized mass production firms appears to have significant implications for the structure of industrial relations in Japan, for it is this sector, along with large enterprises, that could provide the organized union movement with a stable base.

Accordingly, it can be said that collective bargaining relationships have tended to become institutionalized in the sectors of large and medium-sized firms. The union movement has been particularly active during the period of rapid economic growth, and labor disputes now occur most frequently at enterprises with one hundred to four hundred employees. It should be noted that, although most unions in this sector are enterprise unions, many of them tend to look for horizontal alliances. Increasing competition with lower labor costs exerts pressure to improve efficiency in the production process. As a result, work standards and working conditions tend to be compared by both companies and unions, and the unions are working toward standardization. Industrywide conference departments or committees on work standards within the industrial unions, such as steel, metal, textiles, and chemicals, gained in importance during the period of economic growth. Whether the unions in this sector will turn to alliance with large enterprisewide unions, as was the case of Nissan and Toyota automobile companies, or to industrywide federations, as in the textile and metal industries, has become an important question, the answer to which will shape the structure of the labor movement as a whole (see Chapters 7 and 8). If the former, extended enterprisewide industrial relations will be the pattern for big business; if the latter, the pattern will be toward more industry-wide contractual industrial relations. Also, against a background of labor shortages, industrial relations in the medium-sized enterprises will continue to exert considerable pressure to upgrade working conditions in the sector of small and very small enterprises.

In relating type of enterprise to patterns of industrial relations, however, one should note still another pattern which has highly significant implications for the future. Since around 1960, the number of bankruptcies has increased markedly among both medium-sized and small firms. Profitability has declined in small firms employing unskilled labor in such industries as construction, civil engineering, food, textiles, wood products, leather, and ceramics. Together with the decline of small businesses in the commercial sector, huge "border" zones were formed with varied orientations of unionism. In the 1940s and 1950s, as the differential in wages and working conditions between large and small firms grew wider, the number of labor disputes increased and national centers of the labor movement strengthened their attempts to organize workers in the medium and small sectors. These attempts were, by and large, successful around 1960. In turn, the government enacted a series of laws aimed at improving working conditions in the small and medium-sized enterprises, such as the Minimum Wage Law of 1959, enabling minimum wages to be established by agreement among employers; the Retirement Fund Act for Medium and Small Enterprises; and the Cooperative Agency for Retirement Funds of Medium and Small Enterprises. Moreover, employers in small and medium-sized enterprises began to work toward improving their personnel relations—a movement that was speeded up considerably by the growing labor shortage. Many of the workers have found a way to solve their problems at least in part, through labor mobility. Thus, since about 1960, industrial relations in small and medium-sized enterprises have been relatively calm.

Dilemmas of Management

In the process of Japan's industrialization, capitalism was imported from the Western world by the political elite during the early Meiji period and was fostered and developed in the private sector by the business elite in close coordination with the government. The zaibatsu firms soon developed, and a market economy evolved in which the ability to compete was limited to those firms.

The lower-grade samurai class provided the first generation of political elite which performed the grand-scale entrepreneurial functions in the early Meiji period; the business elite were townspeople who had family-business backgrounds. Thus, the intra-enterprise social structure that developed had many of the characteristics of the patrimonial bureaucracy of the shogunate and *daimyō* undertakings and the business enterprises of the large merchants.

The patrimonial bureaucracy and the social structures of prewar Japanese enterprises had a strong institutional basis. Their political foundation was the patrimonial state of imperial Japan. Socially, there was an abundant supply of workers with argicultural backgrounds. The attempt to organize and develop a labor movement eventually failed due to both political oppression and the introduction of industrial familialism as the guideline for labor relations policies within the patrimonial bureaucratic structure as adapted to modern private industry.

After World War II, many of the leading large enterprises ceased to be family properties and a greater degree of "control by management" developed. The managerial stratum at large firms, coordinating its activities with the government's economic policies, led the recovery and growth of postwar Japan and, in the process, established itself firmly at the peak of the power elite in society.

The formal patrimonial character of large enterprises disappeared with the end of World War II, but postwar industrial relations continued to be conditioned by the legacy of patrimonial bureaucraty that included leadership composed largely of work group leaders and senior permanent workers. At the enterprise level the unions are primarily functional in structure and cooperate with management.

Intensification of interenterprise competition, changes in technology, and general sociocultural changes that took place revealed dysfunctional aspects of the by now quasi-patrimonial bureaucratic social structure—the inherent limits of its formal rationality and its inefficient use of manpower. Thus, it became necessary to reorganize the intra-enterprise social structure, and, at the same time, to make changes in the industrial relations ideology and personnel policies.

Throughout the prewar and postwar years, the structure and function of the national employer associations paralleled, at least in part, the divided functional controls mechanisms within the quasipatrimonial structure of the enterprise. However, management reorganization, especially in some leading enterprises in the heavy and chemical industries, may exert pressures for reorganizing the structure of employer associations at the national level. The trend within large industry toward general staffs to integrate personnel, financial, and other policies and to establish long-range plans appears to have generated the recent appeals of several leading managers in the Keizai Dōyūkai for the establishment of an integrated and unified Japan Industrial Federation. Although unification does not appear to be likely in the foreseeable future, the fact that such a proposal was made suggests that the environment for managers at large firms is changing. The increasing need to reorganize the industrial structure at the national level and the need for long-range integrated planning at the enterprise level will necessitate still closer coordination between private economic decisions and government economic policies. If coordination is to be achieved, a stronger stand by the employers and closer cooperation among them, which could be brought about through a unified national front, appear to be necessary.

These trends are reflected in the "new managerial ideals" and the emerging new orientations in personnel policies. However, the new orientations contain inherent dilemmas. Whereas the ideology of the welfare state stresses the need for intensive social investment, this is in direct conflict with the reality of enterprise egoism of large firms which demands priority for capital expenditure to facilitate expansion and rationalization of the firm. Although the ideology of a pluralistic society emphasizes the importance of institutionalized countervailing forces to secure a wide consensus in developing rules, such a process is inconsistent with the de facto orientation of preserving enterprise-wide unionism, an institution that ties the union and also the worker to an overcommitment to the enterprise. The new policy embracing ability principles stresses the need for efficient staffing but is inherently opposed to the traditional, preferred employment policies of securing the loyalty of workers by offering permanent employment.

These dilemmas may be mitigated in large enterprises by forms of "welfare enterprise," "consultative and participatory" schemes, and ad hoc "Japan-type" layoffs. However, even within the large enterprise sector, the number of firms for which those solutions are practical will probably dwindle, and it goes without saying that solutions of this sort would be difficult for the medium-sized and small firms. With the mounting pressure for reorganization of the industrial structure and the prospects for continuing technological progress, the dilemmas of the managerial stratum will become even more complex and eventually will call for some new patterns in industrial relations. Already by the early 70s trends of the increasing significance of labor relations at the national, industrial and workshop levels, in addition to the transactions at the enterprise level, could be observed. These trends are likely to continue despite the persistent resistance of management and their organizations.

7. Workers and Their Organizations

Japanese worker behavior patterns in the work place and in the society at large and the structure and administration of worker organizations are analyzed in this chapter. Rather than offering simply a description of specific features such as union constitutions and bylaws, the perspective here is comparative. However, if Japanese labor unions are judged in terms of the experience and concepts of Western industrial relations systems, they may be misunderstood. The local union in the United States does not correspond to the "unit union," the basic structural unit of organization in Japan, which usually is organized within a given enterprise and consists of the employees of that enterprise only. Nor is the American national union the equivalent of the Japanese "industrial union." Although 36 percent of all Japanese wage and salary earners are organized in labor unions which have a total membership of more than ten million, it would be misleading to conclude from these figures that the strength of Japanese unions is equal to that of unions in Western countries. Japanese unions are weak; they still lack a strong voice in determining standard employment conditions on either a local or an industrywide basis. Why they have remained organizationally weak and why they are oriented toward political activities are explained in this chapter.

Worker Life and Consciousness

The number of Japanese wage and salary earners in 1968 was 31,480,000, double the number in the work force immediately after the end of World War II. While this increase indicates the great Japanese industrial expansion since the war, it should also be recognized that the Japanese economy has a dual structure with a much larger underdeveloped sector than is present in advanced Western nations. As of 1968, there were 18,500,000 Japanese classified as self-employed (3,860,000 in agricultural and 5,980,000 in nonagricultural employment) and unpaid family workers (5,140,000 agricultural and 3,520,000 nonagricultural). Most of the self-employed operate small businesses employing five persons or less.

Although in recent years the wage labor market has become increasingly dependent on new school graduates and those who move from one job to another, historically the major source was migrants from farm villages. The latter are still dominant in the present labor force, and as a result most Japanese workers are influenced by the traditional culture of the farm village. In other words, even though nuclear families are becoming more common because of urbanization, a premodern consciousness of paternalism developed and rooted in the family system and the kinship community of the farm village remains among many industrial workers. Such worker consciousness fosters ready acceptance of simple paternalism in small businesses and paternalistic management in large industry. In Japanese farm villages, family members are still regulated by the *ie* (household) system in which control over several generations of the family centers around the direct descendants of a patriarch. Under this system, members of the household subordinate their individuality to a stratified hierarchical structure.

In a modern industry, no such kinship relationship exists between the manager and the managed; instead, the real relationship between the two is one of exchange of labor for remuneration. When the household system is applied in modern industry, however, the employer alone, like the patriarch, sets the expectations of workers regarding their service to the company. Thus, large enterprises and local or national government emphasize fringe benefits and welfare facilities for employees in an attempt to promote villagelike familialism in industry, and many workers respond affirmatively to this kind of management policy. This "artificial" paternalism in industry is analogous to the paternalism of the household system in farming villages.

On the other hand, masses of workers in large industry have become aware of their status as wage earners and their "class" interests, which they have learned from the experience of labor movements in other countries. At times, dissatisfied with merely bargaining over the amount of their remuneration, they have sought to reform the existing society.

Therefore, it may be said that Japanese workers are ambivalent, attempting on the one hand to maintain the traditional system and on the other to reform it. This ambivalence is reflected in many aspects of premodern society and traditional culture that remain in Japanese industrialization. Such traditional elements have become a part of the workers' lives through their daily experiences and their family ties as well as through external pressures in industry. However, the young workers who have grown up since the war in a new social environment and under a democratic school system tend to be conscious of a concept of individualism that conflicts with the notion of the family system. Where a majority of workers in an enterprise are less than thirty years old, paternalism in industry may have to give way to a new policy geared to the expectations of these young people.

Worker Living Standards

Generally speaking, worker social status and living standards have significantly improved with economic growth. Workers were regarded as being in the lowest social class with a low educational level during the Meiji era (1868–1912), but as industrialization proceeded key employees in large enterprises received secondary education. However, there was a clear distinction in social status between *shokuin* (white-collar workers) and *kōin* (blue-collar work-

Table 7.1
Rate of Increase in Disposable Income and Consumption by Income Bracket, 1951–1968

Income Bracket	Disposable Income				Consumption			
	1955/1951	1959/1955	1964/1959	1968/1964	1955/1951	1959/1955	1964/1959	1968/1964
I	109.4	27.6	80.3	65.6	49.1	18.5	77.5	56.8
II	76.7	29.0	74.3	54.3	59.8	23.2	71.5	51.2
III	73.6	30.6	67.0	52.6	59.4	36.1	63.6	49.2
IV	71.6	30.6	68.9	50.6	61.1	24.4	60.4	46.3
V	67.6	35.8	68.4	48.2	67.0	26.8	60.8	39.7

SOURCES: 1951–64 data, Ministry of Labor, *White Paper on Labor—1965* (Tokyo: Ministry of Labor, 1966), p. 394; 1968 data, Economic Planning Agency, *Economic White Paper—1969* (Tokyo: Economic Planning Agency, 1970), pp. 258, 268.

ers) that corresponded to a difference in educational background.

Meanwhile, social reform and the extensive growth of organized labor after World War II served to elevate the worker's status in general and to narrow the difference in social status between white- and blue-collar workers. As shown in Table 7.1, income differentials narrowed as incomes in lower brackets greatly increased from 1951 to 1955, but consumption in the higher brackets increased relatively to widen consumption differentials during the period. From 1955 to 1959, both income and consumption differentials widened, but from 1959 to 1964 both again narrowed as a result of rapid economic growth. Thus, the recent economic growth has generally elevated Japanese living standards, which, despite changes in Japanese eating habits and food prices, have risen year after year except in the immediate postwar period.[1] Some deficiencies remain, however, in the lower income brackets.

A public opinion survey of the household economy conducted by the Prime Minister's Office in 1958 disclosed the true feelings of the Japanese people concerning changes in their living standards. Only 19 percent of the respondents answered that their standard of living had improved since prewar days, while 46 percent answered that prewar living was better. Eighteen percent responded "unchanged" and 17 percent "unknown." These responses no doubt reflected the respondents' current desire to consume; nonetheless, they seem incompatible with the results shown in Table 7.1. This may be due to the fact that the consumption increase in each bracket was largely for purchases of durable goods. Thus, those in lower income brackets tended to feel more burdened in their household economy, as a result of the drastic changes in the structure of consumer life in the postwar period.

The average size of a worker's family is smaller than that of a farmer, averaging only 3.6 members per family in large cities in recent years. The pattern of worker family life is seen in the wage earner's life cycle. At age 24 to 26 a male worker generally marries a woman two to three years younger than himself. Within a few years they spend increasing amounts on infant rearing, education, housing, and other household expenses. For example, in cases

1. Prime Minister's Office, *Survey on Household Economy* (Tokyo: Prime Minister's Office, 1966).

where the family has two children, the father usually is 53 years old when the second child graduates from high school. If there are three children, the father is 55 years old when the third child graduates from high school. If the second or third child goes on to college, the father is 57 to 59 years old at the time of graduation. Thus, educational expenses increase after the father becomes 30 years old, mounting until beyond his retirement, usually at age 55. Since, in general, promotion is heavily determined by educational background, Japanese workers are extremely eager to send their children to higher schools. Moreover, household expenditures further increase if the worker has to support his parents. In any event, living expenses reach a peak when workers are in their forties and fifties. As a result, the propensity for saving among workers increases rapidly after 24 years of age or so and reaches its peak, at a high rate of 37.8 percent, at the age of 35 to 37. The saving rate drops slightly to 32.9 percent around the age of 45 but again rises to 35.5 percent between 55 and 59. After 65 years of age, it drops sharply to 17.3 percent. Thus, there are three important transitional periods in the worker's life cycle—age 30, age 45 to 54, and age 60 to 64—when workers need to build or repair their homes, purchase durable goods, educate their children, buy real estate, marry off their children, and so forth.[2] Consequently, worker propensity for consumption decreases between the ages of 35 and 60, whereas it is relatively high under age 25 and over age 60.

Because of the prevailing type of retirement system, those who leave companies at retirement age constitute 86.5 percent of all persons leaving jobs between the ages of 50 and 64.[3] Since the average life span has increased to 70 years for men and 74 years for women, workers who reach retirement age face unusual difficulties in supporting themselves thereafter.

The most serious problem in the livelihood of Japanese workers is housing. Many houses were destroyed in the war, and public housing investment has been insufficient. Rapid urbanization and

2. Ministry of Labor, *White Paper on Labor—1965* (Tokyo: Ministry of Labor, 1966), p. 292; and Kokumin Seikatsu Kenkyūsho (Institute for National Life), *Kakeishutai no raifu saikuru jittai* [The actual situation of the life cycle of household economy] (Tokyo: Kokumin Seikatsu Kenkyūsho, 1965). See also Chapter 12.

3. Ministry of Labor, *White Paper on Labor—1963* (Tokyo: Ministry of Labor, 1964).

the scarcity of land in Japan have inflated land prices enormously. The most difficult achievement for a worker is to own his own home. Those younger than 30 rarely own their own homes, but home ownership rapidly increases around the time the first child is born and continues to increase with the size of the family. A considerable proportion of people, however, have to rent houses or rooms or live in company residences. Workers employed in public service or large corporations tend to have their own homes and also have more opportunity to obtain residences provided by enterprises. They are more privileged than workers in small and medium-sized firms.[4]

Worker Consciousness

As mentioned above, although the worker's standard of living has improved on the whole, considerable hardships remain for people in the lower income brackets, and income differentials are much wider than in Western countries. These aspects of the livelihood of Japanese workers seriously affect their attitudes in the workshop and on the job.[5]

About 40 percent of all Japanese workers are employed in large private corporations with five hundred or more employees or in government and public service. Although there are an increasing number of exceptions, many regular workers still come from farm areas after school graduation, are employed through careful selection and personal connections, and are assigned to training in the corporation's school or to on-the-job training. Usually, after spending three to five years in acquiring occupational skills, they adapt to the enterprise's occupational hierarchy based on educational level and length of service and commit themselves to the enterprise for an indefinite period. At the same time, the enterprise provides its employees with a variety of welfare facilities and

4. Ministry of Health and Welfare, *White Paper on Welfare—1962* (Tokyo: Ministry of Health and Welfare, 1963), p. 61.
5. Hitoshi Matsuo, "Soshiki rōdōsha no ishiki chōsa" [Research on the consciousness of organized workers], *Nihon Rōdō Kyōkai Zasshi*, Tokyo, 1967; Takeshi Nakajo, "Gijutsu kakushin to seinenso rōdōsha" [Technological innovation and younger workers], *Nihon Rōdō Kyōkai Zasshi*, Tokyo, May 1967.

special allowances such as housing, recreation, cultural facilities, medical care, semi-annual seasonal bonuses, and retirement allowances and pensions based on age and length of service. Many large companies and agencies also provide substantial discounts in house rent, utility charges, commodities, lunches, haircuts, movies, and so forth. Thus, for most regular employees in these enterprises, family life is only an extension of the work place and is closely tied to the enterprise. All of these benefits tend to encourage worker loyalty to the enterprise. As a consequence, employees in large private and public corporations or in government service enjoy far more employment security and higher wages than workers in small businesses or in daily or temporary work.

Differences in consciousness of various aspects of the work situation among employees in large private and public corporations or government tend to reflect the job hierarchy by educational level and by blue- or white-collar occupational status. A survey aimed at assessing the feeling of "belonging" revealed a greater number of blue-collar than white-collar workers answering affirmatively to the question "Is the interest of workers compatible with that of management?" Among both blue- and white-collar workers, however, affirmative replies tended to increase with age of the respondents. As for consciousness of their rights, 80 percent of the white-collar workers answered that social security is a natural right, although older workers were less inclined than the younger ones to answer in this way. However, more white-collar than blue-collar workers answered that they should avoid strikes, as did more older workers than younger ones. To the question "Are workers and employers (capitalists) in class conflict?" more blue-collar than white-collar workers responded affirmatively.

The survey also showed that white-collar workers tend to be highly conscious of general, abstract rights, even though they are likely to oppose conflicts of interest with employers, primarily because they are closer to the position of the employer. On the other hand, their consciousness of rights is evident in dissatisfaction with the work situation. As for political activities, more white-collar than blue-collar workers reacted negatively to disinterest in political activities, indicating keen interest in political participation in any form.

According to this survey, workers' consciousness tended to vary, depending upon age, occupational status, and the like, but there was no significant difference among workers in their answers to questions about interest in their jobs, sense of being worthwhile, and worker loyalty. On the other hand, young workers were more concerned than older workers about having a happy family life, and they tended to view their jobs as a means to achieving this goal.[6] This tendency among young workers may be due to drastic changes in their values in the postwar period, away from the ideas of obedience to the sovereign and filial love and duty of the prewar days.[7]

In small businesses, the employer in many cases has to function as a worker as well as a manager, and he tends to work along with his family employees. Even when he employs persons other than family members, they usually live at his residence like members of a family. In this situation, hired employees work for the employer at the latter's discretion while learning occupational skills on the job, and they often change employers in order to take advantage of opportunities to acquire skills in a shorter time.

Small business usually is labor intensive, and what little capital it has usually is in the form of obsolete machinery. These firms are highly vulnerable to business fluctuations, and they maintain themselves by keeping labor costs low. Members of the employer's family working in the business receive no regular wages or salaries, and there tends to be no distinction between business and household accounts. The hired employees generally expect little in the way of wages and benefits but look forward to becoming independent managers in the future. For this reason, a majority of young workers in small businesses tend to find this work interesting, in spite of the poor employment conditions.[8]

Under these circumstances, workers in small businesses have little interest in unionism and little commitment to a given em-

6. Waseda University, Seisan Kenkyūsho (Institute of Industrial Production), *Sarari man no ishiki* [The consciousness of salaried men] (Tokyo: Waseda University, 1960).
7. Shojiro Ujihara, *Gendai seinen mondai* [Problems of contemporary youth] (Tokyo, 1960).
8. Ibid.

ployer. Their rate of mobility is high, and the promotion of organized workers is quite low in this industrial sector.

Temporary and subcontract workers also have little employment security, as they may be discharged at any time. Although
they are often employed by large enterprises, they receive fewer
length-of-service benefits than regular workers, and they have
only very limited access to fringe benefits and welfare facilities.
Minimum wages, agreed upon by employers, provide them with
hardly more than the unemployment benefits of public relief
workers. Their employment conditions are comparable to those
of workers in small businesses.

Daily workers, of which there are three types, make up still
another group. First are the traditional craftsmen, common in the
building trades and in the longshore industry, whose current
employment status emerged from the *oyakata* system which broke
down under the impact of technological and social change. Many
craftsmen are organized either in craft-type unions or in *gōdō rōso*
(combined unions, i.e., a union formed by all eligible wage and
salary employees in the area without regard to craft or other
status) among small and medium-sized industries. Second are the
common laborers, unskilled workers, and janitors, and the third
group is composed of persons unemployed as the result of being
repatriates, war widows, divorced women, or unsuccessful self-
employed and family workers. Daily workers of the second and
third types find it difficult to obtain jobs and therefore come to the
Public Employment Security Offices for unemployment relief or
casual jobs on relief projects. Workers in the third category have
been organized by the All-Japan Day Workers' Union, or Zen-
nichijirō, to bargain collectively with the Public Employment
Security Office.

Worker Organizations

The living conditions and consciousness of workers affect the
nature and function of their organizations. Before World War II,

employers and government so oppressed unions that workers in large industries and public service were permitted only to have joint consultation councils within the enterprise or to carry out sporadic militant activities and short-lived strikes. In small businesses, professional organizers took the lead in forming unions outside the enterprises, under slogans of lawful action and labor-management cooperation. The number of union members was quite small, reaching, at its peak, only 7 percent of the labor force, with a membership of 400,000. These unionists formed the nucleus of the prewar Sōdōmei, or Japan General Federation of Trade Unions.

Leftist leaders also organized workers within each work place at large enterprises, first through the Nihon Rōdō-kumiai Hyōgi-kai, or Japan Trade Union Council, which was subsequently dissolved, and later through the underground Zen-Nihon Rōdō-kumiai Kyōgikai, or All-Japan Trade Union Council. These organizations advocated establishment of autonomous factory committees and councils of factory representatives and succeeded to a considerable extent in carrying out strikes. However, these strikes resulted in the organization of only the radical and revolutionary workers, and the other workers had to be persuaded again and again to join in strike action.[9]

Immediately after World War II it became possible for the leftist unions to reach the masses of workers and to organize them effectively in enterprise-wide unions. What emerged was Sanbetsu, or the All-Japan Congress of Industrial Unions, a national federation of unions organized by industry. Sanbetsu's rule that persons from outside the enterprise work force should be excluded from union leadership as far as possible was widely accepted by leaders within the enterprises. These leaders also were encouraged to be sympathetic to and to join the Japan Communist Party, and they were soon assigned to party "fractions" within the unions. Thus many union leaders at the enterprise level were induced to organize along Communist Party lines, and they

9. Mentioned here are only the two main federations of the pre-World War II days. There were several other intermediate federations, each of which supported different proletarian parties and maintained diversity in the labor union movement.

were successful in promoting radical worker movements for several years after the war. The result was that the Japan Communist Party began to visualize a revolution in Japan and to mobilize masses of workers in an effort to develop radical political struggles.

However, there was a limit to the potential for such a radical movement in large enterprises because many workers, having been trained by and become committed to the company over a long period, could not bring themselves to engage fully in revolutionary activities. These workers, especially clerical employees who were closely associated with the employer, gradually dropped away from the radical labor movement. As a consequence, there remained only those who had been mistreated by the company during the war or were communists or party sympathizers. When the Occupation mounted its "red purge," there was a drastic change in the direction of the workers' movement, which witnessed the successful development of the Minshūka Dōmei, or National Liaison Council for Democratization.

Nevertheless, the premodern status system and other traditional practices that persisted within and outside industry gave rise to a revolutionary ideology among workers. Accordingly, Sōhyō, the General Council of Trade Unions of Japan, organized after the "red purge" as a moderate national center, has continued to be critical of Japanese conservatism and capitalism and to support the Japan Socialist Party. While it is true that the majority of workers are committed to their enterprise, when they are organized on an industrial or national basis they tend also to be critical of the existing society. This is the dual nature of Japanese workers.

The Japanese labor movement is based mainly on exclusive organization of employees in large private and public corporations and the government who are highly conscious of belonging to their enterprises. Should a union become independent of the enterprise and engage in radical "class struggle" against the enterprise, it usually faces opposition from its own members as well as from the employer. Therefore, unions at this level tend to move from a radical toward a moderate position. How to attain sustained organizational autonomy within the enterprise framework is a grave problem for Japanese unionism.

The Scale of Worker Organizations

In 1969 union membership reached 11,248,601, or 35.2 percent of the total number of wage and salary earners in Japan. There were 58,812 unit unions (*tani kumiai*), the smallest labor union organization on a plantwide basis with its own constitution and independent activities. When the unit unions in the same enterprise are combined, the result is a total of 29,611 single-entity unions (*tanitsu kumiai*).

Two-hundred-eighty-eight single-entity unions have memberships of 5,000 or more each; 1,314 have more than 1,000 but fewer than 5,000 members; and 1,383 have between 500 and 999 members. Together, these 2,985 unions of relatively large size, while amounting to less than 10 percent of the total number of single-entity unions, account for 76.2 percent of total union membership.[10] Given the organizational basis of the unions, labor union size corresponds closely to enterprise size.

Ninety-six percent of all enterprises with 1,000 or more employees recognize their labor unions, but the rate of recognition is lower among the smaller enterprises: 22 percent in enterprises with 50–99 workers; 11 percent for the 30–49-employee class; and 1.5 percent for those with 29 or fewer employees. Labor union organization in the small and medium-sized enterprise is unlikely, due primarily to the traditional paternalism in that industrial sector, lack of understanding of labor unions, insecurity of employment, lack of able leadership, and poor financing of union administration. The absence of craft unionism is a significant indication of these conditions. Since 1956 the national centers have become active in organizing workers in the small industry sector, but their successes have been slow in coming and meager. Therefore, it can be said that the Japanese labor movement has been led by unions in the large enterprises and in the public or government sectors.

10. Ministry of Labor, *Rōdō kumiai kihonchōsa hōkoku, 1969* [Basic survey report on labor unions, 1969] (Tokyo: Ministry of Labor, 1970), p. 16.

The Extent of Worker Organizations

In 1969, 37.7 percent of all union members were in manufacturing, 18.3 percent in transportation and communication, where public corporations play a dominant role, 11.4 percent in services, including education, and 10.0 percent in public or government employment. Percentages in other industries were negligible.[11] Generally speaking, the more highly concentrated an industry, the more likely it is that its workers are organized. Where public or government employees are involved in an industry, there is likely to be a labor union. As large enterprises employ more workers the rate of organization among them in most cases goes up as a result of union shop practices. From 1961 to 1969, the percentage of organized workers in the declining coal- and metal-mining industries fell from 90.3 percent to 73.3 percent. On the other hand, during the same period the rate of organization increased in transportation, communication, and public utilities from 74.0 to 67.7 percent, in manufacturing from 34.6 to 38.8 percent, in public and government services from 64.7 to 70.9 percent, and in commercial trades from 14.2 to 17.2 percent.[12]

Labor unions composed exclusively of regular workers comprise 85.3 percent of all labor unions and account for 82.5 percent of the total membership. Labor unions organized with both regular and temporary workers together account for 11.9 percent of the total membership, while unions organized exclusively by temporary or daily workers account for only 0.4 percent.

In principle, many unions claim to have eliminated discrimination with regard to employment conditions between regular and temporary or subcontract workers. In practice, however, a wide gap remains. Because temporary and subcontract workers function as a safety valve for adjusting employment to business fluctuations, it is very difficult for enterprise-level unions of regular workers to admit temporary and subcontract workers into their organizations. The labor shortage in recent years, however, has helped to raise temporary workers to regular worker status or to substitute

11. Ibid., p. 15.
12. Ibid.

Table 7.2
Labor Unions and Membership by Law Applied, 1965 and 1969

Law Applied	Number of Unions (%)		Total Membership (%)	
	1965	1969	1965	1969
Trade Union Law	22,966	25,254	7,208,896	8,226,156
	(83.4)	(85.2)	(71.0)	(73.1)
Public Corporation and National Enterprise Labor Relations Law	56	24	1,005,109	1,038,403
	(0.2)	(.08)	(9.9)	(1.7)
Local Public Enterprise Labor Relations Law	433	565	176,755	183,035
	(1.5)	(1.9)	(1.7)	(9.2)
National Public Service Law	392	404	256,098	284,051
	(1.4)	(1.3)	(2.5)	(2.5)
Local Public Service Law	3,678	3,361	1,500,014	1,516,956
	(13.4)	(11.3)	(14.8)	(13.5)
Total	27,525	29,611	10,146,872	11,248,601

Sources: Ministry of Labor, *Rōdō kumiai kihonchōsa hōkoku, 1965* [Basic survey report on labor unions, 1965] (Tokyo: Ministry of Labor, 1966), p. 23; *Rōdō kumiai kihonchōsa hōkoku, 1969* (Tokyo: Ministry of Labor, 1970), pp. 21, 78–79.

subcontract workers. Despite these changes, the labor movement has been predominantly in the hands of regular workers closely committed to the enterprise for life and therefore reluctant to open their unions to others whose employment situation is less secure.

Male union members make up 72.7 percent of the total.[13] Of the females, the majority are young unmarried girls; middle-aged female workers are very rare, although their number is increasing gradually. Female members are in the majority, however, in the government monopoly tobacco industry and in textiles, garment manufacturing, and medical services, a reflection of the important role of female labor in these industries, dating from before the 1930s, when women comprised the majority of the industrial labor force.

The laws protecting the right to organize in Japan are different for industries in the private and public sector. Public workers are divided into public service and government corporation employment, and public service is further subdivided into national and local service employment. As discussed in Chapter 8, collective bargaining by public employees is partially restricted by law, and strikes by public employees are prohibited. Despite these restrictions, public employee unions are organized on a national level and play a leading role in the Japanese labor movement. Organized public employees comprise 26.9 percent of total union membership and 71.0 percent of the union membership in Sōhyō. Worker organizations by appropriate labor law coverage are summarized in Table 7.2.

Types of Labor Unions

In prewar Japan there were some craft unions, but none was strong enough to set wage standards for the craft in the labor market. Furthermore, as was pointed out in Chapter 2, by the time of World War II, all labor unions were forced to dissolve and reorganize into the Sangyō Hōkokukai (Association for Ser-

13. Prime Minister's Office, *1963 nen rōdōryoku kihonchōsa* [1963 basic labor force survey] (Tokyo: Prime Minister's Office, 1964).

vice to the State through Industry) as part of the wartime mobilization. After the war, labor unions organizing all the workers within a given enterprise sprang up in great numbers.

As already noted, more than 90 percent of all labor unions in Japan are organized on an enterprise basis, and the enterprise union is an outstanding feature of the Japanese labor movement. The All-Japan Seamen's Union, or Kaiin, an industrial union, is an exception. Several other unions, such as the National Federation of Metal Industry Trade Unions, or Zenkindōmei, the All-Japan Harbor Workers' Union, or Zenkōwan, and the All-Japan Property Insurance Labor Union, or Zensonpo, are classified as industrial unions because members affiliate individually with them, but actually they are also enterprise unions.

The few craft unions in Japan that correspond to craft unions in Western countries are found among carpenters, plasterers, and other building trades, dye workers, harbor workers, and female domestics. These unions came to function primarily as labor-supply centers after private employment exchanges were prohibited by law. There are also several unions based on a specific craft line, such as the locomotive engineers and machinists, but they restrict their bargaining activities to single employers. In this sense, they may hardly be called craft unions. Wage earners and the self-employed in construction, restaurants, barbershops, and other service industries have organized trade associations but these too are far from being labor unions. Such associations are often sponsored by conservative politicians as a means of obtaining votes in elections. On the other hand, recent technological changes have had a significant impact on craftsmen and their organizations. As craftsmanship has become less important in industry, the traditional organizations based on master-servant relationships have been reorganized gradually into modern labor organizations.[14]

When workers are employed in enterprises too small for them to be able to form labor unions on an enterprise basis, they sometimes establish unions outside the firms but within a given geographic area. This type of organization, called *gōdō rōso* (combined union),

14. Shojiro Ujihara, "Nihon no rōdō kumiai," [Japanese trade unions], in Toru Ariizumi, ed., *Nihon rōshikankei* [Japanese industrial relations] (Tokyo: University of Tokyo Press, 1963), pp. 45–49.

developed before the war and produced many of the well-known union leaders of that time. Such unions have again become common since about 1955 due to the organizing activities of national centers and industrial unions through local branches of the latter. However, their growth has been very slow because of the gulf between this type of worker organization in the smaller-sized enterprises and the unions in large enterprises. The experience of the latter is not always helpful to the former. Worker organizations in small enterprises are inevitably handicapped by financial difficulties due to business fluctuations and bankruptcies. There is also considerable mobility among workers in small companies who move from one to another, hardly creating solid ground for the development of a strong and competent leadership from their own ranks.

There are three types of *gōdō rōso*: industrial, occupational (craft-based), and general. The general *gōdō rōso* organizes workers in various types of industries and occupations, but since there are few common interests among the members it is difficult to maintain organizational integrity. Industrial and occupational *gōdō rōso* have succeeded in bargaining collectively with individual employers or their associations in some cases. They have common grounds for negotiation with employers and may become more widespread in the future.

Unions of the Unemployed

As previously mentioned, there is also a union of workers registered at the Employment Security Offices throughout the country who work as casual day labor on unemployment relief programs. Most are repatriates, war widows, and discharged workers. In spite of the placement service of the Employment Security Offices, many of these workers remain casual laborers continually dependent on work relief projects. Their union bargains with the offices for wage increases and bonus payments.[15]

15. Ibid. The union is the *Zen-Nihon Jiyū Rōdō-kumiai* (All-Japan Day Workers' Union), which had a membership of 158,000 in 1967.

Enterprise Unions

The most important feature of Japanese labor unions is enterprise unionism. An enterprise union is organized autonomously by workers within a given enterprise. Such unions are widespread and dominant not only in large private industry and the public sector but also in small and medium-sized enterprises.

The major characteristics of an enterprise union are as follows. (1) It includes all regular employees in an enterprise or industrial establishment regardless of occupation or job status. In many cases it embraces both blue- and white-collar workers and lower-level management. Immediately after the war, when the labor movement mushroomed, even the middle management people were included. (2) Since the membership of the enterprise union in most cases is confined to regular employees, temporary and subcontract workers are usually excluded. (3) Regular employees automatically join the union even where there is an open shop, and their union dues are usually collected through automatic check-offs. Consequently, many unions tend to neglect activities at the grass roots, which often creates various internal problems. (4) Union offices and other administrative facilities are commonly provided by the company. (5) Leaders of the enterprise union are elected from among the regular employees in the enterprise. The elected officials usually maintain their employment relationship with the enterprise while devoting themselves to union activities. Becoming a union officer does not mean giving up promotions in the enterprise. On the contrary, it often leads to promising careers within management. In the public service sector, however, many union leaders have in recent years been discharged by the enterprise for unlawful strike action and no longer have an employment relationship with the enterprise.[16] (6) The organizational structure of the enterprise union inevitably corresponds to the organization of the enterprise, facilitating the maintenance of the union's

16. Following the long controversy over and adoption of ILO Convention 87, new laws drastically limited the number and employment tenure of those elected full-time union officials. Especially hard hit was the Japan Teachers' Union, or Nikkyōso. See Chapters 4 and 8.

organizational integrity but at the same time making the union vulnerable to employer intervention.

Why has enterprise unionism been so predominant? First, "paternalism" continues to pervade industries of all sizes. It is persistent on the part of employers, while workers expect its benefits as a matter of course and respond by being strongly conscious of the closed "communities." Since prewar days, employers in large industry have tried to confine employee organization to single enterprises and have developed labor-management consultation systems and employee welfare facilities based on the enterprise. During the war labor and management were forced to cooperate with each other for war production. Later, during the postwar period of inflation and shortages of goods, as workers spontaneously and rapidly organized labor unions with the help of Occupation policies, they inevitably organized on an enterprise basis as a result of their earlier experience.

A second reason the Japanese labor union could not be organized on any basis other than the enterprise was the very wide variation in working conditions and employment security among firms. Interfirm differentials made it especially difficult for workers to unite industrywide.

Third, there have been deficiencies in public investment in a social security system, housing development programs, and the like. As a result, workers in both large private industry and the public sector have been seriously concerned about guaranteed livelihoods and have demanded such guarantees from their employers.

For the labor movement as a whole, enterprise unionism has had a number of consequences: (1) As all employees in an enterprise are organized together, conflicts of interest within the enterprise union are frequent. Such conflict often leads to splits between those workers who stand firm against the employer and those who are more cooperative with the employer, or between blue-collar workers and white-collar employees. (2) New employees, who automatically join the union upon joining the enterprise, are generally indifferent to the union and have no clear-cut consciousness of being a union member. Consequently, the union tends to be an instrument solely for the leadership. (3) Union leadership tends to change frequently so that there is little possibility for experienced, competent, and responsible leaders to emerge or develop. (4) When the union is organized in a small firm, it is apt to be weak and inactive. (5) Since the union organization is confined within an enterprise, the scope of union activities tends to be narrow. (6) Because of the nature of the enterprise union organization, it is rather ineffective in determining wage rates of individual union members, and once general increases in base pay are agreed upon, individual wage-rate determination is usually left to the employer's discretion. (7) As there are no distinctive occupational demarcations among union members, it is rather easy for the employer to transfer workers at will. (8) Since the union is so closely attached to the enterprise, it is sometimes very difficult for an employer to merge his business with another. Merger is less difficult when the unions involved belong to the same national center or industrial federation, but when they do not, intense strife between the unions often occurs. These conflicts of interest may generate union splits.[17]

In the case of multiplant enterprises, workers are usually organized in a unit union at each plant and these units often form a federation within the enterprise. The federation is a type of enterprise union, since it is confined to employees of the enterprise. The federation often bargains collectively to standardize employment conditions throughout the enterprise. In many cases such organizations turn out to be strong unions.

The strength of the enterprise union federation is largely determined by its power relationship to the national level union organization to which it is affiliated (usually an industrial union) and to its own unit unions. If the enterprise federation is directly involved in the national organization, as in the case of the unions at Toshiba and Hitachi Electric Companies, it tends to become powerful. In most cases, however, there is no such involvement in the national organization; rather, the federation functions as a supplementary agent for the higher organization while the unit unions belong to the national organization. In the steel industry,

17. Severe conflicts of this nature occurred in 1966 in the merger involving the three Mitsubishi Heavy Industry companies and the Nissan and the Prince Automobile companies.

for example, the Japanese Federation of Iron and Steel Workers' Unions, or Tekkōrōren, an industrial union, has the right to call and end a strike, while the member enterprise federations carry on the actual bargaining. However, when an industrial union has the power to bargain with individual employers, it often competes with the enterprise union federations for bargaining rights. In such cases, it is not unusual for an enterprise federation to threaten to withdraw from the industrial union.[18]

Of course, there are cases in which neither unit unions nor their enterprise federation belong to a national organization. These are "pure" enterprise unions. Also, there are cases in which unit unions belong to national organizations with or without affiliation by its enterprise federation. Here constant internal strife within the enterprise federation tends to occur, and sometimes the unit unions break away from the federation.

Generally speaking, the enterprise federation is the center of union activities for strikes and collective bargaining. As a result, it usually maintains greater organizational unity than the industrial union.

The Industrial Union

The structure of the Japanese industrial union differs from those in Western countries, with the exception of the All-Japan Seamen's Union. The industrial union in Japan typically is an industry-wide federation of unit unions and/or enterprise union federations organized within the large oligopolistic companies in a given industry. Generally it is loosely organized, although the looseness varies from industry to industry. Furthermore, its policies and activities are often dominated by the powerful member unions.

The unions of public workers can be regarded as equivalent to industrial unions. Most public employee unions in Japan are huge. For example, the National Railway Workers' Union, or Kokurō, the All-Japan Telecommunication Workers' Union, or Zendentsū, the Japan Postal Workers' Union, or Zentei, the

18. For example, this has frequently occurred in the steel workers' and textile workers' unions.

Japan Teachers' Union, or Nikkyōso, and the All-Japan Prefectural and Municipal Workers' Union, or Jichirō, are as large as or larger than the private industrywide federations and are key opinion leaders in the national center.

The All-Japan Seamen's Union is the only industrial union of the Western type. Seamen belong to this union as individuals, regardless of the size of the company that employs them. The union has the responsibility for bargaining over wage rates and other employment conditions.

The seamen are organized on an industrial basis for several reasons: (1) A seamen's union organized on occupational lines existed before the war. (2) During the war, the maritime companies were integrated into a single national maritime committee, and management of the maritime industry became unified. This unification has continued since the war and the committee bargains with the union for the industry. (3) The required government procedures for qualifying and licensing seamen make it easy for the union to control job entry. The union is relatively free from the pressures of surplus labor and industrial paternalism, and thus it is able to control the labor market. (4) The leadership of this union is oriented toward practical strategies rather than toward abstract ideologies of class struggle. (5) The union is well financed and disciplined.

Activities of the Industrial Union

The Japanese industrial union is usually engaged in workers' education, public relations, assistance in strikes, research, organizing the unorganized, and orientation for member unions. Furthermore, it is often involved in promoting industrywide or nationwide political campaigns in collaboration with the national center.

In general, there is an intermediary organization between the industrial union and its member enterprise unions. This is the regional federation of unions formed on the basis of one or more prefectures. Its function is to assist member unions in the region, to interpret and relay orders of the industrial union to member unions, and to help them carry out the orders. The intermediate organization is merely a supplementary administrative unit for communication between the industrial union and member enter-prise unions.

Since the industrial union in Japan is a loose federation of enterprise unions, it is not effective for establishing standard em-ployment conditions on an industrywide basis. For this reason, the member unions of industrial unions devise joint struggle actions in which they adjust the strength of the action to each particular situation.[19] When the leadership of an industrial union is too involved in ideological orientation and overlooks the fact that it is only a loose federation, unit unions often break away from the federation. These cases result in either a weakening of the indus-trial union or the creation of a rival industrial union.

In spite of such organizational weakness, under the present conditions joint-struggle action is increasingly required; that is, the realization of union demands through enterprise unionism has been limited because of intensified competition among big firms and their drive to minimize labor costs. Thus, it is expected that the industrial union will play an increasingly important role in integrating the bargaining processes of the member enterprise unions.

Industrial unions also cooperate through interindustry liaison councils or joint-struggle committees. This type of cooperation is common in the metal, longshore, banking and finance, transpor-tation, commercial trades, food, medical, chemical, and mass com-munication industries. Recently the International Metalworkers Federation–Japan Council (IMF-JC) has been established by a number of industrial unions. Some of these interindustry organi-zations are oriented toward radicalism, but most are designed to participate in international trade secretariats.

Such interindustry organizations are also common in the public sector. There are joint-struggle committees of national and local public service employees and of national and local government corporation employees. Since these unions bargain with the gov-ernment and request the Public Corporation Labor Relations Commission or the National Personnel Authority (NPA) to settle disputes, they are readily oriented toward joint action. As final

19. In this respect, see Hideaki Okamoto, "Spring Offensive and Gōka-Rōren," *Japan Labor Bulletin*, May 1966.

decisions on collective agreements always depend on the approval of the Diet, such joint action often involves political strife and tends to intensify the political preoccupation of public employee unions (see also Chapters 8 and 9).

In recent years there has been an increase in the formation of industrial combinations (for example, the petrochemical industry) and mergers of large companies, disregarding traditional financial ties. This trend is a great challenge to the unions, requiring increased cooperation and coordination among industrial unions and including the possibility of merger or reorganization into larger industrial unions. For example, two industrial unions in the chemical industry have planned mergers; nine electric power industry unions have formed a single federation; and the General Federation of Private Railway Workers' Unions of Japan, or Shitetsusōren, and other overland transportation workers' unions have been integrated. Such organizational integration is also under way among affiliates of Dōmei, the Japanese Confederation of Labor, while almost one million metal industry workers have been organized in the IMF-JC.

The National Centers

There were four major national centers in Japan as of 1969: Sōhyō, with 37.8 percent of the total number of organized workers; Dōmei, with 17.4 percent; Shinsanbetsu, or the National Federation of Industrial Organizations, with 0.6 percent; and Chūritsu-rōren, or the Federation of Independent Unions, with 12.0 percent. In addition to these, unaffiliated national unions account for about 8 percent of the total membership, and independent enterprise unions for 33.4 percent. As only 39.0 percent of Sōhyō's membership is in the private sector, public employees are well in the majority in the largest national center.[20]

Dōmei was organized in 1954 by unions that had belonged to Sōdōmei before and after the war and by unions of seamen, textile workers, and electric power workers. In contrast to Sōhyō, 93.0

20. Ministry of Labor, *Basic Survey Report on Labor Unions, 1970* (Tokyo: Ministry of Labor, 1971), p. 20.

percent of Dōmei's affiliated union members work in private industry. The member unions formerly affiliated with Sōdōmei are primarily in small and medium-sized industry.

Shinsanbetsu is actually so small that it does not warrant being called a national center. However, its organizational goals and strategies are distinctive, deriving from the time Sanbetsu disintegrated in the late 1940s and centering on wage policy and labor unification.

Chūritsurōren is composed primarily of unions that once belonged to the old Sanbetsu. It is a loose national center of enterprise union federations and is still organizationally weak, although since 1961 it has employed full-time officers. Some 99.9 percent of its affiliated union members work in private industry.

Formally, each national center is organized by member industrial unions, but in fact it also involves direct participation of enterprise union federations and unit unions. Sōhyō, in particular, comprises the enterprise union organizations that mushroomed immediately after the war and were affiliated with Sanbetsu. As a result, it tends to be dominated by large, powerful member unions to the neglect of small member unions.

Considerable rivalry exists among the four national centers, especially between Sōhyō and Dōmei. The reasons for such rivalry are deeply rooted and pervasive, involving long-established relationships between the unions and the political parties they have respectively supported since prewar days, conflicting ideologies of class struggle, and differences in practical union strategies. While integration of the national centers or cooperative action is often proposed, it hardly appears feasible in the very near future.

The national center does not play the role its member unions do on a day-to-day basis. Its major function is to provide guidelines for the total labor movement and to communicate with and influence its affiliates. More specifically, it assumes leadership in nationwide joint wage struggles, representations to the government, mass demonstrations, and international relations and exchange programs, and it provides support for the reform parties. In essence, it is a liaison council and does not have power to control and discipline member unions. This weakness poses grave problems with regard to organizational integration of member unions and effectiveness at the national level.

Lower units of the national center are the district councils (in the case of Sōhyō) or district federations (in the case of Dōmei) and about 1,200 local labor union councils made up of both affiliated and unaffiliated unions. These regional organizations give support to weak unions in the area. However, they tend to be ignored by the large enterprise unions which are closely tied to their own enterprise union federations or industrial unions; nonetheless, the enterprise unions do offer substantial financial support and union personnel. The regional organizations have functioned primarily to mobilize union members in an area for regional joint struggles and to support and campaign for regional candidates of political parties backed by the national union.

Internal Union Functioning

As already mentioned, various kinds of conflict occur between the different levels of labor union organization in Japan. In addition, there are many conflicting interests even within the same level. Therefore, the actual functioning of unions cannot be understood merely by studying the provisions of union constitutions which specify various governing bodies and their functions. Thus, the actual decision-making structure of a typical union will be described below.

Administrative Machinery

The union constitution typically provides a structure for union government. The major governing bodies are for decision making, execution, auditing, and union discipline, while supplementary divisions include a secretariat, the financial department, and other services. Generally speaking, since at the level of the unit union rank-and-file members are automatically organized and their concern with the union is slight, decisions adopted at membership meetings usually follow proposals of the officials, except when tension between labor and management is extremely high. At the industrial union level or higher, the decision-making body, usually called a convention, is composed of the representatives of each unit union or industrial union; it is important in that it is the scene of conflicts among the unit unions or the industrial unions.

Within the large unit unions, sectional or departmental meetings for each interest group are held in an effort to adjust interunion conflicts between company consciousness and union consciousness, over ideologies, and among separate interest factions, such as blue-collar and white-collar workers, different jobholders, and those of different ages, sexes, and educational backgrounds. When coordination fails, a union split may occur, such as, for example, the split of the locomotive workers away from the National Railway Workers' Union and of the white-collar workers from enterprise unions in coal mining.

The Trade Union Law provides that each level of the union must hold meetings of the decision-making body, or convention, more than once annually in order to maintain its legal recognition. The law also requires that the convention take up any questions on dissolution of the union and the operation of welfare and mutual aid funds. Other subjects on which decisions may be made are (1) business reports; (2) amendments to the bylaws and constitution; (3) union activity policy; (4) budgeting and settlement of accounts; (5) election of officers; (6) execution of strikes; and (7) ratification of the collective agreement.[21] Because of the members' lack of concern with unions, few unit unions at the lower level hold general membership meetings more than once a year.

Between conventions, meetings of such intermediate decision-making bodies as the central committee and the councillors or union delegates are held fairly frequently. The responsibilities of these groups are broader than mere execution of policy agreed upon at the general membership meetings, but their power and authority relationships with the convention are unclear. In addi-

21. It is observed that practically all union conventions have stereotyped proceedings, including such items.

tion, some decisions are made at meetings of the three top-ranking union officials (president, vice-president, and secretary-general or chief clerk) and of the departmental chiefs. Thus the relationship between decision and execution within the total union organization is obscure.

The conventions, on occasion, delegate decisions regarding strikes to the union officials in anticipation of possible struggles in the coming year, although recently this practice has been under reconsideration.[22] The number of representatives of each unit union to the convention of its industrial union is decided either by a simple proportional representation system or by a successive diminution system as the organization grows in number.[23] The union's bylaws tend to provide for an executive committee to carry out decisions made at the general convention or at the central committee meeting. As a result, the executive committee plays a key role in the actual operation of the union, sometimes neglecting the opinion of the rank and file. Most members of executive committees of national unions are full-time officers and at the same time are in charge of union departments such as general administration, finance, education and propaganda, research, organization, struggle policy, legal matters, welfare, recreation, or female and young workers.

Centralization of power in the three top-ranking officials is considerably weaker than in European or American unions, probably because of the authority vested in the executive committee. Such a tendency is also common in other general organizations in Japan. The reason for this is that group leaders are afraid of being isolated from the collective will of the members of the group and try to avoid internal conflict as much as possible. In addition, the Japanese union has the potential for great internal conflict among its many different components.

Another responsibility of the convention is to establish a struggle committee, whose membership overlaps with the executive committee or the struggle policy department; as a result, its responsi-

22. For example, Tekkōrōren and other federations hold membership votes on strikes at the plant or enterprise level.

23. Coal miners', private railway, synthetic chemical, and textile unions have proportional representation with some allowance for small unions. Steel workers and others have a successive diminution system.

bility also is unclear. Its major function is to coordinate conflicting interests among the different enterprise unions or to raise the morale of members in the subordinate organizations in case of a struggle.

What is clear from the above description is that, in comparison with European or American unions, the Japanese union has many overlapping bodies among which power is spread and responsibility ill-defined.

Most unions have an auditing body which audits accounts only formally and does not inspect the actual conduct of business or content of assets.[24] When internal union conflict is intense, however, the right to audit is often used as a means to attack the opposing faction.

A disciplinary body is not usually found in Japanese unions, although notable exceptions are the Seamen's Union and the All-Monopoly Corporation Workers' Union, or Zensenbai, in tobacco. In most cases, disciplinary decisions are made at the union convention. In the unit union, the executive body sometimes possesses disciplinary power, but there have been few cases of meting out punishment and then only as a tactic in a factional struggle, as will be discussed later.

Officers and Staff

It is characteristic of Japanese unions that many full-time officers maintain their employment relationships with the company, and they are guaranteed the right to return to their jobs whenever they wish. However, when an officer is discharged or retires from the company and accordingly loses his company position, he can no longer remain a union member or officer. During the so-called red purge in 1950, more than ten thousand active members and officers were discharged from companies and, as a result, ousted from their unions. Many public worker union officers also have been discharged for participating in disputes prohibited by law. There have been cases where the employer

24. The law provides that a certified public accountant audit the union finances.

refused to approve the union when it elected discharged employees to office. Such unions subsequently created jobs for professional full-time officers having no employment relationship with the employer.[25] In the large industrial union or the national center some leaders actually become career officers after being elected to the position for several terms.[26]

Officers usually rotate, and union positions are regarded as jobs in the company. This tendency is stronger among the white-collar officers for whom the union position is regarded as a step toward promotion within the company. As a result, distrust of white-collar officers by the rank-and-file members has increased, and the proportion of blue-collar officers has grown.

One exception to the custom of elected officers was found in the former Sōdōmei, now a part of Dōmei. Sōdōmei was controlled by "outside" professional leaders from prewar days who insisted upon fixed principles for union activity. As a result, it was not favored by the large enterprise unions formed after the war—one reason it was unable to increase its membership.

In general, the tenure of union officers is short and officer professionalization is uncommon. In one sense, this turnover in the leadership is a result of acceptance of the concept of union democracy, but it has its drawbacks as well. The officers' sense of responsibility is not great, and it is difficult to establish a long-term plan for the union. Furthermore, the experience necessary for union operation, increasingly complex and difficult, does not accumulate. Rather, persons elected are those who are skillful at winning superficial and temporary popularity among members, which does not contribute to the sound development of the union. Many unions have reconsidered and eliminated these drawbacks, but only after considerable internal unrest and conflict over the leadership. Since around 1960 the number of industrial unions and national centers adopting two-year terms of office has been notably increasing.

Where tenure of union officers is prolonged, these officers often become members of the local government assembly or officials of

25. Most public corporation workers' unions have leaders of this type.
26. Many top leaders of industrial unions and of the national centers are career officers; for example, Ohta, Takano, Takita, and others.

the local labor bank, cooperative association, or some other organization that has a relationship with the union. These connections guarantee their livelihood after retirement from the union. Also, career officers of a national center or industrial union who are not interested in returning to their former company jobs seek to become members of the Diet or officers of a union-related organization or in a subsidiary of the company in which they had been employed.

The average age of the majority of union officers, although it varies with the level of organization, is around thirty-five. The next age group includes those in their forties, but in large enterprises where the number of young workers is increasing leaders in their twenties are growing in number. A substantial number of the present-day leaders became officers during the 1946–48 period when they were young and when the number of unions was greatly increasing. About half have remained at their positions. During the period of confusion when Sanbetsu was replaced by Sōhyō, there was a considerable change of leadership. Those who became leaders at that time have continued to be leaders. Those who became workers during and right after the war constitute the bulk of the union leadership today.

Since the power of the leader reflects the solidarity of the union, he needs the support of the majority of the members. For this reason, the relationships among different groups in the union and the means of representation of their different interests become important factors in deciding who assumes the union leadership. In a union where the average age of the members is high, relatively old people occupy most of the leadership positions. In national organizations where length of service of the leaders is long, those who obtain the support of the influential enterprise unions or industrial unions usually are elected to leadership.

For several years after the war the percentage of union leaders with college and high school educations was high, but this percentage has decreased and the percentage of former middle school graduates and new high school graduates has greatly increased. In the industrial unions and national centers, the average age of the officers is high and primary school graduates and upper elementary school graduates constitute a majority.

Clerks are usually employed by unions to assist with executive functions. If we call the union officer "line," then the clerk should be called "staff." Only 14 percent of all unions have full-time clerks, but among the unions with a thousand or more members, the rate rises to 90 percent.[27] Clerks are drawn either from among the union members, with the company's approval, or from outside. At the enterprise union level, the number of those employed from outside is small and they cannot become union members. The clerk who has served with the union for a long time is thoroughly acquainted with the situation or activities of the union and is very able, but his pay and position usually are low and there is no way open for him to become an officer. Accordingly, few able college graduates become clerks, although they are needed. However, an exception is the white-collar unions where turnover of officers is frequent. Here the clerks have power and a strong voice in union affairs. Also, Sōdōmei traditionally gave union membership status to clerks and appointed them as officers.

Discipline

As noted, discipline within the union is weak. One reason for this is that, as a reaction to the extreme control and oppression of the prewar days, postwar democracy was seen as complete egalitarianism and unlimited freedom. As enforcement of social rules and order relaxed, the coexistence of freedom and discipline became difficult to manage. While a greater balance emerged as the economy stabilized, even today the egalitarian tendency remains.

There are union shop clauses in many labor agreements at the enterprise level. In most cases, however, they provide that expulsion from the union for violation of union rules will not necessarily result in discharge from the company. Usually there is a conditional clause to the effect that, if there is a legitimate reason for the management to continue to employ the worker ousted from the union, then the union cannot force his discharge. Such a union

27. Ministry of Labor, Survey of Labor Agreements, (Tokyo: Ministry of Labor, 1962).

security system is called the "loophole" union shop. Thus, among violators of union rules, only those whom the employer agrees to discharge will be discharged. This implies that the role of the union as a force independent of the employer is not yet fully recognized.

In the industrial union or national center, expulsion of an affiliated union for a disciplinary reason is possible by decision of the convention. Actually, however, expulsion tends to weaken the upper-level organization, and there is the further possibility that the expelled union may affiliate with a rival organization. Therefore, exercise of discipline is not easily resorted to even at this level, basically because an industrial union is a loose federation of enterprise unions or their federations and has no power to control the labor market.

The Japanese union whose disciplinary power is weak at every level needs the voluntary support of its members for successful operation. Activists within the union form groups according to their political consciousness or desire for given union policies. Such groups function as factions within the union, and the activists control rank-and-file members through such factions. In other words, the union operates without any formal discipline system enforced by the union itself. This is the reason the mainstream of the union sticks to highly political educational or political party activities and to abstract class conflict theory even though these activities have little connection with and are sometimes contrary to the actual union movement.

Union Finance

The structure of union financing is significant in the sense that it reflects the power structure of the union. Since union finance and union organization are two sides of the same coin in Japan, the ability of the upper-level organization to raise funds is weak compared with the enterprise union. Generally speaking, dues tend to be high in unions that are more active and secure more benefits for members. In 1965, the highest dues were those of the miners; monthly dues were ¥728, or more than 1.7 percent of the average wage. The lowest monthly dues were those of the textile union—¥210, or 0.71 percent of the average wage. In most unions monthly dues ranged from ¥300 to ¥500, while the overall average was ¥422, or 1 percent of the average wage.[28]

The amount of union dues is either a fixed percentage of average wages or a fixed amount. In some cases both methods are used jointly. The fixed amount is generally used in smaller unions, and dues at the headquarters of virtually all industrial unions are paid by the fixed amount method. The check-off system is employed by a majority of unions and obtains for 79.9 percent of total union membership. In mining, manufacturing, and commerce more than 90 percent of the members are covered by check-off. By size of union membership, 89.5 percent of the members of unions with a thousand or more members have their dues checked off, but as the size of the union declines, the percentage of union membership covered by this system decreases.[29]

For budgeting purposes, dues are allocated to a general account and to special accounts. The latter include expenses for struggles, to relieve victims of strikes (i.e., those who are discharged or penalized by the company for their activities),[30] for political enlightenment, disaster relief, mutual aid, and so forth. The number of such items is largest among the public employee unions.

There are various means of allocating union dues to the organizations at each level. Generally, in private industry the unit union within the enterprise collects the dues and delivers a portion to the enterprise federation, the district headquarters, and the industrial union. The industrial union delivers a portion in turn to the national center. Usually the unit union retains 70 to 90 percent of the dues collected. Payment to the upper-level organizations is supposedly made on a per capita membership basis as decided by each upper-level organization, but most unit unions pay for a number lower than their actual memberships. This underreporting

28. Ministry of Labor, *Rōdō kumiai kihonchōsa hōkoku, 1965* [Basic survey report on labor unions, 1965] (Tokyo: Ministry of Labor, 1966), pp. 26, 68–69.
  29. Ibid., pp. 26–27.
  30. See pp. 253 and 255.

is called the "concealed paddy field," an expression derived from the traditional practice of the farmer of underreporting his cultivated acreage in order to reduce his land taxes. For this reason, the upper-level organization is financially weak and always has to concede to the lower-level industrial union or the enterprise union. Again, the Seamen's Union is an exception, as union dues are collected directly by the national headquarters, which then allocates funds to the branches or chapters according to the headquarters' activity schedule. Most of the collected dues (80 percent) are retained by the national headquarters.

In addition to the Seamen's Union, public employee unions such as the National Railway Workers' Union, the Postal Workers' Union, the National Telecommunication Workers' Union, the Prefectural and Municipal Workers' Union, and the Teachers' Union, also collect dues directly at the national headquarters and then allocate them to the lower-level organizations. In these unions local activities are strong, since nearly 40 percent of the dues are allocated to the district organizations. Of 13 national unions whose budgets totaled more than ¥100,000,000 in 1962, 9 were public unions. Also, of 14 industrial unions whose per capita budget was over ¥1,000, 13 were public employee unions.[31]

In the private sector, with a few exceptions such as the Seamen's Union or the Japan Federation of Textile Workers' Unions (Zensendōmei), the majority of the industrial unions have relatively small budgets—even smaller than those of affiliated enterprise unions. This is another factor that makes it difficult for national unions to perform industrywide services.

Differences in the financial ability of each industrial union are well reflected in union activities. Although most unions in the private industries are legally guaranteed the right to strike, the struggle funds of their industrial unions are hardly sufficient even to support an industrywide strike for a few days. Accordingly, their unified struggles are always appeals for support, and what they are able to accomplish is at most sporadic shop meetings during working hours, limited-time strikes, or partial strikes. However, the Seamen's Union, since it has ample strike funds, conducts

31. Ministry of Labor, *Rōdō kumiai kihonchōsa hōkoku, 1962* [Basic survey report on labor unions, 1962] (Tokyo: Ministry of Labor, 1963).

long-term industrywide strikes under the strong control of its headquarters.

Since strikes by public employees are prohibited, their unions have used various forms of struggle which have effects similar to strikes. These struggles, however, result in many "victims" of discharges, wage reductions, or work suspensions. Therefore, public employee unions have collected and accumulated large amounts of funds to relieve these victims. Such funds, amounting to 40 percent of the total budget of the national headquarters, insure the union membership against dangers connected with the struggle. It is quite reasonable to assume that this centralization of finances as well as power has been a source of radicalism among these unions.

The management of union finances is another important problem. Generally, the status of the person in charge of finances is extremely low in the union, and the actual decisions to use funds are made primarily by the three top-ranking officers. In most unions, budgeting and balancing of accounts are not directly related to the actual activities of the union, and formal allocation of authority for expenditures is completely neglected in actual operations. When a large deficit occurs, it is not a question of individual responsibility but is usually settled by political dealing among the factions within the union.

This characteristic of Japanese union operations is common to other organizations in Japanese society as well. It reflects the Japanese tendency to avoid any public consideration of financial problems in detail. A major example of loose and unreasonable control of union funds is the deficit of several hundred thousand yen accumulated over several years in publishing the Sōhyō weekly magazine. Heated discussions raged over whether the deficit should be covered by the leading unions. The problem was settled after negotiations among the factions without any attempt to fix responsibility for the deficit or to improve financial management and auditing within the union. This case also disclosed the possibility that the high-ranking officers, even though their constitutional power is weak, may actually have unlimited power to spend or borrow funds without relying upon the officer in charge of finance or the provisions concerning financial control.

Political Action and International Relationships

As the influence of the labor union increases, its social status also grows and its area of activities broadens. Collective bargaining and labor disputes for the purpose of improving working conditions, strengthening and enlarging organization, or educational activities are discussed in Chapters 8 and 9. This section will discuss only union political activities and international relations.

Legislative Activities

The fact that Japanese unions with the help of national centers and influential industrial unions are active in "progressive" political activities has attracted international attention, even though European unions also support labor parties. The rather unique Japanese characteristics concern the area and methods of union political action.

The Japanese labor movement has tended to develop political activities because the working conditions of public employees, who comprise an important part of the movement, are for the most part decided by legislation. Sōhyō, which occupies the mainstream of the Japanese labor movement, stresses political action, in addition to economic strikes, to improve the wage rates of employees of the government, the public corporations, and the national enterprises.

Furthermore, since legislation concerning working conditions is inadequate, demands to improve or enact laws necessarily take a political form. These demands include legislative enactment of a minimum wage system on a nationwide basis rather than the existing employer agreements by industry and by area; improvement of labor standards, particularly shortening of work hours; and changes in energy policies to solve employment problems in the declining coal-mining industry. To achieve these demands, the unions sponsor demonstrations of large numbers of union members, offer opinions at various kinds of administrative committees, and support Diet activities of related political parties.

Each union actively supports the struggle for labor's rights, as the union regards protection of the rights and freedoms guaranteed by legislation at the end of the war as the basis for worker efforts to improve living standards. Unions opposed the order to stop strikes issued by the Occupation forces in 1948, amendments to the labor laws in 1952, and the Strike Restriction Law in 1953 as depriving the workers of their guaranteed rights. The struggle for rights became increasingly active when union officers of the National Railway Workers' Union and the National Railway Locomotive Engineers' Union, Dōryokusha, were discharged as a result of the *Shuntō* (Spring Labor Offensive) struggle in 1957. Later, it developed into an international struggle for the ratification of International Labor Organization (ILO) Convention 87.

Activities opposing police oppression heightened, and many cases have been disputed in the courts. Sōhyō established a defense council, with a famous lawyer as its chief, and sent 164 lawyers throughout the country to argue in courts. In 1959, the Postal Workers' Union, followed by Sōhyō in 1960, established a special committee for recovering the right to strike in connection with the ILO convention problem. At the same time that Sōhyō began to accumulate funds for this activity, it also appealed to the ILO[32] and successfully gained support from the International Confederation of Free Trade Unions (ICFTU) and other international union organizations. In 1958, the four national centers— Sōhyō, Dōmei, Shinsanbetsu, and Chūritsurōren—established a union conference to promote ratification of the ILO convention.

Along with the appeal to the ILO, preparations also were undertaken to recover the right of public employee unions to strike. The leading public employee unions have assessed struggle funds (including funds to relieve the victims) of ¥100 per member per month since 1961. With many union members participating in illegal strikes, expenses for the relief of those punished by dis-

---

32. The appeal to the ILO in 1957 was presented at the ILO's Fortieth General Session in the form of a resolution to stimulate ratification of Convention 87. It was followed by appeals each year on Japanese government violation of workers' rights to organize and freedom of association. Public employee unions sponsored the appeals. See Alice H. Cook, "The International Labor Organization and Japanese Politics," *Industrial and Labor Relations Review*, (October 1965): pp. 41–57.

charge, suspension, or wage reduction reached one billion and several hundred million yen each time such a struggle was carried out.

The Peace Movement

National memories of the war damage are still very strong, and some extremely active peace movements center around opposition to the atomic bomb. Unions have always promoted such movements, although they have not always taken the same position. Sōhyō, together with the Japan Socialist Party, advocates a stance of positive neutrality for Japan, while Dōmei, together with the Democratic Socialist Party, supports Japan's position as a member of the free nation group. The anti-mainstream faction within Sōhyō, like the Japan Communist Party, demands a policy denouncing American imperialism. As a result, the peace movement is similarly complicated and confused.

As the core of the National Conference for the Promotion of Peace, Sōhyō developed such movements as the anti-atomic bomb movement, the anti-military base movement, the anti-Japan-Korea Normalization Conference movement, and the movement for the protection of a peaceful constitution or the anti-Japan-United States Security Treaty movement. However, since the anti-atomic bomb movement split over the treaty limiting nuclear testing by the United States, the United Kingdom, and the Soviet Union, Sōhyō's peace movement has become less active. Dōmei, in opposition to Sōhyō's radical peace movement, has organized its own anti-nuclear weapon movement or constitution-preservation movement. As a result, labor's peace movement has been further split, encouraging inactivity.

Unions and Political Parties

In prewar days, many union leaders were also proletarian party leaders. Accordingly, through the activities of these leaders, conflicts and splits within the party were carried over into the union and vice versa. Such relationships have continued to a certain degree in the postwar labor movement.

The conflict between the Japan Socialist Party and the Communist Party right after the war was reflected in the conflict between Sōdōmei and Sanbetsu, and two separate labor movements developed. Later, labor united under Sōhyō, but by 1950 it had split again into two groups influenced by the break of the Socialist Party into right and left wings. The right-wing socialists were the stronger immediately after the split, but the left wing increased its Diet representation from election to election with support from Sōhyō, and its strength soon exceeded that of the right wing. In the 1950 and 1951 elections, Sōhyō helped the left wing by providing not only funds but also influential leaders as electoral candidates; most of them were elected to public office.

During the period of conflict within Sōhyō over leadership, the Socialist Party supported the big industrial union group which succeeded in winning. Also, during the period of conflict within the Socialist Party in 1959, Sōhyō actively supported the movement to split the party. As a result, the Democratic Socialist Party was born, and the present-day relationship was established; that is, the majority of Sōhyō, Shinsanbetsu, and Chūritsurōren affiliates support the Japan Socialist Party, while Dōmei supports the Democratic Socialist Party. Most of the independent federations not affiliated with a national center as well as the enterprise unions support the Japan Socialist Party. Although in 1960 Sōhyō advocated a Japanese type of unionism which distinguished between union and party activities, it actually has strengthened its ties with the Japan Socialist Party.

The Communist Party, excluded from the labor movement, no longer has a base from which to penetrate union leadership, but it still tries to influence the leaders to adopt radical policies. Also, the penetration of the youth groups by the Communist Minsei (Democratic Youth League) at the lower union levels has been remarkable. Minsei develops a wide range of activities, from recreation to ideological study, taking advantage of young people's frustration under the present system.

Union Support for Political Parties

Both Sōhyō and Dōmei have a policy of giving exclusive support to a political party through resolutions at their general conventions or at the conventions of their lower-level organizations. Theoretically, they make a distinction between the party and the union because of the multiplicity of factions and interests within the union membership, but actually most unions support the Japan Socialist Party and cooperate with other reform parties as necessary. In most instances, Sōhyō is very critical of the Democratic Socialist Party.

Dōmei, as a matter of course, supports the Democratic Socialist Party but follows a policy of mutual nonintervention by party or union, denying the union the use of the party as a means to attain its goals. Dōmei's attitude toward the Japan Socialist Party is critical, and it argues that the Socialists stick to the old ideologies and do not recognize that conditions have changed. It also maintains strong opposition to the Communist Party.

Party support at the industrial union level is more complex. The following outline summarizes union attitudes toward the parties:

1. Unions that support the Japan Socialist Party
   a. Those that support the Japan Socialist Party only (private railways, coal mining, trucking, chemical association, national railways, locomotive, postal, telecommunication and electric machine workers)
   b. Those that support the Japan Socialist Party and cooperate with other reform parties when necessary (Sōhyō, synthetic chemical workers, metal-mining workers, banking and insurance workers, teachers, prefectural and municipal employees)
   c. Those that primarily support the Japan Socialist Party and cooperate with other reform parties (steel workers, Shin-sanbetsu)
2. Unions that support both the Japan Socialist Party and the Communist Party

     a. Those that support both parties (relief laborers, automobile drivers, paper and pulp workers, harbor workers, and construction workers)

     b. Those that cooperate with both parties (casualty insurance workers)

     c. Those that cooperate with all progressive parties (metal workers, automobile transport workers)

3. Unions that support the Democratic Socialist Party

     a. Those that support the Democratic Socialist Party only (textile workers, seamen, new coal miners, new national railway workers)

     b. Those that support the Democratic Socialist Party and cooperate with the Japan Socialist Party when necessary (electric power workers, shipbuilding workers)

     c. Those that support both the Democratic Socialist Party and the Japan Socialist Party (automobile workers)[33]

Resolution of party support at the union convention does not necessarily lead to all-out support by the union membership. In elections, the decision by the rank-and-file members as to whom to vote for is greatly influenced by recommendations from the activists who are informally connected with the parties and by the personalities of the candidates. In this sense those who are most likely to be supported by the union membership are candidates who have been officers of the union concerned. Therefore, officers of enterprise unions that have large memberships in one electoral district or officers of an industrial union with large memberships all over the nation are in very advantageous positions politically.

    Within Sōhyō, the Japan Socialist Party forms the Socialist Party Members' Conference, composed of the party members who are also officers of the twenty-two Sōhyō-affiliated industrial unions. Through this organization the Socialist Party tries to expand its influence within Sōhyō. Since the majority of the party's members are union members, the Socialist Party relies heavily upon the unions.

    During elections for the two houses of the Diet, local assemblies,

33. Ministry of Labor, *Present Situation of the Labor Movement and Industrial Relations* (Tokyo: Ministry of Labor, 1964), pp. 1296–97.

and other public offices, including prefectural governors and mayors, Sōhyō, the majority of whose membership are public employees, conducts very active campaigns. In the House of Representatives election in 1952, right after the split of the Socialist Party, the power of the two wings was balanced. Later, with the strong support of the Sōhyō-affiliated industrial unions, which included supplying candidates for the party, the left-wing Japan Socialist Party steadily increased its strength each year. As a result, a majority of the upper house Socialist Party members are former officers of Sōhyō-affiliated unions. In the House of Representatives, such members increased from 34 in 1958 to 55 in 1963, and have become the largest single power in the Japan Socialist Party. In particular, such giant public employee unions as the Teachers' Union, the National Railway Workers' Union, and the Postal Workers' Union occupy 25, 13, and 9 seats respectively in both houses combined.

For the purpose of election campaigns and of raising money for political activities, leading industrial unions establish political activity committees which develop independent election campaigns to support the party or union-nominated candidates with money collected by the union. The Japan Socialist Party receives several hundred million yen from these sources for each election.

Because the union political movement is so active, the Japan Socialist Party does not act independently but instead depends upon union activities. As a result, the party is criticized as being merely the political department of the union. Indeed, there is a strong correlation between areas where union membership is strong and areas where the party obtains a large number of votes. Such close ties between the union and the party inhibit the party's efforts to establish its own policies and approaches to groups other than the organized workers, thus limiting the consolidation of the party's influence and the expansion of its power base.

In the 1968 general elections, the Japan Socialist Party lost eight seats in the House of Councillors (upper house) while the other parties, Social Democratic, Kōmei (Clean Government), and Communist, made gains. Again in the 1969 elections for the legislative body of Tokyo and the House of Representatives the

Liberal-Democratic, Kōmei, and Communist parties gained in representation and the Socialists alone lost seats. It is difficult to judge the trend of the "progressive" parties from these election results except to say that the multiparty system apparently is cutting into Socialist support. There may be several reasons for this tendency: (1) Along with rapid socioeconomic change, the attitude and consciousness of workers are changing and they are showing more interest in daily issues such as prices and taxes and less interest in problems such as the security pact which are emphasized by the Socialists. (2) Many large unions in private industry have partially withdrawn, or weakened, their support for the Japan Socialist Party. (3) The Socialist appeal to the mass of citizens who do not belong to unions has not improved at all.

Participation in Government Committees

In addition to election campaigns, another form of union political activity is participation in various kinds of central and local government administrative bodies and committees. There are several types of such committees, including the employment council, and the committees on industrial accident prevention, the social security system, labor dispute settlement, labor standards, the minimum wage system, job stabilization, and vocational training, most of which are directly concerned with the workers' interests. However, union participation is very low in committees for the purpose of basic economic planning. In this respect, the Japanese labor movement is different from its European counterparts, and the fact that it has in effect been barred from economic policy discussions is one reason Japanese unions basically assume a posture of confrontation vis-à-vis the current social and economic system. In other words, the labor movement has become a strong power in society, but it is not yet accepted as one of the major forces in society; rather, it is accepted negatively as a necessary evil in contemporary Japan.

International Relations of the Union

Japanese unionism has always tried to import the experience of labor movements in advanced countries. After the dissolution of the first organization, which attempted to pattern itself after the American Federation of Labor (AFL) in the 1890s, the new union movement, modeled after British trade unionism, started in 1912 under the name of the Friendly Society. Later, through links with the AFL, the Japanese labor movement was influenced by business unionism. In the period following World War I, syndicalism, as represented by the Confederation Générale du Travail and by the Industrial Workers of the World, became dominant, while the communist labor movement theory, Bolshevism, also came into prominence. As conflict arose between the left-wing Profintern and the right-wing Amsterdam groups, a middle group emerged. At about the time the left-wing movement was prohibited and disappeared, the nationalistic union movement rose and the Sangyō Hōkokukai was organized as a national mobilization institution. This association was similar to the German Labor Front.

The Japanese labor movement continued to reflect the experience of the advanced countries in the postwar period. Changes in the World Federation of Trade Unions, the American Congress of Industrial Organizations, the AFL, and the ICFTU greatly influenced the Japanese unions.

Today, their international relationships are seen in various affiliations. Dōmei, composed of the prewar Sōdōmei, textile workers, seamen, electric power workers, and so on, is affiliated with the ICFTU. Sōhyō, following the principle of neutralism, does not participate in the ICFTU, but Sōhyō-affiliated unions—coal miners, metal-mining workers, broadcasting workers, postal workers, and metropolitan transportation workers—do belong.

Even more unions belong to international industrial organizations affiliated with ICFTU. The Metal-Mining Workers and the Coal-Mine Workers belong to the International Miners' Federation; the Postal and the Telecommunication Workers to the International Postal, Telecommunication and Telephone Service Workers' Federation; the Textile Workers to the International

Textile and Garment Workers' Federation; the Synthetic Chemical Workers to the International Petroleum and Chemical Workers' Federation; the Electric Machinery Workers, Automobile Workers, Shipbuilding Workers, Metal Workers, and Steel Workers belong to IMF-JC; and the Seamen, National Railway Workers, and Private Railway Workers belong to the International Transport Workers' Federation.

Sōhyō's neutralist attitude is delicate. It is influenced by the fact that most of the unions in the Afro-Asian countries do not necessarily support the ICFTU, that Japan is located near the communist-controlled continent, and that anti-American feelings remain among the Japanese people in general. Representatives of twenty-six industrial unions affiliated with Sōhyō, such as Metal Workers, Paper and Pulp Workers, and Printing Workers, are preparing to join the WFTU, while construction workers, workers on public relief projects, and truck drivers already belong to their respective international industrial organizations of the WFTU.

In addition to the organizational affiliations mentioned, Japanese unions have developed many exchange programs with unions in both Western and communist nations. Among the Western nations, exchange with ICFTU-affiliated and American unions are most frequent. During the 1952–63 period, 608 union representatives visited foreign countries and, in addition, the Japan Productivity Center sent 756 unionists abroad during the 1955–62 period.

A total of 2,200 representatives, or 315 groups, visited communist countries during the 1951–63 period, traveling to such countries as the People's Republic of China, the Soviet Union, East Germany, and North Korea. The number of representatives of WFTU-affiliated unions who visited Japan between 1953 and 1963 amounted to 388, or 77 groups. Most of them came from the Soviet Union, mainland China, and other communist countries, but 46 people were from noncommunist countries.

The figures cited in the paragraph above do not necessarily mean that the Japanese union leaders are pro-communist, but they do indicate that the communist countries, especially the Soviet Union and mainland China, attach importance to the Japanese unions and actively try to influence them.

Tensions and Perspectives

The factors causing tension and contributing to change in the lives and consciousness of workers, and therefore in their organizations, are many. The following are the most notable: the rapid shift in the industrial structure from primary to secondary and tertiary industry, accompanied by rapid urbanization; continuing technological innovation; the continuing labor shortage (the demand, especially for young workers, exceeds the supply); higher incomes in every wage bracket (the number of workers in the lowest bracket has been decreasing rapidly in recent years); and the intensification of both domestic and international competition, particularly the liberalization of capital flow. These factors have improved the relative position of workers in society and have intensified their attachment to their companies, but the same factors have also increased the workers' need for protection as the growing pressure of competition fosters an enterprise rationalization policy. This trend is observed in the so-called fluidity of labor unions in very recent years. Thus far the established organizations are maintaining their dominant positions in the face of the challenge from factors contributing to change, but Japanese labor is confronting a type of transition it has never before experienced.

The unions themselves may be too inflexible to adjust to the rapid changes in industrial society, and as the average standard of living and social status of Japanese workers rise, they will increase their opposition to rigidly ideological or class-conscious unionism. Young workers in particular, who were the source of union militancy in the past, are becoming increasingly uninterested in unionism. In recent national elections many of them supported the conservative Liberal-Democratic Party rather than the Socialists, as they apparently found the young talent of the former more attractive than the traditional Socialist trade-unionist candidates. This development has marked a great change and a reversal in the revolutionary or reformist commitment of young workers. They and other workers are no longer tied to anticapitalism or socialism but make their own selections among candidates on the basis of their personal circumstances.

Nonetheless, enterprise unionism is maintaining its dominance, at least in form, and there appears to be no progress toward intra-industrial integration in the face of rapid industrialization. Rather, many enterprise units have dropped out of militant industrial organizations and have consolidated within the framework of their respective enterprises. This unit organization reflects a sensitivity to the competitive pressure among enterprises. The capital liberalization issue intensifies this tendency and influences an enterprise unit in the direction of more concern with the mutual interest of management and labor and less with the class struggle. (Developments in the synthetic chemical, paper-pulp, metal-mining, and casualty insurance industries are examples of this trend.) Among enterprise unions there are increasing signs of joint consultation machinery being established; about 80 percent of all union contracts provide for joint consultation, an indication of union intent to have a voice in management. The effect of this trend may be an improvement in the Japanese pattern of modernization and democratization, and the consolidation of unionism as a social institution.

These trends among labor unions may lead to a reorganization of union affiliation above the national center framework. The IMF-JC is the outstanding example of the increasing activities of ICFTU trade federations in Japan. The IMF-JC has been successful in gaining the support of Tekkōrōren (steel workers), Denkirōren (electric machine workers), Zōsensōren (shipbuilding workers), Jidōsharōren (automobile workers), and others. The council does not operate as a national center or industrial union but rather acts independently with regard to struggle policy and has taken a leading role in wage determination in recent years.

In a number of districts and regions, conferences and meetings of private industry unions have been held by steel workers, electric machine workers, and others. This movement can be attributed to the critical reaction of private sector unions to the radical anti-capitalistic activities of some public workers' unions in Sōhyō.

All of these trends lead to a strengthening of trade unionism and a shift in the power balance among the national centers. Dōmei, in recent years, has had more affiliated members than Sōhyō in the private sector. The trends also may be an indication of the impact of industrialization on the labor union movement, and as economic development continues unions and managements may become cooperative rather than remaining deadlocked in confrontation.

This fluid situation among unions, reflecting changes in both workers and their unions, has greatly influenced labor's political activities. The Socialists, supported by Sōhyō, lost the past two national elections of members of the lower and upper houses of the Diet, while the Democratic Socialists, supported by Dōmei, the Communists, and Kōmeitō increased the number of seats they held in the Diet. This Socialist loss could be attributed to the decrease in Sōhyō-union support of the party, among other factors. Many unions, from left to right, oppose the Sōhyō unions' resolutions for exclusive support of the Japan Socialist Party, and some of them have even refused their support. As already mentioned, young workers are not interested in the Socialist ideological program and do not follow the leaders' directions in voting.

Neither the Socialist nor the Sōhyō leaders, nor their activist followers, are yet able to grasp this change in behavior among the younger generation. At the same time, the Japan Socialist Party has taken so much for granted the support of the Sōhyō and Chūritsurōren unions that they have neglected to adjust their policies and activities to keep pace with the rapid changes in plants and firms—and in the minds of people—while the other political parties have responded to social change by making the necessary adjustments.

Changes in the positions of unions with regard to political parties will surely have an effect on Sōhyō and its affiliated unions as well as on the labor movement. Unless these unions are reorganized and consolidated into a unified organization, they can never expect to see the Socialists or their allies gain the majority of seats in the Diet necessary to take over the responsibility of the government. Sōka Gakkai has announced plans to organize its own unions even though its programs are not yet clear. While the effect of this policy cannot be discussed here, it surely will reduce the power of unions supporting political parties. Many unions may choose to support Kōmeitō as a reform party; one of the largest steel unions already has so chosen. All of these factors indicate that labor's political front has become quite fluid; and, as parties supported by labor increase in diversity, the conservative Liberal-Democratic Party will have the advantage until some unification is achieved among unions and reform parties.

The "internationalization period" is a very popular term in Japan. In line with this trend, labor also has increased its international activities, East and West, North and South. A majority of unions support the ICFTU and particularly its industrial federations. The best example is the IMF-JC. But they also are trying to maintain friendly relations with unions in socialist countries and with WFTU-affiliated unions. Even the anticommunist Dōmei approved a visit by a leader of one of its affiliated unions to the Soviet Union to attend a union convention.

The interest of Japanese unions in their counterparts in Asia and Africa is increasing as they respond to the expectation that Japan, as the sole industrialized nation in the area, should assume a leading role in those countries. Many labor union conferences and seminars have been held. Japanese unions are expected to carry out their part in technical training, which is urgently needed in these countries for industrialization. If they are able to maintain and to expand their international activities, they are assured of being able to develop their democratic practices in industry as well as in their nation.

8. Collective Bargaining

The Context

For the most part, collective bargaining as a rule-making procedure has developed in Japan only since World War II, and it therefore has a history of barely more than twenty-five years. Before the war the labor movement was extremely weak and unstable, as it faced government and employers' policies designed to suppress unions. In these circumstances collective bargaining generally served only to secure recognition for a union and seldom functioned as a method of determining employment conditions. An exception was the All-Japan Seamen's Union, or Kaiin, which was quite successful in developing industrywide bargaining. After the war, the labor movement was unleashed and collective bargaining was established as a constitutional right. However, with few exceptions, it was a completely new experience for both workers and employers.

The concept of collective bargaining was quite different from the traditional attitudes, values, and customs that governed relations between Japanese workers and employers. The notions that workers, through their unions, were to be regarded as the equals of their employers in negotiations and that the price of labor should be determined jointly through union-management bargaining were psychologically alien to both. The traditional Japanese employer-employee relationship was not a contractual one between free and independent citizens but rather a relationship between master and servant or between family head and his dependents. Thus it was a status relationship of control and subordination. Employment conditions were decided for the most part by arbitrary decisions of the employer; they were not bargainable or negotiable. Collective bargaining between union and employer to determine employment conditions meant a radical change in traditional industrial relations and challenged long-established management authority. Individual workers who were unable to rid themselves of the traditional feelings of subordination found it virtually impossible to accept this challenge.

For example, grievance procedures are provided for in many labor contracts but, although they tend to be increasingly used, they seldom work well, for a number of reasons: the idea and consciousness of job property rights are lacking in Japan; provisions on job content, promotion, demotion, and transfer in the labor contract or agreement are very ambiguous; and most grievances are not arbitrable. Essentially, grievance procedures are ineffective because the Japanese worker finds it very difficult to demand satisfaction of his personal wants and to interact with his employer on an individual basis. He often can confront the employer only as a member of a group.

Thus, collective bargaining usually has been conducted only when a confrontation has developed between union and employer, and collective bargaining, in turn, aggravates the tension. In this sense, collective bargaining is a form of "industrial conflict" and is not clearly separable from other forms of conflict. It becomes one of the few ways to present workers' demands or dissatisfactions and to secure employer compliance with the labor agreement. At the same time, it is a means by which the union obtains employer concessions through group pressure rather than through negotiating peacefully toward the goal of "give-and-take" or compromise. As a result, collective bargaining in Japan has been characterized by confrontation by and through force rather than by discussion and negotiation.

This characteristic was typical during the three- or four-year period immediately after the war when the labor movement took the form of a radical, revolutionary movement against the existing political, economic, and social order. In the labor offensive then led by Sanbetsu, or the All-Japan Congress of Industrial Unions Organizations, which was controlled by the Japan Communist Party, collective bargaining developed as part of the struggle against management and the government and became one of the tactics used in efforts to force workers' demands upon them, sometimes with threats of violence by masses of employees. At times revolutionary unionists, in the name of collective bargaining, crowded around the employer in a "people's court" and accused him of "crimes;" physical violence often was the result. More frequently, however, the union would send as many representatives as possible to the negotiating table. The bargaining committee members wore red bands around their heads as a symbol of their determination to wage a struggle, while union members shouted labor songs in a mass demonstration outside the bargaining room. Some of these practices are still popular today.

In the twenty-five years since the war, union and management have accumulated collective bargaining experience and have become familiar with bargaining practices. As a result, most of the early features of collective bargaining have disappeared, and bargaining has become more businesslike. At least in large-scale industry, where union organization has stabilized and employers have genuinely accepted collective bargaining, the aggressive practices that characterized the early postwar period have gradually disappeared. However, even now, in large-scale industry, if an intense situation such as massive displacement develops, or if a union split occurs, collective bargaining tends to be bitterly antagonistic. In small and medium-sized industry, where modern industrial relations with solidly established union organizations have not yet matured, the violent form of collective bargaining is not unusual.

The Distinction between Collective Bargaining and Strikes

Because collective bargaining in Japan is a form of confrontation, there is a unique relationship between bargaining and strikes.

A strike often breaks out during negotiations. For example, in the annual Spring Labor Offensive for wage increases, the union usually decides its strike schedule at the same time it formulates demands. These plans are drawn up by the executive committee of the union and decided by the convention, the central committee, or other union decision-making bodies, or by a direct referendum of union members. Commonly, a scheduled strike occurs during the bargaining process and is intended to improve or hasten the employer's response to the union's demands and to force concessions. It is usually brief and more of a demonstration than a work stoppage. It is common practice for the employer not to negotiate seriously unless the union takes some kind of action.

Therefore, most strikes in Japan are not the result of a deadlock in bargaining or failure to reach agreement but are a means for the union to bring about serious and bona fide collective bargaining. In this sense, a demonstration strike is often the preparatory stage for bargaining; it is held for a short, prescheduled time, such as one or two hours, a half-day, or a day, and it serves to rally the union members and to convince the employer of the union's determination. The strike is a more dramatic form of expressing the membership's determination in the struggle than alternative devices such as displaying banners, arm bands, and signs calling for worker solidarity or full acceptance of the union's demands. The duration of a strike, twenty-four or forty-eight hours or even an unlimited period, usually depends on the degree to which the employer makes concessions and on the union's power and organizational stability. In most cases, the employer tends to approach the union's demands gradually, paying attention to the union's power and the conditions offered by other companies or in other industries. At the initial stage of bargaining the positions of union and management are far apart, and there seems to be little possibility for proposals and counterproposals to develop into workable negotiations. The union typically makes demands it knows to be unrealistic, and the employer responds in terms he knows are unacceptable. Thus, it is power rather than reason that often dominates collective bargaining in Japan. The process can be better understood by detailed reference to the stages of development in a typical case.

Stage I

In preparation for the Spring Labor Offensive of 1966, the central committee of a national industrial federation of unions in the shipbuilding industry decided on the following wage demands at their meetings on February 22, 23, and 24: (1) a uniform wage increase of ¥5,000 per month, not including the periodic wage increment scheduled annually under the established age and length-of-service wage formulas; (2) an industrywide minimum monthly wage of ¥17,000 for 15-year-olds; (3) a 39-hour work week (7 hours a day Monday to Friday plus 4 hours on Saturday); and (4) extension of the retirement age from 55 to 57.

On March 10 the member unions presented these demands to their respective employers, asking for a reply by March 22. In the meantime, the member unions were requested to grant to the leadership of the industrial federation by April 1 the right to order a strike and also to end it. The member unions gave their approval.

Stage II

The respective employers refused to answer the union demands in specific terms on March 22. The unions then held workshop meetings protesting the employers' refusal and adopted the tactic of refusing overtime work. The federation also decided to strike for a half-day on April 16 and to continue to refuse overtime work on and after April 17. Beginning on April 11, the various employers made separate offers, ranging from ¥1,000 to ¥1,500, excluding the periodic regular increase. As these offers were far below the original demands of the unions, the federation ordered a full 24-hour strike to be held sometime between April 20 and 23, followed by repeated short, partial strikes to last no longer than 1 hour each.

Stage III

For the last development in these negotiations, let us examine the case of Company B of the joint employer group. Having refused the proposal of Company B, the enterprise union struck for 36 hours on April 22 and again for 24 hours on April 26. In the meantime, negotiations continued. On April 29, the employer proposed an increase of ¥3,150, including the periodic increase. This, too, was rejected by the enterprise union, which struck for 36 hours on May 2. When no further agreement was reached, the enterprise union conducted a "partial" strike on May 7 in which only a portion of the membership participated. This was followed by an 18-hour strike, in which all members participated, and later by a series of partial strikes.

In the meantime, Company A proposed an increase of ¥3,200, the largest offer thus far made, and its enterprise union accepted. The federation and the enterprise union in Company B were then in a difficult position. As the enterprise union in Company A broke away from the federation's united policy and action, the federation resolved to stay with a demand for more than ¥3,200. However, since Company A was one of the most influential employers in the industry, the settlement negotiated there tended to place a ceiling on the negotiations at other companies. Therefore, the federation permitted the other unions to reduce their wage increase demand from the original ¥5,000 to ¥3,500, including the periodic increase. Finally, the enterprise union in Company B accepted the employer's offer of ¥3,500, including the periodic increase. The dispute ended on May 14.

Enterprise-Level Bargaining

Collective bargaining in Japan tends to consist of negotiations between representatives of the employer and of his employees within the more or less closed community of the enterprise rather than between autonomous and independent bodies designated as union and management negotiators. It is a procedure of confrontation, accommodation, and reconciliation. The process involves an increase in tension leading to a break in the familial ties between the employer and the employees within a particular enterprise and leaves a scar in the subsequent healing. The employer is inclined to confine collective bargaining within the enterprise and is reluctant to permit "outsiders" or "strangers" to become involved. The enterprise union shares the employer's attitude in most cases, though it seemingly advocates industrywide bargaining.

These attitudes explain, in part, why joint consultation systems are easily established in Japanese enterprises. In contrast to the situation in Western countries, where the labor union is usually formed outside the enterprise, in Japan employee representatives who participate in the joint consultation system are almost always union officials who at the same time are employees of the company. For this reason, the boundary between joint consultation and collective bargaining is generally indistinct, and it is not unusual for joint consultation to precede collective bargaining or to serve as an alternative to it. In most cases, the same items are discussed in both systems, and if an agreement is not reached in the joint consultation process, the issue is referred to collective bargaining. One difference is, however, that there are no strikes during the joint consultation process.

Joint consultation serves as an information and communication channel between the employer and employees and as an effective instrument in the search for mutual understanding and cooperation at the enterprise level. Management can explain to the union details of its policies, the production schedule, and the firm's financial situation. Because it speaks to the enterprise union as an "inside" organization, it generally refuses labor-management consultation at the industrial level since this would involve "outsiders."

As long as labor-management tensions and disputes are dealt with inside the community formed by a particular enterprise, the two parties can reach mutual understanding and establish a cooperative relationship. If an outside union is involved in the process of collective bargaining at the enterprise level, the implicit trust, which sometimes amounts to collusion, between the employer and the employees is disrupted. The employers try to avoid allowing outsiders to take part in internal negotiations, both because they would lose face and because the collective bargaining process would then become more complicated.

The Role of Employers' Organizations Policies

Since collective bargaining tends to be confined within the enterprise in Japan, employers' organizations are rarely involved directly in the bargaining process. Only in an exceptional case will employer organizations accede to the demands of strong national unions for industrywide bargaining. In some cases they have been forced to do so by the labor relations commissions. The structure of employers' organizations varies by type of industry, and in general an employers' organization is not designed to deal with labor-management relations problems as such. It may become concerned with labor relations in order to respond to the integrated movement of labor unions, but as a rule such organizations are reluctant to become bargaining agents, though they often exchange information or consult informally about wages and other matters. In this context, the policy of the Japan employers' associations has been support for bargaining only within enterprises. They approve of joint consultation within the enterprise and disapprove of any form of collective relations at the industry level. In coping with the annual Spring Labor Offensive, which will be discussed later, Nikkeiren, the Japan Federation of Employers' Associations, has advocated employer solidarity against the integrated labor union movement, but this position does not contradict its determined policy to confine collective bargaining within enterprises.

The Demand for Standardization and Intra-enterprise Collective Bargaining

One of the most important reasons collective bargaining tends to be confined within single enterprises is that the features of wages, welfare programs, and other basic employment conditions are peculiar to each enterprise. Thus, since the workers' basic solidarity rests on common interest "inside the enterprise" to which the employees belong, the union of employees in an enterprise has become the basic unit of labor organization and holds the most important position in the power structure of labor unions in Japan.

It does not follow, however, that collective bargaining confined within an enterprise actually indicates that either the practice of determining employment conditions or the conditions themselves are totally different and independent from those within other enterprises. As detailed in Chapter 10, unions and managements in most cases consider the "prevailing price" when concluding their own agreements. From the standpoint of the union, it is possible to satisfy its members by guaranteeing the prevailing wage or its equivalent among competitive firms in the same industry.

Since employers and employees within an enterprise are considered close-knit members of the same community, organizations at levels higher than the enterprise are of secondary importance to them. On the other hand, as in other social situations in Japan, deviations from the pattern followed by the social group to which others of the same status belong are considered undesirable. Thus, in the case of collective bargaining, it is considered irresponsible for an employer to give his employees a wage increase well above the prevailing level. It is also regrettable if he decides on a wage lower than the prevailing level.

In this way unions and managements actually tend neither to proceed autonomously in wage negotiations nor to settle without regard to situations in other companies. They tend to enter into serious bargaining by carefully comparing their own situation with developments or results of bargaining in rival companies in the same product market or similar companies in other industries. This tendency has become more explicit with the increase during the last decade of industrywide coordination in the Spring Labor Offensive negotiations.

In this situation, it is difficult for the upper levels of both union and management organizations to choose the union and the management that are to take the lead in setting the pattern or the initiative in determining the prevailing wage. (The pattern setter is also called the "top batter" in Japan.) Difficulty arises since it is necessary for the pattern setter to endure a strike and to make other sacrifices and to assume the "social responsibility" for effectively setting the framework for negotiations in other industries or rival companies. Naturally, both unions and managements are reluctant to play such a role. Hence, they tend to seek the involvement of a third party, such as the Central Labor Relations Commission or the National Enterprise and Public Corporation Labor Relations Commission. In this case the role of the third party becomes very important, since it often is the one that eventually sets the prevailing wage, thus relieving the union and management of this "responsibility."[1]

Union Membership and the Coverage of Collective Bargaining

It should be noted that not all union members in Japan are covered by collective bargaining. A considerable number are legally excluded from or limited in their participation in collective bargaining for reasons discussed in Chapter 4. Since this matter relates to an evaluation of the role of collective bargaining in Japan as a decision-making mechanism, especially in the determination of wages, it is necessary to discuss it here in greater detail.

The first and foremost limitation on union members' participation in collective bargaining is determined by the legal framework of industrial relations in Japan's public sector. There are roughly four million workers directly or indirectly involved in wage determination awards of the National Personnel Authority (NPA) and the National Enterprise and Public Corporation Labor Relations Commission. These workers amount to about one-seventh of the

---

1. It should be noted that the heavy dependence of both parties on public machinery in the settlement of wage disputes has been decreasing since 1965. Particularly during the past several years, it has been the policy of both the Central Labor Relations Commission and the National Enterprise and Public Corporation Labor Relations Commission to follow the pattern set by collective bargaining in private industries, rather than trying to take the lead themselves. This has been the case at least for the Spring Labor Offensives from 1965 to 1968, when the unions in public corporations and government enterprises have been not pattern-setters but pattern-followers. Although many factors have contributed to this tendency, the most important is the continuing prosperity of the private industries which has enabled them to be "generous" in meeting unions' demands. If the economic situation were to worsen, the public dispute settlement machinery would probably be used to set patterns.

total number of wage and salary earners in Japan. About three million of these public employees are organized, comprising 30 percent of all organized labor in Japan. Sōhyō, the General Council of Trade Unions of Japan, has organized the majority of these workers and is often criticized for its tendency toward political activities. However, as the political struggles of these unions may be seen as a substitute for their restricted economic struggles, it is necessary to discuss them as a decision-making mechanism, especially in the determination of wages.

The proportion of unionized national and local civil servants is relatively large, constituting 17.3 percent of all organized labor in Japan as of 1966. These civil servants have no legal right to bargain over contracts or to strike, and, if they attempt to do either, they are subject to disciplinary measures by the authority in question, including suspension and discharge.

Their union activities are also heavily restricted by law. Thus, their unions can neither bargain over wages, other employment conditions, and personnel problems nor take other forms of collective action. Therefore, the National Personnel Authority for national public service personnel and the local personnel commissions for local public service employees play the crucial role in wage adjustments. If the NPA finds in its Survey of Wage Conditions in Private Industry that wage levels in the private sector exceed those in the public sector by 5 percent or more, it recommends wage adjustments to the Diet and the Cabinet. Such a recommendation becomes effective only when the law regulating wages for central government public employees is revised and the necessary budgetary arrangements are made. It is, of course, the decision of the government and the Diet whether or not the wage adjustment is put into effect. If it is, the wages of local public employees are automatically adjusted through the local personnel commissions. The adjustment is also applied or used as a reference for employees in semipublic corporations, special corporations, affiliates of the government offices, private hospitals, and private schools.[2]

2. Semipublic corporations and affiliates of government offices are organizations founded by the government mainly for social investment: for example, housing, highway construction, scholarships for higher education, vocational training, etc. There are

Thus, although the NPA's role in wage determination is quite important, it can only offer recommendations, and the actual decision making is in the hands of the government. In fact, since 1949 NPA recommendations have never been accepted and put into effect unchanged. Often, adjustments have been delayed or postponed for months beyond the date recommended for implementation.

Public employees' unions have opposed the method used by the NPA in making the private sector wage level survey, and they have also opposed the specific content of NPA recommendations as well as the government's failure to accept NPA recommendations without change.[3] Their opposition, however, has been limited to merely demonstrative action. They have been unable to create a situation in which they can have a voice in or take part in wage determination through collective bargaining.

As stated in Chapter 7, the proportion of organized workers in national and local government enterprises and public corporations, aside from civil servants, was 11.4 percent of all organized labor in Japan as of 1966. Under special labor relations laws, these public enterprise workers have the right to bargain collectively, but they do not have the right to strike. Actually, however, they frequently engage in brief work stoppages and slowdowns. As these activities are illegal, union officials who order them or who agitate for them and the union members who take part are punished by discharge, transfer, wage reductions, suspension of wage increases, reprimands, and in other ways.

In spite of the prohibition, the National Railway Workers' Union (Kokurō), the National Railway Locomotive Engineers' Union (Dōryokusha), the Japan Postal Workers' Union (Zentei), the All-Japan Telecommunication Workers' Union (Zendentsū),

---

also public corporations (*kōdan* or *kōsha*) financed by national or local governments but not covered by the Public Corporation Labor Relations Law, since strikes in these corporations would not affect society to any significant degree. The NPA recommendation is used as a "standard" not only in these public corporations but also in private ones such as universities and hospitals where the bargaining power of unions generally is weak.

3. Unions do not oppose the *use* of the private sector wage survey. Their complaint is that the survey includes medium-sized and small enterprises as well as large ones, and they demand that the wage comparison should cover only wages paid by firms with more than 500 or 1,000 employees.

and other major unions have frequently struck, but each time they have done so they have received "mass punishment," In each instance, the unions have had to pay out a great deal in relief funds to those members who were punished. A relief fund differs from a strike fund in that it is usually designed to compensate workers for earnings lost during the strike; it covers wages and allowances that punished members otherwise could have received had they continued their employment. Because such union payments are large, the financial cost to the union tends to be a restraining factor in mounting illegal strikes.

Another factor impinges on the functional effectiveness of unions in the public corporations—the fact that the other bargaining party, the public corporation, cannot make a responsible decision in negotiations over employment conditions, much less implement a decision, since it is tightly controlled by government budgeting and financing. In this sense, collective bargaining in the public sector has little substance.

For this reason, both union and management in national enterprises and public corporations must depend on the National Enterprise and Public Corporation Labor Relations Commission for the solution of their disputes. As in the case of the NPA for public service employers, awards of the commission do not become effective until first the government and then the Diet approve the necessary financial arrangements. It is only since 1957 that the government has officially adopted a policy of fully respecting commission awards. Until that year, the Diet often refused to effectuate them.

Under these circumstances, wage adjustment for public employees becomes a process involving highly political questions rather than a process of economic bargaining. As cases in point, the publicly owned corporations in the public transportation and communication industries are virtual monopolies and are public utilities which directly affect the daily lives of the people.[4] Wage

4. The reason unions in the publicly owned transportation and communication enterprises do not have the right to strike although unions in the private sector have that right is not so much a matter of principle as it is a matter of politics. At the time General MacArthur issued the SCAP order depriving civil servants of the rights to bargain collectively and to strike, in his letter of July 22, 1948, to the prime minister, the employees of the national railways, post and telecommunications, and tobacco

adjustment here involves control of utility prices, budgets, and finances by the Diet and local governments. These public corporations are relatively free, at least thus far, from domestic and international competition and business fluctuations, and the prices for their services are determined by political processes rather than by the market economy. For example, wages are not set by pure economic calculations as part of the cost of the service; rather they are politically determined with little consideration given to a balanced relationship of wage costs to corporation profits. In other words, the constantly fluctuating market factors have little to do with wage decisions. Unions and managements in public corporations share an interest in raising service prices under government control, and therefore there is a possibility that they may engage in collusion in the struggle for wage increases. More often than not, the unions in this sector wage "political struggles" against the government in order to push their demands, which could hardly be met through their restricted bargaining.

As strikes in industries such as national railways, postal services, and telecommunications affect not only economic activities but also the daily lives of the people, social and political pressures are brought to bear in order to settle disputes in these industries as quickly as possible. Thus the need for public labor relations commissions to intervene as a third party is underlined. In these industries also, wage determination is political in nature, having little to do with the balance of economic bargaining power of union and management.

---

monopolies held the status of civil servants employed by the government. Later, the national railways and tobacco monopolies, and eventually the telecommunication services as well, were reorganized into public corporations and their employees were no longer classified as civil servants. Their right to strike, however, still was prohibited. Had it been otherwise, the aim of SCAP's political maneuver, that is, to ban strike activities by the strong, leftist-led unions in these enterprises, would not have been accomplished. This special restriction on employees of public corporations was applied later to employees of other government enterprises, such as the post office, national forestry, and mint. However, it would be difficult to extend the restriction to private industries because the right to strike is one of labor's basic rights guaranteed by the constitution, and there has been no adequate justification for a restriction on this constitutional right of workers in the private sector. Strikes by the private railway workers' unions are certainly a public nuisance, but they have never been of a magnitude and duration to constitute enough of a threat to public welfare to warrant further government restriction.

The restrictions and limitations on bargaining also pertain to private utilities such as the private railway, electric power, gas and water supply, medical and hospital service, and shipping industries. Private railways are monopolies in local areas, providing indispensable service to commuters into and out of the large cities. Their importance has been growing with rapid urbanization, crowded housing conditions, and difficult traffic problems. Supply and demand for their service are inelastic and relatively free from business fluctuations; their fares therefore are controlled by the government in the same way as are the fares of national enterprises and public corporations. The social impact of a strike in the private railway industry is so great as to require settlement as quickly as possible, and for this reason, the Central Labor Relations Commission (CLRC), the national adjustment board for private industries, tends to intervene in an effort to effect a settlement of a dispute.[5]

What this means is that, although until recently autonomous union-management collective bargaining has not worked very well in wage determination in the private railway industry, wage settlements, usually reached after a CLRC award, have indirectly but strongly influenced collective bargaining in other private industries.

The second, but no less important, limitation on union members' participation in collective bargaining pertains to the large number of small, independent enterprise unions that exist in small and medium-sized industries. As of 1966 there were approximately 17,000 unions with memberships of less than one hundred each, with an aggregate membership of about 720,000 workers. It is highly doubtful whether these small enterprise unions are able to function as bargaining agents for their members since, as a rule, they lack adequate power and leadership to carry on bargaining effectively. The aforementioned attitude of Japanese employers in general, that is, fear of and hostility toward collective bargaining, and the workers' traditional consciousness of subordination

5. In the Spring Labor Offensive of 1966, union and management refused an award of the commission and finally reached agreement through negotiations. In this case, however, the agreement was based essentially on the previously rejected award of the commission.

nurtured in the long-established master-servant relationship are particularly strong in the small and medium-sized industries. Under such circumstances the majority of these small enterprise unions tend to exist only nominally, without fulfilling their bargaining role. The situation may be different if a small enterprise union is an affiliate of some parent body, either regional or industrial. As a matter of fact, however, most are not in a position to resist or overcome their employers' hostility to such affiliation, which the employers feel would result in the possible intrusion of "outsiders" into the employer-employee relationship within the enterprise.

Collective Bargaining and the Collective Agreement

Collective bargaining in Japan is not necessarily a negotiation over the terms of a written agreement since a formal labor contract does not always result. It often ends with only an implicit understanding between union and management, partly because some unions are not yet familiar with the concept and practice of contract negotiation, and partly because some managements strongly resist committing themselves to a written contract, though they may recognize the union. This situation appears to be more conspicuous among small and medium-sized firms than among large companies. In order to conclude a collective agreement in written form, it is necessary for the union to become strong enough to convince management of its power. In other words, the existence of a collective agreement tends to be an approximate index of the degree to which collective bargaining actually works.

Since not all Japanese labor unions have contracts, the number of workers covered by contracts is actually less than the number of union members. In the United States the situation is reversed, since collective agreements are often applied to a firm's nonunion employees as well as to union members.

As discussed above, public employees' unions cannot conclude collective agreements. Table 8.1 shows the proportion of eligible

Table 8.1
Unit Unions and the Conclusion of Collective Agreements

Year	Unions Legally Eligible to Conclude Collective Agreements		Unions with Collective Agreements			
	Number of Unions	Number of Union Members	Number of Unions	Rate of Conclusion[a]	Number of Unions	Rate of Application[b]
1955	24,929	4,860,368	16,182	64.9%	3,797,573	78.1%
1956	26,851	5,000,591	17,095	63.7%	3,856,436	77.1%
1957	28,634	5,205,066	18,370	64.2%	4,042,317	77.7%
1958	30,006	5,419,084	19,302	64.3%	4,231,965	78.1%
1959	31,091	5,585,710	16,843	63.8%	4,347,178	77.8%
1960	32,994	5,992,654	20,947	63.5%	4,658,239	77.7%
1961	36,295	6,568,405	22,859	63.0%	5,105,956	77.7%
1962	39,034	7,156,699	24,303	62.3%	5,532,748	77.3%
1963	41,317	7,585,653	25,937	62.8%	5,873,870	77.4%
1964	43,023	7,906,026	27,849	64.7%	6,271,606	79.3%
1965	44,462	8,293,757	29,135	65.5%	6,594,324	79.5%
1966	45,503	8,501,101	31,603	69.5%	6,975,759	82.1%
1967	46,948	8,721,742	33,708	71.8%	7,281,723	83.5%
1968	48,323	9,015,961	35,291	73.0%	7,581,063	84.2%

Source: Ministry of Labor, *Rōdō kumiai kihonchōsa hōkoku* [Basic survey report on labor unions] (Tokyo, published annually).

a.   Rate of conclusion = $\dfrac{\text{no. of unions with collective agreements}}{\text{no. of unions legally eligible to conclude collective agreements}} \times 100$

b.   Rate of application = $\dfrac{\text{no. of members of unions with collective agreements}}{\text{no. of members of unions legally eligible to conclude collective agreements}} \times 100$

Table 8.2
Rate of Conclusion and Application of Collective Agreements by Size of Union.

Number of Union Members	Single-Entity Labor Unions[a]							
	Rate of Conclusion[b]				Rate of Application[b]			
	1963	1964	1965	1968	1963	1964	1965	1968
1,000 persons and over	80.8	82.2	82.3	85.5	76.1	77.9	77.6	81.6
500–900 persons	75.4	77.3	76.8	80.4	75.7	77.7	77.5	80.9
300–499 persons	67.7	71.1	71.9	76.1	68.3	71.3	72.3	76.6
100–299 persons	58.6	60.8	60.6	70.4	60.7	62.4	61.8	71.4
30–99 persons	44.7	48.6	49.7	60.3	45.9	50.0	51.2	61.3
Fewer than 30 persons	34.6	36.6	38.0	48.2	36.5	38.9	40.5	51.0
Total	49.3	52.1	53.0	62.5	71.6	73.6	73.7	78.6

SOURCE: Ministry of Labor, *Rōdō kumiai kihonchōsa hōkoku* [Basic survey on labor unions].
a. *Tanitsu kumiai*; see Chapter 7, p. 229, for a discussion of this form.
b. For explanation, see notes to Table 8.1, above.

unions and union members actually covered by labor contracts and indicates that the proportion has been increasing steadily over the past several years. Table 8.2 shows the proportion by number of union members and type of union; it implies that, the larger the union, the greater the possibility that it has concluded a labor contract covering its membership.

The subject matter of collective bargaining in Japan is quite flexible. What is bargainable and what is an exclusive management prerogative are major issues between union and management and tend to be affected by the general political and economic climate and the balance of power between the parties, including government.

As collective bargaining is accepted by union and management as a practice regulating the relations between them and as it develops into an established institutional practice, order appears in the subject matter of the bargaining.

Immediately after World War II, unions fought not only for economic demands, such as substantial wage increases, but also over such major noneconomic issues as union recognition, freedom of union activities, and guarantee of the union's right to strike. Furthermore, they demanded displacement of top management and other supervisors unfavorable to the union and other reforms in management organization, all in the name of "management democratization." They also made political demands, such as the overthrow of the Yoshida Cabinet, which individual employers could hardly meet.

Since about 1950, however, a more normal and practical pattern of collective bargaining has developed. By that year the communists were rapidly losing their foothold in the labor movement, and more moderate and democratic leadership had taken over, a development encouraged by SCAP and the Japanese government. Management utilized this opportunity to revitalize its prerogatives in labor relations and turned its attention to efforts to roll back the labor offensive.

During the period of rapid economic growth since 1955, unions have increasingly emphasized economic rather than political activities. The bargaining issues have tended to be such economic problems as wages, working hours, size of work force, welfare facilities, and safety and health. Furthermore, the national labor centers and national industrial federations of unions have made efforts to develop standardized conditions among affiliated unions by pushing for uniform basic employment standards for wages, working hours, retirement age, retirement allowance, and paid vacations. In the case of the maritime industry, where industrywide bargaining is most fully developed, enterprise pension funds have been pooled to integrate their administration on an industrial basis.

Characteristics of Collective Agreements in Japan

Reflecting the structure of unions and the scope of bargaining, the overwhelming majority of collective agreements are negotiated between an individual enterprise and its enterprise union. It is very rare for a national union to become a party to a collective agreement. Most written agreements provide exclusive bargaining rights for the enterprise union, a provision which, from the standpoint of the union, could serve to discourage the formation of "second" or rival unions. Actually, however, it serves to permit the employer to exclude "outsiders," such as the national union, from the bargaining situation.

The content of a labor contract can be divided into two parts. One is concerned with the labor union as a party to the contract and covers union recognition, membership eligibility, union security, union officers, union activities, collective bargaining, procedures for calling and terminating strikes, and so forth. In effect, the provisions prescribe and define the status of the union as an organization. The other part incorporates the provisions covering working hours and employment conditions of workers in general. It is characteristic of the Japanese labor contract that the first part is spelled out in detail, but the latter part is ill-defined and lacks specification.

There are many reasons for this disparity. It may be viewed as consistent with a general emphasis upon status relations in all aspects of Japanese society, an observation often made by foreign scholars. Indeed, it may be said that workers' interest in defining precisely the content of the job and the corresponding compensation may not be as strong or as well developed in Japan as in Western countries whether on an individual or a collective basis. The reason for this may become clear later through a detailed discussion of wage negotiations.

Job security is one of the most important concerns of Japanese workers, but "job" here does not necessarily mean a specific job, that is, work which requires specific skills, knowledge, and experience, and which corresponds exactly to fixed compensation for that work. Rather, it means the worker's state of being employed by a particular company. The status of being an employee of the company guarantees the Japanese worker various rewards according to his educational background, length of service, occupational position, and the actual work he may do. If he loses status as an employee, he suffers serious economic damage.

Therefore, what the Japanese worker expects most from his union is employment security in the company and control of the employer's otherwise arbitrary power which may affect his employment security. Of course, he expects his union to work for improvements in his employment conditions, especially his wages, working hours, and welfare facilities, but he is most concerned with employment security. The overwhelming importance of employment security to workers is the reason Japanese labor unions carry on protracted and bitter strikes against reduction of work forces or massive displacements, while strikes for wages are generally of short duration. Transfer of workers is also a bargaining issue, but since transfer guarantees continuous employment of the worker in the company it seldom becomes a bitter issue in dispute.

Thus, union recognition and security issues constitute the major part of the labor contract because of the union's deep concern with the employer's policy and attitude vis-à-vis unionization of his workers. Many labor contracts also include provisions specifying rights already guaranteed by the Trade Union Law. Such contract provisions are designed to confirm the employer's bona fide commitment to union recognition.[6]

6. This may not be unique to the Japanese labor contract. A major goal or dominant note in American industrial relations in the 1930's was union recognition. It

What is most characteristic of the Japanese labor contract is that provisions relating to the status of the union as an organization—union security, membership eligibility, union officers, and so forth—are intended primarily to maintain the framework of the enterprise union. Thus, the "union shop" clause is quite prevalent, as are provisions for check-off of union dues. Employers readily accept these provisions because the union is composed solely of permanent regular employees of the given enterprise.

Basic employment conditions, especially workers' wages, are not specified in detail in labor contracts, primarily because of the Japanese method of wage determination, the wage system, the composition of wages, and the rapid economic changes since World War II.

Since a labor contract is designed to confirm the respective status of union and management, it must be stable over a considerable period of time. However, the postwar period in which collective bargaining has developed in Japan has been one of turbulent economic development. It began with serious inflation after the war, followed by severe contraction, and then a business boom and recession during and after the Korean War. Since 1955, the economy has experienced continued rapid growth, although with occasional recessions, rising prices, and changing consumption patterns, especially during the 1960s. Under these conditions, both unions and management have been cautious about committing themselves to fixed wage agreements over long periods, preferring to retain maximum flexibility. Thus, the duration of a wage agreement in Japan is generally only one year, and it usually takes the form of a separate memorandum, rather than being part of the labor contract.

As noted earlier, management frequently is reluctant to make the wage agreement explicit and to write out the provisions in a formal way for fear of limiting its discretionary latitude to decide the wages of individual workers. This is particularly the case where unions are not powerful enough to force the management to change its attitude toward wage contracts. In addition, there are some cases where union and management agree not to make

should be remembered that it has been only a short time since labor relations based on labor unions became an institution in Japanese society.

a fully detailed wage agreement lest "outsiders," that is, parent organizations on both sides or controlling authorities, discover the actual content of the agreement. This practice often occurs in plants of multiplant corporations or in public corporations where wage disputes are resolved through an implicit understanding between the union and the management at the plant level. Here the management may be in a position to utilize some additional monetary resources to grant wage increases higher than those agreed upon at the corporation level. However, the most important factor accounting for the general absence of minutely specific wage agreements in Japan is the unique feature of "collectively negotiated wages."

Characteristics of Wage Negotiations

To what extent collective bargaining actually determines wages and what portion of the wage composite it determines are difficult questions. As described in detail in Chapter 10, in Japan there is almost no equivalent of Western wage rates by job or skill, except in such industries as construction, stevedoring, taxi driving, and the like, and for certain categories of workers such as temporary or part-time. In the total wage or salary of a worker, the main component is the so-called basic pay, determined by a combination of factors, such as his educational background, age, years of service, occupational experience, sex, and work performance. The way of combining these factors is highly particular to a specific firm and, of course, is also particular to the personal attributes of the individual employee. What is publicly known about a worker's wage is only his starting pay in the company and the average annual or periodic increment. In applying the annual or periodic increment to individual employees, the employer often uses a personal rating or performance evaluation system.[7]

Under these circumstances, union wage bargaining is not

7. See Chapter 10. See also Shōjirō Ujihara, "Nihon no chingin kettei" [Wage determination in Japan], in *Nihon no rōshi kankei* [Industrial relations in Japan], (Tokyo: University of Tokyo Press, 1961), pt. 2, pp. 211–30.

negotiation over the wage or job rates, as in Western countries, but is instead concerned with the starting wage and the so-called average amount of wage of all employees in a particular enterprise. This average, or "base wage," is calculated by dividing the enterprise's total wage bill by the number of employees. Any increase in this base wage is called a "base-up." In this context, a wage negotiation has two aspects: the amount of the base-up, and the principle to be followed in distributing among individual employees whatever amount is agreed upon.

The primary concern of the union is the amount of the base-up, that is, the total amount of funds to be applied to the wage increase. When this amount is determined, it does not mean that the wage rates of individual employees in the company have also been determined. There are certain principles and factors affecting the method of distributing the wage increment among individual employees, and these vary from company to company. Variations are due to differing wage components, differing proportions of the components in the total wage, and differing methods of determining each component in particular enterprises. Hence, the predominant form of collective bargaining on wages restricts the scope of the negotiation to the enterprise. If national industrial federations of unions have been able to do anything, it has been to standardize the size of base-ups among affiliated enterprise unions and to standardize the starting wage for new school graduates. As a rule, however, these upper-level union bodies cannot exercise any direct influence on intrafirm wage structures, wage payment systems, and the composition of factors that actually determine the wages of individual employees.

Coupled with the structural problem of the enterprise union, such a method of wage negotiation often causes internal union conflict among different groups of employees with different interests. White-collar employees, blue-collar workers, employees with different grades of skill and different educational backgrounds, and different age groups are all members of the single enterprise union, and as a rule they have no separate sectional representation or separate bargaining units. In this situation, the distribution of the average wage increment becomes a problem. Up to now the majority of union members have been blue-collar workers, and an egalitarian ideology has been dominant in the Japanese union movement. But recently, because of the tightening labor market situation and because technical changes have been occurring very rapidly, younger and skilled workers have been placed in a more favorable position than before. Consequently, the distribution of the wage fund has favored blue-collar workers, and wage differentials between blue- and white-collar workers have become narrower than in other industrialized countries. This development has produced increased discontent among white-collar workers, especially technical and professional employees who usually are college or university graduates. On the other hand, wage differentials by age have been narrowing among both blue- and white-collar workers, which also tends to create dissatisfaction on the part of employees in both the younger and the older age groups, although for opposite reasons. Such conflicts of interest among employee groups tend to weaken the union's solidarity and to encourage employers' "divide and rule" strategies.

To overcome or alleviate such difficulties, unions have been demanding flat-rate increases "plus;" that is, across-the-board increases plus a certain amount of money to be used to adjust the existing pattern of intra-firm wage differentials. Since employers are, in most cases, reluctant to apply the flat-rate increase, a part of the negotiated base-up fund is set aside to adjust the wage system and wage differentials in the enterprise.[8]

Structure and Types of Collective Bargaining

As elaborated in Chapter 6, the power structure of organized labor is highly decentralized, and the enterprise union or the enterprise federation of unions generally has almost untrammeled authority. Therefore, the most important level of collective bargaining is at the intra-enterprise level; that is, the shop, the plant, and the firm or corporation. Negotiations by industry and district

8. There is a statistical survey on the method of distributing the acquired wage increase fund. See Central Labor Relations Commission, "Chingin jijō chōsa" [Wage situation survey] *Chūō Rōdō Jihō*, no. 466 (Tokyo: Rōi Kyōkai, March 1968).

provide almost no alternatives to enterprise-level bargaining. However, the national or district federation of unions attempts in various degrees to coordinate enterprise bargaining on an industrial or district basis. The All-Japan Seamen's Union is the only national industrial union that has achieved the exclusive right to bargain collectively on an industry-wide basis.

A combination of factors determines the scope of bargaining as between the shop, the plant, and the firm or corporation level of a given enterprise. On the part of management, factors such as size of the firm, the locus of decision-making authority, management policies with respect to industrial relations, product market structure, and geographical areas in which the firm operates may all be important. In the case of a multiplant corporation, location of respective plants, product versatility, and differences in technology and profitability among the plants may also be significant. On the part of the enterprise union, its organizational structure, administrative machinery, and relationship with the national union or district federation, and the structure and integrity of the union leadership may determine the scope of its bargaining.

One characteristic of Japanese collective bargaining is that the structure of the levels in intra-enterprise bargaining not only tends to vary from enterprise to enterprise but also tends to shift or change within a given enterprise. In most cases the pattern is not stabilized. There seem to be two reasons for this instability. One, as mentioned earlier, is that provisions, particularly the procedural rules, for collective bargaining are not specifically defined or detailed in the labor contract. Another reason may be that the grievance machinery, if it exists, seldom works well, and it is difficult to determine whether labor disputes or problems should be settled in the process of bargaining over the terms of the agreement or dealt with through the grievance-handling procedure. In actuality, these problems are solved either by negotiating directly on an ad hoc basis or by the worker withdrawing his grievance. Since collective bargaining usually takes the form of a struggle, ad hoc negotiation at the shop level often becomes a workshop struggle which only militant unions and union members are able and willing to conduct.

Another factor that tends to make the intra-enterprise bargaining structure quite unstable is management policy. Management decision-making power over general industrial relations problems and basic employment conditions is apt to be centralized in the personnel or industrial relations department at the administrative headquarters, but the more concrete and specific problems that may arise from day to day in the workshop are usually handled at the shop level. Yet the distribution of power or authority in such minor decision making is still ambiguous and flexible. Foremen, for example, have functions and authority very different from their counterparts in the United States.[9] Generally speaking, if the union is militant at the shop level, the employer tends to shift decision-making power to the upper levels of management. If the union is weak and lacking in internal solidarity, the employer tends to move the decision-making power to lower levels of management and to make on-the-spot settlements if possible. Due to such management policies and to the tendency for union organization at the workshop level to be weak, collective bargaining is apt to shift from the shop level to the level of the plant or enterprise.

In single-plant enterprises, the structure of collective bargaining is obviously simple, but in a multiplant corporation the relationship between plant-level and corporation-level bargaining is complicated. As mentioned above, the bargaining level tends to be determined by the degree to which management decision-making power is centralized with regard to industrial relations problems and the degree to which decisions on employment conditions and union activities apply to the whole enterprise. Furthermore, the relationship between collective bargaining at the plant level and the enterprise level also depends on the extent to which the enterprisewide union federation maintains integrity and on the extent to which union authority or power is centralized in the enterprise federation rather than remaining at the level of the separate plants.

As a general trend, however, intra-enterprise bargaining more

9. The Japanese foreman, *shokuchō* or *kumichō*, usually is a member of the enterprise union, and he has no distinct function as an agent of management. In many cases, he is a spokesman for workers in the workshop, playing the role of go-between in union-management relations. See Chapter 11.

or less centers around the head office of management and the headquarters of the enterprise federation because basic employment conditions, such as starting rates, straight-time pay, annual or periodic increments, retirement age, health insurance, housing, pensions, retirement allowances, semi-annual seasonal bonuses, working hours, and paid holidays are uniformly applied to all employees in the enterprise.

Before World War II, the locus of decision-making power differed according to the employee's educational background and occupational status. For example, all employment conditions of clerical workers with university educations were decided by the head office, while those of clerical employees with only high school educations were determined by their respective plant managers. The employment conditions of manual workers with elementary school educations were determined by the foreman or the head of the workshop. This pattern of decision-making authority is still maintained to some extent, but for the most part it has disappeared, due primarily to (1) the unions' struggles to eliminate the status system, (2) the rising educational level of employees, (3) the formation of a more uniform national labor market, (4) the establishment of standards for starting wages and salaries, and (5) the growth of unified wage struggles by unions.

Bargaining at the level of the firm's head office and the enterprise federation deals with general principles on terms and conditions of employment rather than with those minute issues related directly to daily operations at the plant level. Wide latitude is left to the lower levels of management and union to apply these general criteria to separate plants or to individual employees. For example, employee rating systems administered by management play an important role in determining wage increments for each worker within a given plant, and this decision significantly affects the basic wage of individual workers. Furthermore, since incentive wage rates are based on group rather than individual performance, the method of deciding group incentive rates and of distributing earnings to individual employees is another negotiable item at the plant level. Work-load assignments, manpower allocations, overtime arrangements, transfers, promotions, and demotions of manual workers and lower clerical workers are also negotiated primarily on a plantwide basis. If the problems are not solved in plantwide negotiations, they move up to the enterprisewide level. This is also true for disputes over union activities.[10]

National and Industrywide Bargaining

Labor unions are increasingly becoming involved with national or district unions in collective bargaining because the involvement of the higher levels of union organization adds to the power of the lower unions, which are otherwise generally weak when divided into separate intra-enterprise units for bargaining. An example is the so-called united or group bargaining on an industrywide basis which has developed in the Spring Offensive wage drives. The involvement of upper organizations in collective bargaining may also increase the control and power of national unions over enterprise-level affiliates, but it does not necessarily mean the presence of national union representatives at the bargaining table. Instead, it can take the form of programming union demands or policy for intra-enterprise bargaining, coordinating the unions' industrial actions, strike or other, and controlling dates of agreement and agreed-upon terms. In this latter context, the role of central federations or industrial and national unions in intra-enterprise bargaining has significantly increased during the last decade.[11]

However, the range of enterprises covered in united or group bargaining varies. Since the decision to participate is voluntary, the structure and number of employer bargaining groups who may participate frequently changes.

Industrywide bargaining has long been established between the All-Japan Seamen's Union, or Kaiin, and four associations of shipping corporations. It is also prevalent between employers in

10. Kazuo Okochi et al., eds., *Rōdō kumiai no kōzō to kinō* [The structure and function of labor unions] (Tokyo: University of Tokyo Press, 1959).

11. Taishiro Shirai, "The Changing Pattern of Collective Bargaining in Japan," in *Changing Pattern of Industrial Relations: Proceedings of the International Conference on Industrial Relations* (Tokyo: Japan Institute of Labor, 1966).

the cotton textile, chemical fabric, and wool industries, and the corresponding departments of the Japan Federation of Textile Workers' Unions, or Zensendōmei; between the private railway employers' association and the General Federation of Private Railway Workers' Unions of Japan, or Shitetsusōren; employers in the coal-mining industry and the Japan Coal Miners' Union, or Tanrō; employers in the metal mining industry and the Federation of All-Japan Metal Mine Labor Unions, or Zenkō; and some employers in the synthetic chemical industry and the Japanese Federation of Synthetic Chemical Workers' Unions, or Gōkarōren.

Nevertheless, except for the seamen, the role of these higher-level union organizations in collective bargaining is still restricted and unstable, not only because of the hostile attitude of employers toward outsider involvement, but also because the enterprise unions themselves, and especially the enterprise federations of unions, tend to be very reluctant to involve outside unions. Their view is that the participation of higher-level union organizations may result in encroachment upon the sovereignty that they now enjoy. Such reluctance tends to be greatest in large enterprise unions which have abundant financial resources and are capable of being independent and self-governing.

Second, the industrial or national union cannot force affiliates to take part in the united struggles it organizes. There is no way it can discipline member unions that do not participate, nor can it discipline unions if they break away from the united front or if they settle upon terms that the national union does not accept. The only recourse left to the national union in such cases is to criticize the deviant. In recent years the most common form of deviation has been settlements involving long-term wage guarantees. In these cases, a specific enterprise union makes an agreement not to strike during a certain period—usually three years—and to cooperate with the employer in the execution of a long-range production plan. In return, the employer promises fixed wage increments during the period, to be based principally on wage increases agreed upon by other employers and unions in the Spring Labor Offensive. Thus, the union signing such an agreement does not itself strike but enjoys benefits that result from bargaining at other enterprises—like a "free rider."

Third, if the national or industrial union actually involves itself in collective bargaining at the enterprise level, its function tends to be limited to negotiation over such general items as the starting pay of new school graduates, average wage increments, base-ups, bonuses, and retirement benefits. Even in these cases, negotiations on an industrial basis can meet only a part of the workers' demands.

The employer is in a similar situation. His desire to avoid the intrusion of outside unions and to maintain the independence of intra-enterprise bargaining is encouraged by employers' organizations. Employers also have responded to the unions' united Spring Labor Offensive by coordinating their actions and policies, sometimes formally and sometimes informally. Formally, individual employers may entrust their bargaining rights to the employers' association, or representatives of the employers' association may attend the negotiations of its member employers. Informally, the employers' group or association assists by conducting an information exchange among its members and advising on adjustment of bargaining policies. The formal bargaining method usually develops in response to union pressure.

The degree to which industrial union federations and employers' associations are involved in collective bargaining tends to vary from case to case, the major patterns being centralized or unified bargaining, group bargaining, and so-called diagonal or radial bargaining. These types reflect the degrees of participation by national or industrial unions in the bargaining procedure.

Centralized or unified bargaining is conducted between an industrial union or federation and an employers' association at the national level. Examples are the negotiations between the All-Japan Seamen's Union and the four shipowners' associations, and between the Local Textile Department of the Japan Federation of Textile Workers' Unions (Zensendōmei) and the Federation of Local Textile Industries (Menkoren). In the case of the private railway industry, where the degree of centralization and uniformity is not as great as in the previous two cases, only those employers who have entrusted their bargaining rights to the employers' association and the corresponding unions are covered by united bargaining. This coverage varies from time to time.

Group bargaining is a less formalized pattern of industrial bargaining. It is conducted by groups composed of several employers and their enterprise unions at the same place and the same time. In some cases delegates of the national unions attend the group bargaining and sign the agreement. This pattern is widespread among unions in the Japan Federation of Textile Workers' Unions, the General Federation of Private Railway Workers' Unions of Japan, and unions organized among taxi drivers.

An important version of group bargaining is the case where no formal procedure for industrywide bargaining is agreed upon but managements of large corporations simultaneously offer uniform wage increases. An example is the "one-shot offer" of the Big Five companies in the steel industry. This practice, which has been followed for several years, cannot be considered bargaining on an industry basis, but it has the effect of industrywide wage determination, as the one-shot offer of the big steel companies has a significant impact on wage determination not only in other companies in the steel industry but also in other industries such as shipbuilding, automobiles, and electric machines.

So-called diagonal or radial bargaining is an intra-enterprise negotiation in which delegates from the national union participate. This pattern of bargaining usually occurs in unions of the Japan Coal Miners' Union, the National Union of Coal Mine Workers (Zentankō), the Japanese Federation of Synthetic Chemical Workers' Unions, as well as in unions in the glass industry and the foreign banks. Though representatives of the national union attend the intra-enterprise negotiations, representatives of the employers' association do not participate. In the case of the synthetic chemical industry, delegates of the national union involved in the intra-enterprise negotiations are limited to those who are employees of the enterprise and at the same time are officers of the national union. Thus, the degree to which the national union participates is much lower than that in the other types of bargaining, and in many cases there is little difference from intra-enterprise bargaining.

The patterns of bargaining described above are sometimes conducted on an area or district basis, especially in small and medium-sized industries. Examples of areawide bargaining are the negotiations between the All-Japan Seamen's Union and the inland and coastal shipowners and between local employers or employers' associations and district branches of the Japan Federation of Textile Workers' Unions, the General Federation of Private Railway Workers' Unions of Japan, the Japan Coal Miners' Union, the National Federation of Printing and Publishing Industry Workers' Unions (Zeninsōren), the All-Japan Harbor Workers' Union (Zenkōwan), and the National Federation of Metal Industry Trade Unions (Zenkindōmei).

Prospects for Industrywide Bargaining

It appears that the development of industrywide bargaining in Japan will depend mainly upon government policy, the state of the labor market, the structure of industry, management policy, and union leadership. Each of these factors will be considered in turn.

One reason the All-Japan Seamen's Union has been able to maintain effective industrywide bargaining is the extensive government assistance and control of the maritime industry which dates from long before World War II. As a result, terms and conditions of employment of seamen were standardized on an industrywide basis, and interfirm differentials in employment conditions became negligible. Government influence, then, coupled with the open labor market for seamen, served to establish the practice of industrywide bargaining in that industry.[12]

Government control was widespread in almost all strategic industries immediately after World War II, covering such indus-

---

12. As explained in previous chapters, the All-Japan Seamen's Union is not a federation of enterprise unions but a single national industrial union. For more detailed reasons for centralized industrywide bargaining, see "Labor Relations in the Japanese Maritime Industry," *Japan Labor Bulletin*, vol. 5, no. 2 (Feb. 1966).

trial activities as product price determination, supply of raw materials, wage setting as a component of production cost, and the distribution of consumer food to workers. As government control meant some degree of uniformity in deciding upon and administering employment terms among enterprises, it often resulted in the collaboration of unions and managements in their bargaining. At least, government controls created common political and economic grounds on which the labor union could demand industrywide bargaining and the employer could accept it.

For example, the All-Japan Electric Industry Workers' Union, one of the most advanced unions at that time, could conduct industrywide bargaining immediately after the war because a quasi-governmental agency controlled the electric power industry. This union declined and ceased to function in industrywide bargaining primarily because the electric power industry was decentralized to the present nine separate corporations.

The same thing can be said about the coal-mining, cotton textile, and private railway industries, all of which were more or less under government control and, as a result, developed industrywide bargaining to a considerable extent. Government control over prices and indirectly over labor costs was a major factor in the development of industrywide bargaining in these industries.

Second, the development of industrywide bargaining will depend, to a significant extent, on the structure of the labor market, labor mobility, and skill development in an industry. For example, the work place of seamen is the vessel rather than a given enterprise. Seamen frequently board and leave ships, their schedules are irregular, and crews move from vessel to vessel, regardless of who may own or operate the ship. Such conditions have contributed to the development of a horizontal and unified labor market structure. Also, maritime skills, including those of both high-grade officers and rated seamen, are developed not through training within a given enterprise but at government-operated colleges and schools. Consequently, skills are standardized, and there is a single source of labor.

Conditions such as these contribute to the beginnings of industrywide bargaining in certain industries, in contrast with most other industries in which the dominant type of workers' organization is an enterprise-wide union, largely attributable to the practice of lifetime employment commitments and to training confined within a company, with a consequent lack of horizontal and uniform labor markets.

In the case of coal miners, harbor workers, and taxi drivers, skills are relatively similar and independent of the peculiarities of their individual employers; thus, their labor mobility is comparatively high. In the textile industry, female workers with junior high school educations constitute the bulk of the labor force, and as these workers have no lifetime commitment to the company in the industry, the turnover rate is high. Furthermore, in the period of rapid economic growth since 1955, the shortage of young workers has become quite acute, serving to create a uniform level of starting wages for new school graduates on a nationwide and industrywide basis.

Third, the scope of industry influences the extent of development of industrywide bargaining. The Japanese industrial union in the private sector is organized as a rule among groups of rival companies in the same product market. Therefore, these companies tend to have more or less similar productivity, technological levels, and employment conditions. If an industrial union includes unions in small and medium-sized industry as well as in large industry (i.e., the Japan Coal Miners' Union, the General Federation of Private Railway Workers' Unions of Japan, and the Japan Federation of Textile Workers' Unions), it tends to develop separate bargaining units for unions negotiating with firms in each size category. Thus, what is called industrywide bargaining may actually be inter-enterprise bargaining covering a separate group of enterprises of similar size and with similar operating or financial conditions but which are rivals in the same product market.[13]

In other words, if similar conditions do not prevail among

13. For the scope, structure and function of industrywide wage negotiations, see Kazuo Koike, *Nihon no chingin kōshō* [Wage negotiations in Japan] (Tokyo: University of Tokyo Press, 1962), and Kazuo Okochi, ed., *Sangyōbetsu chingin kettei no kikō* [The structure of industrywide wage determination] (Tokyo: Japan Institute of Labor, 1965).

employers, the possibility of developing industrywide bargaining is slight. Also, if there is a significant change in conditions that once were similar, industrywide bargaining tends to break down. For example, industrywide bargaining will be very difficult to maintain if a member enterprise becomes a multi-industrial corporation by diversifying its production and if the union organization and its bargaining structure cannot adjust to this change. It is also very difficult to establish or maintain if a few member enterprises become far advanced in technology and assume an oligopolistic position in the market. In that case the managements would be able to discourage their enterprise unions from joining in the demand for industrywide bargaining by offering far better employment conditions than could be expected from the industrywide bargaining. Enterprise unions in turn would become less dependent upon their parent bodies and less interested in joint action by unions at the industry level, simultaneously becoming more interested in maintaining or improving the enterprise's position in market competition. Within the context of enterprise unionism with its peculiar behavior nurtured by the length-of-service wage system, unions would not "play off" competing managements, as is done by some American unions through "whipsawing," but rather would tend to emphasize the common interests of management and labor. These are a few of the reasons industrywide bargaining has been difficult to establish even among such technologically similar industries as steel, automobiles, shipbuilding, and electrical machinery.

Fourth, union leadership constitutes a problem for the achievement of industrywide bargaining. Whether or not an industrial union or federation is consolidated and integrated organizationally is a decisive factor. The enterprise union or federation usually has a high degree of autonomy, and leaders of the large enterprise unions or federations usually have great authority or power and are reluctant to delegate their bargaining function to the industrial or national union. Industrial unions that have been successful in industrywide bargaining tend to have powerful personalities in leadership positions. Only if such leadership exists in the industrial union will its affiliates accept its authority. And, if the union organization is not internally cohesive, it can hardly persuade reluctant employers to accept industrywide bargaining.

These, then, are the main factors. It is a rare union that exhibits all four characteristics and can develop industrywide bargaining in the face of employer opposition. One institutional factor that may compensate for the weakness of the union lies in the dispute settlement function of the Central Labor Relations Commission. Even if the employer insists upon bargaining only at the level of his own enterprise, the unions can still organize a united industrywide struggle and involve the Central Labor Relations Commission. In such a case, the commission substantially encourages industrywide bargaining by recommending uniform and simultaneous settlements for the individual companies and enterprise unions concerned.

In a similar vein, the Spring Labor Offensive serves as an institutional force for unified collective bargaining efforts.[14] As an established method of reaching an agreement on wages, the Spring Labor Offensive has had a number of results that depart significantly from the enterprise orientation of collective bargaining. First, wage levels have been greatly increased. Between 1960 and 1966 the annual average wage increase has been more than 10 percent in nominal terms and more than 4 percent in real terms. The wide gap between nominal and real wages is due to soaring prices. In any case, it is one of the highest rates of wage increase among advanced countries. Of course, this increase rate was not solely the result of the Spring Labor Offensives. Coupled with the recent rapid economic growth, labor shortages have become acute, starting pay for new school graduates has increased significantly, and consumer prices have risen enormously. All of these are potent factors in pushing up the wage level. But it is only on the occasion of the Spring Labor Offensive that unions have been able to take advantage of these factors in order to obtain wage increases.

Second, as a result of the Spring Labor Offensive, wage increases have become more standardized on an inter-industry basis and among various unions, and the effect has spilled over even to

14. See Chapter 9 for a full description and analysis of the Spring Labor Offensive.

the unorganized sector. This standardization has come about because both unions with strong bargaining power and those that were weaker joined together in the wage-hike drive. What is significant about the joint drive is that it has tended to provide workers in the small and medium-sized industries with a social atmosphere that supports their bargaining efforts. Thus, wage disputes have become a more normal phenomenon than before in Japanese industrial relations.

Third, the role of higher-level union organization in collective bargaining has increased greatly. Whether or not the industrial federation joins in at the bargaining table, it has become more important as a leader or coordinator of enterprise union activities, and a gradual change has been taking place in the power structure of union organization in Japan. Furthermore, as the Spring Labor Offensive covers almost all industry and functions substantially as wage bargaining on a national economy basis, it has tended to heighten the prestige of the national union centers and their leaders.

Fourth, one of the most important results of the Spring Labor Offensive thus far may be that it has opened to the public various aspects of industrial relations that used to be private matters of particular enterprises. Consequently, it has aroused wider public interest in and a deeper understanding of industrial relations problems. Discussions between the leaders of the Japanese Federation of Employers' Associations (Nikkeiren) and of national union centers, and meetings between high government officials and union leaders are widely televised and increasingly attract large audiences.

Conclusions

Collective bargaining in Japan is a practice that has developed quite rapidly during the relatively brief years of the postwar period. It is now an established mechanism for determining wages and other employment conditions, at least in the large-industry sector. Whether coverage will continue to grow or not depends on expansion of union organization in the future.

This prospect faces several obstacles. One is that the ratio of organized labor to the total number of employed workers is leveling off. Another is the political question of extending coverage of collective bargaining to the public sector. The prospects for this do not appear very favorable in view of the likely continuation of the majority position of the conservative Liberal-Democratic Party in the government in the foreseeable future.

The enterprise form of union organization also impedes the development of bargaining power among Japanese unions. This weakness has been overcome considerably by the united Spring Labor Offensive for wage increases. However, its development is too recent to permit firm conclusions as to whether or not such united action may radically change the power structure of Japanese labor unions and broaden the industrial union's leadership role in collective bargaining.

It may be said that Japan's high economic growth, coupled with rapid technological developments, tends to create factors that lead in opposite directions. On the one hand, the changing labor market situation, that is, an acute labor shortage and increased labor mobility, tends to promote collective bargaining on a basis wider than the enterprise in order to facilitate labor mobility. If the traditional length-of-service system of industrial reward in Japan were to decline, the institutional foundation of enterprise unionism would be eroded and this might lead to a change in union organization and its power structure. Thus far, however, there is little evidence that unions are taking the initiative in developing the more sophisticated policies and the new leadership that would be required to meet and utilize the changing situation in order to strengthen their bargaining power.

On the other hand, the increasing concentration of capital and the strengthening of oligopolistic controls over the market may be important factors supporting enterprise-level bargaining. The merger of enterprises often disrupts the union organization and frequently results in stronger enterprise unions or enterprisewide federations and weaker industrial unions or federations. Some oligopolistic enterprises tend to create privileged enterprise unions which can enjoy far better employment conditions than other unions. Thus the framework of intra-enterprise bargaining, buttressed by the persistent support of employers, is strengthened. It is possible that even intra-enterprise bargaining may be lost, replaced by a joint consultation system in the enterprise. Through the joint consultation system, management succeeds, in many cases, in taking the lead in labor relations and in inducing the union to respond with no-strike commitments. Should that be the case, there would be even less possibility for industrial unions to exert a meaningful influence on the enterprise union.

9. Labor Disputes

Statistics on labor disputes in Japan since the end of World War II reveal some general trends in the development of the Japanese system of labor relations. Thus, this chapter will begin with a review and analysis of these statistics. Then we will offer an explanation of the trends they reveal, examine the principal issues in labor disputes—wages and discharges—and, finally, discuss the relationship between labor disputes and labor relations.

Labor Disputes Since World War II[1]

The first trend that emerges from the statistics on labor disputes is seen in Fig. 9.1. The data indicate that peaks in the frequency of labor disputes closely correspond to peaks in the number of workers involved, although, as will be explained below, the latter shows sharper fluctuations than the former. Peaks occurred in 1948, 1952, 1957, and 1961. The issues and events involved will be described in greater detail later in the chapter, but here we will mention briefly the major disputes comprising each of these four peaks.

1. Sources for the data that follow are *Rōdō tōkei nenpō* [Yearbook of labor statistics] for 1946–65, and *Rōdō sōgi tōkei chōsa nenhōkoku* [Yearbook of labor dispute statistics] for 1961 and thereafter, all published by the Ministry of Labor, Division of Labor Statistics and Research.

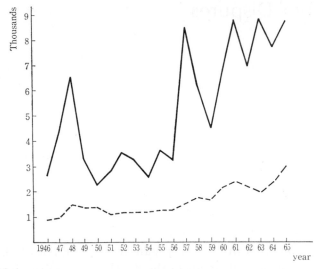

Fig. 9.1.
Trends in the number of labor disputes and workers involved, 1946–65. Solid line: number of workers involved. Broken line: number of labor disputes.

The 1948 peak resulted from a number of circumstances arising out of the postwar confusion. Labor unions were organized very rapidly after enforcement of the Trade Union Law in March 1946, and by August of that year Sōdōmei and Sanbetsu had been established as national labor centers. Sanbetsu launched its struggles in October and Sōdōmei launched its at the end of 1946. When a general strike planned for February 1, 1947, was banned by order of General MacArthur, Sanbetsu changed to guerrilla tactics. It again attempted to organize a general strike in March 1948, but this one, too, was banned by SCAP. When a general strike was attempted three times in July 1948, SCAP issued a general order prohibiting all public employees from engaging in strikes. This order met with considerable resistance from labor unions, especially the National Railway Workers' Union (Koku-rō), which adopted a "walk-out" strategy.[2] The most critical confrontations between labor and management were expected during the summer of 1949, as a reaction to massive discharges

2. Workers walked off their jobs rather than sitting down.

that had taken place in both public and private industries. Rather than overt confrontations, however, a series of mysterious events occurred: the Shimoyama case, in which President Shimoyama of the National Railway Corporation was found dead on July 5; the Mitaka case, in which an electric train without a motorman went out of control in Mitaka, Tokyo, on July 15; and the Matsukawa case, in which a National Railway train was overturned in Matsukawa, Fukushima Prefecture, on August 17.

The 1952 peak occurred in the context of the end of the Allied Occupation. Although the labor movement had retreated after losing its battles against massive discharges in 1949, it had regained its strength by the end of the Korean War and at the time of the peace treaty. The movement strongly advocated an overall treaty rather than a separate agreement, which the government and the conservative party supported. Furthermore, it was pressing for improvement in working conditions which had deteriorated during the recession of 1949–51. From April to June 1952, organized labor called for general strikes against passage of the Subversive Activity Prevention Law and revision of the labor relations laws. In the autumn, the Japan Electric Power Workers' Union, or Densan, and the Japan Coal Miners' Union, or Tanrō, struck for better working conditions; the latter strike lasted sixty-three days.

The 1957 peak was associated with the growth of the Spring Labor Offensive. In 1954, Nikkeiren, the Japan Federation of Employers' Associations, had made public its wage policy based on a system of annual or regular wage increases. The labor relations commissions followed this policy in adjusting wage disputes, and the National Personnel Authority (NPA), despite its recognition of the need for wage increases for national public service employees, made no recommendations for raises because of the state of the Japanese economy at the time. Beginning in 1955, eight industrial unions in the private sector formed a joint wage struggle council. These included the Japan Coal Miners' Union, the General Federation of Private Railway Workers' Unions of Japan (Shitetsusōren), the Japanese Federation of Synthetic Chemical Workers' Unions (Gōkarōren), the National Federation of Paper and Pulp Industry Workers' Unions (Kamiparōren), the

Japan Electric Power Workers' Union, the All-Japan Federation of Electric Machine Workers' Unions (Denkirōren), the National Trade Union of Metal and Engineering Workers' Unions (Zenkoku Kinzoku), and the Japanese Federation of Chemical Industry Workers' Unions (Kagakudōmei). A joint committee of the public corporation workers' unions, called the Kōkyōkigyōtai Rōdō-kumiai Kyōgikai, which had been formed in 1953, also joined this wage struggle council. Thus began the union alignment for the *Shuntō*, or Spring Labor Offensive. In 1957 major unions in the public corporations, although legally deprived of the right to strike, staged strikes to express dissatisfaction with the failure to implement arbitration awards. The chairman of the National Railway Workers' Union, who had been discharged as a result of this strike, was reelected to his post and demanded collective bargaining with the National Railway Corporation. However, the corporation rejected this demand on the basis of the article in the Public Corporation and National Enterprise Labor Relations Law that specified that only employees of the corporation were eligible for union office. As a result, numerous strikes took place protesting the discharge of union officers and demanding collective bargaining. It was these actions that developed into the struggle for ratification of International Labor Organization Convention No. 87. Also, during 1957, the All-Japan Seamen's Union (Kaiin Kumiai) and the Japan Federation of Textile Workers' Unions (Zensen-dōmei) struck for shorter hours.

The 1961 peak was the result of the very rapid development of the Spring Labor Offensive under the economic growth policy of the Ikeda Cabinet. From 1960 to 1961, the number of labor disputes in the annual offensive increased from 425 to 700 and the number of workers involved from 1,960,000 to 3,030,000. At the same time the number of disputes accompanied by work stoppages grew from 296 to 501, the number of workers involved from 306,933 to 1,037,784, and the number of man-days lost from 756,916 to 3,316,420. Moreover, 110,000 workers were discharged in the coal-mining industry, provoking struggles against discharge in that industry. Many labor disputes also occurred in hospitals.

As shown in Fig. 9.2, the peaks for the ratio of union members'

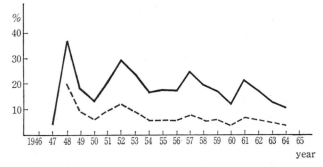

Fig. 9.2.
Union member and employee involvement in strikes, 1946–65. Solid line: workers involved in strikes as a percentage of total union membership. Broken line: workers involved in strikes as a percentage of nonagricultural employment.

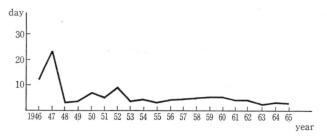

Fig. 9.3.
Duration of strikes, 1946–65.

involvement parallel those for the ratio of employees' involvement. These peaks have gradually fallen during the 1960s.

Duration of strikes, measured by man-days idle per worker involved in work stoppages, does not correspond to the peak of labor disputes that occurred in 1961 (see Fig. 9.3), because the typical duration pattern of strikes changed after 1955, as we shall explain later in this chapter. Since that time, most strikes have been short, although both the number of strikes and the number of workers involved have increased.

Man-days lost due to strikes of union members, measured by working days lost per hundred union members, have shown a diminishing trend since 1955 (see Fig. 9.4). The percentages of man-days lost by strikes of both union members and nonagricul-

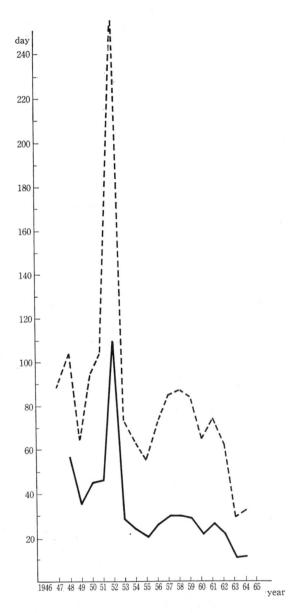

Fig. 9.4.
Man-days lost due to strikes. Solid line: man-days lost per hundred union members. Broken line: man-days lost per hundred nonagricultural workers.

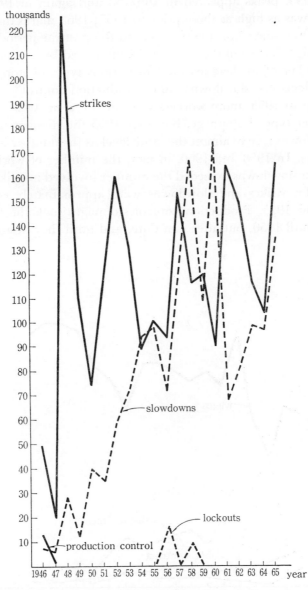

Fig. 9.5.
Number of workers involved by form of labor disputes.

tural employees were highest in 1952, following the 1948 peak. After 1955, peaks appeared in 1957–58 and again in 1961, but neither was as high as those prior to 1955; 1963 marks the lowest level in man-days lost due to strikes in the postwar period.

The significance of the year 1955 is indicated by an analysis of the number of workers involved in various types of stoppages—strikes, lockouts, slowdowns, and "production control" (see Fig. 9.5). Up to 1955, more workers were involved in strikes than in any other type of stoppage, but after 1955 the number involved in slowdowns rose to almost the same level as the number involved in strikes. In 1958 and 1960, in fact, the number of workers involved in slowdowns exceeded the number involved in strikes. The figures for strikes and slowdowns were approximately equal in 1954 and 1955. Production control stoppages took the form of strikes until 1950, but after that date, and until they disappeared

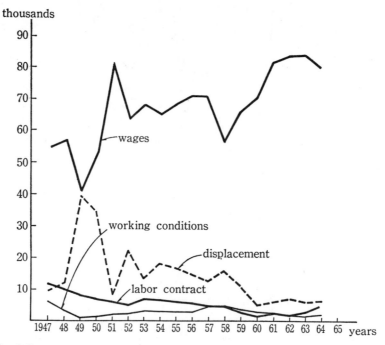

Fig. 9.6.
Number of labor disputes by major demand issues.

in 1955, the sit-down technique was used. The peaks for lockouts occurred in 1956 and 1958.

The trend of labor disputes according to issues is set out in Fig. 9.6. About 1 percent of the strikes each year have been over union recognition—reflection of persistent problems in organizing unions in small and medium-sized firms. The major issues, however, have been wages, discharges, labor contracts, and working conditions. As is clear from the figure, strikes over wages have occurred most frequently, followed by strikes against discharges.

If the percentage of labor contracts concluded indicates the degree of stability in labor-management relations, then the number of strikes over labor contracts suggests instability in Japanese labor-management relations. As labor contracts in Japan usually are negotiated separately from wage agreements, their duration does not coincide with the periods for wage agreements. The number of disputes over labor contracts, however, has been steadily decreasing, and in general it may be said that employer recognition of workers as members of enterprise unions has gradually become commonplace.

With the initiation of the Spring Labor Offensive in 1955, wage disputes have become more frequent, although the type of action appears to have shifted from strikes to slowdowns, and those strikes that have occurred have been shorter. Since 1955, moreover, disputes over discharge have tended to be settled within large enterprises through transfers of displaced employees; and displacement problems have seldom developed into labor disputes in small firms because of the number of bankruptcies among such firms.

Though disputes over wages make up a major proportion of the total number, disputes over hours and other working conditions are rare. The figures indicate that disputes over working conditions increased to some extent in 1957 and 1958 and again in 1963 and 1964, but in actuality these increases are very minor and indicate that labor unions have no influence on the issue of work hours of their members.

In summary, the statistics suggest that it is most appropriate to deal with labor disputes over wages and discharges as the two predominant types of issue, and to separate the analysis into two distinct periods, before and after 1955.[3]

Disputes Before and After 1955

According to the statistics reviewed above, Japan's experience with labor disputes does not seem to be an exception to Arthur M. Ross's proposition that in many industrialized countries strike activities tend to decline over time. Even if such a generalization is compatible with an apparent trend, however, in order to understand the reasons for and methods of labor disputes in a nation, the theory must explain how internal contradictions and conflicts in industrial relations are adjusted or become adapted to the society in which they exist.

The strikes in the period from the end of World War II until 1955 may be subdivided into two categories: those conducted by Sanbetsu in the early years and later ones led by Sōhyō, the General Council of Trade Unions of Japan. Strikes in both categories were led by the most radical national labor center in existence at the time.

From 1946 to 1949, the major labor disputes included the following: demonstrations for increased rice rations and for production control in May 1946; strikes of the National Railway Workers' Union against discharges in July 1946; strikes of the All-Japan Seamen's Union against discharges in September 1946; Sanbetsu's October Struggle in 1946; the Winter Struggle of Sōdōmei in 1946; the February 1, 1947, General Strike; the March Struggle and the July Struggle of the Japan Postal Workers' Union (Zentei) in 1948; the Tohō Strike in April 1948; walkouts of the National Railway Workers' Union in August and September 1948; and struggles over the above-mentioned Shimoyama,

3. For the view that 1955 was an epoch-making year, see Wakao Fujita, "Shōwa nijūkyū nen ikō no rōdō-kumiai undō" [The labor union movement after 1954] in *Shakaikagaku no kihonmondai* [Basic problems in the social sciences] (Tokyo: Institute of Social Science, University of Tokyo, 1963); and Wakao Fujita and Shōbei Shota, eds., *Sengō Nihon no rōdō sōgi* [Labor disputes in postwar Japan] (Tokyo: Ochanomizu Shobo, 1963), pp. 645–51.

Mitaka, and Matsukawa cases and the protection of industry in June 1949.

In 1946 the labor unions won all their strikes against discharges. Wage struggles began with Sanbetsu's October Struggle in 1946, developing in 1947 into the February 1 General Strike and then into the March Struggle and July Struggle of the Japan Postal Workers' Union. After the February 1 General Strike, other general strikes were led by government employees' unions. When government employees, and especially workers in government corporations, were deprived of the right to strike in July 1948, they conducted walkouts in protest.

The Tohō Strike of March 1948 was the first one actively opposed by management. When a massive number of workers were discharged in both public service and private industries in June 1949, with the support of SCAP, the protest strikes were led by Sanbetsu or one of its major member unions.

Strikes in the form of production control occurred frequently

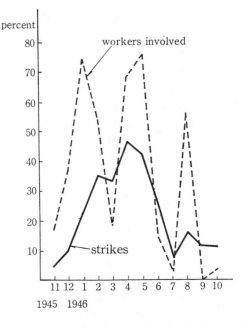

Fig. 9.7.
Number of production control and workers involved. (Percent)

soon after the end of the war, the largest number of workers involved in disputes being 73,000 in March 1946 and 37,000 in May 1946. As shown in Fig. 9.7, production control strikes occurred most frequently in April and May 1946, comprising 46.8 percent and 42.6 percent of the disputes accompanied by dispute tactics, respectively.

The first May Day observance since 1935 took the form of a major demonstration on May 1, 1946, followed by "Food May Day" on May 19. This was the month when "Give-Us-Rice" demonstrations took place quite frequently in conjunction with production control strikes. These activities, at least in part, were a reaction to the inflation of the immediate postwar period, and the production control strikes were an expression of the resistance of workers who had been ill-treated under the *nenkō* system. In addition, the leader of the emerging radical unions appeared most frequently from among those blue-or white-collar worker groups that had previously been kept at a distance by superior management power.

Demonstrations demanding rice stemmed from poverty on a national scale, and their leadership was identical with that of the labor unions. Together, they developed into an organized movement which was a prelude to industrial union organization in Japan. Sanbetsu, formed in August 1946, organized the Industry Recovery Council, which developed a general strike strategy and aimed at the further development of an organized labor movement. Furthermore, the newly organized industrial unions joined the October Struggle of 1946 and helped plan the February 1 (1947) General Strike, which was to be led by the Joint Struggle Committee of the National and Local Government Employees' Unions, or Kyōtō, with the backing of the Joint Struggle Committee of National Labor Unions, or Zentō. The government unions' joint committee called a general strike for February 1 with the aim of replacing the government with a "democratic" one. Their declaration was identical to a Communist Party announcement that urged establishment of a democratic people's government.

The general strike movement later peaked again with the regional people's struggles of Sanbetsu in March 1948 (the so-called ¥2,920 "base-up" struggle which aimed at a ¥2,920 increase in base pay), and in July 1948 (the ¥5,200 "base-up" struggle). These two peaks were due primarily to the activities of the unions of national and local government workers, especially the Japan Postal Workers' Union. Although the issue in these strikes was wages, a more typical general strike issue was set forth in the policy statement of the fourth convention of Sanbetsu in November 1948, calling for strikes against discharges. The aim of this "industry protection struggle" policy was to speed up the recovery of production through joint worker struggles to control workshops on a regional and national basis. Its objectives were to develop a political struggle in both metropolitan and rural areas and to prevent Japanese industries from becoming subcontractors of international capital. Under this policy, Japan's financial organizations and major industries were to be nationalized and turned over to the Japanese people.

Thus, the policies and strike actions of Sanbetsu were revolutionary. The labor unions, planning the February 1 General Strike, affiliated to form Zenrōren, the National Liaison Council of Labor Unions. The council encompassed Sanbetsu, Sōdōmei, Nihon Rōdō Kumiai Kaigi, or the Japanese Congress of Labor Unions, and several independent unions, then was designed to integrate the labor front for joint action on issues of common interest. In this period, it played a significant role in carrying out revolutionary strikes.

A number of splits occurred in 1948 in industrial and local Sanbetsu unions, from which emerged a movement called the Minshuka Dōmei, or the National Liaison Council for Democratization. The outbreak of the Korean War in June 1950 was followed by the "red purge" in Japan, which lasted until the end of that year; Zenrōren was outlawed, and Sōdōmei split into two groups. Portions of Minshuka Dōmei and of the former Sōdōmei then reorganized and formed Sōhyō. SCAP assisted the successful organization of the new federation.

From 1950 to 1952, labor demonstrated against the proposed United States-Japan Peace Treaty and Mutual Security Agreement, and Sōhyō became increasingly militant over the treaty issue. Soon after its formation, Sōhyō adopted its policy of four principles for peace: a total peace treaty, maintenance of Japan's neutrality, opposition to military bases on Japanese soil, and opposition to Japan's rearmament.

Major strikes of this period included a strike by the Ube Nitrogenous Fertilizer Union, an affiliate of the Japanese Federation of Synthetic Chemical Workers' Unions (Gōkarōren), at the beginning of 1952; general strikes against passage of the Subversive Activity Prevention Law and revision of the labor relations law during April and June of 1952; a 63-day strike by the Japan Coal Miners' Union and a strike by the Japan Electric Power Workers' Union in the fall of 1952; a strike by the branch of the National Automobile Workers' Union (Zenji) at the Nissan Automobile Company in 1953; a 113-day strike by the Mitsui Coal Mine Workers' Union Federation, a member of the Japan Coal Miners' Union in 1953; strikes by union branches of the Japanese Federation of Iron and Steel Workers' Unions (Tekkōrōren) at the Amagasaki Steel Company and the Muroran Plant of Nihon Steel Company in 1954; and strikes by local bank employees, workers at the Ōmi Silk Company, and stock market workers in 1954. At the same time, union agitation against American military bases in Japan continued.

Looking at these strikes in more detail, the General Strike in 1952 actually was the first general strike of the postwar period. The February 1 General Strike and the March and July Struggles in 1948 had been concerned with wage issues and were led by government employees. The General Strike, however, demonstrated that it had become nearly impossible to organize a general strike over wages alone. Although the public service workers had been deprived of their right to strike, their wage levels were set at approximately the average for all industries, and wage determination for them played a part in wage control in general. Moreover, as wage differentials widened in private industry, it became almost impossible for labor unions in the private sector to organize a general strike even though they retained the right to strike.

The Japan Electric Power Workers' Union and the Japan Coal Miners' Union, which were among the strongest national unions at the time, struck in an effort to force an improvement of deteriorating work conditions that occurred during the general retreat of unions during 1950 and 1951. The electric power strike resulted in a split in the union, and the coal strike ended with maintenance of previous work loads at a slight wage increase.

The Ōmi Silk Company strike is an example of a labor dispute in small and medium-sized industry. Two factors contributed to it: (1) the impact of the reorganization of large companies upon small and medium-sized companies, and (2) the influence of the union movement in large companies upon workers subjected to old-fashioned labor-management practices in the smaller companies and just becoming aware of their substandard working conditions. This type of labor dispute became increasingly severe around 1959; the same circumstances brought on labor disputes in hospitals around 1961.

Labor disputes in which displacement was the issue occurred at a time when Japanese employers had gained strength as a result of the Korean War boom. In 1953, the strike of a branch of the National Automobile Workers' Union at the Nissan Automobile Company took place over the union's demand for a revision of the *nenkō* wage system. This strike, like others during the period, had the following features. Workers, upon receiving notices of discharge, ignored the notices and continued to report to work. The employer then locked out the entire work force. The next development was a split among the union members and creation of a "second" union. Thereupon, the employer canceled the lock-out for members of the second union and called them back into the plant in order to start production. At this point, violence often occurred as members of the two union groups confronted each other, and police or thugs were called in to protect the second union members. In the end, members of the second union usually succeeded in breaking through the picket line into the factory, and production was resumed. The original union group gradually became a minority, as more and more members returned to work.

Various struggles against American military bases at Uchinada, Asama, and Myogi took place in 1953, along with strikes by workers discharged from the special procurement industries after the Korean War. In 1955, for example, there was a mass discharge of Japanese workers employed by the United States army. Struggles against military bases occurred in Sunagawa, Daitakane, and

Kita-Fuji in 1955, and at Sōmagahara in 1957, while labor disputes continued into 1958 in the special procurement industries and American army employment. In order to reevaluate and lead the above-mentioned strikes, Sōhyō organized the People's Council for a Peaceful Economy (Heiwa Keizai Kokumin Kaigi Undō), which aimed at opposing the political and economic system under the United States-Japan Mutual Security Agreement.

Turning now to the decade from 1955 to 1965, major labor disputes included: the introduction of the annual Spring Labor Offensive, or *Shuntō*, strategy in 1955; the struggle against the military bases at Sunagawa in 1956; strikes of public enterprise and public corporation employees in March 1957 and the dispute of the Niigata branch of the National Railway Workers' Union and of the Kijima Coal Mine Company in July 1957; the struggles of the Japan Teachers' Union, or Nikkyōso, against the efficiency rating system and the Ōji Paper Company strike in 1958; strikes in small and medium-sized companies in 1959; struggles against the United States-Japan Mutual Security Agreement and the Mitsui Miike Coal Mine strike in 1960; struggles for a change of government policy toward the coal-mining industry, strikes in hospitals, and the Nittan Takamatsu Coal Mine strike in 1961; a strike at the Minamata plant of the Shin-Nihon Chisso (nitrogenous fertilizer) Company in 1962; and a general strike planned for April 17, 1964.

Examining these disputes in more detail, the strikes at the Kijima, Mitsui Miike, and Nittan Takamatsu coal mines and the struggles for a policy change toward the coal-mining industry were disputes in opposition to industrial reorganization and worker displacement resulting from the decline of the coal-mining industry, which was no longer able to compete with petroleum imports from abroad. The strikes at these mines were conducted by three of the strongest member unions of the Japan Coal Miners' Union, and, although the strikes nominally were against displacement, they were actually directed toward national industrial policy.

The strike of the public enterprise and public corporation employees in March 1957 broke out because of bitter union resentment against the failure, over a period of several years, to put arbitration decisions into effect. Also, the struggle protesting the discharge of employees involved in these strikes was an expression of opposition to Article 17 of the Public Corporation and National Enterprise Labor Relations Law, which prohibits these workers from striking. These events marked the beginning of the movement by organized labor for ratification of ILO Convention No. 87.

The issue in the strike at the Ōji Paper Company in 1958 was management's proposed revision of the labor contract, which the workers viewed as an attempt to restrict union activities further; the struggle of the Japan Teachers' Union in 1958 was in opposition to the establishment of an efficiency rating system for public school teachers. All of these disputes were worker protests against employer-imposed restrictions on union activities.

The Spring Labor Offensive strategy formally began in 1955 and was countered later by the employers' "stable wage" policy (*antei chingin hōshiki*). The strike at the Minamata plant of the Shin-Nihon Chisso Company was an example of the workers' resistance to the "stable wage" policy. Although the union split on this occasion, members of the first union were able peacefully to persuade second union members not to cross the picket line.

The Spring Labor Offensive strategy of lining up all unions took the form of a general strike over wages on April 17, 1964. As it turned out, however, this general strike was not carried out, since, just before it was to take place, opposition arose within Sōhyō from a faction dominated by the Japan Communist Party. As a result, the strike was settled by negotiation at the top labor-government level.

The struggle against the Sunagawa military bases in 1956 was a continuation of a movement that began in 1953, but it differed in the sense that it was directly led by the leaders of the Socialist and Communist Parties and not by the labor union leaders as had been the case before. Labor disputes in small and medium-sized companies began to develop after 1954 and occurred frequently in the decade from 1955 to 1965, increasing and intensifying particularly in 1959. Hospital workers, as mentioned above, struck frequently in 1961.

The major characteristics of labor disputes since 1955 may be summarized as follows: (1) unions have tended to use the Spring Labor Offensive strategy or general strikes for their wage struggles;[4] (2) in the workers' struggles against industrial reorganization and displacement, the unions have tended to press policy changes on an industrial basis; (3) organized demonstrations against military bases have been directly led by the leaders of left-wing political parties rather than by union leaders, although the latter have supported these struggles; (4) strikes have appeared with increasing frequency and intensity in small and medium-sized companies;[5] (5) labor disputes seem to have become shorter in duration.

Thus, the labor movement and labor disputes in Japan since 1955 appear to be different in nature from those of the earlier revolutionary and retreat periods. On the whole, the labor movement and labor disputes since 1955 seem to have acquired the characteristics of "Japanese trade unionism" advocated by the mainstream faction of Sōhyō in 1960.

Wage Disputes

Japanese wage disputes may also be divided into two types: those occurring before and those after the epoch-making year of 1955. The differences lie in the theories behind wage demands, the forms of settlement, and the groups of union members supporting the disputes. An understanding of wage demands can be gained by contrasting the movements—revolutionary unionism and "Japanese trade unionism"—that dominated each period.

Under revolutionary unionism, from the end of the war until 1955, wage demands were based on theoretical living costs. Immediately after the war, labor unions demanded large wage increases, ranging from two to five times the then current wages. The Japan Electric Power Workers' Union, Densan, an enterprise

4. In the Spring Labor Offensive, as a rule, a "top batter" is selected to lead the campaign. As a result, there has been an increase in slowdowns as well as short strikes lasting less than four hours.

5. The effect of these strikes has often been to drive small companies into bankruptcy.

union in a government-owned corporation, succeeded, after a strike, in negotiating a *minimum* wage system based on the worker's age and number of family members. However, the Japan Coal Miners' Union, Tanrō, in a similar wage struggle during January and March 1947, was unsuccessful, in spite of the pressure generated by the February 1 General Strike. The miners' wage struggle finally ended with an agreement on a system of *average* wage increases. This settlement was due primarily to the fact that Tanrō is a federation of numerous enterprise unions, which makes it difficult to formulate for all member unions a single standard system based on the worker's age and number of family members. After these unsuccessful struggles, most unions demanded the Densan-type of minimum wage system, but most settlements were for the Tanrō-type system of average wages.

The minimum wage system based on age and family size was also called the "system of theoretical living costs." That is, living costs per capita were estimated, based on the number of calories a person consumes in a given length of time. The necessary calories were then converted into a sum based on prevailing food prices. This sum, in turn, determined the wages paid to a worker. The idea originated in the antiwar resistance movement during World War II,[6] when *nenkō* wages of the prewar days, which were increased regularly according to the worker's length of service in order to encourage loyalty to the company, became a type of minimum wage based on age and family size for workers entering a company immediately after school graduation and remaining in service for a long period. The wages were determined not by collective bargaining but by the unilateral decision of the employer. As labor shortages grew increasingly severe in the wartime economy, however, large firms found that they had to have another source of employees in addition to new school graduates, and they began to recruit workers who had been employed elsewhere for several years. These workers were paid at rates lower than those of workers who were employed upon school graduation; and, as their numbers grew, their discontent over this discrimination also increased. During the wartime inflation period,

6. Masakichi Andō, *Saitei chingin no kisoteki kenkyū* [A basic study of minimum wages] (Tokyo: Diamond-sha, 1941).

the problem of discrimination was alleviated by the establishment of family cost-of-living and temporary flat-rate allowances, the base rate being kept unchanged. Thus originated the system of minimum wages based on age and family size. The wage increments at that time, however, never caught up with inflation, and the antiwar resistance movement consequently stimulated the establishment of the concept of minimum wages by age and family size, at least in principle, and a guarantee that the labor force would be maintained at the size required for war.

The wage demand of Densan was based on these ideas. After the war many union leaders emerged from the ranks of the workers who had been recruited from other companies; for them, wages based on the theoretical living cost meant in effect elimination of wage discrimination which favored those who had been hired upon school graduation. Thus, inflation was not the only reason for the demand for wages based on age and family size related to a theoretical cost of living.

There were a number of reasons why the wage struggles usually ended with the unions accepting the system of average wage increases. First, wide variation existed in wage systems from one company to another, although there were certain standards based on educational level, age, and family size. Second, the base rate continued to be a key wage component, but it was not based on job content or on uniform criteria in common among the companies in the same industry. Third, when an industrial union and an association of employers negotiated over wages, the total wage bill would be calculated by determining an average wage and multiplying this amount by the number of workers (see Chapter 10 for further discussion). Finally, the Katayama Cabinet, formed after the February 1 General Strike, developed a wage policy that prescribed an average wage by "type" of industry, "type" being a subclassification of an industry. The mining industry, for example, is classified into coal and nonferrous metal mining. The classification chosen was based on the industrial unit that had been subjected to production and price controls during the war. The average wage policy was designed in effect to guarantee the employer a certain profit, taking into account material and labor costs. The labor cost established made up the wage fund to be paid to the workers and was calculated on the basis of the average wage per employee. It is reasonable to assume that the wage policy of the Katayama Cabinet served as a prototype for settling wage disputes. Until 1949, the Densan-type wage demand played an important role in conducting wage negotiations, but the Tanrō-type average wage was the important one in settling disputes.

The role of public service employees' unions in wage disputes should not be overlooked. As was mentioned earlier, the Joint Struggle Committee of the National and Local Government Employees' Unions (Kyōtō) directed the February 1 General Strike and the Joint Struggle Committee of National Labor Unions (Zentō) backed it. In the general strikes of March and July 1948, the Japan Postal Workers' Union, a public employees' union and a major force in Sanbetsu, took the lead. Although these general strikes were not carried out because of SCAP bans, they were quite successful as wage struggles. The fact that public service employees' unions played key roles in these wage disputes is due to the character of the Japanese industrial structure. After the Meiji era began, major modern industries were first managed by the government but eventually, one after another, they were turned over to private ownership. Before World War II, the weapons industry, the national railways, the postal service, and the telephone and telecommunication industry, however, continued to be government-operated. With the end of the war, the weapons industry ceased to exist, but the other government enterprises were still very important to the Japanese economy. Furthermore, as labor unions were organized on an enterprise basis, the National Railway Workers' Union and the Japan Postal Workers' Union, among government enterprises, became two of the largest unions in Japan.

In 1952, Sōhyō issued its wage-struggle program for a "minimum healthy and cultural living" in support of union struggles for wage increases based on theoretical living costs. This program was the rallying cry of the campaign to recover prewar wage levels. The goal was a minimum take-home pay of ¥70,000 per month based upon the "market-basket" method of computation, since government figures in the Consumers' Price Index were not believed to reflect reality. Wage demands based on the market-basket method were adopted by many industrial unions as a worker thirty years of age did not benefit as much as older workers from the system of wage distribution based on the average wage. As a solution to the problem, there emerged a method of making flat-rate wage increases where by the total amount of wages negotiated was distributed equally among workers, regardless of theoretical living coasts or age and length of service. This method was adopted by some industrial unions such as the Japanese Federation of Synthetic Chemical Workers' Unions, the General Federation of Private Railway Workers' Unions of Japan, the Japan Federation of Press Workers' Unions, the National Federation of Paper and Pulp Industry Workers' Unions, the Japanese Federation of Chemical Industry Workers' Unions, and the National Railway Workers' Union. However, the flat-rate wage increase was not usually sufficient for workers with families. Therefore, the method was modified and took the form of a "flat-rate increase plus alpha," the latter factor representing increases in family allowances and having the effect of diminishing wage differentials. This formula developed into a minimum wage guarantee based on age for those workers who had not been hired upon school graduation. Thus, between 1952 and 1954 there were persistent union demands for wages based on theoretical living costs, although variations began to be introduced in the latter part of the period.

Wage demands based on theoretical living costs had been the wage policy of unions in Sanbetsu until 1949 and of Sōhyō after 1950. At the same time, however, there were wage struggles conducted by rival groups. Sōdōmei followed a policy of demanding wages based on "actual" living costs as well as advocating equal pay for equal work by sex. The main difference between Sōdōmei and Sanbetsu lay in strategy: the latter backed its demands by means of general strikes, while the former strove for wage gains through collective bargaining or joint labor-management consultation. Sōdōmei's idea was to avoid labor militancy and to bargain for wage increases with employers who fully comprehended the state of the Japanese economy after the war. This idea also reflected the prewar experiences of labor union leaders who had found that strikes often aroused strong resistance from middle management, and the conviction that more could be gained by talking with and convincing top management personnel, who were often more intellectual and paternalistic than middle management. Furthermore, wages based on actual living costs often resulted in greater wage gains for the older workers, thereby isolating and discouraging militant young union members.

In 1954, when Japan at last reemerged from the ashes of war damage, Nikkeiren, the Japan Federation of Employers' Associations, announced three new wage principles: (1) no wage increases should be granted if they would result in raised commodity prices; (2) no wage increase should be granted if they would exceed the employer's ability to pay; and (3) no wage increases should be granted if they were not accompanied by increases in labor productivity. In reality, this policy sought to revive the system of regular periodical wage increases within the framework of the second principle. In fact, most wage disputes that year were settled according to the system of regular annual wage increases despite prolonged union struggles, in some cases extending into the spring of 1955. As the result of this situation, Kaoru Ohta, then vice-president of Sōhyō, decided that a massive wage struggle would be most effective, and he organized five industrial unions in the private sector into a joint council to conduct a spring offensive for wage increases. The five were the Japan Coal Miners' Union, the Japanese Federation of Synthetic Chemical Workers' Unions, the General Federation of Private Railway Workers' Unions of Japan, the National Federation of Paper and Pulp Industry Workers' Unions, and the Japan Electric Power Workers' Union. Three more industrial unions were added to the joint council in 1955: the All-Japan Federation of Electric Machine Workers' Unions, the National Trade Union of Metal and Engineering Workers' Unions, and the Japanese Federation of Chemical Industry Workers' Unions. These eight became the key force in the 1955 struggle. A year later, the General Council of Public Corporation and National Enterprise Workers' Unions, or Kōrōkyō, also participated in the joint council, thus completing the struggle organization for the annual Spring Offensive.

Immediately after the war, there were four wage disputes each year. Wage struggles in the spring (for contracts that ran from

March to September) and in the fall (for contracts that ran from October to March) were conducted over base rates. Struggles for bonus allowances took place in June and December. Between 1952 and 1955, some unions reduced the number of wage struggles to three a year: one for an increase in the base rate and two for bonus allowances; this procedure became increasingly widespread after the Spring Labor Offensive was established in 1955.

As mentioned, the favored demands in the Spring Offensives were "flat-rate increases plus alpha" and a minimum wage guarantee based on age. This type of increase was designed to interest the younger workers in the wage struggles, since, under any other wage payment method, they would be the ones to benefit the least, and they were supposed to be the central force carrying on the wage struggles. This strategy was also called the "individual wage demand" in the sense that the wage increase demanded at the beginning of the wage struggle was the amount to be received by each individual worker. If adopted, it had the effect, under the nenkō system, of restricting the employer's unilateral power to decide upon the wage distribution and of eliminating his power to discriminate against union activists. A minimum wage guarantee based on age served to reduce wage discriminatory differentials between workers hired immediately upon school graduation and those hired later. Therefore, the Spring Labor Offensive seems to have had as its goal the restriction of employer arbitrariness in wage determination within the framework of the nenkō wage system, although Sōhyō claims that the approach actually was designed to destroy the system.

In recent years there has been a shift in the emphasis of the Spring Offensives. Technological change has been introduced rapidly in industrial plants, a great deal of money has been invested in production equipment, and more and more new school graduates have been employed. These developments have meant increases in the number of young workers or union members. However, although these young workers join the unions, most of them tend to be indifferent toward them. Union leaders have attempted to interest the young workers in union activities, but they have failed because of basic differences in values or points of view. Since the end of the war, young workers have been and are being educated under an entirely new school system, and many are now employed in technologically advanced plants, working at jobs more important than those of some of the older workers. For this reason, they often think that they should receive higher pay.

Sōhyō attempted to ease this situation by demanding increases in starting wages and improved treatment for young union members. While a principal Sōhyō slogan is "equal pay for equal work," this principle often meets with opposition from older union members, who argue that if larger proportions of wage gains are given to young workers less will be available for senior workers. As a solution, Kaoru Ohta, as president of Sōhyō, proposed to conduct struggles for wage increases large enough to satisfy both young and old workers. This strategy was followed in the period of rapid economic growth and following the 1960 struggle against the United States-Japan Mutual Security Pact. Sōhyō asserts that the *nenkō* system exemplifies Japan's low wage policy and that large wage increases can destroy both the low wage policy and the *nenkō* system.

The Japanese Trade Union Congress was inaugurated in 1954 as a national center in competition with Sōhyō and was reorganized in 1964 as the Japanese Confederation of Labor (later renamed Dōmei). This organization has worked out its own strategy for wage struggles.

The Spring Labor Offensive, or "schedule struggle," method of bargaining calls for a key industrial union to set a strike date in the spring and for other unions to consult together to determine their own strike schedules. Zenrō's criticism of this approach, and Dōmei's current criticism, is that it disregards the principle that each individual union should conduct its own wage struggle. Dōmei proposes instead that first strikes should take place only after negotiations have reached a deadlock, and it argues that the Spring Offensive nullifies the negotiation process by scheduling the strike dates in advance. It also claims that, because the Spring Offensive consists of concerted strike action by unions under the direction of Sōhyō, it therefore tends to destroy the autonomy of affiliated unions. Accordingly, Dōmei's policy is to respect the autonomy of each member union and merely to give approval to individual union decisions as to dates of wage struggles, amount of wage demand, and so forth.

In spite of these policy differences, the number of unions participating in the joint struggle council of the Spring Labor Offensive, organized by Sōhyō and joined by the Federation of Independent Unions (Chūritsurōren), has grown. Even some Dōmei unions have joined. On the whole, however, Dōmei's strategy is to avoid strikes as much as possible but also to gain as great a wage increase as obtained by Sōhyō in the Spring Offensive.

Disputes over Discharge

The character of labor disputes over discharge has also changed since 1955. While disputes over discharge occurred earlier in coal mining, the causes of the disputes after 1955 were different, reflecting the changing economic situation of an industry that had continually declined and had seen 110,000 workers discharged. Since displacement after 1955 was due to technological change and the introduction of new equipment, the more recent disputes essentially involved bargaining over transfers of the displaced workers to new operations. The focus, however, moved from the large to the small and medium-sized companies, many of which have since gone bankrupt. Thus, disputes have on the whole become smaller in scale for the obvious reason that, the smaller the firm, the less likely it is that a union is organized within it.

Immediately after the end of World War II, employers were anxious to reorganize the war industries and to get them back into normal production. However, some war industries ceased to operate, displacing a large number of workers, and no reorganization plan was clearly established until the time of the Draper Mission to Japan in March 1948.

The labor unions strongly resisted displacement caused by industrial reorganization. As we have seen in previous chapters, under the *nenkō* system of the prewar days, lifetime employment had been accepted by all employees; workers served a company until retirement age. Those who were hostile to the company usually were discriminated against and, rather than suffer a loss of face as a result of a discharge, they would choose "voluntary retirement." The discharge of such workers helped to maintain the pyramidal structure of the company's work force, based on age or length of service. Thus, there had developed a peculiar personnel management system in which the employer could make arbitrary and discriminatory decisions. When this system was applied to workers through competitive promotion, it helped to establish the practice of automatic discharge of any workers who appeared hostile to the employer. During the war, however, because of the labor shortage, hostile workers were fired only in unusual cases. It was many of these hostile workers who later became militant union leaders at the end of the war, demanding concrete lifetime employment for workers in enterprises rather than an abstract full employment as in the prewar days. When Japanese unions advocated "full employment," they actually meant continuous employment of union members in a particular company until retirement, not "full employment" by definition.

In August 1946, when Sanbetsu was organized, the strategy of the center in working for full employment was to create an Industry Recovery Movement Council. Sōdōmei, the competing national center at that time, proposed an Economic Recovery Movement Council. The councils were similar in that they included representatives of labor, management, and scholars and in that they planned to organize individual enterprise unions by region and industry for affiliation with the central council. However, they differed in emphasis. Sanbetsu stressed industrial rather than regional organizations and attempted to achieve worker demands by means of general strikes. Sōdōmei emphasized regional organizations and settlement of disputes by means of joint consultation councils within individual enterprises.

After the February 1 (1947) General Strike, the Katayama Cabinet, backed primarily by the Socialist Party, created an Economic Recovery Council, as proposed by Sōdōmei groups affiliated with the Socialist Party. The problem of Sanbetsu participation in the council's program was partially solved when that center agreed to cooperate under certain conditions. However, in March 1948 antagonism between representatives of the two national centers intensified, eventuating in the breakdown of the council before any noticeable results were achieved.

In general, strong union resistance to displacement persisted until the summer of 1949, making it difficult for employers to embark on reorganization of their production processes. Earlier, as has already been noted, unions had attempted to control production directly. When the National Railway Corporation announced a plan to displace 17,000 workers in July 1946, the National Railway Workers' Union initially forced the corporation to postpone the discharges until September and finally succeeded in forcing the employer to abandon this displacement plan. Maritime employers at one time planned to drop 40,000 seamen who were not needed because so many ships had been lost in the war, but the All-Japan Seamen's Union called a general strike and succeeded in forcing the employers to abandon their displacement plan. In this period, the Tōhō Movie Company was the only large corporation that was successful in carrying out discharges, in spite of a strike in August 1948. This strike began with the closing of the company's Kinuta Studio, accomplished only after four American army tanks, one cavalry squadron, three airplanes, and 1,800 armed police surrounded the studio.

In order to reorganize the administrative and industrial wartime system, public service and government corporations began to discharge employees in 1949, after enactment of a law fixing the number of personnel in the administrative organs.

Labor disputes in opposition to displacements were led by Sanbetsu under its Industry Protection Struggle policy, which aimed at placing major strategic industries under the control of a people's government. In this scheme, individual plants and regions were also to be organized under control of the people's government, and plans were advanced to establish councils for key industries (e.g., the Council for Protection of the Communication Industry, Council for Protection of the Keihin [Tokyo-Yokohama] Industrial Region), and in local company towns for local industries. The objective was to prevent exercise of arbitrary management authority at lower levels, such as the company, plant, or workshop.

These struggles against displacement proved unsuccessful in the wake of a series of improbable events in the summer of 1949—the Shimoyama case (July 5), the Mitaka case (July 15), and the Matsukawa case (August 1), mentioned earlier in this chapter. Owing to these episodes, social insecurity prevailed, and as a consequence no militant union struggles against displacement developed.

Two factors combined to defeat these struggles: (1) Occupation policies and activities that assisted employers; (2) some successful efforts by employers to produce internal union splits by often excluding middle-aged and older workers from displacement lists and providing them with augmented wage increases. Furthermore, with the impetus of the Korean War boom, employers regained their strength, and, after the peace treaty was concluded, they became powerful enough to put production reorganization into effect through displacements. Displacement drives thus took place in waves over six-month periods in each industry, continuing until 1954.

After 1954 major union struggles against displacement included several of those mentioned earlier in this chapter: the strike at the Ube Nitrogenous Fertilizer Company early in 1952, the 113-day strike by the Mitsui Coal Mine Workers' Union Federation in 1953, and the strikes at the Amagasaki Steel Company and the Muroran plant of the Nihon Steel Company in 1954. The strike at the Nissan Automobile Company in 1953, already described, may be added to this list.

Labor disputes against displacement often took the form of community struggles. In Japan, the economies of many towns are dependent upon the few large firms located there, so a mass discharge in any one of them can severely affect a whole community. As noted earlier, union struggles against displacement often attracted the sympathy of the towns people, such as merchants and shopkeepers, and an entire community might turn against the employers. This was the type of strike the Industry Protection Councils intended to use to force public ownership of strategic industries. The strategy, however, was not successful because enthusiasm and support outside the labor movement were less widespread than in 1946, when everyone was eager to escape from hunger. Following the First Land Reform in February 1946 and the Second in July 1946, guaranteeing the farmers' status as owner-operators, farmers ended their earlier partnership with the labor movement. Also, employer attempts to favor older workers in order to reinforce their loyalty to the company resulted, as intended, in union splits, so the unions themselves often lacked the support necessary for the kind of concerted uprisings that they had launched in the struggles for production control and to secure rice in April and May 1946. Finally, although wage struggles could be initiated by the unions, displacement depended on the initiative of the employers, who could discharge workers from each plant at different times over a prolonged period in order to avoid concerted opposition of all the plant unions.

Other inflammatory events also served to discourage or nullify the union struggles. After 1950, strikes similar to the Industry Protection Struggle occurred frequently. For example, the strike at the Ube Nitrogenous Fertilizer Company over discharges (including Kaoru Ohta, then vice-president of Sōhyō) developed into a citywide struggle and was successful. The strike at the Miike, Yamano, Tagawa, Bibai, Sunagawa, and Ashibetsu mines of the Mitsui Mining Company was successful after a 113-day struggle. The struggle was conducted jointly by blue- and white-collar workers, who prevented the implementation of a plan to displace 5,838 workers, including 1,001 white-collar employees. However, many other struggles did not end in victories for the unions.

Various signs of the decline of revolutionary unionism began to appear in these unsuccessful struggles. In labor disputes immediately after the war, the workers' objective was to take over production, but in later disputes "production control" was replaced by a variation on the sit-down technique: *kyōkō shūrō*, literally, "forceful report to work," in which workers daily came to work and reported to their work places even though they had been told to stay at home because there was no work for them to do. Displaced workers also reported for work in order to prevent any discrimination against friends. In such cases, the employer often locked out all workers, making it difficult for the union members to communicate with their leaders, since the usual site of such communications was within the work place. At the same time employers, as we have seen, often attempted to take advantage of communication problems among the union members by organizing a second union. At this juncture, violent confrontations would occur between the forces of the first union and the forces of the second, who were protected by armed police and hired thugs. In the Miike strike in 1960, for example, thugs stabbed one union member to death, and after the second union members resumed work members of the first union surrounded the mine property to cut off food supplies. A violent confrontation between the two groups took place several days later. When production at Miike resumed, however, internal disputes flared among the first union members, many of whom left the union. In the end, the first union became a minority organization, and displaced workers found that the only way to secure relief was to appeal to the courts.

In 1953, as mentioned above, the Mitsui Coal Mine Workers' Union Federation defeated a displacement plan after a 113-day strike. The federation then hoped to extend its struggle under the policy slogan "participation in management," which became a subject of debate within Sōhyō. From this debate emerged the federation proposal to ask for a labor contract prohibiting the premodern characteristics of coal-mine management; the labor contract would demand that employers present their long-range plans to the unions in order to preclude unfair displacement. Meanwhile, opponents of the federation within Sōhyō decided to adopt a "labor plan" patterned after the Italian method of worker struggles against discharge. After a strike was lost in the summer of 1954, and the "labor plan" method apparently was achieving no fruitful results, the union strategy turned to the more promising "labor contract" approach. This method was adopted in 1947 and 1948 by two little-known unions, the Mitsui Coal Mine Workers' Union Federation, as part of the Japan Coal Miners' Union, and the Hokuriku Private Railway Workers' Union, an affiliate of the General Federation of Private Railway Workers' Unions of Japan. The two enterprise unions gave direction to the labor movement from 1955 onward, strengthening the organization of virtually all of Japan's unions. The focus of the new approach was to make labor redundancy and displacement the subject of collective bargaining.

Typical of the disputes over displacement after 1955 was a series of strikes in coal mining. Unsuccessful in attempts to compete with petroleum, the industry declined to such an extent that 110,000 workers had to be discharged. As mentioned, the series of strikes in the industry reflected economic conditions after 1955, but in nature they seemed very close to the strikes that occurred from 1950 to 1955.

Examples of such disputes over displacement were the strike of the Kijima Coal Mine Workers' Union in 1957, which followed the successful methods used by the Mitsui Coal Mine Workers' Union Federation in 1953, and the bitter, prolonged strike of the Miike Coal Mine Workers' Union of the latter federation in 1959–60. These strikes did not arise because of mass discharges but rather were skirmishes that preceded later disputes over large-scale displacements.

The Miike strike, the larger of the two in scale, marked the termination of communal struggles that had developed between 1950 and 1955. The change in Sōhyō's struggle strategy reflected accumulated experience from the strikes at the Muroran plant of the Nihon Steel Corporation in 1954, at the Ōji Paper Company in 1958, and at the Miike mines in 1960. The new policy aimed at counteracting the employer's "second union" strategy by emphasizing the union's attempt to bargain collectively over the reorganization of the work force after a great many workers had already been displaced. The Miike management, however, rejected the union's attempt to bargain, resorted to a lockout, and succeeded in creating a second union.

One prominent characteristic of the labor disputes after 1954 was the development of improved strike support.[7] For example, the strike at the Muroran plant of the Nihon Steel Corporation had the support of the Hokkaido Regional Council of Trade Unions and Sōhyō, and, to a lesser degree, of the Japanese Federation of Iron and Steel Workers' Unions, or Tekkōrōren. By contrast, the strike at the Ōji Paper Company was supported primarily by the National Federation of Paper and Pulp Industry

7. For further details, see Wakao Fujita, "Sengō Nihon rōdō sōgiron" [Labor disputes in postwar Japan], in *Shakaikagaku Kenkyū* [Journal of social science], 17, no. 2 (1965).

Workers' Unions, and, to a lesser degree, by the Hokkaido Regional Council and Sōhyō. The key supporting union organizations in
the Miike strike were even more clearly identified; the Japan Coal
Miners' Union, an industrial union, took full responsibility for the
strike, backed by Sōhyō. Also, there tended to be an increase in
strike assistance in terms of both strike fund contributions and the
dispatch of officers from supporting unions. Labor banks were
more fully utilized to meet shortages in strike funds. The problem
in the Miike strike, however, was that the supporting industrial
union could not effectively carry out a strike on an industrywide
basis. In addition, communal struggles had ceased to be successful
around 1953. People in the community where a strike broke out
no longer offered unanimous support; rather, they separated into
opposing groups much like the union members splitting into first
and second unions.

In the developing industries, where a great deal of money was
being invested in technological change and the introduction of
new equipment, still different features of labor disputes emerged.
In the declining industries, such as coal mining, the tendency was
to close down an old plant and to build or open a new one, causing
serious problems of mass displacement. In the developing industries, however, many young workers were employed at new
plants, and, in order to avoid disputes over the discharge issue,
there tended to be no rapid displacement of personnel at plants to
be closed down. Instead, employers simply ceased hiring new employees at the old plants and allowed the work force to decline by
attrition as workers retired. In case the business situation worsened
and the plant had to be closed, there remained the possibility for
the labor union to struggle for fair transfer of workers to new
plants.

Following the unsuccessful Miike strike, another coal strike took
place in 1961 at the Takamatsu mine of the Nihon Coal Mine
Company. The process of closing unproductive mines had by now
brought about the discharge of a total of 110,000 miners, and to
cope with the situation, the labor unions decided to struggle for a
new *overall national policy for the industry*. Sōhyō had already pro-
grammed a *long-range economic policy* which dealt in part with the
coal-mining industry, but in 1961 the Coal Miners' Union went

further by advocating more government protection of the industry and preparation for an emergency stoppage of petroleum imports.

After a coal study commission was organized in 1962, unions and employers in the industry joined in appealing to the commission for protective measures, making it difficult for unions to oppose strongly the policies of the employers and the government by means of strikes. Therefore, the unions decided to send masses of union members to metropolitan Tokyo to engage in demonstrations aimed at bringing the union demands to public attention. This episode shows that even the Coal Miners' Union, a powerful industrial union, had to rely on appeals to the public rather than on its own economic strike power.

Meanwhile, trade liberalization after 1959 had severe effects upon domestic industries, forcing further rationalization to achieve increased efficiency in order to meet international competition. Consequently, even developing industries often found it necessary to close down old plants and build new ones. In these industries, union struggles for transfers of workers became especially frequent and persistent during the period from 1955 to 1960. Moreover, since employers had been decentralizing their business organizations into self-contained units, the unions sought the transfer of union members from the old to the new installations as well as better working conditions for their members in the new plants. This kind of problem, however, could be solved within the enterprise, so that since 1960 industrial unions have supported few disputes over displacement.

Labor disputes over displacement, however, became widespread in the small and medium-sized companies, but in this sector both this type of dispute as well as those over wage increases often resulted in the bankruptcy of a firm. Figures on labor disputes over plant shutdowns or displacement by size of enterprise clearly indicate a correlation between the frequency of disputes over displacement in unionized plants and the size of the firm. Since, the smaller the firm, the less likely it is that a labor union is organized, however, the actual number of disputes of this kind may be greatly underestimated. For this reason it may be said that disputes over displacement have become more common in the small and medi-

um-sized companies and are declining in the large enterprise
sector.

Enterprise Unionism and Labor Disputes

Japanese labor unions have been characterized, in this study
and elsewhere, as enterprise unions. The relationship between
enterprise unions and labor disputes is seen in the following characteristics.

1. The Sit-Down Strike

Japanese business, in terms of industrial sociology, is organized
according to an enterprise family system, and from the standpoint
of labor relations the governing rule of the system is that length of
service is the criterion for value judgments. As a result, especially
in large enterprises, the relationships characteristic of a closed
society prevail. In judging a member, for example, the enterprise
to which he belongs, the position he occupies in the enterprise, and
how long he has served the enterprise are more important criteria
than the ability he has demonstrated. Those who transfer from
one enterprise to another are thought of as "wavering" or capri-
cious.

For this reason, as we have seen in earlier chapters, labor unions
are organized on an enterprise basis. The prerequisite for union
organization is not that workers have job interests in common
beyond the enterprise organization but that they belong to (or
work for) the same enterprise. This is especially true in large
enterprises. Although there are some labor unions organized on a
job basis, they do not occupy strong positions in the Japanese labor
union movement. Since the end of World War II, the organizational unit that has comprised the bulk of the labor union movement is the plant- or office-level organization of all employees;
these units are further organized in an enterprise federation or
enterprisewide union, or *kigyōren*.

The basic strategy of these unions in disputes is always to try to
occupy the plant. Instead of "plant occupation," it might be more

accurate to call this type of action a sit-down strike. Although this technique is basic, statistics indicate that the conventional strike with workers walking off their jobs is more frequent. But even in the cases of walk-outs, when disputes reach a critical stage, the central strategy is to enter and occupy the plant.

The following paragraphs include comments on this problem with regard to postwar developments. As has been noted, many business or production control disputes occurred immediately after the war. Some observers explain this phenomenon as a movement for social revolution, while others are convinced it was necessary to combat inflation. Since the latter explanation is convenient for the purposes of objective description, it will be adopted here to a certain degree. However, in attempting to grasp the essence of Japanese labor disputes—their meanings or motives—this explanation does not suffice. At the end of the war, when inflation was severe and employers were unable to reorganize for economic reconstruction, sit-down strikes took the form of business or production control; but after employers had worked out a way to move toward reconstruction of the Japanese economy, strengthened by the Korea War boom, business or production control could no longer occur in the large enterprises, although it may have been possible in small companies. At this stage, sit-down strikes took the form of discharged employees reporting for work and refusing to leave. When they were locked out, the dispute then became a walk-out strike. Especially when a union uses the walk-out to circumvent an employer's lockout strategy, then the walk-out strike in its true sense appears to be the basic strategy in labor disputes. In such cases, relationships between the first and second unions must also be taken into consideration. The return to the plant of members of the second union in order to resume production and the subsequent withdrawal of members from the first union provide proof of the strong attachment of union members to their enterprise.

2. Living Expenses during Disputes

"Family-system" management was also reflected in the practice of labor unions, once a dispute was settled, of demanding payments for their members' living expenses during the dispute, and the employer's agreeing to make such payments. For SCAP people engaged in labor relations affairs, this practice was difficult to understand. Dr. Itsutaro Suehiro, then chairman of the Central Labor Relations Commission, explained Japanese labor disputes by comparing them to quarrels between husband and wife. Even during quarrels, the wife lives on the husband's income. Translating this idea into labor relations terms, since Japanese labor disputes take place within the context of lifetime employment, it follows that minimum expenses to maintain the living standards of workers during the disputes should be paid, although such payments were not called wages so long as the principle of "no work, no pay" prevailed.[8] It was on the premise of the lifetime employment guarantee that unions demanded payment of expenses during disputes and companies acceded to these demands.

From 1950 to 1955, American-type labor relations and agreements were most strongly advocated by the Ministry of Labor, and as a result the practice of paying expenses during disputes apparently ceased temporarily. After 1955, however, this practice reappeared in the form of "payment of recovery funds," as part of the terms of settlement suggested by labor relations commissions in bitter labor disputes.[9] The "payment of recovery funds" has the following meaning: since the union members are too exhausted to work after a long dispute, in order to stop the dispute and get production started again, the workers must obtain enough staple food to restore their physical stamina so they will be fit for productive work. Formally, "recovery funds" are not payments for expenses during the dispute period, as in the past, but rather are payments for future expenses. This new designation, however, is merely a euphemism; essentially, "recovery funds" are simply a different form of paying for expenses incurred during a dispute.

8. Itsutaro Suehiro, *Rōdōhō no hanashi* [Lectures on labor law] (Tokyo: Nihon Hyoronsha, 1947), p.45
9. For example, in the Mitsui Miike dispute of 1960.

3. Internal Union Factionalism

Factional relationships within enterprise unions are also important to observe as they affect or contribute to union splits in struggle situations.

As has been explained in detail in Chapter 7, the total work force—everyone in a plant or office except certain managers (usually above the department manager level)—constitutes the basic unit of an enterprise labor union. Thus, the union typically includes both office and manual workers, regardless of differences in their jobs.

In such an organization it is difficult for the members to reach unanimous decisions, since the value system based upon length of service in the plant is apt to be the primary influence upon employee attitudes. The more difficult the problem, the more difficult it is for a union to reach an unanimous decision. Unanimity, as the term is used here, means not that there are no negative votes on an issue, but that there is at least considerable stability and predictability in union decision making by majority rule over a long period of time.

Generally speaking, however, in an enterprise union, antagonism between clerical and manual workers tends to arise during wage struggles, and clerical workers can always be counted on to oppose the wage demands of the manual workers. Antagonism within the union is even more apparent in antidischarge issues than in wage struggles. In one newspaper union, for example, there are separate factions of printers, reporters, and sales workers. In manufacturing, in addition to the clerical-manual antagonism, the lower-level managers also form a factional group. Such factions can be considered to be based on different job interests within an all-inclusive union, but there can be other explanations. Educational background, which is largely identical with job classes among both clerical and manual workers, and age can also be pointed to as contributing factors. Generally speaking, young workers are militant, while middle-aged and older workers are conservative.

In addition to job interests, education, and age, still another point of conflict must be noted—whether or not to comply with the length-of-service value system. Because of this last factor the so-called vertical shift phenomenon occurs; it cannot be explained simply by job, education, and age. To explain: The second union, as noted, functions as a strike-breaking organization. Therefore, in Japanese labor disputes, the union usually has a potential strike-breaking group within itself. Outside strike-breakers whom the company hires in disputes are not actually production workers but are hired thugs who serve as bodyguards for second union members trying to break through the picket line of first union members and their sympathizers.

The characteristics of picketing in Japanese disputes should be explained at this point. The original purpose of picketing, of course, is to dissuade possible strike-breakers or to inform the general public and other workers of the reasons for the dispute. As Japanese strike-breakers include union members, they participate in the decision making of the union before a strike takes place. When they reach the point of forming a second union, there is no longer any possibility of persuading them peacefully to change their minds. As a result, the picket line which the first union forms aims at preventing the second union members from entering the plant. The line is an attempt at forceful prevention. Pickets do not carry placards, but instead they appeal to citizens and other union members through handbills which they pass out.

There is still another possible explanation of the formation of a second union, if we assume that, by breaking a strike, workers who might otherwise be discharged are assured by the employer that they will keep their jobs. According to this explanation, before it is decided who will be discharged when personnel curtailment is about to take place, some of the potential unemployed join with workers who expect to be retained to form the second union. In so doing, the potential unemployed workers avoid discharge. However, this reasoning is unsatisfactory as an explanation of the motivations behind the formation of second unions. The previous explanation of conflict between different groups of employees—those loyal to the union and those who would betray it—is probably more reliable.

Although Japanese picketing has often taken the form of scrimmages, this does not mean that there are no attempts at peaceful persuasion. In the dispute at the Minamata plant of the Shin-Nihon Chisso Company in 1962, led by the Japanese Federation of Synthetic Chemical Workers' Unions (a union which uses some of the most rational approaches among Japanese labor organizations), the first union and its sympathizers did use persuasive picketing when second union members tried to enter the plant.

4. General Strikes

There is no one definition of a general strike in Japan. Even a strike that extends beyond an individual enterprise is often called a general strike. In this presentation, however, a general strike is defined as a large-scale struggle intended to influence not only labor-management relations but also governmental policies. Therefore, the definition covers, for example, strikes calling for social change, amendments to labor laws, or changes in wage policies of labor relations commissions.

According to this definition, there have been five general strike attempts since the end of the war: (1) the February 1 General Strike, 1947; (2) the March Struggle, 1948, for a ¥2,900 increase in base pay; (3) the July Struggle, 1948, for a ¥5,200 increase in base pay; (4) the Rōtō Strike, in 1952; and (5) the April 17 Strike, in 1964.

Of these five, only the Rōtō Strike, in opposition to passage of the Subversive Activity Prevention Law and amendments to the labor relations laws, actually occurred. The other four were wage struggles. It is not accurate to conclude from this experience, however, that general strikes on wage issues are difficult to carry out in Japan. The first three strikes on the list, called during the Occupation and before the signing of the peace treaty, were thwarted by SCAP prohibitions.

The characteristics of Japanese general strikes can be understood from the following review of events. First, during the postwar period, especially until anti-inflation policies were initiated in 1949, conditions were favorable for carrying out a general strike for wage increases. Because inflation was so intense, there was a strong universal desire to remedy extremely adverse conditions, especially before the intra-union splits developed. What made it impossible was the unyielding opposition of the Occupation.

Second, after 1950, a general strike over wage issues became difficult because wage differentials among enterprises became more pronounced and policy differences within the labor movement posed an obstacle to unified action among union members. These differences were especially evident with regard to wage problems. Under these circumstances, the wage issue, which otherwise might unify the workers, did not directly influence them as individuals. A general strike was possible only over problems unrelated to differences in viewpoints among individual workers; an issue had to be of common concern to all in the sense that the workers' future interests were involved. Possible amendments to the labor laws constituted such an issue.

This does not mean that wage issues were no longer a problem. For example, in the 1964 Spring Labor Offensive, Sōhyō set April 17 as the date for a general strike which was to be the greatest demonstration since the Spring Offensives began in 1955. However, Sōhyō was unable to carry out the strike because, as noted, the Communist factional group withdrew its support on April 8, just before the scheduled date of the strike. Since the wage-increase struggle of the Spring Offensive aims to permit as many unions as possible to participate in strikes by setting strike dates in advance, the Spring Offensive itself is a form of general strike. The reason it usually does not develop into an actual general strike is that there is a tendency for pattern bargaining to take place among national industrial federations or national unions; the General Federation of Private Railway Workers' Unions, for example, often sets a pattern which other unions follow. In the case of the 1964 Spring Offensive, however, there was to be no pattern-setting national union and, therefore, a general strike came very close to being an actuality.

5. Discontinuity in Labor Union Movement

Any review of the development of the labor union movement

over the past twenty years reveals a large degree of discontinuity. The experiences of the movement have not been cumulative as common property of the unions. The high turnover among union officers is evidence for this point.

When the revolutionary labor movement collapsed shortly after the war, the "leading-union" movement appeared from among unions that formerly had been unknown or regarded as company unions. The Hokuriku Railway Workers' Union of the General Federation of Private Railway Workers' Unions and the Miike Coal Miners' Union of the Japan Coal Miners' Union are examples of unions that served as pattern setters in union organization at the plant level during the early period, 1953–58. However, when these unions lost their positions of leadership around 1960, a job wage plan (anti-*nenkō*) appeared in the Matsushita Electric Workers' Union of the All-Japan Federation of Electric Machine Workers' Unions, or Denkirōren, an affiliate of Chūritsurōren.

Such phenomena occurred because the labor unions that had been leaders for a period lost their hegemony as a result of the ascendancy of second unions before they had time to adapt to changing economic or political conditions. Still another reason is that, before a union is able to accumulate enough experience to assume leadership within a national organization, it is often replaced by a second union within its company. Experience is not cumulative because the leaders of the national union are composed of representatives of enterprise unions. Therefore, even if the leader of a union that is replaced by a second union stays on as an officer of the national union, he can no longer play a leading role in the national labor movement.

The result of these experiences is that the fighting spirit, or even the ideas generated at the lower levels of the labor movement, does not break through to the top. Typical of this failure was the labor plan and the long-term economic policy struggle of Sōhyō in 1954. As described above, in 1953 the Mitsui Coal Mine Workers' Union Federation of the Japan Coal Miners' Union, after a 113-day strike, succeeded in defeating a personnel curtailment plan of the company, and in 1954 the union further concluded an agreement with the management for an examination of the company's long-term development plan. There was a possibility at that moment that this struggle "from below" would develop into a full-employment movement in the coal-mining industry. However, a group within Sōhyō, hoping to imitate the Italian labor plan, rejected this form of struggle and later proposed a long-time economic policy planned by Sōhyō itself. Thus, it made no effort to develop the autonomous struggles at the lower levels into a full-employment movement.

It appears that union leadership in Japan is constantly trying to imitate foreign labor movements. Formation of industrial policy, an important problem for unions today, is advocated by those who have studied European union movements. It is not based upon the experience, successful or unsuccessful, gained in policy-change struggles such as those conducted by the Japan Coal Miners' Union in 1962.

Labor Disputes and Labor Relations

Japan's postwar labor disputes have reflected the contradictions and strains of prewar labor relations, partly because the employers were severely stricken by the defeat in the war and more importantly because after the enactment of the labor laws workers were guaranteed the right to form a labor movement.

Those who promoted the labor movement, especially Sanbetsu in the immediate postwar period (up to 1949), were workers who had been unfavorably treated under the length-of-service system based upon status due to one's educational background, and who would have been discharged if it had not been for labor shortages during the war. Now these workers were not even discharged for taking an active role in the labor union movement, since self-organization had become a guaranteed right. Further, this movement led to kangaroo court negotiations and labor disputes of the business or production control type. The goal of Sanbetsu in developing this movement on a nationwide scale was to achieve people's administration of important industries; the basis of the movement was the work place or area controlled by the people.

In opposition to this movement, in 1949, government and employers opened the way to personnel curtailment in administrative organs and in private enterprise with the support of the Occupation. Later, they proceeded with displacement on their own, almost completing it by 1954 or 1955 (see Fig. 9.8).

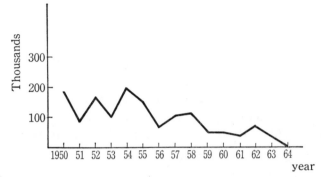

Fig. 9.8.
Number of displaced workers in manufacturing industry, 1950–64.

The problem here is to determine what happened to labor-management relations during the labor union movement's so-called regressive period. The central force of the militant labor union was a small group of middle-aged workers who had been unfavorably treated under the prewar length-of-service system;

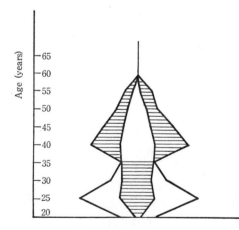

Fig. 9.9.
Employment structure of the National Railway Corporation by age, 1948 and 1966.

the followers were a great many young workers who were employed in large numbers in the enterprises during the postwar period. The young workers were usually organized in youth departments set up by each union; these departments were dominated by the Young Men's Communist League.

According to Fig. 9.9, the largest number of union members fell in the 20–24-year-old age group in 1948; in 1966 the 35–39-year-old group was the largest. Although workers under 30 years of age made up 63 percent of the work force in 1948, the percentage had decreased to 21 percent by 1966. Workers over 35 years of age accounted for only 27 percent of the work force in 1948, but by 1966 they had increased to 70 percent. In 1948 the central group of the revolutionary labor union movement in the National Railway Workers' Union was under 30 years of age; the group then made up 62.9 percent of the work force.

The method the employers used to break this revolutionary work force was to give preferential treatment to the middle-aged and older militant workers. In concrete terms, this meant favorable wage increases and exclusion from personnel curtailments. By these means, employers succeeded in increasing the loyalty of the middle-aged and older workers to the enterprises and in separating them from the militant young forces within the unions. This policy, which was designed to weaken the militant labor union in the enterprise, resulted in successive union splits during 1948.

The length-of-service system was greatly influenced by this policy. That is, in prewar labor relations, the "guarantee of lifetime employment" was only an ideal, for in fact employers relied on the system of voluntary retirement or other special methods of discharge in order to thin the ranks of older employees and maintain pyramidal employment structures. However, when the middle-aged and older workers came to be treated favorably, idealized lifetime employment became real lifetime employment in postwar labor relations. What James C. Abegglen pointed to as a "lifetime commitment" in *The Japanese Factory* was brought about by the above developments.[10]

10. James C. Abegglen, *The Japanese Factory* (New York: Free Press, 1958).

The method of discharge also changed, since the former means of maintaining the pyramidal employment structure in an enterprise could no longer be used and the employer was not able to induce "voluntary" retirement. In the prewar days, since most discharges were handled as voluntary retirements, there were few cases in which court suits were filed; since the war, those who have been discharged under work rules have often filed suits.

Although court suits over discharge have been frequent, employers and employees have not yet found a way to adjust the work force by means of layoff and recall based on seniority. Although idealized lifetime employment has become real lifetime employment, promotion is not based upon seniority but continues to be decided arbitrarily by the employer. As a result, employers find it easy to take advantage of competition for promotions among union members in order to provoke splits within the unions.

Sōhyō was formed in 1950 in an effect to go along with the employer policy of giving favorable treatment to middle-aged and older workers. From 1950 to 1955, when personnel curtailment due to readjustment of enterprises had not yet been completed, union activists were always the target of discharge. While Sōhyō at first took advantage of the policy and encouraged the purge of activists who had belonged to Sanbetsu unions, later the activists in the Sōhyō unions found themselves the targets. Formation in 1954 of Zenrō Kaigi (forerunner of Dōmei), by a group of unionists who split away from Sōhyō, can be regarded as yet another attempt to go along with employer discharge policies.

Between the end of the war and 1955 forms of *status* discrimination based upon educational background were eliminated. However, *job* discrimination according to educational background has existed throughout the pre- and postwar periods and has functioned as channel for mass energy. No matter how poor the family from which a Japanese boy comes, so long as he does well in school, he has the opportunity to enter a higher-level school. As all graduates of the famous universities are expected to hold jobs with high social status, the percentage of students entering schools of a higher grade in an attempt to achieve a higher status has increased markedly; this as well as other factors have led to a rise in the overall level of education.

University graduates still get the managerial jobs, and those with less than a high school education are assigned to operative jobs. The remarkable increase in the number of university and high school graduates, however, has resulted in a decline in their respective social positions. High school graduates are now employed as operatives in heavy industry; they are also employed in clerical positions, whereas before the war only middle school graduates were employed in these jobs. Thus, it can be said that the prewar status-oriented length-of-service system based upon educational background changed to a job-oriented length-of-service system based upon educational background. That it is still a length-of-service system means that individual promotion is not carried out by seniority but depends upon the arbitrary will of the employer. Even when criteria for promoting employees or union members are expressed in terms of a merit system, length-of-service values still constitute the decisive factor. Promotion competition among union members thus becomes a factor in the formation of second unions, through which employers continue to exercise control over the unions.

Since 1955, the introduction of new technology as well as capital investment has made lifetime employment, concretely expressed in the preponderance of middle-aged and older workers in the work force, a deterrent to rationalization, and emphasis has been placed upon the employment of young workers.

The age structure of the work force in 1948 and in 1966, as

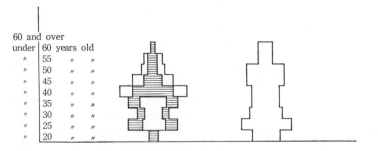

Fig. 9.10.
Employment structure by age of the National Railway Corporation, the Telegraph & Telephone Public Corporation and private firms.

shown in Fig. 9.10, demonstrates two typical patterns of enterprise expansion under the lifetime employment system. However, the change in age composition has differed among enterprises. For example, the age structure of the Telegraph and Telephone Corporation is similar to the 1948 pattern shown in Fig. 9.9, since enterprise expansion there has been achieved by employment of new school graduates. By contrast, in the National Railway Corporation's structure, the largest number of workers fall in the 40–45-year-old age group. These structural differences brought on a stormy debate over wage policy among the unions belonging to the General Council of Public Corporation and National Enterprise Workers' Unions at the 1964 Sōhyō convention.

The age structure in private enterprises is a mixture of the 1948 and 1966 types, reflecting the industrial mix of enterprises that are not expanding and do not employ new workers and those that are expanding and do employ young workers as well as a mixture of employees in old and in new plants.

Unions are attempting to take advantage of the increased need for young workers by demanding increases in wages for young workers and by using this demand as a lever to win wage increases for the middle-aged and older workers as well. The Spring Offensive is nothing but bargaining over annual wage increases. The number of enterprises that have adopted the annual wage increase system has been increasing; therefore, the scope of the Spring Offensive has been broadening. The essence of the new job wage system is that employers attempt to meet the wage demands of the young workers by holding down increases for the middle-aged and older workers. In larger enterprises, an employer does not attempt to discharge the middle-aged and older workers, but rather, through collective bargaining with the union, he tries to transfer them, as much as possible, whenever the company expands its facilities.[11] These workers, together with a large number of young workers, constituted the typical 1948 work force. Therefore, except in a declining industry such as coal mining, disputes over readjustments and personnel curtailments have decreased in number. The national union does not concern itself

11. In prewar days transfers were made arbitrarily by employers without resort to collective bargaining.

with this problem. Instead, transfers are settled by negotiations between the enterprise and the enterprise union.

Technological change, capital investment, and rationalization have also tended to promote the establishment of independent auxiliary businesses and subsidiary enterprises as well as mergers of established companies. In the former case, the principal production activities continue to be carried on by the parent company, some of the company's personnel can be allocated to its subsidiaries. Thus, the subsidiaries provide jobs for some of the parent company's redundant middle-aged and older workers. Such arrangements do not become a source of trouble but are settled through collective bargaining within the enterprise.

In mergers, differences in the nature of the unions in each plant or work place sometimes create a barrier which the employers try to overcome by suppressing active opposition within the unions. If a dispute occurs, the employer can take advantage of it by encouraging the formation of a second union in the hope that the group opposing the readjustment or merger will become a minority. Examples of mergers in recent years are the Ishikawajima Heavy Industries-Harima Shipbuilding merger, the Nissan Automobile Company-Prince Motor Company merger, and the merger of several companies to form New Mitsubishi Heavy Industries.

As a whole, Japanese labor unionism, particularly as developed by Sōhyō, favors the following policies: the annual Spring Labor Offensive for employers' regular wage increase policy; differentials in the wage distribution means of fixed-amount allocations; a minimum wage guarantee by age for workers not regularly employed (i.e., workers not employed immediately after school graduation); and collective bargaining over the transfer of displaced middle-aged and older workers to new plants of the company or its subsidiaries. This type of movement is characteristic of the recent boom period (due partly to the Vietnam War) in contrast to the period of personnel curtailment before 1955.

At the same time that large enterprises carry out capital investment and technological changes, some small enterprises go bankrupt because they are unable to manage the necessary business readjustment. Since the rate of union organization in these enterprises is low, labor disputes over business readjustment or personnel curtailment either do not occur or do not attract public attention. However, the tension in labor relations caused by bankruptcies has created some concern within the labor union movement, which has encouraged efforts toward unionization of small units.

As indicated in Chapter 7, there is a great gap in the rate of unionization between the enterprises employing more than one hundred workers and those employing fewer than a hundred. The reason for this gap is that Japanese unions are organized at the plant or work place level. A certain number of employees are necessary to maintain a union financially. It is difficult to organize an independent plant union covering all employees in an enterprise that employs fewer than a hundred workers. As a result, it becomes necessary to organize an amalgamated union, composed of employees of several enterprises. This idea was already recognized around 1955 as a principle of organization. During that period, owing partly to the fact that the Japan Communist Party adopted the position of not recognizing Sōhyō as the leader of the unified labor union movement, when an activist in a small enterprise was discharged, his supporters formed an "anonymous" amalgamated labor union. The disputes in the small enterprises carried on by an "anonymous" amalgamated union, which is supported by a number of sympathizing unions, often take a form similar to a kangaroo court.

The most decisive influence upon Japanese labor relations since 1955 has been the decrease in the growth of the labor force. Since 1947, which has been called the year of the baby boom, the birth rate has fallen. By 1963, when those persons born in 1947 entered the labor force, the problem of a developing labor shortage was apparent. Given the decline in the number of new school graduates seeking employment since the mid-1960s, it may be necessary to make changes in the system of labor relations based upon length of service. As an illustration, the wage agreement which the Matsushita Electric Workers' Union concluded with the company in 1966 established wages by job on the premise that a twenty-five-year-old worker is a full-fledged worker, and the minimum wages formerly guaranteed by age were replaced by guaranteed minimum wages by job. The reason for the conclusion of this agreement was that, as it became difficult for the company to employ young women workers, it recruited middle-aged women who had fulfilled their child-rearing obligations. Under the former system of wage determination, the age factor had functioned to keep the wage rates of young workers low. Since this same factor functioned to provide high wage rates for newly employed middle-aged workers, the job wage agreement was concluded for the purpose of excluding the age factor from wage determination.

This wage agreement, which sets a standard rate for the twenty-five-year-old worker, changes the guaranteed minimum wage by age under the former length-of-service wage system but is also different from "the job wage system," which combines a base rate under the length-of-service wage system with a job wage rate. The job wage system is a kind of allowance controllable as circumstances change, and it is often used to adjust the wage fund by holding down wage increases for middle-aged and older workers and converting the savings into wage increases for young workers. This method can be carried out successfully in enterprises where there are relatively few middle-aged and older workers; in enterprises with many older workers in the labor force, however, it is impossible to implement.

It cannot be denied that the labor shortage has had a profound effect on the length-of-service wage system. Since 1962, when people first became aware of absolute shortages in the labor force, the organization of "anonymous" amalgamated labor unions has occurred, and the base rates have begun to rise as a result of disputes initiated by such unions. In 1964, when Japan joined the Organization for Economic Cooperation and Development, capital liberalization became necessary, and this brought about a fundamental change in labor-management relations. A solution to these problems might require a more fundamental readjustment of labor relations than the change that occurred in 1955, but it may still be too early to discuss this problem.

10. The Industrial Reward System: Wages and Benefits

Japan's wage system in general is quite different from the wage systems of Western countries. In the West wages usually take the form of base rates only, whereas in Japan they are the sum of a variety of payments. The Japanese worker, in most cases, receives not only a base rate but also an individual efficiency rate, a group incentive rate, and job duty allowances for occupational position, diligence, and so on. There are also other payments such as family regional living-cost and housing allowances. All these wage items, taken together, are called the *chingin taikei*, or wage system.

Wage Components

The wage system has its roots in Japan's history. It may be said that the major purpose of the system has been to keep the base rates as low as possible. The place of a worker on the ascending scale of base rates, the cornerstone of the personnel management system, explicitly indicates his status in the work place, a feature of the wage system that Japanese employers have never changed. As the base rate is also a basis for calculating the worker's retirement allowance, employers have felt it necessary to keep it as low as possible in order to minimize the cost of such allowances. On the occasion of wage increases in times of rising prices, they have preferred to add a variety of allowances rather than to increase base rates.

The concept of a living wage based on traditional family-paternalism may have been still another factor that contributed to the peculiar Japanese wage system. The family allowance as a part of wages was introduced after World War I and has spread rapidly since that time. It has contributed significantly to the wage system's paternalistic features.

Finally, whereas wage rates in Western countries are based essentially on occupational skill, in Japan they are characteristically determined by the worker's age, length of service, and occupational status (and, since World War II, his educational background). In other words, the wage rates of Japanese permanent employees increase by an annual increment that raises the wage of each individual according to his age and length of service.

This characteristic is often called *nenkō-chingin* (seniority wage). It does not necessarily follow, however, that the Japanese wage system is totally unrelated to occupational skill or job performance. For example, it is assumed that workers who have completed higher educational levels may be able to achieve higher skill levels or that older workers with longer service may be more skilled than younger workers. In Japan, however, occupational skill is measured only by factors of educational background, age, and length of service and is not used directly to determine the wage rate. Thus, a worker's level of occupational skill can deviate from his level in terms of such factors as educational background, age, and length of service. A typical example is the case in which an employee reaches a plateau in his occupational skill level while his wage rate continues to rise as his age and length of service increase. On the other hand, it is also common for an employee to reach a skill level where he is more competent and efficient than an older employee, but to be paid less because he is younger and has a shorter period of service with the company.

The post-World War II wage system in Japan differs in several ways from that of prewar Japan. For example, formerly the employer set wage rates at his own discretion without reference to any standard. However, certain objective standards for wage determination emerged after the war. In addition, the base rate as a proportion of total wages also has increased, while job rates, which had only negligible use in prewar days, have become more popular in recent years. Despite these changes, however, the basic features of the wage system have remained unaltered.

Major features of the Japanese wage system can be described by reference to the *Survey Report on Wage Components*, issued by the Ministry of Labor in 1965. This survey covered about 4,000 establishments, in various types of industry, selected from among those employing more than 30 persons. The basic findings, shown in Table 10.1, illustrate recent changes in the composition of wages.

Table 10.1[a]

Composition of Wages, 1963–1965 (by percent)

		1963[b]		1964[b]		1965[b]
A. Regular wages						
Base rate:		81.5		82.3		83.6
Type I[c]	7.5		8.8		9.4	
Type II[d]	8.7		7.2		9.0	
Type III[e]	65.3		66.3		65.2	
Incentive rate		8.0		7.1		6.1
Allowances:						
Job-duty		2.9		3.1		3.1
Living		5.5		5.7		5.8
Encouragement		1.5		1.4		1.2
Others		0.6		0.4		0.2
Total		100.0		100.0		100.0
B. Total wages						
Regular wages[b]		87.5		87.9		89.1
Overtime pay		11.8		11.5		10.3
Other payments		0.7		0.6		0.6
Total		100.0		100.0		100.0

SOURCE: Ministry of Labor *Kyūyo kōsei chōsa-hōkoku* [Survey Report on Wage Components] (Tokyo: Ministry of Labor, 1965).

a. Regular wages exclude overtime wages and non-contractual wage payments.

b. As of September.

c. Based on age, length-of-service, education, and/or job experience.

d. Based on job rank, job skills, and job type.

e. Based on a comprehensive determination including factors in Types I and II (see Table 10.2).

First, as the upper section of Table 10.1 indicates, the base rate as a proportion of total regular or contracted wage payments is significantly larger today than in the past, having risen to 81.5 percent in 1963 and to 83.6 percent in 1965. The lower section of the table shows, moreover, that regular or contracted wages account for more than 85 percent of total wages, including over-time. In earlier years, the base rate was proportionately much lower, being supplemented by various other wage items. According-ing to a Ministry of Labor survey on wage composition in 1948, the base rate then averaged only 38.5 percent of total regular wages. Since then it has increased steadily, reaching 72.2 percent in 1953, 78.2 percent in 1955, and finally, as noted, 83.6 percent in 1965.

This increase in the relative share of the base rate is due prima-rily to simplification of the wage system achieved by integrating or eliminating various payments or allowances and establishing new base rates derived from job rates. Such a tendency indicates that the Japanese wage system is approaching Western systems but, as Table 10.1 shows, various carry-overs from the earlier days, such as incentive rates and living allowances, remain.

Another noteworthy feature of the wage composition pattern is that the group incentive rate, as a proportion of total regular wages, decreased to 8.0 percent in 1963 and further to 6.1 percent in 1965. This incentive rate was considerably greater in the period immediately after World War II. For example, the Ministry of Labor's "Survey on Wage Components" in 1951 showed that the group incentive rate (including the encouragement allowance) was 17.8 percent of total regular wages. The incentive rate at that time, the so-called *seisan hōshōsei*, or reward-for-production pay-ment system, was a certain proportion of the total sales or produc-tion of an enterprise, distributed to individual employees on the basis of their base rates. As the base rates were essentially deter-mined by length of service, the incentive rate turned out to be quite different from the original concept of a reward for individual efficiency.

One reason the incentive rate percentage gradually decreased is that productivity increases, resulting from technological innovation, made it unnecessary to continue such group incentives as reward-for-production payments. It also should be noted that the group incentive plan never really fit into the Japanese wage system, since it was designed to reward the worker for efficiency and was unrelated to his age, length of service, and educational background. In Japan, however, a worker's incentive rate is affected by his length of service, and no matter how efficient he may be he is paid less if he is younger and his service is shorter, thus weakening the incentive feature of the payment. Since the *nenkō* wage system does not conform to the original purpose of the incentive rate, as long as the system continues to be emphasized, it is inevitable that this type of incentive rate will be gradually eliminated.

The lack of congruence between *nenkō* wages and the incentive rate has created a tendency for Japanese enterprises to neglect the development of standard work schedules and standard working hours. Needless to say, these standards are essential for the successful operation of incentive systems, as incentive rates are based on the quality and quantity of workers' production. Scientific management may also need to be introduced into the enterprise if incentives are to be used, but if the incentive rate does not conform to the *nenkō* wage system scientific management will not be required.

In order to discuss the Japanese wage system in more detail, let us examine the wage components in selected establishments by size. Table 10.2 shows, among other things, that comprehensively determined base rates are most widely used, regardless of the size of an establishment. These rates are determined by such factors as age, educational level, length of service, years of organizational experience, ability, job duties, service merit, and degree of diligence. The three subtypes are labeled A, B, and C.

In comprehensively determined base rate A, the factors of ability and service-merit are evaluated according to a personnel plan based on systematic standards. A comparison of the result of this evaluation with a wage table determines the base rate. This type of rate is used in almost 40 percent of establishments with 500 or more employees, in more than 15 percent of those with 100 to

Table 10.2
Distribution of Base Rates and Incentive Rates by Size of Establishment in Manufacturing, 1963–65 (in percentages of establishments)

Wage Component[b]	1963[a]			1964[a]			1965[a]		
	500 emp. & over	100–499 emp.	30–99 emp.	500 emp. & over	100–499 emp.	30–99 emp.	500 emp. & over	100–499 emp.	30–99 emp.
Base Rate[b]									
Type I: Age	13.0	7.0	3.0	12.5	9.1	5.1	13.9	9.3	6.4
Length of service	15.3	12.9	9.8	14.4	13.4	11.5	15.2	15.2	11.5
Education	2.8	3.1	0.5	3.1	3.0	0.9	3.1	2.6	1.0
Age, length of service, education	9.1	10.8	12.7	11.5	12.0	9.1	11.1	12.2	9.7
Type II: Job-duty	12.5	3.8	0.4	13.1	2.2	0.2	14.4	2.5	0.2
Job-skill A[c]	17.9	8.0	1.2	21.2	8.3	1.6	23.3	8.1	2.1
Job-skill B[d]	5.5	2.5	1.4	3.2	2.1	0.8	2.0	2.2	0.7
Job-type	7.2	2.9	2.6	5.7	1.6	1.4	5.5	2.6	2.0
Type III: Comprehensively determined									
A	22.5	8.8	2.3	31.9	12.2	3.9	38.8	16.7	5.0
B	20.2	10.2	2.1	19.8	9.8	2.1	22.1	13.4	5.4
C	53.9	73.0	84.3	46.7	70.9	86.3	37.9	62.1	81.2
Incentive Rate									
Individual	15.9	15.6	20.4	13.9	14.6	14.3	9.4	16.0	13.7
Group	19.0	16.8	14.1	18.1	17.0	12.1	17.3	13.2	10.6

SOURCE: Ministry of Labor, *Kyōyo kōsei chōsa hōkoku* (1965).
a. As of September.
b. See Table 10.1 for explanation.
c. Based on ability and job-ranking.
d. Based on ability without job-ranking.

499 employees, and in about 5 percent of firms with 30 to 99 employees. Thus, the larger the establishment, the more widely this method of base-rate wage determination is used. The rate is determined objectively to some extent, since it is based on both a systematic personnel evaluation plan and an established wage table. Such a method of modern personnel management is not prevalent in small and medium-sized enterprises, however.

In comprehensively determined base rate B, the establishment uses a personnel evaluation plan but not a wage table. This type is used in more than 20 percent of establishments with 500 or more employees, in close to 15 percent of those with 100 to 499 employees, and in just over 5 percent of firms with 30 to 99 employees. Thus, like subtype A, it is also used more widely in large companies than in smaller companies. In this case, however, the standards for determining the rate are less objective than for subtype A, and the system for wage determination is not as modern.

Comprehensively determined base rate C is a comprehensive evaluation without any systematic standards. It is used in more than 35 percent of establishments with 500 or more employees, in over 60 percent of firms with 100 to 499 employees, and in at least 80 percent of small companies with 30 to 99 employees. Thus, unlike subtypes A and B, C is more prevalent in small and medium-sized than in large enterprises. In no sense is it based on objective standards; instead, it is determined entirely by the employer's discretion, although the labor market is considered to some extent. The fact that this kind of wage payment is widespread not only in the small and medium-sized companies but also in large companies indicates that the Japanese wage system retains premodern characteristics.

As also seen in Table 10.2, there are four other types of basic wage payments: the job-duty rate (determined by job evaluation), job-skill rate A (determined by ability in performance with job ranking), job-skill rate B (determined by ability in performance without job ranking), and job-type rate (rate of trade or occupation). The job-duty rate (*shokumukyū*) is found in almost 15 percent of establishments with 500 or more employees, in 2.5 percent of those with 100 to 499 employees, and in a mere 0.2 percent of firms with 30 to 99 employees. Thus, it may be said that although

the job-duty rate has been introduced into the Japanese wage
system, it is quite rare even in large companies, and its use is almost negligible in small and medium-sized companies. As it is
determined on the basis of the job, it is inconsistent with the *nenkō*
wage.

Job-skill rate A, based on ability and a job-ranking system,
prevails in almost 25 percent of the establishments with 500 or
more employees, a higher percentage than for the job-duty rate.
Moreover, it is used in over 8 percent of establishments with 100
to 499 employees and 2 percent of those with 30 to 99 employees.
While these percentages are a bit higher than the job-duty rate
even in small and medium-sized firms, job-skill rate A is not in
common usage.

Job-skill rate B, which is based on ability but not on a job-
ranking system, is used in only a little more than 2 percent of
establishments with 500 or more employees, over 2 percent of
companies with 100 to 499 employees, and less than 1 percent of
those with 30 to 99 employees. Thus, this rate type is also quite
rare in firms of all sizes. While the job-skill rates, like the job-duty
rates, are based on occupational skill rankings, they still rely primarily on the worker's age and length of service and secondarily
on his occupational skill. Thus, real differences in occupational
skill are only partially reflected in these rates.

The Wage System in Public Employment

The wage system for public or civil service personnel represents
an attempt to base wages on job rankings. This system was
established in 1948 through collective bargaining agreements between unions and the government which provided an average
wage of ¥2,920 per month. Prior to this development, there had
been eight wage components for public service employees; therefore, the system of determining wages was extremely complicated.
The "Rule on New Salaries" adopted in 1948 reduced the number
of wage components to four: basic salary, living allowance, work-
place allowance, and special duty allowance.

The basic salary is, of course, the key component. The rule is that salary payment is based on the degree of complexity, difficulty, and responsibility of the job, and on the work load, working hours, working environment, and other working conditions. This rule seemingly indicates that the concept of job rates was introduced into the wage system of the public workers. Occupations of public service employees are grouped into fifteen classes which are again subdivided into several grades, depending on the specific job content; the rate range for employees in the same grade or class is determined by this job-ranking system.

The reasons for grouping the occupations into fifteen classes are of interest. The classifying procedure started with definitions of the occupational class, proceeded to an analysis of the difficulty, degree of responsibility, qualifying prerequisites, physical conditions, and working environment of each specific occupation, and finally ended with comparisons of each job analysis with the job definition in order to determine job rank. This method amounts to job classification according to a job-evaluation plan.

In fact, however, a detailed job analysis was not made of the occupations of the public service employees. Instead, the so-called Method of Estimation by Occupational Class was employed as an expedient means of classifying and analyzing the occupations. By this method, the higher officers were classed as follows, in descending order: the vice-minister in each ministry is in Class 15; the director of each bureau, such as the Government Monopoly Bureau, Class 14; the director of each bureau within a ministry, Class 13; the department chief in each ministry, Class 11; the private secretary, Class 10 or 11. On the other hand, clerical employees were classified according to their personal qualifications (mainly, educational level) and a table for estimating length of service. For example, clerical employees in Class 4 were those who had an elementary school education and had served more than six years, those who had a high school education and had served more than five years, or those who had a higher technical school education and had served more than one year. Employees in Class 7 must have had an elementary school education and served more than thirteen years, a high school education and served more than ten years, a higher technical school education and served more than seven years, or a college or university education and served more than four years. Thus, as the Method of Estimation by Occupational Class shows, the job ranking of public service employees was influenced to a great extent by the *nenkō* system.

Moreover, although the job ranks of employees in Class 9 and above were classified by occupational status, their promotion was based on educational level and length of service. Therefore, it may be said that the job-ranking system for public employees in all classes is a *nenkō* system in substance, but in a different form.

The salary range in each occupational class from Class 5 to Class 9, moreover, was divided into ten grades; each of the other classes was divided into seven grades. Salary increases, therefore, have been of two types—one within the same occupational class and one as the result of promotion to a higher class. A salary increase within the same occupational class is based on length of experience on the job; that is to say, increases are given every six months in Classes 1 to 5, every nine months in Classes 6 to 9, and once a year in Classes 10 to 13. Salaries in Class 14 are increased every eighteen months. In case of promotion to a higher class, the salary is based on the rate of the lowest grade in the higher class.

The salary range within grades tends to be broader than the job rate range in Western countries. The wider range in Japan is flexible enough to take into account salary determination by the *nenkō* system. In spite of this, there is an increasing number of cases in which the rate range is not completely differentiated by the *nenkō* system, and wage increases are not always possible for employees with longer service. If a wage increase is impossible for some reason, it causes a great deal of discontent among the employees because they expect regular increases. Consequently, in 1957, the fifteen-class system was modified into an eight-class system, and the rate range for each class was broadened. For example, it now takes sixteen years to rise from the bottom to the top grade in Class 6, so there is no longer a problem of suspending wage increases for employees with long service who cannot be promoted to a higher class.

At present, the salary table is divided into as many as sixteen classes within each department, such as administration, tax revenue, public safety, maritime transportation, education, scientific research, medical care, and so on. For example, on the salary table for administrative departments, occupations are grouped into eight classes, and in each class there are rate ranges of from fifteen to eighteen grades. An employee's progress through the grades is based on age and length of service. Furthermore, the classes themselves are also differentiated by the *nenkō* system. Therefore, though the wage system of public service employees is called a job-rate system, it actually is an example of such a system modified for Japanese industrial society.

Nonetheless, it should be remembered that the method of wage determination in public service employment is different from that in private industry. Since public service employees at both the national and local levels have been deprived of their right to strike and to bargain collectively since the revision of the National Public Service Law in 1948, the national or local governments have unilateral power to determine salaries of these employees, based on the recommendation of the National Personnel Authority (NPA). The NPA compiles its recommendations once a year, on the basis of its surveys comparing wages of public service employees with those of employees in private industry, starting salaries and special allowances in private industry, and consumer prices and living costs. These recommendations, however, have often been ignored or their effectuation postponed by the government.

The National Railway Corporation also introduced a job-ranking system in 1948. While the job-ranking of public service employees was based on a method of job classification, a point system is used in the job-ranking of national railway employees. The elements and weight for job-rankings are as follows:
1. Experience, training, and qualifications—15 points
2. Responsibility—10 points
3. Degree of risk—5 points
4. Physical conditions—5 points
5. Working environment—5 points
Based on this job evaluation plan, the occupations of national railway employees were divided into 12 classes and 38 grades. (Nonclerical workers were divided into 10 classes.) The relation-

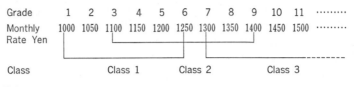

Fig. 10.1

ship between grades and classes was as follows: The grade ranged from a monthly rate of ¥1,000 in Grade 1 to ¥10,000 in Grade 70, with a flat increase of ¥50 from grade to grade. How classes were related to grades is illustrated in Fig. 10.1.

As in the case of public service employees, the job-ranking system of national railway workers made it impossible for all employees to receive regular wage increases, which, of course, gave rise to discontent. Thus, in 1951, the 12 classes were reorganized into 7 classes, and minimum and maximum rates were set for each class. In the case of station employees, for example, Class 1 is divided into 27 grades, Class 2 ranges from Grade 5 to 30, Class 3 ranges from Grade 7 to 33, Class 4 ranges from Grade 7 to 36, Class 5 ranges from Grade 9 to 39, and Class 6 ranges from Grade 19 to 42.

Since 1959, the National Railway Corporation has made an effort to put more weight on the job rate in order to establish a more rational wage system which takes into consideration such factors as changing job content and employee attitudes. As the National Railway Workers' Union (Kokurō)[1] opposed such a management policy, rationalization of the wage system proved unsuccessful until the management revised it again in 1964 to specify the job groups in more detail. In the revision, occupations were divided into nine job groups, from A to I. Job Group A includes apprentices and unskilled workers (*rōmushoku*). Job Group B is defined as Job Group A workers with more than ten years of service. Regular employees (*kakarishoku*) are in Job Group C. Job Group D is composed of supervisory employees for nonclerical work. Job Groups E and F include technical employees and

---

1. Kokutetsu Rōdōkumiai.

highly skilled workers. Job Groups G and higher are for professional staff and upper managerial personnel, including the managers at each work place. There are maximum and minimum limits on wage rates in each job group.

The Base Rate Table for national railway employees has four occupational areas: (1) general work, (2) medical care, (3) locomotive engineers, and (4) navigation and special tasks. However, the wage rates for a majority of the employees are determined by reference to the Base Rate Table for general work. A Base Rate Table is formulated for each of five job ranks. Thus, Base Rate Table 1 is applied to employees engaged in the lowest level of general work, and Base Rate Tables 2, 3, 4, and 5 are applied to employees at higher levels. It may be said that in most cases employees rise as far as Table 3. Base Rate Table 1, for example, ranges from the lowest grade, Grade 1 (¥12,200), to the highest grade, Grade 48 (¥49,300). In cases where the wage differential between grades is less than ¥500, the wage rate increases every six months. If the wage gap between grades is more than ¥900, the wage rate increases once a year. Though this is called a job-duty rate system, there is wide flexibility in the rate ranges. In this sense, it may be said that the wage system for the national railway workers retains the characteristics of the *nenkō* wage system.

Wage Systems in Large-Scale Private Enterprises

On the whole, the wage system in large industry is still premodern. Most large enterprises employ a comprehensively determined wage rate based on personal characteristics of age, length of service, educational level, occupational skill, and experience of the employee. Therefore, there are few rational standards for wage determination based on job criteria, and in most cases the employer determines individual wage rates unilaterally. Usually he adds a variety of allowances to the base rate, and in certain types of industry he adds incentive rates. On the occasion of the regular or annual wage increases, the employers usually use some type of personal evaluation plan, so that they gradually are coming to employ modern techniques to overcome irrationality in methods of wage determination. While the *nenkō* system is used without exception in large industry, rapid technological innovations and the scarcity of new school graduates in the labor market since 1955 have created conditions that require a reform of the system.

First, technological change has brought a shift in the quality of labor and a polarization of occupational skills. What has emerged is unskilled labor, on the one hand, and new types of skilled workers in master control and maintenance work, on the other. These new skilled workers are qualitatively different from the conventional skilled workers who acquired the knowledge and techniques necessary to perform their jobs through long experience. The new skilled workers are required to have a certain amount of education or knowledge, particular nonmanual skills, dexterity, punctuality, conscientiousness, and perception. These skills tend to contain objective elements, and since they can be mastered within a short period, they can hardly depend on length of service. Therefore, they are likely to be conspicuously inappropriate to the *nenkō* wage system, in which length of service correlates with level of skill. Furthermore, these new skilled jobs are usually performed by young workers who are products of the postwar education system, who tend to demand rights without hesitation and to view things realistically, and who, consequently, often are critical of the *nenkō* system. Thus, it may be said that environmental conditions have emerged which call for modification of the *nenkō* wage system and the introduction of job-duty and/or job-skill rates.

Second, the *nenkō* wage system is based on labor markets in which the supply of new graduates from junior high schools, high schools, and colleges or universities is abundant and constitutes the main source of recruitment. Because ample supplies of new school graduates were always available in the past, the starting pay level generally could be kept low. However, as these workers grew older, their living expenses tended to increase, and therefore their wages also had to be increased regularly. Moreover, large companies needed to provide employees with skill training and thus encouraged their long service in a given firm. As a result, industry emphasized rewards for long service and, coupling this idea with the familistic ideology peculiar to Japan, developed the *nenkō* wage system based on age and length of service.

Since 1955, however, the supply of new school graduates has become increasingly short, and the level of starting pay has been creeping up. Consequently, wage differentials by age have narrowed to a great extent, as will be shown in more detail later. This narrowing obviously means that the basis of the *nenkō* system is gradually being eroded. It is especially conspicuous in the small and medium-sized enterprises, but it has also occurred in large firms since 1964. In other words, conditions for maintaining the *nenkō* system have continued longer in large firms. Consequently, only a few enterprises have introduced the job-duty or job-skill rate, usually modified to retain features of the *nenkō* system. Described below are typical examples of enterprises that introduced job-rate systems.

A Case of Job-Duty Rates

On the occasion of the Spring Labor Offensive in 1962, the Yahata, Fuji, and Nihonkōkan Steel Companies joined in introducing job-duty rates. As these three companies have a great influence on the Japanese economy, their action was a noteworthy event. Among the reasons for introducing the new system, technological change in the steel industry may have been the most important. New equipment introduced into steel mills changed jobs from conventional manual labor to visual and control work. At the same time, the new equipment enabled people to master their jobs in a shorter period. Such a change in the quality of the labor required accentuated the contradiction between the new methods and the *nenkō* wage system. Under these circumstances, the problem of how to revise the *nenkō* wage system emerged.

In the case of Yahata Steel, although the company introduced the job-rate system, it did not totally replace the *nenkō* system. Before 1962, the company's wage system was composed of two items, a base rate and an incentive rate. These items had equal weight in the total wage payment. The base rate was a typical *nenkō*-type wage, based on the age and length of service of the employee. The incentive rate was a group incentive, based on production in each plant, and was distributed to individual employees according to their base rates and the result of personnel evaluation. Thus, the incentive rate actually had no relationship to the efficiency of individual employees, since it was related to their age and length of service.

In making the change, the company chose 194 jobs from which standards were developed for the evaluation of 9,000 jobs. Elements and weights in the job evaluation were as follows:

Qualifications	Basic knowledge	20 percent
	Experience	20 percent
Responsibility	Responsibility	20 percent
Effort	Decision making	10 percent
	Mental load	10 percent
	Physical load	10 percent
Environmental conditions	Working environment	5 percent
	Safety	5 percent

Based on the above elements, the job evaluation was made according to a point system. The occupations were divided into twenty classes; each class was then subdivided into three grades—low, medium, and high—and a wage rate was set for each grade. Thus the company adopted a rate-range system.

Within this system, when an employee is assigned to an occupational class, he first receives the wage rate for the lowest grade within that class. In six months the job is reevaluated, and he is promoted to the medium grade. After three years in the medium grade, the evaluation is conducted again for promotion to the highest grade. In promotions from the low to the medium grade, employees absent more than fifteen days per month on the average or punished by suspension or other penalty during the six months' period are denied promotion. In the case of promotion from the medium to the highest grade, those absent more than five days per month on the average or punished by a reduction in wages or other penalty, or evaluated as "unqualified" for the job, are denied promotion.

Although the company's job-duty rate in this wage system is apparently modern, it retains the base-rate feature of the *nenkō* system, and the method for determining the incentive rate is also based on age and length of service of the employee. This kind of job-duty rate system is called the "coexistent" type (coexistent with the *nenkō* system), and is typical of a job-duty rate system modified for the Japanese situation.

The management plan is to increase the job-duty rate as a proportion of total wages with every wage increase, and eventually to replace the *nenkō* system completely with the job-duty rate system. In fact, the proportion of job-duty rates has increased gradually since 1962 and is now more than 20 percent of the total wage payment.

A Case of Job-Skill Rates

The job-skill rate, which has also been introduced in large companies, is designed to produce wages reflecting the ability of individual employees to perform their jobs. Thus, a job-skill rate is determined individually for each employee; this differs from the job-duty rate which is set for the job that the employee performs. It is not usual in Japan for a company to employ an individual to perform a particular job; rather, companies usually hire new school graduates all at one time, once a year. Consequently, it does not necessarily follow that they find the right person for various jobs. Here emerges the need for taking into account the ability of individual employees to perform a job, as the job-duty rate is insufficient for rational wage determination. In this situation, the job-skill rate has been introduced in some large companies as in the following case of the Isuzu Automobile Company.

Isuzu has been using the job-skill rate system since 1960, when it revised the wage component which was formerly based on an employee's age and length of service. The change was promoted primarily by the rigorous automation of the production process and centralization of management by means of computer and data-processing methods. As automation drastically simplified the production operation and, therefore, job content, it enabled a worker to become skilled enough to perform a job within three or four years. For example, in the casting department highly

skilled workers who might need fifteen or twenty years of experience are still required, but in fewer numbers. Since under the
previous *nenkō* system, the length-of-service rate increased annually
without an upper limit, employees' wage rates often deviated
greatly from their actual skills.

In these circumstances, Isuzu substituted the job-skill rate for
the base rate. The main feature of the new wage system is that a
job-skill classification was established. The work force is first
divided into white-collar employees (clerical employees and
engineers) and blue-collar workers. Blue-collar workers are classified as follows:

1. Supervisory
   F1: *hanchō* (crew chief) and equivalent
   F2: *kuchō*[2] (group chief) and equivalent
2. Special and technical:
   AF: personnel extremely competent in skill, knowledge, and
       ability for a job, and recognized as equivalent to the
       hanchō
3. General
   L1: workers competent to do a specific job or to be an ap-
       prentice for the job
   L2: workers competent to perform basic operations as their
       job duties
   L3: workers with potential to become highly skilled work-
       men and supervisory personnel
   L4: workers competent to perform supervisory jobs, to be-
       come so qualified in a short period, or already highly
       skilled

Among these occupational classes, F1, for example, requires
a minimum of one year's experience, while AF requires three or
four years of experience. In this way, the conventional factors of
age and length of service are replaced by factors of job skill and
occupational experience.

Although the new wage schedule is based on occupational
classes, the blue-collar class L1, for example, is further divided by
length of service ranging from one to forty-one years. In other

---

2. Otherwise also referred to as *Kumichō* and *Kochō*.

words, the *nenkō* system influences determination of job rates. Furthermore, there are a maximum and a minimum rate for each service period. The actual rate for each employee is somewhere between the length-of-service maximum and minimum rates, depending on the number of points (60 to 100) that he gets in his performance evaluation. This range allows his base rate to reflect his occupational ability. As a result, even though employees may be in the same occupational class and may have served for an equal length of time, they may receive different wages—the so-called individualized rate.

The Wage System in Small and Medium-Sized Enterprises

Before World War II, no objective standards existed for determining wage rates in small and medium-sized enterprises in Japan, and the employer usually set wages at his own discretion. Many of these companies were satellites of or subcontractors for larger firms and sold their products to the parent company for a fixed price per unit. Whether or not the firm was a subcontractor, the wage a worker received depended upon the sale price of the product and thus was a variation of a piece-rate wage system.

Typical examples are the so-called *tatakiwake*, in which the management retained 50 percent of the gross sales receipts and used 50 percent for workers' wages, and the *shiburoku*, in which 40 percent went to management and 60 percent to the workers in wage payment. A skilled journeyman would receive the maximum share (50 or 60 percent) of the sale price of the products he produced; and if he himself were a labor subcontractor within the company, he would have to pay unskilled workers or apprentices working for him out of his own wages. The unskilled workers and apprentices had a set wage rate and were paid by either the employer, the skilled journeyman, or both. Their wage rates never varied, even if they worked overtime, and the rate was completely unrelated to the quality or quantity of their labor.

This discretionary method of wage determination is still practiced in many small and medium-sized enterprises. Wage rules often are obscure, and in many cases no wage system is yet established. Even where there are wage rules, they seldom constitute objective standards for setting the base rate. Usually, the employers determine the rate comprehensively, taking into account such factors as age, length of service, skill, experience, and educational level of the employee. A few examples of the wage system in such enterprises are described in the following paragraphs.

A small company in the food industry has the following components in its standard wage: base rate (78.9 percent of the standard wage), consumers' price adjustment allowance (6 percent), efficiency allowance (6.4 percent), subsidy for commuting (5.4 percent), responsibility allowance (0.3 percent), and regular attendance allowance (3 percent). Overtime payment may be part of total wages but is not a standard component. The base rate is set comprehensively, taking into account such factors as educational level, experience, and skill of the employee, while the consumers' price allowance is differentiated according to his occupational position. The efficiency allowance is, of course, based on merit.

Another firm, in the cotton textile industry, developed the following wage system: base rate (80.5 percent of the standard wage), responsibility allowance (2.3 percent), efficiency rate (14 percent), paid vacation allowance (2.1 percent), and special duty allowance (1.1 percent). Overtime pay is a nonstandard payment. There is no rule governing wage increases. The average annual wage increase is ¥604 (¥2,500 maximum and ¥130 minimum). The base rate is determined by such factors as employee's skill, experience, length of service, and educational level. The maximum responsibility allowance is ¥7,000 and the minimum is ¥700. The efficiency rate is set for each production process, depending on the total amount of production.

Minimum Wages

The Minimum Wage Law, enacted in Japan in 1959, provides four methods for setting minimum wages. First, according to

Article 9, a minimum wage may be decided by agreement among employers concerned, subject to the approval of both a tripartite Minimum Wage Council established by the law and the labor minister or the director of the Prefectural Labor Standards Bureau. Second, a regional minimum wage agreement among employers may be extended to cover other employers in the area, provided the majority of the employers concerned apply for the extension and the appropriate Minimum Wage Council and the labor minister or the director of the Prefectural Labor Standards Bureau give their approval. Third, a regional labor agreement may also be extended to the majority of employers and workers in the region by decision of the labor minister or the director of the Prefectural Labor Standards Bureau, based on the opinion of the appropriate Minimum Wage Council. Fourth, Minimum Wage Councils may set minimum wage rates when the labor minister or the director of the Prefectural Labor Standards Bureau requests a council to investigate the need for improving working conditions in a specific industry, occupation, or region but recognizes the difficulty of following the other procedures.

Among these methods, the agreement among employers is used most frequently. In this procedure, it should be noted, employers *alone* reach legal minimum wage agreements and the workers concerned play no role. As a result, Sōhyō[3] (the General Council of Trade Unions of Japan), Dōmei[4] (the Japanese Confederation of Labor), and other union federations have been demanding a revision of the existing Minimum Wage Law. Revision of the law is also an issue pending before the Central Minimum Wage Council.

Since the Minimum Wage Law was established, more and more agreements among employers have been legalized—996 by the end of 1962. Among these agreements, 959 were put into effect by the first method (initial employer agreements), 34 by the second method (extension of an agreement in effect), and three by the third method (extension of an existing labor contract). These agreements together covered 115,924 employers and 1,779,624 workers in 1962. The textile industry is predominant in terms of coverage by such minimum wage agreements—a total of 427,417

3. Nihon Rōdōkumiai Sōhyōgikai.
4. Zen-nihon Rōdō Sōdōmei.

workers—while the machine manufacturing industry is next, with 148,440 workers. The food-processing industry has 142,477 workers covered by such agreements, followed by the lumber and woodcraft industry, the ceramic products industry, and the service industry. Most agreements are in manufacturing industries; they are less extensive in the commercial trades and services where cheap labor predominates.

The general level of minimum wages has increased gradually in recent years. It was about ¥200 per day in 1960–61. By 1962 it had risen to between ¥250 and ¥279, reflecting the rising level of starting pay due primarily to the tightness of the labor market for new school graduates. That is to say, without any agreement among employers, recruitment of new school graduates would have been more difficult. On the other hand, the government encouraged such agreements and established a plan to expand the number of workers covered to 2,530,000 between 1961 and the end of 1964. Actually, the number covered rose to more than 2,920,000 by March 1964, greatly surpassing the expressed goal.

However, many important problems have arisen in the process. Imbalances appeared among industries or regions as agreements were developed among employers. The minimum wage level prescribed by the agreements still was lower than the general wage level, and the minimum wage agreements were reviewed and revised so rarely that they tended to become ineffective over time.

Under these circumstances, the Ministry of Labor asked the Central Minimum Wage Council (1) to make a systematic selection of industries to which minimum wage agreements could be applied effectively; (2) to establish a minimum wage scale for nationwide adjustments; and (3) to make the best use of all methods for determining minimum wages. The minimum daily wage scale recommended by the council was as follows:

Industry	Region A	Region B	Region C
A	¥480–440	¥460–420	¥440–400
B	¥440–400	¥420–380	¥400–360

(Industry A was a relatively high-wage industry; Industry B relatively low wage.) This minimum wage scale eventually may be useful in bringing the agreed minimum wage level up to the general wage level and in removing the imbalances among industries or regions.

Fringe Benefits

The most important fringe benefits in Japan are bonuses, retirement allowances, and worker welfare facilities. The bonus is an allowance, separate from the monthly wage payment, which is paid during the summer and again at the end of each year. Both the payment and the timing of it can be traced to the former custom in Japan of giving expensive presents to others at the midsummer *Bon* Festival and at the year end. Originally it was a kind of incentive recognition of an employee's achievements and a reward for his loyalty to the employer. At the same time, bonus payments to employees were necessary in part to make up for low wages. Therefore, before World War II, they served to supplement workers' incomes substantially. After the war, the incentive and benevolent features of the bonus were diluted, and it now serves primarily as an income supplement. As the general wage level has risen steadily, the bonus has come to be an established part of the guaranteed income for the worker. Thus, it is now paid regularly, regardless of business fluctuations.

In the *1965 Monthly Labor Statistics*, the Labor Ministry reported that the average bonus payment in all industries was 3.27 times a worker's monthly wage—1.3 times being paid in summer and 1.6 times at the year end. The largest bonus payments were made in the banking and insurance industry—5.04 times the monthly wage, while public utilities (electric power, gas, and water supply) paid 4.65 times. In terms of size of enterprise, large enterprises employing more than 500 workers paid on the average 3.55 times the monthly wage; small companies, with 5 to 29 employees, paid only 1.55 times. Thus, as can be seen, the Japanese bonus is a considerable amount, much larger than the Christmas or profit-sharing bonus usually provided in Western countries. As bonus payments have become an established custom, they may be integrated into the regular monthly wage payments.

In Japan, the origin of retirement allowances may be traced to two traditional customs, *noren wake* and *manki shoyō*. *Noren wake* was a custom whereby the employer set up an employee in business after the latter had undergone a long period of training in the employer's work place. The *manki shoyō*, or enforced savings plan, was originally designed to discourage labor turnover; the employees were paid their savings in a lump sum only when they retired from the company.

The present type of lump-sum retirement allowance became widespread after World War I, when employers lacked sufficient numbers of engineers and skilled workers. The retirement allowance was a device to encourage these workers to stay in the enterprise as long as possible, and as it justified the so-called lifetime employment practice, it became an important element in the strategy of keeping skilled personnel. Expecting a considerable allowance at the time they retired, workers became committed to long service with a given company.

Since World War II, the retirement allowance has become a bargaining issue along with wages, bonuses, and other factors in terms of the principle of equality between labor and management. Whereas before the war the allowance was paid as an employer benevolence, now every worker believes he has a legal right to it in order to guarantee his livelihood after retirement.

The method of calculating retirement allowances is usually to multiply the employee's monthly base rate of pay by his length of service in months and by a numerical indicator of the reason for his retirement. Length of service, usually computed in years in determining the base rate, is converted to total months of service in the retirement allowance formula. The "reasons for retirement" vary, however. For example, if the worker retires at the normal retirement age of 55, the reason is weighted as 1; if he retires voluntarily before age 55, it may range from 0.5 to 0.8; if he retires before age 55 at the request of the company, it may be as high as 1.5. As indicated by such a formula, the longer an employee's service, the higher his base rate, the greater his number of months of service, and thus the larger the retirement allowance he receives.

A survey of retirement allowances, temporary allowances, and pensions carried out by the Secretariat of the Central Labor Relations Commission in 1965 showed the relationship between the retirement allowance and length of service. For example, a male clerical worker with a college education in a large company could expect to receive ¥75,936 (2.4 times his monthly pay) after three years of service; ¥1,035,312 (15.5 times) after fifteen years of service; and ¥5,043,685 (42.5 times) after thirty years of service.

While virtually all large companies have retirement allowances for employees, they were relatively rare in small and medium-sized firms until 1959, when the Retirement Fund Act for Medium and Small Enterprises was put into effect. A substantial number of small and medium-sized companies then joined in the mutual aid system for the payment of retirement allowances so that, by the end of February 1965, 78,324 establishments, with a total of 1,052,549 employees, were participating. There usually is a great difference in the amount of the retirement allowance paid by small and medium-sized companies and that paid by large industry. A recent survey by the Labor Department of the metropolitan Tokyo government shows that an employee with a college education employed in large industry received an average of ¥4,690,000, while a comparable employee in a small or medium-sized industry would receive only ¥2,030,000.

Retirement allowances as a proportion of total labor costs amounted to 2.8 percent in the latter half of 1955, 3.6 percent in 1960, and 3.9 percent in 1964. This growth in the retirement allowance fund is due to the overall aging of the work force and the consequent lengthening of employee service, both of which have increased the retirement payment percentage and the base rate on which it is calculated.

Employers in large industry have become concerned about the burden that the steadily increasing retirement allowances will impose on them; in an effort to hold retirement allowances at the present rate and thus prevent this burden from becoming heavier, they have devised enterprise pension plans to spread out the payments. These plans, in which pensions usually supplement the retirement allowance, have developed gradually since 1955.

Since enactment of tax reform legislation in 1962, private pensions and pension installments have been recognized as "qualified pensions" and are thus exempt from tax as a loss in a company's accounts. Thanks to this tax reform, private pension plans have developed greatly since then; the number of pension plans recognized as "qualified pensions" numbered 5,644 in 1965.

This type of plan, of course, is designed to pay pensions to those who retire from the company at the age limit, but it has increasingly come to serve also for paying pensions to those who retire before the age limit. The amount of a pension varies widely, depending on its content: whether it is paid for a specified period or for a lifetime; whether or not the recipient has contributed to the pension fund, and if so, what percentage he has contributed; and whether or not there is a retirement allowance program in addition to the pension plan. Usually the pension payments range between ¥10,000 and ¥20,000 per month. The old age pension prescribed by the Welfare Pension Insurance Law is about ¥10,000 per month. Thus, monthly payments ranging from ¥20,000 to ¥30,000 in total are guaranteed for those covered by pensions as well as by the law.

Employees' welfare facilities are by definition the totality of many benefits in kind that the employer voluntarily provides for his employees in addition to wages and other monetary payments. The origin of welfare facilities in modern Japanese industry goes back to the mutual aid systems developed by the Kanebo Textile Company, the National Railway Corporation, and other establishments during the Meiji period. At that time, employee dormitory systems were prevalent in textile mills and at coal and metal mines to prevent workers from leaving their work places and to commit them to the companies. After World War I, this system was further developed by providing such benefits as discount purchases, money loans, company savings, and company housing. The welfare facilities developed at that time were an important aspect of employer policy to encourage lifetime employment commitment, just as were the retirement allowance and the *nenkō* wage system.

Welfare facilities stemmed from the employer's benevolence, and they formed the basis of the paternalistic management ideology. Needless to say, these welfare facilities were designed and operated as part of the employer's policy of confining workers within the enterprise and preventing labor unions from penetrating. Furthermore, they served to compensate for insufficient unemployment benefits, pensions, family allowances, and social security and for low wages. All of these protective measures were expected to commit employees to the enterprise and encourage loyalty.

Although welfare facilities seemingly remained unchanged after World War II, some features have changed to a significant degree. One goal of the labor union movement after the war was to weaken the paternalistic management ideology and its benevolent features characterized by welfare facilities. The labor movement tended to stress that improvement of the welfare facilities raised the workers' real wages, and therefore it attempted as much as possible to include welfare facilities as issues in bargaining over the labor contract. At the same time, the unions made an effort to participate in the administration of the welfare facilities in order to weaken the employer's paternalistic policies. Of course, this union pressure was resisted by the employers, and conflict over the issue intensified. It may be said, however, that such conflict actually served rather positively to improve the system of welfare facilities after World War II.

Several facets of welfare allowances and facilities have developed considerably during the postwar period. These include especially housing allowances for employee families and unmarried employees; employee dormitories; commuting expenses such as bus fares; physical check-ups and medical care in hospitals, health centers, and so forth; such services as haircuts and baths; nursery facilities and feeding rooms; food service such as cafeterias and dining halls; and discount sale shops for commodities, tea rooms, and other recreational, sporting, and cultural facilities. (see Table 10.3) The cost of these facilities is referred to as welfare expenses "outside the law" (*hōteigai fukurihi*) in contrast to employer payments for health insurance and unemployment insurance which are welfare expenses "inside the law" (*hōtei fukurihi*). According to the Ministry of Labor's 1965 *Survey on Labor Costs*, these expenses as a proportion of the total wage package then amounted to 5.2 percent on the average—6.1 percent in large enterprises and 4.3 percent in small enterprises (30 to 99 em-

Table 10.3
Welfare Programs by Size of Enterprise, 1964 (percent)

Type of Welfare Programs	Size of Enterprise by Number of Employees			
	Total	More than 500 employees	100–499 employees	30–99 employees
Housing	71.0	96.8	83.3	66.5
Barber, bath or shower	71.0	94.0	83.1	66.7
Cultural & recreational facilities	92.4	98.7	94.8	91.5
Sports facilities	67.1	96.8	83.1	61.4
Canteens, other food services	40.5	81.4	53.9	35.4
Medical & health facilities	16.5	85.3	29.9	10.1
General merchandise sales	6.8	65.7	15.8	2.0
Transportation	24.7	54.0	35.7	20.5
Counseling & help for employees' family	15.2	46.6	24.5	11.3
Nursing facilities	0.9	12.6	1.7	0.3
Congratulatory or condolence payments	91.6	99.2	96.3	90.0
Loan system for employees	39.7	82.6	52.6	34.3
Intracompany deposit system	35.1	79.6	49.9	29.7
Group life-insurance system	26.1	33.0	26.0	25.9
Scholarship system for employee children	5.2	19.9	9.7	3.4

SOURCE: Ministry of Labor, Division of Labor Statistics and Research, *Shōwa 30 nen kigy fukushi shisetsu chōsa hōkoku* [Survey of welfare facilities managed by firms] (Tokyo: Ministry of Labor, 1965), p. 11.

ployees). Thus, there is a wide variation in the amount of money that employers spend for welfare facilities. The greatest portion went for housing—2.2 percent of the total. The next largest expense was for food service (0.9 percent), followed by recreational, sporting, and cultural development facilities (0.8 percent), medical care expenses (0.5 percent), and gifts of money as tokens of congratulation and condolence (0.2 percent). According to a *Survey on Welfare Facility Expenses* conducted by Nikkeiren, the Japan Federation of Employers Association, in 1964, welfare expenses both inside and outside the law amounted to 13.5 percent of total labor costs in large companies employing more than 5,000 persons.

As these expenses have increasingly become a burden on the employer, large industry has considered ways of rationalizing welfare facilities. The areas to which they are giving primary attention are housing, food service, commodity-purchasing, and commuting. Employers are especially interested in reducing expenses for housing, the largest single welfare cost. As many employees want to live in inexpensive company residences and at the same time seek better housing in terms of space and design, the employer alone cannot meet their demands for quantity and quality. For this reason, in many cases, he tends to encourage employees to buy or build their own houses and to emphasize the principle that employees should solve their own housing problems and that housing should no longer be the employer's responsibility. Consequently, financial aid plans for worker home ownership have been developed; under these programs loans are made with retirement allowances as security or with savings checked off from employee wages and placed on deposit toward the purchase of a house.

At the same time that large firms are trying to reduce their welfare expenditures, small and medium-sized firms are making an effort to establish and extend them. Welfare facilities in small and medium-sized firms usually are poor compared with those in large firms, and in recent years, the smaller firms have come to need their welfare facilities more than ever in order to attract young workers in the tight labor market.

The External Wage Structure

A major characteristic of the Japanese labor market is that the employer generally relies upon new graduates from junior high schools, high schools, and colleges or universities as the main source for recruitment. Consequently, there is severe competition between large, small, and medium-sized companies for these recruits. The labor market for new graduates in turn has become more or less nationwide, and the national labor market has come to determine the level of starting wages.

A second major feature is that large companies employ new graduates and encourage them to stay within the company for the rest of their lives under the system of lifetime employment. As a result, there is little mobility among workers employed by large companies, and the labor market is internalized to a great extent. In this context, wages tend to be determined separately, company by company.

Third, there is far greater mobility for workers in open labor markets in small and medium-sized companies than in large companies. There is, however, relatively little movement of workers from small and medium-sized to large companies. The labor markets of the two groups are separate and the latter has higher status.

These characteristics—the internalized labor market in the large enterprise sector and stratification of the labor market by size of enterprise—inevitably tend to affect the Japanese pattern of wage determination. There is no standardized wage rate in Japan except for starting pay. At the same time, wages in Japan are not standardized on the basis of types of occupations or job duties. Even if workers have identical jobs, their wages differ depending on their age and length of service. For this reason there is no possibility of standardizing wage rates in the external market, and this is why the problem of interfirm wage differentials is discussed in Japan in terms of differentials by size of firm, type of industry, and region rather than by occupation.

Table 10.4 shows the trend in wage differentials by size of firm in manufacturing industries since 1962. Even though the wide wage differentials by size of firm have been narrowing slightly, they still exist. This feature of interfirm wage differentials is peculiar to Japan and is not as apparent in Western countries. It is due mainly to the stratification of the Japanese labor market by size of firm, in which labor mobility is considerable in the small and medium-sized industry sector where firms employ workers regardless of age and absorb surplus labor from both rural areas and cities. The existence of this surplus labor thus results in a lowering of the industrial wage level. On the other hand, since large industry seldom employs people other than new school graduates and closes itself off from the external market, the enterprise union can exert pressure for wage increases, and under these circumstances, wage differentials by size of industry tend to emerge.

Table 10.4
Wage Differentials in Manufacturing Industries by Size

Year	Total Wage Payment			
	More Than 500 Employees	100–499	30–99	5–29
1962	100.0	77.6	66.7	57.0
1963	100.0	79.6	68.8	58.(?)
1964	100.0	79.0	69.5	60.4
1965	100.0	80.9	7.10	63.2

SOURCE: The Ministry of Labor, *Survey on Monthly Labor Statistics.*

As Table 10.4 shows, however, this narrowing of wage differentials by size of firm since 1962 is due primarily to the tightening of the labor market for young workers and the consequent increase in the starting wage level in the small industry sector. In fact, wages of workers under twenty-five years of age have recently become higher in the small than in the large industry sector. If the shortage of young workers becomes more serious in the future, there will probably be more labor mobility from the small to the large industry sector, and the stratification of the labor market by size of firm will gradually disappear. If this happens, the existing wage differentials by size of firm will narrow even further.

The trend in wage differentials by type of industry since 1962 is shown in Table 10.5. In 1965 the electric power, gas, and water supply industry was highest, followed by the banking and insurance industry; manufacturing industry was the lowest. One outstanding feature in wage differentials by industry is that the wage level in the construction industry has risen considerably since 1962, due largely to the tightening of the labor market for construction workers in the recent construction boom.

Wage differentials by region also show that in the mining industry, with Tokyo as 100, Hyogo Prefecture is 70.5 and Kagawa Prefecture, the lowest, is 40.0. In manufacturing, also with Tokyo as 100, Nagasaki Prefecture is 99.7, Yamaguchi Prefecture 95.7, and Kanagawa Prefecture 94.8; while at the low end, Tottori

Table 10.5
Wage Differentials by Type of Industry, 1962–65

Year	All In-dustries*	Mining	Construc-tion	Manufac-turing	Retail & Wholesale	Banking & Insurance	Transportation & Communication	Electric Power, Gas, Water Supply
1962	100.0	105.6	94.1	92.5	91.3	132.3	119.4	150.2
1963	100.0	103.5	96.7	92.3	92.3	93.5	117.8	148.2
1964	100.0	104.9	99.1	92.4	93.1	126.5	119.0	150.0
1965	100.0	105.8	100.2	91.7	92.6	128.3	119.8	151.5

SOURCE: Ministry of Labor, *Maitsuki kinrō tōkei chōsa hōkoku* [Survey on monthly labor statistics].
* All industries included here employ 30 or more people.

Prefecture is 51.7, Kagoshima Prefecture 58.0, and Yamagata Prefecture 58.6. It may be said that the regions where the wage level is low are usually rural areas that have relatively ample supplies of labor. Wage differentials by region also have tended to narrow recently due to the tightness in the labor market for new school graduates.

Internal Wage Structures

The most important problem in the Japanese internal wage structure is that of wage differentials by age, the primary characteristic of the *nenkō* wage system. Wage differentials by age and by size of firm are shown in Table 10.6.

Table 10.6
Wage Differentials by Type of Industry, 1962–1965

	Over 1,000 Employees					30–99 Employees				
	1954	1958	1961	1964	1965	1954	1958	1961	1964	1965
Age 18 and younger	49.8	53.0	50.4	53.8	57.1	50.4	52.1	56.9	56.6	57.7
18–20	71.5	79.9	78.2	76.9	76.5	73.9	73.6	76.8	76.6	74.9
20–25	100.0	100.0	100.0	100.0	100.0	100.0	100.0	100.0	100.0	100.0
25–30	136.7	146.0	136.7	129.1	126.7	126.4	126.1	126.6	122.1	121.3
30–35	164.3	186.3	182.0	162.7	157.9	146.5	146.7	141.1	131.6	131.8
35–40	184.4	211.2	210.1	191.6	185.4	155.9	159.7	153.5	136.1	133.3
40–50	203.1	238.2	237.0	214.2	208.1	155.2	158.6	153.2	140.2	136.3

SOURCE: Ministry of Labor, *Chingin kōzō kihon tōkei* [Basic survey of wage structure] (Tokyo: Ministry of Labor, 1965).

In large firms employing more than 1,000 people, the wage level of employees 40 to 50 years of age was 4.0 times as high as the wage level of employees 18 years of age and under in 1954, 4.49 times as high in 1958, and 4.70 times as high in 1961. Thus, wage differentials by age widened during the period from 1954 to 1961. These differentials, however, have since narrowed to 3.98 times in 1964 and 3.64 times in 1965.

In firms employing 30 to 99 people, the wage level of employees 40 to 50 years old was 3.07 times as high as the wage level of employees 18 years of age and younger in 1954, 3.04 times in 1958, 2.69 times in 1961, 2.47 times in 1964, and 2.36 times in 1965. Thus, the wage differentials have narrowed continually over the whole period.

This narrowing of wage differentials by age is due largely to the fact that the demand for young workers adaptable to new technology has increased in the process of rapid economic development since 1955; as a consequence, the wage level of workers under 25 years of age has risen. The rising wage level of young workers may be regarded as a threat to the *nenkō* wage system.

The wage levels in Table 10.6 are all average and include employees not hired immediately after their school graduation. Therefore, in order to obtain an accurate picture of the *nenkō* wage system, it is necessary to examine a model wage structure covering regular employees who were hired immediately after their school graduation and continued to work at the same company. Such a wage structure for large and small firms, compiled by the Japanese Chamber of Commerce, is shown in Table 10.7.

Table 10.7

Model Wages in Manufacturing by Size of Firm, 1964 (average monthly wages in yen)

Junior High School Graduates	Over 1,000 Employees	Under 100 Employees
Age 15	¥15,474	¥15,551
16	16,510	17,006
18	19,119	19,836
20	21,698	23,116
22	24,232	26,695
25	28,490	31,284
27	32,913	35,645
30	38,269	40,098
35	46,473	45,081
40	54,664	50,798
45	61,782	54,501
50	67,361	58,069
55	72,866	62,406

SOURCE: Japanese Chamber of Commerce and Industry, *1961-nendo moderu chingin* [Model wage in 1964] (Tokyo: Japanese Chamber of Commerce and Industry, 1965).

Wages in manufacturing firms employing more than 1,000 people continuously increase by age up to the limit of age 55, and the highest wage rate is 4.7 times the lowest rate. Similarly, wages in small manufacturing firms employing fewer than 100 people also increase by age up to age 55. These wage structures clearly show the character of the *nenkō* system. In small firms, however, the rate of increase under *nenkō* is less after age 35 than in the large firms, and there is a difference of approximately ¥10,000 per month at age 55.

These wide wage differentials by age are due primarily to the fact that the main source of labor recruits in Japan are new school graduates. The Ministry of Labor's *White Paper on Labor—1965*, for example, indicates that the 15–19 age bracket accounts for 15 percent of the total population over 15 years of age. The corresponding figure in the United States is 12.3 percent; in West Germany, it is 8 percent. Fifteen- to nineteen-year-olds account for 39 percent of the total work force in Japan, 27 percent in the United States, and 16 percent in West Germany. It is estimated that in the United States, among 14,100,000 newly employed workers, 1,600,000 or 11 percent were the age of high school graduates; in Japan, according to the Ministry of Labor *A Survey on Employment Trends in 1964*, it was estimated that among 3,430,000 newly employed workers, 1,080,000 or 31 percent were new school graduates. Thus, because the number of new school graduates recruited in the Japanese system is so great, their wage level tends to remain low. Only as they get older do their wage rates increase. Furthermore, as the employer encourages long service to the company, he provides an additional length-of-service rate.

As shown in Table 10.8, wages of blue-collar workers in the same age bracket are different if their length of service is different. Obviously, the longer the service, the higher the wage rate, so that the length-of-service factor becomes more important than the age factor. On the other hand, in the length-of-service columns from 0 to 3–4 years in Table 10.8, for example, wage rates of workers age 40 to 49 are the highest, with regard to the age factor. In this way, *nenkō* wages of a worker are determined by a combination of the two factors, age and length of service.

Table 10.8
Average Monthly Contract Cash Earnings in Manufacturing Industry by
Age and Length of Service, 1965 Blue-Collar* (in thousands of yen)

Age	\multicolumn{9}{c}{Length of Service (years)}								
	0	1	2	3–4	5–9	10–14	15–19	20–29	30–
–17	13.8	15.0	16.4	—	—	—	—	—	—
18–19	19.4	19.2	18.7	19.6	—	—	—	—	—
20–24	24.1	24.2	25.0	25.4	27.0	—	—	—	—
25–29	28.3	28.8	29.7	30.5	32.5	35.1	—	—	—
30–34	30.0	31.4	31.8	30.9	36.4	39.5	41.9	46.1	—
35–39	30.3	31.2	32.2	33.8	39.7	42.5	46.6	49.5	—
40–49	30.6	31.1	32.2	33.8	38.5	44.6	49.3	54.8	56.2
50–59	27.5	28.1	28.9	31.6	35.1	41.1	47.4	55.5	56.6
60–	23.1	23.1	24.3	24.8	28.2	30.0	31.2	29.8	33.0

* Male employees who are graduates of junior high schools.
SOURCE: Ministry of Labor, *Chingin kōzō kihon tōkei* [Basic survey of wage structure], 1965.

Table 10.9
Average Monthly Contract Cash Earnings in Manufacturing Industry by
Age and Length of Service, 1965 White-Collar-Clerical* (in thousands of yen)

Age	\multicolumn{9}{c}{Length of Service (years)}								
	0	1	2	3–4	5–9	10–14	15–19	20–29	30–
20–24	24.5	27.8	30.0	27.9	30.4	—	—	—	—
25–29	32.0	31.1	32.3	34.6	39.6	40.7	—	—	—
30–34	42.7	41.8	43.4	44.4	46.7	54.9	50.1	36.4	—
35–39	45.9	53.8	58.9	52.7	56.4	63.4	70.4	54.9	—
40–49	55.4	61.5	66.8	68.8	71.7	74.5	83.4	103.8	69.5
50–59	52.0	68.0	66.7	61.9	73.4	78.3	94.2	116.1	109.6
60–	31.6	32.4	61.4	60.5	47.8	72.4	39.6	94.1	120.5

* Employees who are university graduates.
SOURCE: Ministry of Labor, *Chingin kōzō kihon tōkei* [Basic survey of wage structure], 1965.

As seen in Table 10.9, the increase rate of wages by length of service for clerical employees is much greater than for blue-collar workers. The rate of increase by age is also greater for clerical employees. Employees aged 50 to 59 are the best paid group.

Another problem that cannot be overlooked in the internal wage structure is that of wage differentials by occupational status. According to the *Survey on the Wage Situation in Private Industry by Type of Occupation* (1966), conducted by the National Personnel

Authority, differentials in salaries among management and clerical employees are large and depend upon the job hierarchy. The salary for the highest position is 4.3 times as much as the salary for the lowest. Among engineering personnel, too, the job hierarchy is the same except that the plant manager holds the top position; the salary at the highest position is 3.1 times as high as the salary at the lowest.

In summary, it may be said that in the Japanese *nenkō* wage system, the factors of age, length of service, and occupational status, all of which are personal properties of the employee, are still dominant in wage determination, and the factor of job skill is only indirectly reflected through these three major factors.

11. Personnel Administration at the Industrial Plant Level

A discussion of personnel administration in Japanese industry at the plant level must necessarily begin with an examination of its characteristics as they are affected by and reflect the *nenkō* system of industrial relations. In this chapter that discussion is followed by an analysis of personnel administration and the local union at the plant level, and finally by a description of the trends toward change in some aspects of labor administration and industrial relations in Japan.

The *Nenkō* System at the Plant Level

The *nenkō* system of industrial relations, peculiar to Japan, has been described in other contexts in previous chapters. Here its primary characteristics with regard to personnel administration are summarized under three headings: stratification by employee status, establishment and maintenance of the vertical elite, and the extended family ideology.

Stratification by Employee Status

The Shokuin and the Kōin

The job function of the *shokuin*, or white-collar staff—to carry out the policies established by and under the supervision of top

Status Hierarchy		*Job Hierarchy*		
sanji (councilor)		shachō (president)		
		fukushachō (vice-president)		
fukusanji (vice-councilor)		kōjōchō	buchō	
		(plant super-	(department head of	White-collar ranks
		intendent)	the head office)	
shain[a] (senior employee)		jichō (assistant superintendent)		
		kachō (section chief)		
White-collar	*Blue-collar*	kakarichō (subsection chief)		
junshain[b]		kakariin (subsection member)		
(semi-senior		(white-collar)		
employee)		(blue-collar)		
koin[c]	jōkyū kōin[e]	kōchō (chief worker)		
(junior	(upper-class			Blue-collar ranks
employee)	worker)			
junkoin[d]	Ikkyū kōin[e]	fukukōchō (assistant chief worker)		
(semi-junior	(first-class worker)			
employee)				
minaraiin	nikyū kōin	kōin (worker)		
	(second-class worker)			
	sankyū kōin			
	(third-class worker)			
	minarai kōin			
	(apprentice worker)			

a. In some other firms *shain* are further divided into several titles which correspond to their respective job categories.

b. University graduates become *junshain* after a six-month *koin* period, then are promoted to *shain* after one to three years of service.

c. Employees who graduate from private colleges become *koin* after a six-month *junkoin* period, then are promoted to *junshain* after two to four years of service and to *shain* after four years of service.

d. *Junkoin* (semi-junior employees) are primarily female typists and guards. Female employees with secondary education usually become *junkoin* after three or four years of service.

e. There are opportunities for upper-class *kōin* as chief workers to be promoted to *koin* and *junshain* and for the first-class *kōin* as assistant chiefs to become *jun-koin* and *koin*.

Fig. 11.1
Hierarchies in a Traditional Firm (Ōji Seishi, 1943)

management—is not unlike that of any modern management organization. Under the *nenkō* system, however, the *shokuin* are above the *kōin*, or blue-collar workers, in both status and function, and there is a well-defined gulf which the latter hardly ever bridge. This gulf is defined and reinforced in a number of ways.

First, there is a vertical status system for both the *shokuin* and the *kōin*. For example, as shown in Fig. 11.1, the status system established in 1943 for the *shokuin* at the Ōji Seishi (paper manufacturing) Company begins with the *minariin*, or apprentice staff, and continues upward through the *junkoin* (semi-junior employee), the *koin* (junior employee), the *junshain* (semi-senior employee), and the *shain* (senior employee); above the *shain* are the positions of *fukusanji* (vice-councilor) and *sanji* (councilor), the highest position or status for the *shokuin*.

Kōin positions begin with the *minarai kōin*, or apprentice worker, at the lowest level and continue up the status ladder to third-class, second-class, first-class, and finally upper-class *kōin* or worker. It is possible for a few competent second-, first-, and upper-class workers to be promoted to *koin* positions in the *shokuin* category upon recommendation and under a merit-rating system.

Second, the *shokuin* are paid monthly salaries, whereas the *kōin* receive wages computed at a daily rate. Before World War II only the *shokuin* received semiannual seasonal bonuses.

Third, there is a clear-cut difference between the *shokuin* and *kōin* in terms of the location and size of the housing built and provided by the company for its employees. Many companies, in fact, provide residences only for the *shokuin* and have separate assembly and dining halls for the *shokuin* and *kōin*.

This distinction between the two functional groups has always been based upon the employees' level of formal education. Before World War II, this distinction was so well defined that it corresponded almost completely with the pyramidal structure of formal education. Those who received only elementary or upper-level elementary school (*kōtō shōgakkō*) educations were doomed to stay at the *kōin* status throughout their lives, whereas those who received education beyond this level were employed as *shokuin*.[1]

---

1. In 1945, the number of elementary schools, including upper-level elementary schools, was 26,332; middle schools, 2,048; high schools, 33; business or technical colleges, 316; and universities, 48. These figures were drastically increased as a result of the educational reform after World War II. In 1960, for example, the number of elementary schools was 26,741; junior high schools, 12,986; senior high schools, 4,598; and colleges and universities, 245. For more detail, see Table 1 in *Nihon no kyōiku to seichō* [Japanese growth and education] (Tokyo: Ministry of Education, 1962).

Under the present educational system, most people who complete nine years of compulsory education, or junior high school, are employed as *kōin* or blue-collar workers; persons with more education (high school or college) are hired for the clerical staff as *shokuin*.

This distinction between the *shokuin* and *kōin* by education level corresponds to a job-function distinction in the industrial organization. Let us again take Ōji Seishi as an example. Both the president and the vice-president at the headquarters have the status of *sanji* (councilors). Under them are the department heads (*buchō*) at the company's headquarters, and the plant superintendents (*kōjōchō*), all of whom have the status of vice-councilor (*fuku-sanji*). At each plant there are assistant superintendents (*jichō*), section chiefs (*kachō*), subsection chiefs (*kakarichō*), and subsection staff (*kakariin*). Again, all of these are *shokuin* positions.

Under the *kakarichō* are *kōin* positions in each workshop, in the following order from the top down: the *kōchō*, chief worker, the *fukukōchō* or assistant chief worker, and the *kōin* or manual workers. In other companies, the *kōchō* and *fukukōchō* are often called *kumichō* (group chief), *gochō* (assistant group chief), and *hanchō* (crew chief). After World War II, one of the targets of the labor movement was the abolition of job-status discrimination, and as a result it disappeared in many companies. However, in the period of economic growth after 1952 it returned, and since 1965 it has developed into a job qualification system which is similar to a system of occupational differences.

The several different employee positions within the *shokuin* and *kōin* groups vary in status and remuneration, and each position has particular characteristics. For the *kōin* there are four positions.

Regular kōin employed after graduation. A *kōin* may be classified as a regular employee, a temporary worker, or an outside worker. The regular employee group is further divided, one segment being composed of regular *kōin* who enter the group upon graduation from school. Compulsory education (elementary school) is the requirement for those who entered the labor force before World War II, and junior high school for those who have begun work since the war. There are no variations in the educational require-ments for factory workers. The regular *kōin* who are employed upon graduation from school are expected to work for the company for forty years, starting from age fifteen when they graduate until age fifty-five when they retire. Because of this expected long service, they are generally assumed to be the "key" workers in the factory.

Regular kōin employed according to company needs. Another type of regular employee is one who formerly worked for another company or who was hired by the company for the first time, depending on its need, and at a time other than following school graduation. Large enterprises tend to hire this type of personnel away from the small and medium-sized companies, the medium-sized companies tend to hire them away from the smaller ones, and the small firms hire them from each other. These factory workers who move from one company to another usually have particular occupational experiences and thus are different from workers who are employed directly from school. These workers are called *chū-tosaiyōsha*, for which there is no equivalent English word; it means literally "midterm employee." This literal translation will be used here to identify these workers. In Western countries, workers of this type are usually considered regular employees, but in Japan they are regarded as irregular and inferior in status to those who were employed immediately after their graduation from school.

Temporary workers. In addition to regular *kōin*, the enterprise employs temporary workers, also depending on the company's need. According to the definition in Article 21 of the Labor Standards Law, a temporary worker is one who is employed on a day-to-day basis or whose employment contract is for two months, subject to renewal. In actual practice, however, some temporary workers are employed by a company for many years. The work rules for temporary workers are quite different from those for the regular *kōin*, and although their job duties are similar to those of the regular workers, they can be discharged or laid off at any time. These temporary workers are usually hired from smaller firms or from farming villages.

Outside workers. The outside worker is not by definition an employee of the company; rather he is an employee of a subcontracting firm and therefore is paid by the latter, although he works in the parent company and uses its production equipment. In shipbuilding, these outside workers usually work in a crew under the regular *kōin*, although both groups work together in the shipyard.

Unfortunately there are no nationwide statistics on the distribution of these four types of factory workers. According to a partial survey of several chemical companies, the proportion of regular workers employed by the companies varied from 11.4 percent to 62.7 percent.[2] An incomplete nationwide survey conducted regularly by the Ministry of Labor reports that temporary workers compose about 6 percent of the total manual labor force in manufacturing,[3] but as temporary workers employed for more than two months are excluded from the statistics it is impossible to get a true picture of the percentage of temporary workers from these data. In reality, there may be far more temporary workers than the reported percentage implies. Nor are there any statistics on the number of outside workers. In the shipbuilding industry, outside workers outnumber regular *kōin*.[4]

The job hierarchy of the *shokuin* is based not only on the method of employment, as in the *kōin* category, but also on educational level. As a rule, these employees are graduates of high schools, colleges, or universities. The expectation is that the college graduates will eventually be promoted higher than merely to middle management, and they are carefully assigned to tasks where they will have special training on the job and will become familiar with various functions. High school graduates are expected to remain within the lower management staff, doing certain types of clerical

2. Wakao Fujita, "Kagaku" [The chemical industry] in Kazuo Ōkōchi, ed., *Sangyōbetsu chingin kettei no kikō* [Wage-determining mechanisms by industry] (Tokyo: Rōdō Kyōkai, 1965).
3. Ministry of Labor, *Rōdō ryōku chōsa* [Manpower survey] (Tokyo: Ministry of Labor, 1965).
4. "Zōsengyō ni okeru gijutsu kakushin to rōmu kanri" [Technological innovations and personnel administration in the shipbuilding industry] and "Zōsengyō ni okeru rōdō shijō to chingin" [The labor market and wages in the shipbuilding industry] in *Gijutsu kakushin to rōmu kanri*, University of Tokyo Shakai Kagaku Kenkyūsho (Social Science Institute) ed. (Tokyo: University of Tokyo Press, 1972).

work. Female employees who have completed high school are not expected to work for the company for many years, and therefore most of them are assigned to lower-grade clerical work or to a receptionist's job. Some clerical workers are hired temporarily according to the company's need, but use of this type of personnel is rare. They are usually assigned to cleaning and other custodial work.

Establishment and Maintenance of the Vertical Elite

In Western countries, personnel administration policies are designed mainly for management, and not much attention is paid to workers as an integral part of the industrial elite. Under the *nenkō* system, however, manpower development policies cover not only the managerial elite but also the *kōin* elite. This *kōin* elite is composed of the regular factory workers who are employed after their graduation from school and who are trained and given favored treatment by the company. The personnel administration policies described below are designed for regular factory workers.

As explained in earlier chapters, workers who are employed after their graduation from school as a rule work continuously for the company until they reach retirement age. When the number of employees needs to be reduced for some reason, the temporary and outside workers are the first to be discharged; if further reductions are absolutely necessary, the midterm employees are then dismissed. In this way the company protects the employment security of its regular employees. Lifetime employment security is not explicitly written into labor contracts, work rules, or any other employment contracts, but it is a traditional employment practice which has been upheld by the courts in a series of decisions since 1955. If a regular employee is inadvertently placed on the discharge list, other regular employees raise strong objections and the incident often develops into a serious conflict between labor and management. As the midterm employee *is* a regular employee, he too usually is eligible for lifetime employment, but he is not as firmly established and protected as those who became regular employees upon school graduation.

When young people are employed upon school graduation, they have neither the occupational knowledge necessary for a job nor any occupational experience, since compulsory education in Japan does not include training for specific vocations. Thus the company that hires new school graduates must train them. The large and medium-sized enterprises usually train employees for up to two years at company facilities.

Employees enrolled in a company training program are regarded as students or apprentices and are supposed to acquire the necessary knowledge in the classroom and through practical experience in the training shop. Many of the training programs in operation within large enterprises qualify as schools officially certified by the Ministry of Education.[5] When an employee completes his training, he is assigned to the lowest position in the workshop; his place in the job hierarchy is determined by the year he completes his training. The job to which he is assigned may be determined to some extent by the aptitude he demonstrates during his training course, but in many cases it is decided by the company's production management. A regular employee tends not to reject jobs or occupations in order to pursue a preferred job or occupation. Rather, he is always ready to move from one job to another, at the will and request of the company.[6]

5. According to the Vocational Training Law, training facilities within a company are regarded as the equivalent of a public vocational training center which is financed by the national government.

6. The transfer of production workers among jobs and occupations within a given plant is limited by the number of transferable jobs. However, it is common for workers to be transferred from a job in an old plant to either a similar or quite different job in a newly built plant. For example, in 1961, among 338 workers who were transferred from three old plants to a newly built one, 34.3 percent found their occupations completely changed. The commonest form of change was from maintenance work or some other indirect job to a direct production job. For elaboration, see Nihon Jinbun Kagakukai (Japan Cultural Sciences Academy), *Gijutsu kakushin no shakaiteki eikyō* [Social impacts of technological change] (Tokyo: University of Tokyo Press, 1963).

Transfer among jobs and occupations is more common among clerical and office workers. For example, office workers are frequently moved from one job to another annually. Where lifetime employment is guaranteed and promotions are granted regardless of job or occupation, transfer from one job or occupation to another within

The new employee starts out on a simple job, under the guidance of senior employees; later he moves up to more difficult tasks. Therefore, length of service can be an index of his achievement, and the skill he acquires is not transferable to any other work place or to any other company. This kind of occupational skill is quite different from the industrial skills in Western countries; it may be called the *nenkō* skill (skill improvement under the *nenkō* system).[7]

These regular employees are assigned to jobs with the assurance that they will progress from one job to another as they improve their *nenkō* skills, but their place in the hierarchy of regular employees and, therefore, the timing of their promotions is determined by their length of service, not by the importance of their job duties or occupations. Under the *nenkō* system, there are two types of promotion—status promotion and occupational promotion—and the two are well integrated. In both, length of service is the decisive factor. For example, at Ōji Seishi, a regular *kōin* assigned to his first job is given the status of a third-class worker. After more than six years of service, as a rule, he moves up to become a second-class *kōin*; in ten years he becomes a first-class *kōin*; and after twenty-five years he is eligible to be promoted to upper-class *kōin* status. A *fukukōchō* (assistant chief worker) is appointed from among the second- and first-class *kōin*, and a *kōchō* (chief worker) from the upper-class *kōin* group. Thus, regular factory workers employed upon school graduation are guaranteed successive promotions to these higher positions on the basis of their years of service.

---

the same firm is seldom resisted. Even skilled workers, such as tool makers and die makers, are involved in the transfer system since they, like others, receive no special evaluations.

As a result of technological changes, job enlargement has been pursued under a systematic job-rotation system which provides opportunities for production workers to learn more than two jobs. This flexibility may be one of the reasons industrialization in Japan has proceeded so rapidly even under the *nenkō* system.

7. This problem is discussed in more detail in Masumi Tsuda's, *The Basic Structure of Japanese Labor Relations*: The Research Series of the University of Tokyo Labor Relations Research Group (Tokyo: The Society for the Social Sciences, Musashi University, 1965), and in "The Japanese Wage Structure and Its Significance for International Comparisons, *British Journal of Industrial Relations*, 3, no. 2 (1965).

As previously discussed, length of service also determines a worker's economic status. The initial wage rate of a regular employee and the increases he may expect depend upon the date of his school graduation. Thus, any occupational experience that a midterm employee acquired before he was employed by the company tends to be discounted in determining his wages.

Before World War II, when large enterprises usually found new workers through personal contacts, there was considerable variation in beginning wage rates. After the war the number of job seekers who had completed middle school decreased, so that the labor market came to influence the starting wage rate. However, the wage increase curve still varies greatly among companies.

The wage rate being discussed here is a daily rate for the *kōin* and a monthly salary for the *shokuin*; it is not an hourly rate for a specific job or occupation. Nor does it follow that employees with the same length of service necessarily receive the same amount of pay. Instead, as explained in Chapter 10, there is usually a wage range based on a merit-rating system.

The wage level of employees reflects their position in the job hierarchy. Regular employees hired upon school graduation tend to be guaranteed wages higher than the wage-increase curve as their service to the company lengthens.

The yearly wage increase makes it possible for the income of regular employees to keep pace with increases in their household expenses related to marriage, childbearing, education, and so on. In this sense, wages are not an economic reward for service but rather are company support for the sustenance of employees and their families. The retirement allowance completes the company's support of its employees. Before World War II children were required, under civil law, to support their parents, and the retirement allowance was sufficient for a retiring employee to rent land and build his own home. It was the ideal for a retired worker to build a house and live in it with his children, the children providing the support for the parents. After the war, however, the family system changed, and children tended to become independent of their parents. Furthermore, the price of land rose enormously, as did home construction costs. Under these circumstances, companies now are unable to provide a lump-sum retirement allowance sufficient for an employee to build a suitable house, but the allowance remains important as a part of the company's lifetime support of an employee and it is assumed to be sufficient to cover expenses for him and his wife for the rest of their lives. The allowance increases in proportion to length of service; it is far lower for midterm employees than for regular employees.

Extended Family Ideology

Personnel administration in Japanese industry operates to preserve the *nenkō* system. Table 11.1 and Fig. 11.2 show the hierarchical status of employees in relationship to their respective working conditions and benefits under *nenkō*.

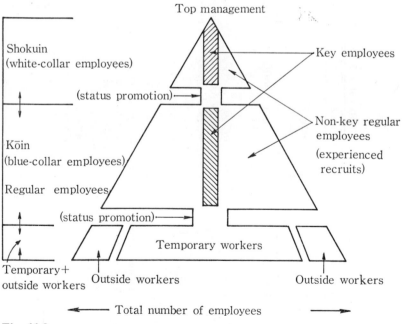

Fig. 11.2.
The Employee Composition of a Japanese Firm.

Table 11.1
The Relationship between Employees' Status and Working Conditions and Benefits under the *Nenkō* System

Employee Status	Source of Supply	Employment Tenure	Firing	Promotion
Regular employees				
Key employees	Immediately after school graduation	Lifetime employment	Not done	Successive promotion
Experienced Recruits	Those with job experience, primarily recruited from smaller firms	Usually lifetime employment; before 1945, no lifetime employment rights	Fired in case of a *severe* recession	Promotion at a slower pace than the key employees
Temporary employees	Those with job experience, primarily residents of agricultural districts, and day laborers in cities; may also include those transferred from smaller firms	Commonly short-term employment; in case of long-term employment, no guarantee of continuous employment	Fired in case of a recession	A small portion are promoted to the rank of the regular employee after selection
Subcontractor's employees (i.e., outside workers)	Employees of a labor supply company, supplied from residents of agricultural districts, day laborers in cities, and employees of tiny establishments	Employed until needed by the parent company	Depends on demand of the parent company	none

(continued)

Table 11.1
(continued)

Employee Status	Wages	Additional Allowances	Welfare Facilities
Regular employees			
Key employees	Nenkō (length of service) wages	Various allowances at a level higher than the minimum level determined by the Labor Standards Law, plus retirement allowance in an amount covering a substantial portion of expenses for the retired employee and his wife for the rest of their lives	Mostly determined by length of service
Experienced recruits	Starting rate is 50–80 percent of that of the key employees in same job, with same educational background, and of same age; thereafter, nenkō wages	Same as the key employees; smaller retirement allowance than that of the key employees, since the amount is dependent upon length of service	In most cases inferior to those of key employees
Temporary employees	Fixed wage rate with slight annual increase	Almost no incidental allowances; no retirement allowance	Almost none
Outside subcontractor's employees	Fixed wage rate by occupation	Depends upon the contract between the parent company and the labor supply company	Use the welfare facilities of the labor supply company

The two employee groups must be integrated by some kind of ideology, and the *nenkō* system supplies it. It is not necessary to go into detail about the Asian family system, which is the traditional ideology of the village community, but the following related point is important. There were two Japanese family systems in the pre-Meiji feudalistic period. One had a family ideology based on Confucianism which was widespread among the samurai class and under which the family members were subordinate to patriarchal authority. The other had the traditional family ideology of farming villages, where patriarchal authority existed but was not as strong, and a cooperative relationship among the family members was dominant.[8] In the early stages of industrialization, the family ideology of the samurai class prevailed in the personnel administration of government enterprises. In the 1900s, after modern Japanese industry was established and the *nenkō* system was introduced, the two ideologies were combined to create a family-nationalistic view (*kazoku kokkakan*) which integrated the idea of subordination to authority with the idea of cooperation; the emperor was the ultimate authority figure. The following two sections elaborate on how the Japanese family ideology has supported the *nenkō* system.

A modern industrial establishment cannot be staffed and run exclusively by members of only one family. Accordingly, the family ideology, if it is applied to a modern company in Japan, must be replicated by the employers. The kinship relation in a family appears as the lifetime-employment commitment to workers, which is limited to employees actually hired by the company and does not include a guarantee of employment to their children. If, however, the children are qualified to work for the company, they receive preferential treatment in the hiring process, thus reducing or eliminating the problem of manpower recruitment for the company. Furthermore, the patriarchal support of the household appears again in the employer's commitment to lifetime sustenance of the regular worker and his family—more concretely,

8. For a detailed discussion of these two types of family ideologies, see Takenobu Kawashima, *Nihon shakai no kazokuteki kōsei* [The family structure in Japanese society] (Tokyo: Nihon Hyōronsha, 1950).

the *nenkō* wage and retirement allowance. In addition, the various kinds of welfare facilities serve this purpose. Successive promotion based on length of service is comparable to the fixed seniority order of a family about which an individual member can do nothing. Thus, as every aspect of the *nenkō* system in industry tends to replicate a feature of the family, it may be inevitable for foreign observers to assume that the system is paternalistic.[9]

The *nenkō* system has its deficiencies. First, as mentioned, it applies completely only to regular employees hired upon school graduation—the "key employees." The midterm employees enjoy some of the benefits of the system, but temporary and outside workers are excluded and probably are the victims of a system which supports the employment security of others. Even those regular blue-collar workers who benefited by the *nenkō* system cannot, however, bridge the status gulf between themselves and the *shokuin* because of their lower educational level, and they almost always are required to remain beneath the *shokuin* class. One way that a few able workers can achieve the higher status is through examination, although here, too, the status gulf seems to be more consolidated than eliminated. Those who are fortunate enough to be promoted to a higher position are given the status of midterm employees in their new positions, and this discrimination tends to discourage competition among employees for status or class promotion. The status system is reinforced by wide differentials in employment conditions among the large, medium-sized, and small companies and by the fact that the employment conditions of temporary workers in large companies often are better than those of regular employees in small companies.

A second deficiency in the *nenkō* system stems from the family ideology of subordination to authority and cooperation. Before World War II, employees who violated work rules suffered severe penalties, the main purpose of which was to rid the company of those employees who offended the subordination principle. Key employees were protected by the *nenkō* system which controlled the promotion schedule and the number of openings in each category.

9. For example, James C. Abegglen, *The Japanese Factory: Aspects of Its Social Organization* (Glencoe: Free Press, 1958). However, his generalization of the *nenkō* system is greatly exaggerated.

Therefore, those employees rarely violated the rules or the principle. On the other hand, the midterm employees had little expectation of promotion to higher positions, however long they might serve the company, and as a consequence they were often actively critical of the employer. Under this discriminatory system, the company could maintain the normal pyramid-type hierarchy system simply by replacing employees, and a massive displacement often occurred in a large company on the occasion of a strike, an action which "offended" the family ideology. One postwar reaction to this discriminatory arrangement was that most of the active leaders of the new unions came from the ranks of the midterm employees, and among their first demands were the abolition of the status system and the dismissal of personnel managers who had been in their positions since prewar days and who were rigid in their personnel policies.

Under the *nenkō* system, employees are not considered separate individuals; they exist only as members of the enterprise which replicates the family, and as long as they submit to the principle of subordination to authority and cooperation, their future livelihood is protected by the company. If they are loyal to senior employees or to persons in higher positions, they learn to perform their jobs and their efficiency increases. The *nenkō* system is the realization of two management goals: production efficiency and maintenance of order in the work place. The phrases *kigyō ikka* (one-enterprise family) or *kigyō wa unmei kyōdōtai de aru* (the enterprise and its employees share a common destiny) denote integration of the family ideology and the *nenkō* system. Thus, personnel administration under the system may be said to be based on collectivism.

The definition of the term as it is used here leads to a discussion of a third possible deficiency of the *nenkō* system. As mentioned in Chapters 2 and 3, Japanese industrialization developed individualism as well as the family ideology among industry personnel. The *nenkō* system in modern industry requires that employees meet only two conditions: the specified educational level and employment directly from school. Once these conditions are met, ambitious employees are provided with opportunities for promotion to higher positions, for which they compete vigorously. Thus individualism functions within the framework of collectivism.

An individualistic ideology could not appear in a pure form in the Japanese industrial milieu, but ability and ambition of individual employees emerge in subgroups or cliques of employees within the company. Cliques have made the *nenkō* system more dynamic, although the system as a whole seems to be rather static. Cliques are formed on the basis of a commonality of education level, place of birth, year of entry into the company, as well as the ambition of individual employees. These groups often compete for leadership in the workshop, the department, the factory, or the company as a whole. They criticize each other for disrupting the order of the company and for inefficiency—a reflection of the "family" integrity of an enterprise and the dynamic situation produced by interfirm competition in the product market, where no rules are explicitly established. In this respect, the existence and function of cliques have often encouraged the growth and development of an enterprise under the *nenkō* system. At the same time they have created severe internal struggles, which might be considered a deficiency.

The above description may serve to provide a total picture of the *nenkō* system, principles of personnel management, and components of personnel administration, all of which are strategic elements of Japanese industrial relations, although they are not easily understood by outside observers. The following section will be devoted to a description of how the system operates and the character of labor union and workshop organizations under the *nenkō* system.

Personnel Administration and the Labor Union at the Plant Level

To facilitate an explanation of personnel administration under the *nenkō* system, it would be useful to take the work organization of a factory as an example—in this case a finishing assembly line of a large machinery manufacturing company, an operation quite similar to a steel-rolling mill, a shipyard, or a chemical plant. The example here cited is from a report made by Shōjirō Ujihara, one of the leading researchers on a project which includes case studies in industries other than machinery manufacturing.[10]

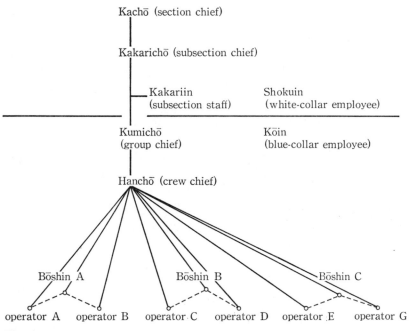

Fig. 11.3.
The Plant Organization of a Large Machinery Firm.

Work Organization and Its Management

The plant organization of this large enterprise, which manufactures diesel engines in the Tokyo-Yokohama area, is shown in Fig. 11.3. At the lowest level is a group of three or four employees who work together as a team; this smallest work unit is called a

10. Research in this area has been pioneered by the University of Tokyo's Social Science Institute in a case study project begun in 1951. For further details, see Shōjirō Ujihara, *Nihon rōdō mondai kenkyū* [A study of labor problems in Japan] (Tokyo: University of Tokyo Press, 1966).

go. The *bōshin* who heads the unit is an older, experienced employee who trains his men, works with them, and guides them as a pace-setter, but he has no formal authority to supervise or manage, nor does he have any responsibility to do so.

At the next level is the *han*, a work unit composed of ten to twenty workers and composed of several *go*. The *hanchō*, the chief of this unit, is the lowest ranking supervisory management personnel and has the authority (1) to maintain equipment, direct work methods, and control the quality of the product in the production process; and (2) to assign tasks to his men, compile basic records to be used as recommendations for wage increases and other merit-rating matters, and settle grievances. However, he has no authority to employ or discharge workers, decide the number of workers in the *han* and their wage rates, judge the merit of individuals, or make decisions on other personnel matters, although he can express his opinion to higher levels of management. He is not concerned with the private lives of the men he supervises.

A *kumi*, composed of one to three *han*, is the largest work unit in the factory and usually includes a whole division processing a particular type of product. The *kumichō*, who is in charge of this unit, is not a production worker but, as manager of the production process, he is responsible for supervising the *hanchō* under him. Using their reports and recommendations, he makes the first authoritative evaluation of workers in the *kumi* and reports the results to the *kakarichō*, or subsection chief. He is also involved in the personal problems of his men outside the work place and is, in fact, the personnel manager of the factory workers in the division.

Above the work organization is the administrative organization staffed by the *shokuin*. The *kakari* (subsection) is the smallest unit of the administrative organization; its members are called *kakariin* or staff. The subsection has various functions ranging from clerical administration, such as accounting and personnel, to production management on the production line and industrial engineering on the production staff. The *kakarichō* or subsection manager has the responsibility for allocating tasks among his staff personnel, for supervising them, and for making the first evaluation of their performance. Usually, however, he has no authority to make decisions in organizational matters, and in this sense he seems to correspond to the *hanchō* among the *kōin*.

A *ka* or section, composed of several subsections, is established in each product division and each occupational group in the plant. The *kachō* or section chief has the final responsibility and authority to make decisions on personnel matters related to factory workers, the subsections of the *shokuin*, and the staffs. A *bu* or department is composed of several sections, and the whole plant organization is composed of several departments.[11] Thus, although the hierarchical status system is very complex, the management structure is relatively uncomplicated.

Table 11.2

Characteristics of Blue-Collar Workers in a Typical Manufacturing Firm

Job Title	Age	Length of Service	Length of Experience	Daily Wage Rates (yen)
Kumichō	38	26	25	250
Hanchō	32	19	19	214
Bōshin B	36	14	14	198
Bōshin A	30	16	16	188
Bōshin C	25	10	6	140
Operator G	42	4	22	177
Operator D	37	3	20	169
Operator C	32	2	17	146
Operator A	27	9	5	139
Operator B	25	6	6	134
Operator E	18	5	5	109
Operator F	19	4	4	109

Wage Administration

The wage system in Japanese industry is characterized by progressive increases in wage rates, with wage differentials tend-

11. For example, the Toyota Automobile Manufacturing Company employed 6,929 people in 1959. Among them, 1,581 were *shokuin*, 3,622 were *kōin*, and 1,726 were temporary workers. In 1960 there were 20 departments, including 6 line departments and 75 sections. In the casting department there were 4 sections, 10 subsections, and 30 *kumi*. For elaboration, see Nihon Jinbun Kagakukai, *Gijutsu kakushin no shakai-teki eikyō*.

ing to correspond to the occupational hierarchy of the employees. The finishing assembly line illustrated in Table 11.2 is again cited as an example in order to clarify the relationship between a factory worker's age, length of service, occupational experience, and wage rates.

Operators E and F, *bōshin* C and A, the *hanchō*, and the *kumichō* are all *kōin* who were employed upon school graduation. These key employees are carefully arranged so that they can be promoted successively and regularly. Furthermore, their age differentials are also carefully arranged in terms of occupational positions. As they have been employed continuously at the work place from the time they were hired by the company, their length of service corresponds to their years of experience. The only exception is *bōshin* C; in spite of his relative youth, his term of service is longer than that of any other worker.

Bōshin B and operators G, D, C, A, and B are midterm employees, and they can be promoted no higher than the *bōshin* level, where they have no authority or responsibility. Operator G is the oldest in the workshop in terms of job experience. As his length of service is short, however, he cannot occupy a supervisory position. Operators D and C are in the same position. They are paid daily, not hourly, wages, and as shown in Table 11.2, their wage rates correspond to those of others of the same occupational status.

In other words, wages increase as the worker climbs the occupational ladder. The differentials tend to correspond more nearly to differences in length of service than to differences in age or years of experience. This factor illustrates a feature of the *nenkō* system which was mentioned in the previous section, and it also demonstrates a feature of wage administration under the system.

In this example there are two exceptions to the pattern described above. First, operators G, D, and C are in one of the highest pay brackets in the worker category, although their length of service is relatively short. The reason is that they are midterm employees, and their wage rates have been adjusted to take account of their ages and years of occupational experience. Adjusting for these variations in personal traits is one of the most important aspects of wage administration. Second, although *bōshin*

C has a principal position among the *bōshin* and his occupational experience is longer than that of anyone else in the worker category, his wage rate is lower than that of operators G, D, and C because, in contrast to the first exception, his rate is adjusted downward to take account of the relatively short duration of his service to the company. However, his wage rate is higher than that of operator B, who is the same age, and that of operator A, who is older but is a midterm employee.

As described in detail in Chapter 10, the *nenkō* system has a unique structure and includes base rates, group incentive allowances, overtime pay, allowances for service on holidays (i.e., special duty allowance), and so on. The overtime pay and allowance for service on a holiday are determined as proportions of the base rate of individual employees, as is the group incentive allowance. Thus the major items of workers' incomes vary according to their base wage rates; exceptions to this formula are family and commuting allowances and other minor items. In sum, the daily wage rate of workers is an indicator not only of status in the workshop but also of their economic status.

Collectivism as a feature of the *nenkō* system is reinforced by workshop practices. As there is no freedom of choice based on seniority, all employees in a workshop are equally eligible for overtime work or service on a holiday. From the viewpoint of the company as a whole, one of the most important personnel policies is equilization of the amount of overtime work or service on a holiday as well as the number of hours or frequency of shift work. Because individual freedom is not considered under this system, neither the low- nor the high-paid workers can try to increase their incomes by increasing the amount of their overtime work.

Labor Union Organization at the Plant Level

The Kawasaki Iron Mill Workers' Union of Nihon Kōkan, one of the largest steel enterprises in Japan, is typical of a plant-level union organization and is considered here as an appropriate example. In 1957 it had a membership of some 13,700 workers at the Kawasaki Iron Mill, one of the company's major installations.

This union, together with the plant-level organizations at three other of the company's mills and the union at the firm's head office, are united in the Nihon Kōkan Workers' Union Federation.[12]

The plant-level union organization is subdivided to correspond in general to the organization of the company. The branch corresponds to the section or department of a company. The smallest subdivision is the *han* or "squad" which consists of more than a hundred members and parallels the company *kakari*. In a union where the work-place organization is well developed, a squad may be further divided to be conterminous with the smaller work units.

Two points should be stressed with regard to the union membership: (1) Only employees who are at the level of *kakarichō* and below are eligible for membership; those who are section managers and above are excluded. An exception to this general rule are employees and group heads who are engaged in personnel administration, labor administration, security, cost accounting, or wage determination; they too may not become union members. In the Kawasaki Iron Mill, approximately one hundred employees are in this category. (2) Only regular employees may be union members; temporary workers are not eligible. It happens that at the Kawasaki Iron Mill the eight hundred temporary workers have organized a union of their own, but this is not the usual practice.

The administrative organization of the Kawasaki Iron Mill Workers' Union is composed of the General Assembly, the Central Committee, and the Executive Committee, augmented by the Secretariat of the departments. The squad, paralleling the *kumi*, is the basic unit for electing delegates to the General Assembly which is convened once a year. One out of every three delegates from each branch is a member of the Central Committee which serves as the legislative body between assemblies. The supreme governing body is the Executive Committee, composed of the full-time officers who serve one-year terms—the president, two vice-presidents, one chief secretary, and about ten Executive Commit-

12. This case was obtained from the report of the research on unions which the University of Tokyo Labor Union Research Office carried out in 1955-58: Kazuo Ōkōchi, Shōjirō Ujihara, and Wakao Fujita, *Rōdō kumiai no kōzō to kinō* [The structure and function of labor unions] (Tokyo: University of Tokyo Press, 1959). The Kawasaki Iron Mill is now part of the Keihin Iron Mill.

tee officers. The chief secretary is in charge of the Secretariat, and one Executive Committee officer heads each department.

Once a year each branch holds a Branch Assembly, nominally the supreme legislative body, but in practice the Branch Managers' Committee is more important, serving both legislative and executive functions between assemblies. Branch officers include a branch director, one or two branch vice-directors, and several managers (the number is proportional to the branch membership); the Jōkō (bar steel) Branch of the Kawasaki union has 60 managers for 1,058 members. All of the branch officers supposedly serve part time, but in practice the director is a full-time officer. A manager is elected from each squad. The director and vice-director are elected by referendum vote of the entire membership of the branch from among the candidates recommended by the Managers' Committee. The branch departments have administrative functions. Chiefs and staff of the departments are appointed by the branch director and vice-director with the approval of the Branch Managers' Committee.

Top level collective bargaining is carried out between the Nihon Kōkan Company, Ltd., and the Nihon Kōkan Workers' Union Federation, where the average amount of the basic wage increase and the method of its calculation, the average amount of the reward-for-production group incentive allowance and the method of its calculation, the average amount of the semiannual seasonal bonus, and important problems related to welfare facilities are negotiated and settled. Then, within the framework of the general agreement, the details of such economic matters as wages, the reward-for-production incentive allowance, and the seasonal bonus are worked out by the management of the Kawasaki Iron Mill and the Kawasaki Mill Workers' Union. Also, during collective bargaining at this level, all matters concerning working conditions, such as hours, production schedule, manning, and transfer, are negotiated, and the result is committed to writing as the collective agreement.

A third level of collective bargaining is conducted between the manager of a department or section of the mill and the branch union. Bargaining at this level is regarded as grievance handling under the collective agreement. At the Jōkō Branch, for example, negotiations concern problems of the average allocation of over-time work, the calculation of hours of work, and the shortage of manpower. Negotiations at this level are complex because the collective agreements are not functional at the department or section level and are so lacking in specificity that local working conditions must be agreed upon separately at each work place. Grievance settlement is not final and binding; therefore, any grievance that is not settled at the branch level is negotiated at the level of the Kawasaki Iron Mill and the Kawasaki Iron Mill Workers' Union, if it is an important problem.

In the Kawasaki union there is no bargaining at the level of the squad, the smallest administrative unit in the union, which corresponds to the company's *kumi*. The union representative at this level is the manager. The squad leader, who is elected from among the managers and represents each squad, is the communication link between the Branch Managers' Committee and the union members. In an active union, the squad leader and the managers are the important union representatives for work-place activities and grievance handling.

Characteristics of Labor Union Officers at the Plant Level

Some of the characteristics of the plant-level union officers in the Jōkō Branch of the Kawasaki Union are shown in Table 11.3. Their average age is slightly more than thirty-six years, an indication that union offices are occupied by employees with long service, when we consider that under the length-of-service system these employees have worked at the company since the time they completed their compulsory education at the age of fifteen. The *average* length of service of union officers also is quite long. Almost all of the squad leaders, who are among the lowest-ranking officers in the work place, are older employees with long service. On the other hand, it can be assumed that among the delegates to the General Assembly and the managers, there are midterm employees who are older but have served for shorter periods of time with the company. The third and most important characteristic is that the proportion of company group and crew chiefs (*kumichō* and

Table 11.3
Characteristics of Typical Plant-Level Union Officers (1957)

Title	Number	Average Age	Average Length of Service	Number of Kumichō & Hanchō	Percentage of Kumichō & Hanchō
Branch director & vice-director	4	36	14	2	50
Central Committee member	12	39	16	6	50
General Assembly delegate	36	36	12	9	25
Hanchō (squad leader)	6	44	20	4	67
Kanji (manager)	61	36	12	16	26

hanchō) among the elected union officers is very high. Such people occupy more than half of the officer's posts if the delegates to the General Assembly and the managers are excluded.

The conclusion that can be drawn from this description of the characteristics of union officers is that the labor union is operated by the company's key employees. As a result, the union is not free to function separately and independently of company policy but rather might be described as "cohesive" with the company.

It is not correct, however, to conclude that the labor union under the length-of-service system is always "grafted on" to the company and perpetually submissive. Other conditions being equal, the labor union experiences the following three stages in sequence. Since the employment structure is shaped like a pyramid, the first stage is one in which the union offices are occupied by members who are older and have served the company for many years, or by those who are in supervisory or leading positions in the company organization; the younger workers who have served for short periods of time form a youth group within the union. If the officers are active, the youth group spearheads union activities; but if the officers are submissive to the company, the union tends to take on the characteristics of a company union.

The second stage is the period when promotion opportunities become fewer as the level of the positions of the majority of the union members in the company's pyramidal organization becomes higher, so that successive promotion is not guaranteed to all key employees, nor are promotions and wage increases guaranteed to the midterm employees. At this stage there will be a number of employees who have served the company more than four years, have acquired skill, and have experience as members of the union, but are not provided sufficient guarantee of promotion and wage increases. If the union is not active enough in representing their interests, they will elect new union leaders from among themselves, present their demands, and oppose objectionable employment policies. It is at this stage that the union is the most active and the union activities extend to the lowest unit in the work place. Of the union officers at the Jōkō Branch of the Kawasaki Union (Table 11.3), 51 percent of the delegates to the General Assembly and the managers are employees who have served between five and ten years, an indication that this union is in the second stage of development. The principal union activists during this period are the midterm employees, and the focus of the movement is the attainment of equal opportunities.

The third stage is the period when opportunities for promotion in the company organization become fewer and fewer, especially at the higher levels, so that middle-aged employees with long service accumulate at subordinate levels. It becomes clear to these people that, unless the company's employment policies are drastically changed, they will have to retire without being promoted. The labor union then becomes an organization of the dissatisfied majority and adopts a very hostile and aggressive stance toward the company. The company counters by promoting a considerable number of these employees, who then become submissive. Factions develop and the union splits. The first union, which is the organization of the dissatisfied majority, goes into battle against the company which responds by discharging many employees in the name of "personnel curtailment." The result is that the first union declines, breaks up, and is absorbed into the second union which is submissive to the company. Thus the employment structure once again has its pyramidal shape, and the second union, which now has become the first union, returns to the first stage. Progress through this three-stage cycle is regarded as typical for a labor union under the length-of-service system.[13]

The Employer's Policies toward the Labor Union

The employer makes every effort to maintain the labor union's cooperation with company policies, but no matter how closely attached the union may be to the company it is an independent organization and is protected by law. Therefore, the company never stops trying to influence not only the union's activities but also every aspect of its organization. Two methods are widely used and are characteristic. The first is the company's effort to influence the election of union officers. At the Kawasaki Iron Mill, for example, and the practice is common in other enterprises, the company works through members of the *kakari* (subsection, the lowest grouping of white-collar workers in the plant) and the *kumichō* to make sure that persons suitable from the company's standpoint are nominated for union offices, and it directs all of the workers to vote for these individuals. This directive is handed down especially to key employees as the policy of the personnel department. Further, in the election of branch union officers, it is possible that department or section chiefs or subsection staff members could nominate persons "unsuitable" from the company's viewpoint. There was a case where candidates recommended by the union Managers' Committee were taken off the ballot and other individuals who had not been recommended by the committee became the candidates. In another company, the principle of secret-ballot voting was replaced by open voting at the work place. Strictly speaking, these actions are unfair labor practices, but they do occur.

As a second method of influencing workers, a company expands its communication system by organizing informal group meetings at the work place. In the Kawasaki Iron Mill, group meetings are set up in each unit of the company organization, often even at the

13. This theory was first presented by Wakao Fujita in Shōjirō Ujihara, Wakao Fujita, and Naomichi Funabashi, *Nihongata rōdō kumiai to nenkō seido* [Japanese type labor unions and the length of service system] (Tokyo: Tōyō Keizai Shinpō-sha, 1960).

han level. Various problems such as additional overtime work, supposedly a subject for union negotiations, are dealt with at the *han* meetings in such a way that the *kakarichō* is able to persuade the employees to abide by any decisions made there, and thus negotiations with the union are bypassed.

The company also frequently develops a network of organizations within the company, based upon the category of employees. At the Toyota Automobile Manufacturing Company, separate meetings of *kumichō* and of *hanchō* are organized on the basis of their status in the company organization, and the meetings function not only as a friendly gathering of colleagues but also as a place to discuss company policies or collective bargaining issues, the results of which are reported to the company. Among the key employees, meetings are organized on the basis of school career or length of service; the purpose and function are the same as the others.[14] As informal meetings and consultations of this kind become more extensive and pervasive within a company, the labor union becomes less and less actively independent.

Changing Aspects of Labor Administration and Industrial Relations at the Plant Level

It must be pointed out that the characteristics of labor administration and industrial relations at the plant level under the length-of-service system, as described above, are not necessarily perpetual and fixed. Since the beginning of the surge in economic development in 1955, and especially since 1960, several factors have emerged that may bring about a great change in labor administration and industrial relations. This section will deal with the most conspicuous among these factors.

As already discussed in Chapters 2 and 3, 1955 marked the beginning of Japan's remarkable economic development, and since that time the heavy and chemical industries have become the heart of Japan's industrial structure. At the enterprise or plant level, this economic development was promoted by changes in

14. According to the above-cited research report by the *Gijutsu kakushin no shakaiteki eikyō,op.cit.*

production control methods based upon technological change as well as changes in management organization.

As production control methods change and production processes come to be controlled in a central control room, many of the functions of the *kachō* and the *kumichō* are no longer the responsibility of the line organization. For example, process and time control are now independent, and the operators who had been supervised by the *kachō* or the *kumichō* are now directed by the control section. Also, such work as transportation, equipment, or maintenance is now assigned to newly established transportation or equipment sections, and oiling of machines in operation processes and grinding of edged tools in machine processes are now done by workers assigned to new filing or grinding sections. Thus, technological changes have created great dislocations in the control system at the plant level so that the responsibility of the head of the line organization has been considerably diminished.

Technological changes have necessitated the abandonment of conventional facilities and machines, the purchase and installation of new facilities, changes in plants and production processes, or the enlargement of research and development sections, all of which require a large capital investment on the part of the company. As the amount of investment funds Japanese companies can draw from reserves is very small, 80 percent of the total must come from borrowed capital; therefore the long-term costs of technological change are enormous.

Two tendencies are apparent in the efforts of Japanese business to minimize these costs. The first is a change in corporate relationships and organization. Formerly, a large company might carry on central production processes in its own plant. Supply and some processing of materials and parts were performed by subsidiary companies established with capital from the parent company, or else such work was subcontracted to small and medium-sized independent firms which contracted for the work of only one of the large companies. This dual structure was the nucleus of the Japanese economy. With progressive technological change and the development of continuous production processes, the large companies have been forced to increase their use of subordinate small and medium-sized firms in order to reduce expenses.

Three types of adjustment have taken place. As an example of the first type, the Tōyō Kōatsu Company concentrated on major production processes and entrusted related business, as much as possible, to subordinate small and medium-sized companies.[15] When its new fertilizer plant using natural gas as the raw material was about to go into production, the company decided to contract with a subsidiary for the development and supply of the natural gas, and to subcontract boiler and pipe manufacturing, plumbing, repair of gauges, and packing and transportation of products to thirteen small firms. All of this work formerly was done in the conventional way by the parent company.

A second type of adjustment is illustrated by the Toyota Automobile Manufacturing Company which subcontracts the production and assembly of parts in small units to small and medium-sized enterprises; the twenty most important of these smaller firms were permitted to move their plants to locations near the parent plants to form areal enterprise groups.[16] An illustration of a third type of adjustment is the electric motor plant of Hitachi Seisaku-sho, which now concentrates on products that can be mass-produced automatically and successively in its own plant and has subcontracting firms handle those that are produced in small quantities or cannot be produced by automatic processes.[17] Each of these types of adjustment compels the subcontracting companies to improve their own technologies and to maintain close relationships with parent companies with regard to quantity and speed of product supply, quality of products, and unit price.

The second way Japanese business has tended to change in response to industrial development is by forming enterprise combinations or industry complexes, often called *kombinatō*. There are nine industry complexes in the petrochemical industry, the major ones being the old zaibatsu companies such as Mitsubishi, Mitsui, and Furukawa. Three of the complexes are composed of enterprises independent of each other. The successful merger of Ishikawajima Heavy Industries and Harima Shipbuilding Com-

15. Ibid., Pt. 2.
16. Ibid., Pt. 1. Toyota Automobile Manufacturing Company had, as of 1958, 7 affiliated corporations, 5 subsidiaries, and 185 subcontracting companies.
17. Mikio Sumiya, ed., *Impact of Technological Change on Labor* (Tokyo: Research Institute on Japanese Industrial Structure, 1966).

pany in 1960, the first merger of mammoth independent companies in Japan, is an example of the formation of enterprise combinations. Sharpened international competition since 1955 has increased the tendency toward this type of change.

Thus it is apparent that changes in the industrial structure brought about by technological change have tended to alter the pattern of enterprise organization as well as the relationships among enterprises in Japan since 1965.

It could be assumed from reading the previous sections that every industrial adjustment or change mentioned influences labor administration and industrial relations at the plant level. The various aspects of change have been the subject of a great deal of research, and six examples can be cited from separate studies conducted since 1955 in the steel, automobile manufacturing, shipbuilding, chemical, power, and telephone communication industries.[18]

Changes in Occupations and Duties

A general effect of technological change in the plant is alteration of the occupations and duties of the employees. Three aspects can be identified. First, in the shipbuilding industry, as a result of the shift from the stratiform to the block-building method, the ironworker and the woodworker, traditionally the principal and most skilled craftsmen, are no longer needed, and the assembly work is now divided into indoor, ground, and building slip work; transportation and material distribution have become independ-

18. On the steel industry, see Masumi Tsuda's report on research in 1956–57, *Rōdō mondai to rōmu kanri* [Labor Problems and Labor Administration] (Kyoto: Minerva Shobo, 1959); on the automobile manufacturing industry, research in 1959: *Gijutsu-kakushin no shakaiteki eikyō*, Pt. 1; on the shipbuilding industry, research started in 1957: University of Tokyo Social Science Institute, *Zōsengyō ni okeru rōdō shijo no kōzō; Structure of Labor Market in the Shipbuilding Industry*, 1963, and *Zōsengyō ni okeru rōdō shijō to chingin*; on the chemical industry, research in 1960: *Gijutsu kakushin no shakaiteki eikyō*, Pt. 2; on the power industry, research in 1959–60: Yasuhiko Ōishi, and Shōji Shiba, *Ōtomeishon to rōdō: Karyokuhatsudensho ni okeru jisshoteki kenkyū* [Automation and labor: A positive study of a steam power plant] (Tokyo: Tōyō Keizai Shinpō-sha, 1961); on the telephone communication industry, research in 1958: Jūji Misumi, and Hachiji Okuda, *Kikaika to Haichitenkan* [Mechanization and Transfer] (Tokyo: Japanese Productivity Center, Productivity Institute, 1958).

ent occupations. Riveting is replaced by electric and gas welding, and as design and cutting of steel materials become further automated, other old occupations will also disappear. This case is an example of the impact of technological change on the occupational structure as traditional occupations are curtailed or disappear and new occupations are created.

Second, work is simplified and objectified by means of written documents or drawings so that the "secret" elements of a journeyman's skill become obsolete. A comparison of the old and the new separation plants in the steel industry illustrates how operations are simplified in the new plant where only a few operators are needed to perform the work, by rotation on three shifts. In the shipbuilding industry, the trades of the iron-and woodworkers, which had been skills with "secret" elements, vanished and were replaced by a standard operation manual outlining the work of operators, each of whom has a separate and independent duty.

Third, in the automobile industry, as a result of the introduction of specialty and transfer machines, the whole operation is simplified, lot production is changed to conveyor production, and the number of cars for which each operator is responsible is increased so that, although the job titles are the same, the jobs themselves are broader. Similar diversification of operation is seen in the power industry, where there is central control; as the breadth of information exchange is widened and regular inspection for defects in the automated processes is necessary, the duties of the operators become diversified.

Such dissolution, curtailment, and reformation of occupations which accompanies the simplification and objectification of job content and the diversification of duties cannot help but influence every aspect of traditional personnel administration under the length-of-service system.

Reduction in the Size of the Operating Unit

Changes in occupations and duties brought about by technological change also reduce the size of operating units needed in the plant. In the chemical industry the number of operators required for the production of ammonia in a new process using natural gas is one-third the number needed in the old facilities which used coal. The new plants have a daily capacity of 120 tons and use three operators per shift for the cracking process and four per shift for the synthetic process; each operator is in charge of a separate part of the graphic panel or patrols a separate section of the plant. Thus, the opportunity for an operating group to work together in the traditional way is eliminated.

The new work-group unit in the shipbuilding industry also is different from what it was before. Not only have the occupations of the iron- and the woodworker disappeared, but as mentioned above the welding of the hull, which formerly was done by a large crew of riveters, is now performed by welding machines operated by one-man units assigned to separate sections.

Such changes in and reductions of the operating group cannot help but weaken the collectivism upon which the length-of-service system traditionally depended.

Curtailment of Promotion Ladders and Supervisory Classes

Iron and wood work in the shipbuilding industry were such highly skilled occupations that workers were ranked in an orderly fashion according to their degree of skill. In each *go* there was a master, a senior workman, a workman, and an apprentice, equivalent to the ranking and order of promotion in the company organization. As these occupations disappeared, so also did the promotional ladder. Riveters also had a promotional ladder based on skill, but the welders who replaced them do not, except for the supervisory position of *hanchō*. In the steel industry there is nothing in the new separation plants similar to the well-defined skill ladders that existed in the old plants.

Changes in occupations and duties also create changes in the rankings of the various occupations. In the automobile foundry, among the molding, melting, casting, core-setting, and mold-repair crews, the molding crew formerly was the top-level assignment. However, when the automatic molding machine was introduced, that job assignment dropped to the bottom of the ranking and a considerable number of temporary workers took over the molding duties.

Changes further influence the managerial and supervisory levels. In hull assembly work in the shipbuilding industry, the installation *shokuchō* supervised several installation *hanchō*, and the process control was handled by the *kakarichō*. After the block-building method was introduced, the installation processes were divided into the indoor, ground, and building slip processes, and a *hanchō*, who was under a *shokuchō*, was appointed for each process. At the same time *shokuchō* were assigned to such direct installation work as lifting, transportation, and equipment as these became independent occupations. This reorganization increased the number of *shokuchō*, but at the same time decreased their standing in the company organization.

Change can bring about a reduction in the supervisory classes also. In one chemical company the supervisory structure below the *kachō* is: *kakarichō*, *kumichō*, *hanchō*. Since this organization is typical of the entire company, a newly established plant will maintain it temporarily, but in the new plant the *hanchō* has the responsibility only of guiding the work of his *han* and the *kakarichō* is a member of the staff of the *kachō*. As a result, real authority and responsibility lie in only two classes, the *kachō* and the *kumichō*, and further changes in the organization are expected. At the same time, the number of supervisory personnel per unit in the organization is diminishing. In the ammonia production section of the old plant of the chemical company, there are one *kachō*, two *kachō-dairi*, five *kakarichō*, and ten *kumichō*, plus eighteen *hanchō* per shift; in the new plant there are one *kachō*, one *kakarichō*, and one *kumichō*, plus two *hanchō* per shift. The ratio of supervisors to operators in the new plant is less than half of what it was in the old one.

Such a reduction in promotion opportunities, together with the reduction in the size of classes and the number of supervisors, means that successive promotion, one of the characteristics of personnel administration under the length-of-service system, is no longer guaranteed for the workers. Thus, the avenue of promotion becomes very narrow. This was the issue in a recent labor-management dispute in the chemical industry, and the employers are well aware of the difficulty and are seeking a solution. In 1958 a system was introduced in some large enterprises in the steel industry to make it possible for *kōin* to become chiefs of production sections. As a result, the *shokuin* will eventually perform only staff functions as far as the production area is concerned. To date, however, no *kōin* has reached the position of chief, so the impact of this new policy on the *shokuin* remains to be seen.

The Tendency to Favor Youth

It was observed during the comparison of the old and new cold strip mills in the steel industry that the companies preferred young workers over the older ones in appointments to key operations in the new plants. This phenomenon was a finding common to all of the research studies discussed here. This preference seems to be a natural consequence of the fact that the new occupations, duties, and operations require more knowledge or a greater capacity to learn than the old workers possess, and that youth is more adaptable, is quicker at mastering skills, and has the higher operating capacity required by the new technology. This practice of promoting young workers has a negative effect on traditional personnel administration under the length-of-service system, and the inevitable result, as the practice is extended, is for highly paid middle-aged and older workers to become redundant in the work place and to be excluded from key operations. A possible solution to this problem was suggested by Nikkeiren, the Japan Federation of Employers' Associations, in 1965 when it proposed a Japanese layoff system for middle-aged and older workers. The proposal had a rather cold reception, but the fact that it was even made was an indication that the employers are conscious of the problem.

Maintenance of Traditional Lifetime Employment

What kind of policies do the employers formulate to respond to the four tendencies for great change described above? First of all, they try to maintain the traditional policy of lifetime employment.

When new technology is to be introduced in a large enterprise, a new plant is established, and the policy of guaranteeing lifetime employment is honored by transferring workers from the old plant to the new one. In the case of the chemical company studied, 76 percent of the workers at the new plant which used natural gas were people who had been transferred from three older plants in Kyūshū and Hokkaidō. This policy of transfer is observed, without exception, in any large company, but even here a tendency toward change can be seen. For example, when a new thermal power plant was activated in 1956, 24 percent of its operators were workers transferred from the old plant. Among those transferred, no specific schooling level was required of workers under thirty years of age, but among those over thirty, the company assigned only workers who had completed middle school under the former education system. The reason was that the new operation required that employees understand the new electric technology and have a knowledge of English, as the equipment was imported. Each year the number of high school graduates who are employed in the new plants is increasing, and the ratio of transferred workers is decreasing. Therefore, it is anticipated that the traditional lifetime employment policy may be modified.

Maintenance of a lifetime employment system contributes to disputes because of various adjustments made at the work place. In one chemical company it became necessary to develop a human relations policy which included informal group meetings called by the *kachō*, closer communication between the *kakarichō* and the *kumichō*, and expansion of company houses and athletic and recreational facilities. In spite of such efforts, there is a marked tendency for youth to transfer among enterprises for at least two reasons. One is their dissatisfaction under the length-of-service system when middle-aged and older workers control the work place and young workers seldom receive the key job assignments— or when, if assigned, their status is not respected. A second reason, observed particularly in the steel or electric machine and apparatus manufacturing industries, is that young workers prefer clean jobs and try to avoid the dirty ones. The tendency to transfer seems to be accelerated by the fact that young workers are in short supply. Therefore, it is a safe general assumption that the lifetime employment system is beginning to crumble as midterm employees become more numerous.

Maintenance of the Traditional Length-of-Service Wage System

In the chemical, power, and automobile manufacturing industries, although great technological changes are occurring at the work place, traditional wage administration principles continue to be perfectly maintained. Thus, a considerable gap exists between wage administration under the length-of-service system and the actual conditions in the work place.

However, even here there are some indications of change. In the steel industry the reward-for-production group incentive allowance, which formerly made up more than half of a worker's total monthly earnings, was allocated according to the amount of his basic wage prior to 1955. After 1955 it was allocated according to the importance of his duties, regardless of age or length of service, and in 1957 the industry established a job-classified wage system based upon job evaluation, which now accounts for approximately 20 percent of a worker's monthly earnings. Since the job-classified wage system provides wage differentials according to the importance of the duties rather than according to age or length of service, the high wages for older workers had to be somewhat modified. This new system is well liked in the steel and electric machine manufacturing industries and is becoming increasingly popular in other industries.

Further, with regard to retirement allowances, which will be discussed further in Chapter 12, there is a tendency for companies to pool retirement allowance funds or to shift to a social security system, so that considerable change is expected in this area also.

Traditional Labor Union Policies

In spite of slogans and declarations, the activities of the labor unions seem to demonstrate that they are supporting the traditional principles of lifetime employment and wages based on length of service. The labor disputes in the telephone communication industry in 1956 furnish evidence for this generalization. The Nippon Telegraph and Telephone Public Corporation announced a plan for automating four southern stations, which involved the transfer of 45 percent of the regular employees to nonautomated stations and service sectors and the discharge of 6 percent of the regular employees and all temporary workers. The local union branches formed a joint counteraction committee to oppose the plan and submitted a demand to the corporation for an increase in personnel to accompany the expansion of exchange service. The atmosphere grew tenser as higher levels of the union organization became involved—the prefectural branch, the district headquarters, and the central headquarters of the All-Japan Telecommunication Workers' Union, or Zendentsū—and criticism and conflict developed between the upper and lower union levels. As a result of negotiations between the district headquarters of the union and the district bureau of the corporation, the union succeeded in reaching a detailed agreement which called for a retraining program to be attached to the original corporation plan, better conditions for the 20 percent of the workers to be transferred, and continued employment for 40 percent of the temporary workers who were scheduled for discharge. The implication of this case is that the Japanese labor union has enough power to defend the guarantees of the lifetime employment system. Additional evidence comes from the coal-mining industry which has declined as a result of keen competition from the petroleum industry. Tanrō, after a fierce struggle, succeeded in getting the government to enact a law providing for the reemployment and retraining of displaced miners for jobs in other industries.

Nevertheless, as a result of the inroads that young workers are making at the work place, a considerable change in union policies will be inevitable. The slowness of unions in making policy adjustments has widened the gap between the rank-and-file members and the leaders, and a turnover in union officers may be expected.

Overall Evaluation of the Changes

It is difficult to foresee whether the traditional length-of-service system in personnel administration and industrial relations will be maintained with minor revisions or whether it will disappear completely. However, the nature of the problem is quite clear.[19]

For example, 93 percent of all manufacturing firms in Japan are small enterprises employing fewer than 29 workers; employees working for such enterprises make up 20 percent of the total number of manufacturing employees. Fifty-three percent of the total number of employees work for firms employing fewer than 300 persons. The *nenkō* system does not exist in the personnel administration of these small companies; rather, their workers are all midterm employees. Thus, it can be assumed that, of the total number of employees of Japanese corporations, only 40 percent are under the length-of-service system.[20] The conclusion must be reached that the key employees under the *nenkō* system of personnel administration are a select elite.

So far we have observed the changing aspects of personnel administration, we have focused upon employers who have introduced new policies and young employees of a new type, and we have anticipated the appearance of union leaders with new policies. But it is not yet clear what is meant by "new" in any of these instances. It is at least certain, however, that "new" is not simply an expression of the ideology or the values of the United States and of Western European countries; instead, it will be defined by how the "new" policies are able to integrate the values and ideology of the length-of-service system which depends upon the traditional familistic ideology.

Many factors operate to generate change in the *nenkō* system. Among them are full-fledged penetration of automation into both production and clerical fields, the decrease in the supply of young workers in the labor market, an increase in the intellectual level of workers as a result of increasing consumption of public education,

19. Detailed forcecasts on the subject are discussed in Masumi Tsuda, *Nenkō teki rō-shi kankei ron* [Nenkō Labor Relations] (Tokyo: Minerva Shobo, 1968).
20. Masumi Tsuda, *The Basic Structure of Japanese Labor Relations, op. cit.* pp. 80–88.

the wide diffusion of the nuclear family system and rapid urbanization, continuous economic development, and a radical change in the industrial structure. At the plant level this change takes the form of "personnel administration based upon ability" and the reorganization of the structure and activity of unions.

"Personnel administration based upon ability" is a concept that has been strongly advocated since the late 1960s. It is considered to be a personnel administration policy that changes the *nenkō* system and at the same time permits Japanese firms to remain competitive internationally. It has two characteristics. First, it is designed to end the evaluation of employees based upon educational background or simply upon length of service. Instead, it seeks to establish the principle of personnel administration based upon ability to perform the job. Second, it is intended to maintain that feature of the *nenkō* system which integrates the individual into the group and rewards the collective and organizational ability, intending thereby to prevent the alienation of individual workers.

In order to achieve this goal, "management by results" and "zero defect" programs have been developed. Also, attempts have been made to curtail middle-management units such as the *bu*, or department, and the *ka*, or section, and instead to form small groups called "project teams" or "task forces," to which a wide range of job authority is delegated. As far as wage structure is concerned, a new system based upon both the *nenkō* wage and a job wage or job-performance ability wage is being developed by increasing the relative weight of the job wage.

The joint labor-management conference is being promoted to replace collective-bargaining and grievance-handling sessions. Cooperative human relations is emphasized more than formal union-management relations. This takes two forms. First, in cases where the union-management relationship is stable, management policy is conveyed to union members through the union communication channel with management taking union reaction into consideration when developing policy. Second, where union-management relations are unstable, management tries to anticipate those problems which the union will raise and to settle them before the union acts. In any case, since wages are increasing at a rapid rate year by year, and working conditions are continuously improving, management has been taking the initiative in plant-level industrial relations.

Due to the various factors bringing about changes in the *nenkō* system, particularly personnel administration based upon ability and changes in plant-level union activities, it is expected that Japanese industrial relations will change. There are at least four possible directions: (1) Maintenance of the basic nature of the *nenkō* system with an effort to adapt it to new developments; most government offices and big zaibatsu enterprises will take this direction. (2) Promotion of both ability-oriented personnel administration and cooperative union-management relations; many big enterprises in the heavy and chemical industries and other developing industries are taking this direction. (3) Establishment of interfirm or industrywide industrial relations which facilitate labor mobility and wage rates based upon the job; although moves in this direction are not yet apparent, it is possible that such a pattern will be established among medium-sized firms in developing industries. (4) Development of class-oriented industrial relations among unemployed and underemployed workers, day laborers, temporary workers, workers in tiny establishments, and potential unemployed workers displaced due to ability-oriented personnel administration; these types of workers remain numerous in spite of rapid economic growth and their demands are primarily political. For the past few years, the Japan Communist Party and other more revolutionary groups have been very active in this field.

The above four directions partially overlap each other, and it is difficult to anticipate the future. As far as plant-level industrial relations patterns are concerned, it appears that cooperative industrial relations will most likely become dominant. In fact, big enterprises in the developing industries are moving in this direction. Also, this direction is an extension or reorganization of the *nenkō* system on a new dimension.

12. Social Security for Workers

The Historical Background of Social Security Measures

The Relief Regulations of 1874, the forerunner of social security in modern Japan, were enacted under the same circumstances as other laws that led to the abandonment of almost all traditional social protection institutions, including the *tomoko kumiai* or mutual aid societies, at the time of the Meiji Restoration of 1868. The regulations stated that it was the "compassionate" duty of people to relieve the poor and the destitute, and that the impoverished innocent were entitled to benefits after subjection to loyalty tests given by the Home Ministry. These regulations continued in force for more than half a century until the Relief Act of 1929 went into effect in 1932.

The conditions of the poor prior to enactment of this "modern" relief legislation is vividly described in *Nihon no kasō shakai* [The lower classes in Japan], written in 1899 by Gennosuke Yokoyama, and in *Shokkō jijō* [Conditions of Labor], issued in 1903 by the Ministry of Agriculture and Industry. According to these accounts, a new kind of pauper emerged after the factory system was introduced, and the economic depression of 1890, considered the first cyclical depression in modern Japan, converted the "poor" in the years after the Meiji Restoration into the lowest class of the industrializing society.

As Japanese heavy industry developed, with munitions manufacturing playing a central role in the industrialization after the turn of the century, the government devised schemes for a compulsory mutual aid society for workers in state-owned industrial establishments. At the same time, certain employers, such as the Kanebo Cotton Spinning Company, introduced on their own mutual aid societies for their employees. Subsequently, these mutual aid schemes, the precedent of which can be traced back to the pre-Meiji type, reemerged, but with the contributions paid jointly by employers and employees. This latter type of mutual aid society is the prototype of the social security schemes that prevail today in the public sector and of the health insurance societies found among large enterprises in the private sector.

Social policy measures slowly but gradually advanced, especially after the Russo-Japanese War of 1904–05. First, the Factory Law of 1911, implemented in 1916, incorporated the principle of employer liability, in recognition of the increase in industrial accidents befalling workers. Second, the Popular Life Insurance Law of 1916, which aimed at assisting the low-income classes, was welcomed by the people with enthusiasm far beyond the lawmakers' expectations. Third, both the state assistance legislation for families of conscripted soldiers and disabled veterans and the Military Relief Law of 1917 constituted important social protection measures. However, the poor and the unemployed were still left to the mercy of the earlier Relief Regulations.

Economic prosperity and industrial development during World War I were followed by social unrest. An "extraordinary event opened a narrow door to the legislation of a social security system in its initial form,"[1] as the Rice Riot of 1918 compelled the government to consider seriously the introduction of social legislation. In 1922, the government succeeded in getting the Diet to adopt the Workers' Health Insurance Law, without substantive debate on its contents;[2] at the same session the Diet had considered but rejected the controversial bill to regulate extremist social movements. Enforcement of the Health Insurance Law was delayed

1. "Social Security System in Japan," *Sōhyō News*, Mar. 15, 1964, p. 15.
2. On December 12, 1921, a draft program for the health insurance bill was referred to an advisory body called the Study Council on Labor Insurance, which on January 16, 1922, submitted to the Minister of Agriculture and Industry an affirmative reply, with certain amendments. On March 13, 1922, the government brought the bill to the lower house of the Imperial Diet, which passed it unanimously on March 15, 1922, then transmitting it to the upper house which also passed it unanimously on March, 25 1922. Thus the law was promulgated on April 22, 1922.

until 1927 because of the great earthquake in the Tokyo-Yokohama area in 1923.

The Universal Male Suffrage Law was enacted in 1925, together with the well-known Public Order Preservation Law, which later provided the government with the legal means to disband leftist political and social organizations arbitrarily. Thus, the introduction of social policy measures was accompanied by the enactment of repressive legislation—a process not unlike the Bismarkian policy for Germany in the 1880s.

It may safely be stated that the 1918 Rice Riot served to awaken the ruling class to the need for some social policy measures in the course of industrialization; to this was added international pressure upon the Japanese government after establishment of the International Labor Organization (ILO) in 1919.[3] Thus, the post-World War I decade witnessed the development of social legislation as well as the growth of the social and labor movement, within the changing environment of industrial growth. The establishment of the Social Department within the Home Ministry in 1922 reflected this tide.

It is worth noting that the implementation of the Health Insurance Law aroused discontent among workers and resulted in a series of industrial disputes in 1926 and 1927.[4] The principal objection of the insured workers was that they were already poorly paid, their contributions were compulsory, and the state subsidies were meager. Also, they objected to the shift of accident compensation

3. For a discussion of the contribution of the ILO to the evolution of labor legislation, labor administration, and the labor movement in Japan, see Iwao F. Ayusawa, *A History of Labor in Modern Japan* (Honolulu: East-West Center Press, 1966), *Industrial Labor in Japan*, International Labor Office, Studies and Reports, Ser. A (Industrial Relations), No. 37 (Geneva: International Labor Office, 1933). In the ILO Japan had been one of eight major industrial countries, which entitled her government to a permanent seat as a member of the governing body.

4. The Japanese Council of Trade Unions, a national center organized by Sōdōmei dissenters in 1925, called a series of strike actions in opposition to the implementation of the Health Insurance Law from late 1926 to early 1927, demanding that (1) the scheme should be financed by capitalists and by state funds, (2) its scope of application and benefit level should be extended and improved, and (3) administration of insurance societies should be entrusted to the workers' representatives. See *Kenkō hoken sanjū nen shi* [Thirty-year history of health insurance] (Tokyo: Zenkoku Shakai-Hoken Kyokai Rengo Kai, 1958), vol. 1, pp. 240–70, and vol. 2, p. 4; *Nihon rōdō nenkan* [The labor yearbook for Japan, 1927] (Osaka: The Ohara Institute for Social Research), p. 144; and Takashi Saguchi, *Nihon shakai hoken shi* [History of social insurance in Japan] (Tokyo: Nihon Hyōron Shinsha, 1957), pp. 153–70.

from the Factory Law requirements to the contributory provisions of the Health Insurance Law, a departure from the principle of employer liability for occupational risks. This conflict, called the "anti-health-insurance struggle" by the Japanese trade union movement, was epoch-making in the sense that for the first time concerted action was staged under the direction of a national labor center.[5]

The worldwide depression of the 1930s was preceded in Japan by a monetary panic in 1927. As the depression and mass unemployment overtook Japan, action was urgently called for, and the period was marked by further development of social policy measures. At the same time an industrial rationalization movement was actively organized by industrialists and financial institutions having taken encouragement from the state.

In 1931 the Workmen's Accident Compensation Insurance Law, providing for employer liability insurance, was enacted, but coverage was limited to employers in public works and in freight loading and unloading. The introduction of this legislation was necessary to cope with mass construction projects undertaken by the government for the relief of unemployed workers.

However, the employers were opposed to the introduction of compulsory unemployment insurance schemes on the grounds that in Japan the practice of voluntarily paying allowances to retiring and dismissed workers had been considerably developed, in contrast with other countries.[6] Moreover, the absence of a national network of employment exchanges would have prevented the effective operation of unemployment insurance. As a result, in 1935 the government made plans to introduce a provident fund scheme as a substitute for unemployment insurance, although employers were opposed even to this because of its compulsory application. Nonetheless, due to the political unrest that followed

5. According to official statistics on labor disputes in the prewar days, the figures in 1926 and 1927 were the second highest, surpassed only by those in 1919 and 1920.
6. Consider, for example, the statement of the National Federation of Industrial Organizations (Zensanren), the central employers' association, made in relation to the items on the agenda Unemployment Insurance and Various Forms of Relief for the Unemployed in the Seventeenth Session of the ILO Conference, Geneva, 1932 Japan Industrial Club, ed., *Nihon Kōgyō kurabu ni-jū-go-nen shi* [A twenty-five-year history of the Japan Industrial Club] (Tokyo: Japan Industrial Club, 1943, 2:878–9).

the Manchurian Incident of 1931 and the assassination of political leaders, among them Prime Minister Inukai in 1932 the government enacted the Retirement Provident Fund Law in 1936. Originally the purpose of this law was to provide statutory benefits to discharged workers, but in 1944 the law was incorporated into the Welfare Pension Insurance Law.

The Sino-Japanese War in 1937 ushered in a semi-war period in Japan which continued until the outbreak of World War II. During this period the government succeeded in enacting a series of social security laws under the name of "wartime social policy." The principal legislation was the following: first, in 1938 the National Health Insurance Law was enacted to establish voluntary state-aided health insurance societies at the local level, mainly for the self-employed, including farmers and peasants and their families. It was one of the relief measures against economic recessions in agricultural areas, but it was also instrumental in recruiting healthy soldiers from among young rural people. This system was to become one of the pillars of subsequent social security legislation. Second, in 1939 came enactment of the Seamen's Insurance Law, a comprehensive scheme covering both short- and long-term risks, including employment injury. Third, in 1941 the government adopted legislation both for health insurance for salaried employees and for workers' pension insurance.

It is important to note also that the Ministry of Welfare was established administratively in 1938 with a view to consolidating and expanding government measures for the labor and social aspects of the economy. Up to then, these functions had been under the jurisdiction of the Home Ministry. Since the latter's principal role was to preserve public order through police power, the separation of the Welfare Ministry indicated a new departure for labor and social policy.

Following this consolidation, the social insurance system in prewar Japan consisted of three parts: the health insurance branch comprising the several schemes for wage earners and salaried employees in the private sector as well as those applied to the general public; the pension insurance branch, consisting of the Workers' Welfare Pension Insurance scheme of 1944, also in the private sector; and the seamen's insurance branch with the special scheme covering a wide range of risks. During the war, while legislation in the overall field of labor remained almost at a standstill, social insurance alone enjoyed further development and made coordinated advances through these different schemes.

However, the steps taken by the government in prewar Japan for the protection of labor in the course of industrialization always lagged behind economic development. Thus, the momentum for social policy measures in Japan came from wars, the Rice Riot, and the worldwide depression, which perhaps indicates a discontinuity in social legislation and explains why the enactment of the workers' health insurance law preceded a workmen's accident compensation insurance scheme.

Moreover, the earlier a social policy measure was adopted, the less distinction was made between a general policy for the poor and a social policy for labor. The first general social insurance scheme was not introduced until 1922, at least thirty years after the appearance of a modern type of unemployment. However, the welfare and assistance services established in the public sector or related to military service (both of which held a favorable position under the Meiji government's policy of a "rich state and strong army") plus the steps taken by employers in large private enterprises were the forerunners of later developments in social security.

One reason for the lag of social policy behind economic growth may have been the traditionalistic policies of the nationalistic elite. This elite always emphasized the family system as a means of integrating the mass of people into national efforts for industrialization. Indeed, it was true that when depressions hit the economy the traditional family system in the villages, from which most workers came to seek employment, served to some extent as a buffer for absorbing the unemployed and mitigating the seriousness of the unemployment problem.

Patriarchal and paternalistic employers had always fiercely opposed social legislation by the state, and this opposition had been effective in restraining the government from enacting new legislation except in periods of social unrest due to political emergencies.

Although the policy of Sōdōmei, the Japan General Federation of Trade Unions, in 1919 included demands for a workers' insurance law as well as universal suffrage, minimum wage regulations, prohibition of night work for minors and women workers, and shorter work hours, the trade union movement in the prewar days had no real influence on the achievement of social policy measures.[7] The Study Council on Labor Insurance, which met in 1921 and prepared the draft for the Workers' Health Insurance Law, included no representative of the labor movement.[8] In fact, most of the unions were concerned with immediate payment of dismissal compensation rather than with unemployment insurance. Also there were virtually no mutual aid societies run by or centered around the trade unions. This state of affairs may be explained by the fact that employers had rejected recognition of trade unions and that the state policy toward the labor movement had been characterized by absolutism within a monolithic nation-state concept. Later, during the semiwar period, all trade unions were obliged to dissolve because of government "persuasion" and the indifference of the mass of the people.

It is very difficult to identify the principal actors responsible for introducing social policy measures in the prewar period. It should be remembered that there was at that time no guarantee that the political leader of the majority party in the Diet would assume the premiership; yet it would not be a mistake to state that, in the case of the Health Insurance Law of 1922, high government officials played a decisive role in bringing about the enactment of

7. Yasoji Kazahaya stated that the Health Insurance Law of 1922 was introduced before the demand for it on the part of the trade union movement had become highlighted. See *Nihon shakai seisaku shi* [The history of social policy in Japan] (Tokyo: Nihon Hyōron-sha) 1937, p. 238.

8. Gen Shimizu stated that the "Study Council on Labor Insurance, which was headed by a high official of the Government as was practiced at that time, was participated in not only by the learned persons, government officials and Diet members, but also by officials of Japan TUC and Japan Seamen's Unions as the matters referred to it were related to labor legislation. This was rather an exceptional thing, and it might be the first example of workers' participation in state bodies"; see *Shakaihoshō to Kanrikikō no henka* (Social Insurance and the Change in Its Administrative Machinery), in *Shakai hoken no hattatsu* [The development of social insurance] (Tokyo: Shakai-hoken Shinbun-sha, 1961), p. 25. However, in the editorial in the *Chūgai Shinbun* for March 18, 1922 (excerpted in *Kenkō hoken san-jū-nen shi*, 1, p. 254), it was pointed out that no member of that council represented labor. Indeed no name of a member representing the labor movement can be found in the list of members of that council, incomplete as it was, which is included in *Kenkō hoken san-jū-nen shi*. It was thus impossible to determine whether the labor member was included in that council.

this legislation.[9] The same may be said about wartime social policy; in this instance the military clique exerted the most important influence.

In any case, there is no doubt that in Japan the government bureaucrats played a very important role in introducing social policy measures. Nonetheless, it should be added that, although Japan ratified few International Labor Organization conventions in the field of social insurance, the international standards set by the ILO and its publications on social insurance enlightened at least the high government officials concerning the need for social policy and provided them with reference materials for use in drafting bills and programs.

Postwar Developments: Japan's System of Social Security and Its Allied Services

The surrender of Japan in 1945 opened the way for further development of social legislation, including social security. The new Constitution of 1946 states explicitly that the people have the right to subsistence and requires the state to promote measures for social security. Thus, various social security measures were enacted and promptly put into effect during the Occupation (1945–52).

In the field of employment injury, a new Workmen's Accident Compensation Insurance Law was passed in 1947 in coordination with the Labor Standards Law of the same year. Employer liability for industrial accidents provided for in the latter law is mandatorily insured through the insurance scheme stipulated in the former. Although this insurance scheme was a continuation of the prewar principle of insuring *employers* rather than *workers*, there were many improvements. The scheme, covering industrial and commercial establishments and run by the government through a network of labor standards offices under the Ministry of Labor, provides benefits financed exclusively by employers' contributions. Thus, the law led to the abolition of the anomalies of the prewar period, when compensation was made under the Workers' Health

9. Saguchi, *Nihon shakai hoken shi, op. cit.* pp. 231–33.

Insurance Law for short-term benefits and under the Workers' Welfare Pension Insurance Law for long-term benefits. In this sense, enactment of the new law opened the way for reorienting both the Workers' Health Insurance Law and the Welfare Pension Insurance Law in the proper direction.

Another important development was the enactment of the Unemployment Insurance Law in 1947. The introduction of unemployment insurance was indeed facilitated by the emergence of a coalition government of Socialists and conservatives. For the first time in the political history of Japan, the Socialists became the leading party in the Diet as the result of general election in May 1947, following promulgation of the new Constitution. The new government had to commit itself to take firm measures against the serious unemployment then assailing the war-devastated economy. The Ministry of Labor, established in September 1947, took jurisdiction over matters directly related to labor conditions, including workmen's accident compensation insurance and unemployment policy measures.

In November 1947, the Diet passed an Unemployment Insurance Law, with only minor amendments to the draft bill introduced by the government. This was a rather unexpected gift for the mass of unemployed in the sense that the law was accompanied by another measure providing that unemployment assistance financed exclusively by state funds would be available during a transitional period of six months until the new insurance scheme became fully operative. However, the enactment of the law at this juncture implied a clever political solution, enabling the government to cope with the increasing social unrest due to mass unemployment. It may be said that this success for the government is attributable in large measure to the attitudes of employers in general, who supported the unemployment insurance scheme. These attitudes were attributable to the prevailing situation. While employers wanted to rationalize their undertakings through personnel reductions, they also sought to salve their consciences and hoped to incur lighter financial burdens because of dismissal allowances for redundant workers.

In this connection, it is also appropriate to refer to unemployment relief work, regulated by the Emergency Unemployment

Countermeasures Law of 1949. There have been two types of unemployment relief work. The first consists of public work projects for the purpose of redeveloping the social infrastructure and involves heavy expenditures of public funds, in hopes of creating effective demand and consequently increasing employment; the law specified that a certain proportion of the positions provided by these projects be reserved for the unemployed. The second type of unemployment relief work consists of projects, also financed by public funds, exclusively for the unemployed. Both types have served as direct measures against unemployment, together with a special unemployment insurance plan for casual day laborers instituted in 1949 as an amendment to the Unemployment Insurance Law of 1947. These unemployment measures, together with assistance for the destitute (under the terms of the Livelihood Protection Law of 1946, to be discussed below), have constituted indispensable elements in the policy of social security during the rapid economic development which took place in the late 1950s.

Paralleling these developments in the legislative field have been efforts in government and academic circles to work out a general policy on social security. In the course of their studies the Beveridge Report, published in the United Kingdom in 1942, and *The Approaches to Social Security*, published by the ILO in the same year, drew much attention. A broad social security policy was first recommended in 1947 by the Statutory Committee for the Study of Social Insurance, which suggested a comprehensive plan embracing the total population and providing extensive or broad coverage of basic needs of the people in their daily lives. This was followed by the *Wandel Report* (a report of a mission of American experts sanctioned by the Occupation Forces) to the government, which had the lasting effect of establishing the Council on Social Security, a permanent statutory organ attached to the Prime Minister's Office. The Council consists of members selected by the government from among various interested circles, including employers' and workers' organizations, and, even though it was merely an advisory body, it soon became a central organ not only in working out broad lines of social security policy, but also in controlling any measure of the government in the field.

The recommendation on social security, submitted to the government in 1950, was the first outcome of the council's studies. Among other things, the recommendation called for establishment of a unified system of social security, comprising not only social insurance schemes but also other programs and services directly financed by the government, such as public assistance, social welfare, and public health, with a view to guaranteeing healthy and decent living standards for the people in case of injury, childbirth, death, disability, old age, unemployment, large numbers of children in a family, and other causes of destitution. Since then, the Japanese system of social security has been considered to consist of four major parts: social insurance schemes, public (social) assistance, public health and medical care, and social welfare services. Notably, the council took the view that the schemes based upon social insurance principles should be the mainstay of social security in Japan, but that they should be supported by allied programs and services. However, the aspirations of the council for a unified system have been repeatedly defeated by the subsequent evolution of makeshift steps. The various government ministries have coped only with exigencies, and the rather privileged classes, such as those employed in the public sector and in large private industry, have resisted a general system of protection against social risks.

One of the most important developments in social security legislation in the early postwar period was the enactment in 1950 of the Livelihood Protection Law mentioned above. The content of this law is in line with the 1950 recommendation of the Council on Social Security, since the bill was drafted in coordination with the council's study. In it, each aspect of the public aid law, which had been hurriedly introduced in 1946, was redeveloped so as to encompass a wide range of basic needs for persons requiring assistance. Thus, subject to a means test, cash benefits are payable for livelihood, housing, education, funerals, and subsistence work in addition to medical benefits in kind for sickness and maternity. Since then, public assistance has served as the floor for protecting any individual. Especially during the period of economic stagnancy and subsequent reconstruction in the 1950s, of necessity it took the central role in the Japanese social security system—probably contrary to the original intention of the council's recommendation.

On the other hand, in the field of social insurance, by 1950 the systems of worker health insurance and of national (or people's) health insurance, both of which had been suffering from the dislocations caused by Japan's defeat and postwar inflation, were reconstituted with all of their provisions substantially improved. The workers' health insurance scheme retained a dual structure, providing health insurance societies mainly for workers employed in large enterprises and a single plan operated by the government (through the Ministry of Welfare) for all other workers. Here again, the suggestions contained in the council's recommendation for covering employees in enterprises with fewer than five employees failed to materialize.

In 1953 a special health insurance scheme was introduced for casual day laborers who up to then had been excluded from coverage under the workers' scheme. However, the conditions of eligibility and level of benefits are inferior to those under the earlier schemes. The introduction of this plan can be attributed to a considerable extent to the political struggle of the trade union movement, in which casual laborers constituted a militant faction by organizing regional and national unions. However, it should be noted that these workers had already been receiving benefits for several years under a special unemployment insurance scheme.

Under the national Health Insurance Law, the city, town, or village—the lowest echelons of public administration—remained the unit for organizing medical protection for all those not covered by other health insurance schemes. Amendments in 1958 required every municipality to establish a health insurance sheme for its inhabitants. Through these means, the long cherished plan of compulsory nationwide medical care insurance coverage was realized in 1961. Health insurance for the total population thus was accomplished through a web of statutory schemes including the workers' schemes under the Health Insurance Law of 1922, the special sheme under Seamen's Insurance Law of 1939, the mutual aid association schemes for central and local government public servants and for employees of state enterprises, and the local inhabitant schemes for the rest of the population.

In the field of old age benefits, more than ten years elapsed before the general scheme for worker welfare pension insurance, which had suffered grave losses in its reserve funds due to currency depreciation, was finally reconstructed in 1954 when new legislation replaced the 1942 law. However, eligibility for benefits ordinarily requires an insured person to pay in for at least twenty years, while the requirements for disability pensions and survivors' benefits are more generous. Because of the long qualifying period and lack of consideration for the very elderly at the time of its inception, the scheme had remained immature a long time since its inception in 1942, and apparently even more time must elapse before it can play its full role and actually secure old-age benefits for the majority of the workers retired.

On the other hand, under the National Pension Law of 1959, a new nationwide pension scheme was introduced for those not yet covered by existing pension schemes. It provides two alternatives. One is a contributory scheme for the general population that went into effect in 1961; the other is a noncontributory plan for persons over seventy years old, the disabled, and mother-and-child households subject to an income test. Payment for the latter began in 1959. As a result, the entire adult population in Japan is potentially covered by one of the existing pension insurance schemes.

Thus, by the early 1960s, fifteen years after the end of the war, the economy had shifted from reconstruction to growth and Japan had become equipped with the devices for social protection in all major branches of social security, with the exception of family allowances. In other words, the government succeeded in providing coverage for all the people under various health and pension insurance schemes, the two most important branches in any national system of social security.

In 1962, at the request of the prime minister, the Council on Social Security again recommended basic principles for coordinating the various existing social security schemes and services. It also provided new guidelines to be followed for developing future social security measures in the context of rapid economic development. Classifying the entire population into three groups—the needy, the low-income, and the ordinary income groups—the council set forth priorities for improvements in the existing programs. It proposed, first, that the benefit level of public (social) assistance under the Livelihood Protection Law should be increased three times within the next ten years for the sake of the needy; second, that the social welfare services, such as those for the disabled, should expand in the interests of the low-income group; and, third, that the provisions of the social insurance schemes should be improved for the ordinary income group. Further, the council set as a ten-year policy goal the raising of the cost of the Japanese system of social security to the current level of West European systems.

In summing up these developments over the past two decades, we may say that, as Japan entered the ranks of the advanced industrial nations during the 1960s, its system of social security has made similar progress at least in quantitative terms. It has achieved coverage for the total population by medical and pension insurance in addition to the basic floor of protection through public assistance, which was already fully operative by the 1950s.

Indeed, the year 1961 can be viewed as marking the beginning of the second phase in the development of social security in postwar Japan. The political targets for medical and pension insurance were realized. Since 1961 the benefit level for public assistance under the Livelihood Protection Law has been improved by more than the increase in the general level of earnings.[10] This was made possible by the adoption of a new method for calculating minimum subsistence. Up to then, the minimum subsistence level, serving as the criterion for providing benefits to needy persons, had been calculated on the basis of a theoretical family budget for a standard beneficiary; but in 1961 the government shifted to a policy of maintaining benefits in proportion to the actual level found in the family expenditure survey.

10. This shift from the theoretical family budget method to the Engel's coefficient method in fixing the minimum protection level for a needy beneficiary may imply a change in emphasis from micro to macro in policy considerations. However, in actuality, this change has resulted in gradually narrowing the gap in living levels between general families and the assisted families up to the present.

In view of these developments, some observers are convinced that social security in Japan has embarked on a road of continuing, long-range improvement. However, it cannot be denied that, compared with the rapidity of economic growth, progress in social security has fallen short of the expectations of the people. Indeed, the proportion of the gross national product going to social security has remained at around 5 percent during the past dozen years,[11] although the favorable economic situation could have been a factor encouraging further evolution of social security. In light of these circumstances, one might speculate that there is a barrier beyond which Japan's system of social security will not be able to pass.

From the political point of view, it should be remembered that steps toward the development of social security in postwar Japan were launched under most unfavorable economic circumstances in the period immediately after the war. This may imply, in the first place, that economic considerations were overridden by political exigencies. Second, a policy that requires unemployed persons to return to their native places, as did that followed by the government during the prewar depression, is no longer tenable in the industrialized economy of present-day Japan. Third, the traditional concept of the family system has become obsolete as an excuse for not adopting social policy measures in the postwar age —even for the conservative government.

In any event, politically speaking, Japan's surrender provided the impetus for the new directions in social security. In fact, during the Occupation period, the basic notion of "the people's right to subsistence," as provided in the new Constitution of 1946, became deeply rooted. Consequently, every government since then has had to pay due respect to the principle, although there have been variations in the concrete forms of expression. This is particularly notable, considering that during the past twenty years or so the political control in Japan has been held by the conservatives.

Technically speaking, development of social security in Japan has been made possible by the existence of a tight network of

11. See ILO, *The Cost of Social Security* 1949–1957, 1958–1963, 1961–1963, and 1964–1966.

public administration. Through a national system of employment exchange services, unemployment insurance schemes for general and casual workers are in operation throughout the country. The same may be said with regard to public assistance for which a national network of welfare offices under the Ministry of Welfare has been created, and with regard to the health and pension insurance schemes for which a separate system of social insurance offices under the same ministry is operated.

However, before making any further evaluation, we must analyze the substance of the Japanese system of social security, especially in view of the fact that the above description gives only a general idea of its historical development.

An Analysis of Social Security in Japan

The recommendation of the Council on Social Security in 1950 included the idea that any scheme, service, or program for social insurance, public assistance, medical care, public sanitation, or social welfare should be treated as part of the overall social security system.

The existing insurance schemes are of two distinct types. One, for employees, is called the employee insurance type; the other, for general citizens, including mainly the self-employed and workers in enterprises with fewer than five employees, is the geographical insurance type. Thus, the major social risks or contingencies in the daily lives of workers—sickness, maternity, old age, invalidity, death of the breadwinner, unemployment, and employment injury including occupational diseases and the like—have been covered by a set of statutory insurance schemes.

However, the missing element is a family allowance scheme, which is nonexistent except for benefits available for physically handicapped children, subject to a means test. Even in the 1950 recommendation of the Council on Social Security, no mention was made of family allowances because the council feared that their introduction would encourage increased birth rates and aggravate the serious population problems in the war-devastated economy. In the course of later economic growth, however, the importance of family allowances has gradually been recognized, and its early adoption was recommended by the Economic Council, a central planning agency, as well as by the Council on Social Security.

To assess the implications of social security in the industrial relations system of Japan, it is useful to describe in detail the nature of the different types of benefits rather than to analyze the various schemes of social security.

Advanced Medical Care

Medical care is provided for all persons through either social insurance or social assistance, available to all needy persons; through public service it is available also to patients with specific diseases, such as tuberculosis and mental illness. As stated earlier, the entire population of Japan was brought under the protection of medical insurance schemes by 1961; therefore, medical care is usually provided on an insurance basis. However, certain gaps are inevitable in the present system of medical insurance because, first, its application lacks coordination and, second, there are some who are unable either to afford insurance contributions or to share certain costs of the benefits provided. In view of this, the system of social assistance has to serve as the last resort for needy persons lacking adequate means, as the benefit level is substantially the same as for social insurance. As a result of this system, there are few who are excluded from medical protection because of their impoverished financial condition.

Within the employee insurance category of the social insurance system (for employed persons and their family members), there are a number of insurance schemes which separately cover ordinary employees in the private sector, seamen, central and local public servants, employees in the public sector, casual day laborers, and so on. Among them, the Health Insurance Law of 1922, set up for ordinary employees in the private sector, outlines two distinct types of coverage. One type is open to workers employed in an industrial or commercial establishment with more than five employees. This may be considered a general scheme for employed persons; at the end of March 1970 it had a membership of 13,150,000. The other type is the health insurance society with coverage based on special schemes established by a single employer or a group of employers for direct employees; in 1970, these societies had a total membership of 9,090,000. Here, it should be noted that employees are covered only through their establishments, since the law stipulates that compliance is the duty of employers. In other words, the insurance is applied to these workers indirectly through their employers. Thus, it has been pointed out that the social insurance policy in Japan has been biased in favor of the employer's convenience in personnel management. This appears to be the case especially when a health insurance society is established within a given undertaking and is operated as if it were one of the welfare facilities afforded by the management.

Under each health insurance scheme, medical benefits are given in kind for illness, without limit in duration. The level of benefits is comparatively high for insured workers. For example, dental prosthesis is available without expense for the insured, although workers bear half the cost of dental care for their family members, and there are small charges for initial consultation and hospitalization.

In maternity cases, neither a pregnant insured worker nor the pregnant dependent of an insured worker receives medical care; instead, lump sum payments are given for general expenses incurred. This is apart from disability compensation during the pre- and postnatal periods for insured women workers. Thus, medical care in insurance schemes has been designed to meet the contingency of sickness. Preventive medicine is afforded only as a supplementary benefit which is especially important in the case of health insurance societies established within undertakings. Since death rates in Japan, especially infant mortality and death due to tuberculosis, have been decreasing year after year with the development of public health and the progress of medical science and technology, it is quite clear that medical care under social security has contributed to the formation and maintenance of a healthy work force. Medical care based on insurance and supported by both social assistance and public service has been firmly built into the daily lives of ordinary people and thus constitutes a central aspect of the Japanese system of social security.

One of the most important problems now at hand is how to finance ever-increasing medical costs. The cost of medical care has been increasing at an amazing rate, greater than the rate of increase of national income and the general level of wages. This is the case especially with the general scheme for ordinary workers administered by the government, which has experienced deficits since 1962 and had accumulated a total deficit of over ¥130,000 million by the end of March 1970. The same situation obtains for some of the health insurance societies, not to mention the smaller insurance schemes for casual day laborers (with a membership of 1,100,000) and seamen (with a membership of 260,000).

The health insurance schemes are financed principally by contributions from the insured and their employers, with occasional subsidies from the state in addition to the regular allocation of state funds for administrative expenses. In the general scheme for ordinary workers, the contribution rate, shared equally by a worker and his employer, is as high as 70 percent of the "wage class" the insured worker belongs to, subject to a ceiling of ¥104,000 a month. In the health insurance societies in the large enterprises, however, the employers contribute more than the employees because the employers consider it advisable to do so from the standpoint of personnel management policy. Generally speaking, because of the higher level of average insurable wages and "good risks," the health insurance societies in the large firms enjoy much more favorable financial conditions than those in the government-administered general scheme for ordinary workers.

The differences in financial condition, however, entail differences in benefit levels among the various schemes. Roughly speaking, the actual level of benefits, in order from the highest to lowest, is as follows: the schemes applied to public servants and public employees, the health insurance society schemes in large enterprises, the general scheme for ordinary workers in the private sector, and the casual day laborers' scheme.

One serious problem stemming from these differences is a lack of coordination among the schemes. This becomes a crucial issue when an insured worker has to change his employment due to dismissal, compulsory retirement, or severance for personal reasons, since medical protection is geared to the place of employment. For example, a person who becomes unemployed is likely to lose the protection of the employee insurance scheme at his former place of employment and thus must shift to a geographical insurance scheme in the area where he resides.

Industrialization and urbanization have undermined the very foundations of the system of geographical health insurance schemes because younger Japanese have been leaving the rural areas in large numbers to take industrial jobs in urban areas. It is feared, as a consequence, that the system of medical care for the population administered to the local geographic levels may not be viable in the future. With rapid industrialization, the younger, more active sector of the population tends to gain coverage in employee insurance schemes within enterprises, thereby "diluting" or weakening the geographical insurance schemes by leaving them with disproportionately large numbers of older participants. This phenomenon is already conspicuous among various health insurance schemes in remote villages.

One of the age-old problems is the relationship of medical practitioners and hospitals to the system of medical insurance. Fees for providing medical benefits have been paid to them by insurers (i.e. the administrations of the respective insurance schemes) after screening by a statutory Medical Payment Fund Board, in accordance with tariff scales for medical fees established by the Ministry of Welfare. However, it has been pointed out that the scales have been biased toward an emphasis on the quantity of pharmaceutical supplies prescribed by medical doctors to the neglect of medical consultations and treatments. This may have had the effect of "downgrading" medical doctors to "retailers of pharmaceutical supplies." In fact, even public hospitals have been supported by revenues from the medical care they currently offer patients, the majority of whom are now insurance beneficiaries.

In view of these serious problems confronting the system of medical insurance in Japan today,[12] a fundamental reorganiza-

12. In 1967, in view of the ever-increasing deficits in the general scheme, the Diet approved a temporary law to increase cost-sharing by patients in medical benefits in kind afforded. The temporary law was abolished when an amendment to increase the

tion which would comprise social insurance, social assistance, and public service, as well as medical practitioners and hospitals, is called for as a prerequisite for entering the next phase of qualitative improvement in social security.

As compensation for loss of earnings due to sickness, injury, or maternity, cash benefits are provided, in addition to medical care, under the employee insurance schemes. Benefit levels are set at about 60 percent of lost wages, according to the wage class to which the insured person belongs. Cash payments are made for suspension of earnings to an insured worker for six months in each case of sickness and for eighteen months in case of tuberculosis. However, persons employed in small establishments with fewer than five employees, for whom there is no compulsory employee insurance scheme, are excluded from this protection unless the employees and their employer have requested it on a voluntary basis. In the case of the general scheme for ordinary workers, broadly speaking, compensation for loss of earnings has amounted to less than 10 percent of the total expenditures for all benefits. This kind of cash benefit presents no serious problem in the Japanese system of social security, except for the unsolved issue of making it available to those not covered on a compulsory basis.

The Pioneering Role of Workmen's Accident Compensation Insurance

Compensation for employment-related injuries is an employer's liability under the Labor Standards Law of 1947, which is buttressed by the Workmen's Accident Compensation Insurance Law of 1947 in the private sector. This insurance scheme is operated by the Ministry of Labor through a national network of labor standard inspection offices. Benefits in the scheme consist of medical care in kind for victims of accidents or occupational diseases resulting from employment; cash payments during temporary work disabilities; and long-term cash compensation in the form of pensions for permanently disabled workers or for survivors of workers fatally injured.

---

charges for initial consultation (¥200) and for hospitalization (¥60 a day) was incorporated in the law in 1969.

Under the insurance scheme, an accident victim's cash benefit is calculated on the basis of his average wages during the three months prior to the accident. Even if the rate of benefit is set at 60 percent of the wage, as is done in the case of short-term accident compensation, actual payment is higher than for sickness insurance because the actual wage of a victim, rather than his wage class, is taken as the basis for calculating the benefit, and there is no ceiling fixed by law. It is understandable that the benefit level for accident insurance is higher than that for other insurance schemes since the contingency dealt with is the loss of earnings due to employment-connected injuries. The law as amended in 1965 adopted automatic adjustments of benefits when the general level of wages increased by 20 percent. This was the first time such adjustments were introduced into the system of social security in Japan.

Benefits under workmen's accident compensation have been financed by contributions paid exclusively by "insured" employers. Contribution rates vary according to the industrial branch to which the employer belongs. The highest rate is 8 percent of the wage bill; the lowest only 0.2 percent. As an incentive for accident prevention, contributions of a company employing more than one hundred workers may be reduced according to an experience rating.

Up to the present, the one criterion for determining the scope of application under the workmen's accident compensation scheme has been the severity of industrial accidents. Accordingly, all establishments are divided into those subject to compulsory application and those whose participation is voluntary. The division explains the large differences in contribution rates among industrial branches and the adoption of the so-called experience rating. At the same time, it has given rise to the situation where an employer who is not in the compulsory category is subject to the liability provisions of the Labor Standards Law. Thus, employers have an incentive to participate voluntarily.

Efforts have been made to improve the workmen's accident insurance scheme by gradually extending the compulsory application so that all wage earners and salaried employees would be covered. This goal was stipulated in the 1970 amendments to the law, which now provides guidelines for the full application of the scheme in the near future by the Ministry of Labor. It is hoped that this will open the way for extending the scope of application of the workers' schemes for health and pension insurance administered by the government (the Ministry of Welfare).

Furthermore, the suggested broadening of coverage for employment injuries to include accidents sustained by workers in commuting to and from their work places would be a pioneering step in the workmen's accident insurance scheme. Workmen's compensation has to some extent played a pioneering role during the past two decades as evidenced by the introduction of the automatic adjustment of benefits in relation to rises in wage levels.

The Unexpected Outcome of Action against Unemployment

Unemployment problems have been dealt with through at least two types of public measures. One is unemployment insurance; the other includes special measures for certain categories of workers, such as those in unemployment relief work, displaced coal miners, and elderly persons. Both types have functioned principally through the national network of employment exchange services, called Public Employment Security Offices (PESO), under the Ministry of Labor.

The Unemployment Insurance Law of 1947 provides for two types of unemployment insurance. One, which is compulsory for regular workers employed in establishments with five or more employees, can be called the general scheme of unemployment insurance. For workers in establishments with fewer than five workers, recourse to voluntary coverage is available as in the case of the general scheme for health insurance. In 1970 the general scheme covered 20,770,000 workers, a majority of all workers in the private sector. The other type is for casual day laborers who are employed either on a day-to-day basis or for contract periods of fewer than thirty days per month. Known as the special scheme for casual day laborers, this program covered a total of 320,000 workers in 1970.

For the convenience of employers in small establishments, the law encourages them to organize unemployment insurance administration associations to perform obligations relating to unemployment insurance for member employers. Such organizations covered 770,000 workers in 1970.

Under the general scheme, the principal unemployment benefit is set at about 60 percent of wages. The maximum benefit is ¥1,400 per day and the minimum is ¥370, to which a family supplement of ¥20 per dependent is added. Benefits are payable on a day-to-day basis, provided the unemployed has been insured for at least six months and has had an interview with a PESO official confirming his unemployed status and willingness to work.

The benefit period ranges from a high of 300 days for workers insured for more than twenty years to a low of 90 days for those insured for at least the minimum period of six months. The adoption of variable benefit periods has been justified on the basis of insurance principles. This reasoning has also been motivated both by the existence of so-called repeated or scheduled beneficiaries among seasonal workers and by the practice of lifetime employment among large enterprises.

In addition, there is a lump-sum payment, called a grant for job placement, payable to an insured worker who obtains a job before half of the benefit period to which he is entitled has elapsed. The amount of this grant is equivalent to unemployment benefits for 50 days when more than two-thirds of his benefit period remains unused, or for 30 days when more than one-half of his benefit period is unused.

Finally, there are sickness benefits payable to qualified unemployed unable to report to the PESO because of illness, moving grants for qualified unemployed who change residence because of job referrals by the PESO, training allowances, and accommodation allowances for trainees who have to live away from their families.

The cost of these benefits is financed both by contributions and by mandatory state subsidies. The rate of contribution is 1.3 percent of wages, subject to a ceiling of ¥80,000 a month, shared equally by the insured worker and his employer. The ratio between contributions and state subsidies has been set at three to one. If the funds accumulated exceed double the annual contribution income, the Minister of Labor may reduce the contribution rate within a specified range after consultation with the Central Council on Employment Security.

The special scheme for casual day laborers, however, provides only unemployment benefits, which are payable to insured persons who have contributed for more than 28 days during the two months preceding unemployment and who are judged by PESO officials as unemployed. The benefits are either ¥760 or ¥500 a day, the higher rate being paid for qualified unemployed whose contributions for the previous two months included at least 24 days of contributions of ¥36 a day rather than ¥24, these being the two rates applicable. Otherwise, the lower benefit only is payable. Thus, benefits vary according to the contribution rate. The benefit period also depends upon the number of days of contribution, the longest being 17 days when contributions have been paid for 44 or more days during the previous two months. Contributions are shared equally by worker and employer.

Generally, due to the favorable economic situation in the past decade, the unemployment rate as the average annual ratio of beneficiaries to the total number of insured has been less than 4 percent for each of the past ten years, except in 1958. Under these circumstances, the unemployment insurance program has enjoyed a favorable financial position, although certain abnormal phenomena have come to the fore.

Under the general scheme, as mentioned above, one problem is that there are numerous seasonal workers who alternate between insured employment and the beneficiary status and thus become so-called repeated or scheduled beneficiaries. In 1965 such persons, mostly migrant workers from agricultural areas, comprised about 35 percent of all beneficiaries although constituting only 3 percent of the total number of legitimately insured workers. They drew 30 percent of all benefit expenditures.[13] To cope with this abnormal situation, provisions were introduced in an amendment to the law in 1970, specifying that special contributions may be levied on employers who rely on seasonal labor. However, these provisions had not yet come into effect at the time of this writing.

13. In fiscal year 1965, the total number of beneficiaries for initial payments was 1,653,000 persons, whereas those receiving repeated or scheduled benefits were estimated at 580,000 (*Shakai hoshō nenkan* [The Social Security Year Book for 1967], p. 68 and Table 67. (Tokyo: Tōyō Keizai Shinpō-sha).

A second problem with the general scheme is the relatively high proportion of women beneficiaries (42 percent) compared with the ratio of women among insured workers (33 percent). This situation may be explained not only by the high unemployment rate among women workers, but also by possible abuses when insured women workers voluntarily quit their jobs because of marriage or childbearing, or for purposes of child care, without seemingly intending to find other jobs.

In the case of the special scheme for casual day laborers, a similar relative increase of women casual workers has been so large that the proportion of women among the insured reached 44 percent in 1965, whereas it was only 15 percent in 1949 when the scheme was first introduced. Moreover, unemployed women workers accounted for 54 percent of the total beneficiaries in 1965.[14]

Third, unemployment insurance seems to play a rather peculiar role where the practice of lifetime commitment is prevalent and the value system tends to regard layoffs as immoral. According to the Ministry of Labor,[15] under the general scheme in 1965 those entitled to benefits for up to 90 days amounted to 43 percent of the total number of beneficiaries; for up to 180 days, 41 percent; for up to 210 days, 10 percent; and for up to 270 days, 6 percent. These different benefit periods correspond to contribution periods of less than nine months, less than five years, less than ten years, and ten years or over, respectively. The majority of beneficiaries thus had records of less than five years of insured employment, which may imply that the general scheme of unemployment insurance has served mostly those who are outside the system of lifetime employment. When this factor is taken into account, it may be understood why the system of unemployment insurance has adopted the principle of varying benefit periods according to contribution period, based, in turn, on the principle of individual equity rather than social adequacy. However, it may also be said that the practice of lifetime employment, so prevalent among large enterprises, has a favorable bearing upon the financial condition of the general scheme.

14. Ibid., pp. 68–69.
15. Ibid., p. 68.

Consequently, the system of unemployment insurance, together with social assistance, may well be expected to effectuate a redistribution of income as economic fluctuations occur. However, as benefit expenditures amounted to ¥184,109 million in the general scheme and ¥4,933 million in the special scheme in fiscal year 1969, such a redistribution represented only a little more than one-third of one percent of the gross national product. In spite of this, it is quite clear that the transfer of income has come to the under-privileged from the privileged groups, industrial branches, or regions.

Apart from the operation of the unemployment insurance schemes, mention must be made of special categories of workers, such as those displaced by technological or structural change in certain industries such as coal mining. The opportunities for new jobs for these workers tend to be narrow under the prevailing practice of lifetime employment among large enterprises. Indeed, records of the labor exchange services of PESO indicate that job opportunities have been open to younger workers, while the older applicants have tended to remain unemployed.

In anticipation of the increasing shortage of younger workers and of increasing displacement due to technological and structural changes accompanying the liberalization of trade and capital transactions in the 1960s, the government began to adopt a positive manpower policy for increased labor mobility, together with a strengthening of the national network of employment exchange services, by introducing centralized electronic data processing in Tokyo. Thus, the Employment Security Law of 1947 was amended in 1963 to allow PESO to take steps to facilitate job placement by providing cash benefits for needy workers and financial subsidies for employers who have recruited such workers. As a special measure for workers displaced by mine closings, cash benefits for up to a three-year unemployment period were introduced. The Employment Policy Law of 1966, which is now the legal frame-work for an active manpower policy, has consolidated the various periodical cash benefits and capital grants for these special catego-ries of unemployed workers by establishing a single scheme of cash benefits for changes in occupation.

The Emergency Unemployment Countermeasures Law of 1949,

originally intended to cope with the consequences of mass unemployment resulting from the Dodge Plan, has continued in existence. As relief work for the unemployed has produced a hard core of "unemployed wage earners working *permanently* in public relief work," the law was amended in 1963 to restore its original purpose by providing the unemployed with vocational guidance and the skill training necessary for prompt reentry into the labor market. This act aroused considerable opposition among casual laborers' unions throughout the country, but in spite of their resistance, which marked a new phase in the trade union struggle for social security, the amendment has successfully reorganized unemployment relief work projects. As a result, the number of so-called permanent unemployment relief workers has decreased, with their union membership also dwindling.

Pension Insurance Schemes

Pension schemes for old age, permanent disability, and survivors have been the weakest link in Japan's system of social security. There are two principal categories: one for employed persons and the second for all others. The Workers' Welfare Pension Insurance Law of 1954, a revision of wartime legislation, provides employed persons in the private sector with a general pension scheme for old age and permanent disability and for their survivors in case of the death of the breadwinner. The scheme is operated by the Ministry of Welfare. In addition, there are a number of pension schemes applicable to particular kinds of employees—seamen, public servants, employees of public corporations, teachers in private schools, and others.

The general scheme is compulsory and is applicable to workers in establishments with five or more employees. However, in spite of the fact that it has existed since 1942, so far it has extended aid to only a small number of pensioners. At the end of fiscal 1969 there were only 472,000 old-age pensioners, 93,000 invalid pensioners, and 442,000 survivor pensioners, although there were 21,236,000 insured workers in the labor force.[16]

16. Quoted from the statistical tables in "Insurance and Pension" in *Kōsei no shikyō*, in Japanese (Welfare Index), 1970, pp. 144–146.

This immature state of the general scheme is attributable, first, to the lack of special considerations that could have been given to the elderly when the scheme was introduced in 1942, and, second, to the comparatively strict adherence to the so-called technical insurance principles that require a worker to make contributions for a minimum of twenty years in order to qualify for a pension. It may be recalled that the scheme was introduced as part of the wartime social policy, which had as one of its purposes to check the then prevailing inflationary pressures by deferring wage payments.

The general scheme was not reorganized until 1954, when a flat-rate component of ¥2,000 a month was introduced into the existing wage-based pension formula in order to improve benefit levels, but the retirement age was raised from 55 to 60 years for regular male workers (55 years for women and coal miners). The strict minimum period necessary to qualify for an old-age pension remained unchanged with a minor improvement. As a result, the adoption of the flat-rate component gave an immediate advantage only to invalids or survivors because of the more liberal qualification period for them than for old-age pensioners.

Again in 1965, further amendments in benefit levels increased the flat-rate component to ¥5,000 a month. This was said to constitute the so-called ¥10,000 a month old-age pension for a standard pensioner, to which a monthly family supplement of ¥400 per dependent is added. In 1969, further improvements in the benefit level was made by amendments to the law which raised contributions in accordance with the legal requirement that the financial provisions of the scheme should be subjected to actuarial and financial review every five years.

The current benefit formula is very complicated; a pension consists of the principal plus family supplements for dependents, and the former in turn consists of the so-called flat-rate (or more exactly *pro rata*) component and a wage-related component. As an example, the monthly old-age pension for an insured worker who retires at the age of sixty, after completing contributions for twenty years, is calculated by the following formula:

Flat-rate component: ¥400 × total number of insured months
   × 1/12

Wage-related component: average monthly insured wages (provided that, when computing the average, the insurable wages before October 1957 are not taken into account, and that any insurable wage of less than ¥10,000 a month shall be taken as ¥10,000) × total number of insured months

Family supplements: ¥1,000 for a wife; ¥600 for the first child; ¥400 each other child

In fact, no radical reform of the pension scheme has been undertaken, and there is little prospect in the near future that such an improvement will have any substantial effect on the number of retiring workers.

In this connection, it may be appropriate to mention the old-age benefits paid to needy aged persons under social assistance. Benefit rates in this system have been increased annually, taking into consideration the general standard of living since 1961. In the case of an aged couple, a male 70 years of age and his spouse, age 67, without income, are entitled, subject to a means test, to ¥21,405 a month, including a cash housing benefit (in Tokyo), in accordance with a scale of benefit rates that took effect April 1, 1969. This benefit level is not only slightly higher than the theoretical rate of an old-age pension under the general scheme for employed persons but is also substantially higher than the actual level of old-age pensions currently paid. The average amount received by old-age pensioners under the scheme outlined in the paragraph above at the end of March 1969 was only ¥8,313 a month.

The mechanics of financing creates such a state of affairs. The cost of the Workers' Welfare Pension Insurance scheme is to be met by long-term contributions, the 1970 rate being 6.2 percent for a regular insured male, shared equally by himself and his employer. In addition, state subsidies are provided to help pay the benefits. However, it is important to point out that the financial system adopted for this pension scheme requires a vast amount of reserve funds accumulated year after year. In fiscal year 1969, the total revenue was ¥779,610 million, including ¥553,604 million in contributions and ¥201,213 million in interest accrued from capital funds; however, expenditures totaled only ¥108,967 million, including ¥98,855 million for benefits. The result was a transfer of ¥669,738 million to the reserve fund, which stood at ¥3,554,000 million at the end of March 1970. Such an abnormal situation will continue in the coming years unless radical steps are taken to bring about an early maturing of the pension scheme.

The multiplicity of statutory pension insurance schemes for the employed, as mentioned, is not wholly attributable to their different origins, because certain schemes split away from the general scheme. Examples are the special pension scheme for teachers in private schools and the scheme for employees in agricultural cooperatives. The two schemes were established as the result of pressure from these particular groups, who had been dissatisfied with the low benefit levels and especially with the meager lump-sum payments for retirement without entitlement to pensions because of insufficient contributions under the general scheme. They were successful in persuading the Diet to establish special schemes, to which their previously credited rights and the accumulated funds pertaining to them were transferred from the general fund.

The amendment of the Workers' Welfare Pension Insurance Law in 1965 opened the way for "contracting out" the wage-related component of an old-age pension for those employed in an enterprise having a more advanced private pension scheme, provided that the provisions of a "welfare pension fund" to be established for this purpose should satisfy certain requirements of the law. The introduction of such a device, which had been requested by Nikkeiren for several years for the purpose of coordinating statutory schemes with private schemes, had been opposed by the trade union movement on the grounds that such a reform would result in further disorganization of the general scheme. But at the final stage of deliberations in the Council on Social Insurance, to which the amendment bill had been referred by the government, the members representing the insured workers had to concede to the proposal because it included general improvements in benefit levels, including an increase in the flat-rate component.

Workers currently benefiting from retirement pensions are mostly privileged former employees in the public sector, where retirement pension schemes have operated to some extent on a paternalistic principle for a longer period than have those in the private sector. The majority of the aged population, however, receive noncontributory pensions under the National Pension Law of 1959, which has provided only ¥2,000 a month since October 1970 if the individual does not qualify for social assistance.[17]

In Japan's system of social security, pensions have lagged behind short-term benefits and medical care; this lag is reflected in the extremely low level of pension expenditures as a percentage of the national income (less than 1 percent). It should be added that the existing pension insurance schemes, including the Workers' Welfare Pension Insurance scheme as well as the national pension scheme introduced in the 1959 law, have indeed contributed, at the expense of the aged population, to the rapid economic development of recent years by allowing the ever-increasing accumulated funds to be used for capital formation and for building up the social infrastructure for industrial development.

The Japanese Pattern of Social Security:
Its Role in Economic Development

In the above sections, after tracing the development of social security in Japan, we have tried to analyze the content of the existing system of social security. On the basis of this analysis, we may single out certain salient features.

In the first place, there are imbalances in development among various branches of the system in affording security against vicissitudes in the course of workers' daily lives. On the one hand, medical insurance has been extensively developed to cover all the population either through employee insurance or geographical insurance, and to offer a high level of medical care in kind with

17. The level of noncontributory welfare pensions for old age has been increased since the scheme's inception in November 1959, as follows:

November 1,1959	¥ 1,000 per month
September 1,1963	1,100 ″ ″
September 1,1965	1,300 ″ ″
January 1,1967	1,500 ″ ″
January 1,1968	1,600 ″ ″
October 1,1968	1,700 ″ ″
January 1,1970	1,800 ″ ″
October 1,1970	2,000 ″ ″

nominal cost-sharing for an insured patient and with substantial cost-sharing for his dependents. This mechanism has been supported by social assistance available to any needy person and by public services available to any patient in case of specific illnesses. Development to an advanced level is also seen in compensation for employment injury, including occupational diseases, and in unemployment insurance. On the other hand, the branches of income security offering long-term benefits, such as old-age, permanent disability, and death of the breadwinner, have lagged behind the short-term schemes, as manifested by their low level of benefits and by immaturity in the case of old-age pensions. Further, we should point out the absence of family allowances. To compensate for these deficiencies in income security, social assistance has played the role of providing the minimum protection for needy families in Japan's system of social security. The fact that expenditures on social security as a percentage of the gross national product in Japan have remained the lowest, except for the United States, among the industrially advanced countries has been attributed to such imbalances among the various branches and to the absence of family allowances.

The contrast between the advanced system of medical protection and the absence of family allowances forms an interesting pattern, since between these two poles are located the advanced short-term benefit branches and the immature long-term benefit branches. Such a spectrum in the existing social security system illustrates that, the more closely the branch circumscribes productive human resources in terms of scope of application, or the more directly the branch is related to the productive work force in terms of the nature of the benefit, the further it has been developed. As a result, old people and children, neither of whom are labor-producing elements in the population, have tended to be placed in an underprivileged position within the total social security system.

This situation has seemingly stemmed from the fact that the notion of social policy in Japan has invariably been identical with the state's labor policy, designed to cope with the unfavorable factors developing in the course of industrialization. Thus, it may be stated that Japan's system of social security has been developed in the light of its economic rationale, narrowly defined. However, such a statement should be viewed in relation to the motivations for introducing particular social security measures in which political exigencies have tended to override economic considerations. This is attested to by the fact that the inception of particular schemes occurred mostly in difficult political periods as the result of social dislocations, such as immediately after World Wars I and II and during the economic depression of the 1930s.

Second, in the method of organizing protection against social risks or contingencies, the principle of social insurance has been constantly resorted to. At first glance, it appears that the existing system consists of a combination of employees' schemes and geographical schemes, classifying the adult population into two groups —employed persons and all others. However, even in the case of employed persons, there are several groupings. In the first place, there is a clear division between those employed permanently in the public sector and those in the private sector. Such a dichotomy may correspond in large measure to labor legislation as a whole. Also, those employed in the private sector have been further divided into various categories for purposes of social security: those employed in large enterprises; regular employees in nonagricultural enterprises with more than five workers; and casual day laborers. There are also special categories of employees, such as seamen.

As a result, those employed in small enterprises, with fewer than five workers, a total of about 3,000,000 workers, have been excluded from any workers' scheme. This exclusion is attributed to the tendency of the Diet to stipulate the obligation of employers to comply with compulsory provisions while disregarding the ability of an individual worker to act on his initiative to come under an insurance scheme. One cannot help feeling that such a tendency is paternalistic in the sense that it regards individual workers as completely passive. If it were the goal of the Diet to attain complete coverage with compulsory application, a method of imposing the total obligation exclusively upon employers, without exception, would be preferable. However, the existing method of compulsory application to employers with five or more employees inevitably entails injustices to certain groups within the working class from the standpoint of equal opportunity for social security protection.

It may be interesting to point out here that those employed in small enterprises have had virtually no means of defending their particular interests and of having their say, since they have not been organized into trade unions. This is in contrast to the casual day laborers, who have had their own unions organized on a horizontal basis and who succeeded in obtaining their own schemes for social protection against unemployment and sickness, as well as protection for their family members.

Here we come back to the issue of the principle of insurance in the context of social security. If workers employed in small enterprises and casual day laborers, whose average level of wages is apparently lower than that of regular employees in well-established enterprises, were to be included in the general scheme of insurance, they would constitute a "bad" risk for insurance purposes. This is why, when casual day laborers requested the protection of health insurance, a special scheme was established for them in 1953 instead of the scope of compulsory application of the then existing general scheme being extended. It cannot be denied that so far the concept of insurance has tended to be rather strictly interpreted. On the other hand, there has been a gradual liberalization in the interpretation, as in the case of the general scheme of pension insurance for employed persons, in which improvements in benefit levels were made by introducing the flat-rate component in favor of low-income workers in 1954, and by increasing it in 1965 and again in 1969.

The insurance principle is liable to give rise to diverse interpretations, depending upon the circumstances. Strict adherence has been pressed by the government with a view to minimizing state subsidies, while the trade union movement has always requested additional allocations from the national treasury. In this connection, it may be added that those in a favorable position have been reluctant to show generosity or tolerance toward the less privileged groups or to attempt to win improvements for the latter by including them in the workers' general scheme or establishing a financial link between the favorable and unfavorable schemes for purposes of compensation.

Third, it has been observed that legislation for social insurance for employed persons has provided employers with an incentive for stabilizing the work force in their enterprises in the sense that the scope of the legislation's application to workers is always defined as the direct employers of those workers; rights to benefits are conditional upon the workers' present (in case of medical and sickness benefits) or former (especially in case of unemployment insurance) status as employees in a particular enterprise; and benefit amounts are fixed more or less proportional to the size and duration of contributions paid. These elements contribute to bringing about close relationships between the insured workers and their employers. This is particularly the case in large enterprises where there are health insurance societies and schemes of "welfare pension fund." These schemes have been geared in large measure to the personnel policy of the employers and have tended to support the "compartmentalization" of the system of social security for employed persons. Consequently, they have perpetuated the grouping of employed persons into privileged, intermediate, and underprivileged classes, contrary to the solidarity principle inherent in social security.

Under these circumstances it would hardly be possible for the existing system of social security designed for the privileged group to rid itself of the influence of the practice of excessive commitment of employees to their particular enterprises, although the transformation of the labor market under a full employment economy encourages increased mobility of labor, which is a goal of an active manpower policy. In this connection, it should be appreciated that in 1963, with a view to redressing the possible injustice of the loss of pension rights when an insured person moves from one pension scheme to another, legislation to maintain those rights was adopted, the principle being to provide for totaling the various periods of coverage of an insured person under different successive pension schemes.

Fourth, compartmentalization of the different schemes among various groups within the working class, especially in the areas of medical and pension insurance, tends to narrow the redistribution of income. Indeed, a number of studies show that only a small degree of income redistribution has been observed in favor of the lowest strata of income classes.[18] This is due mainly to unemployment insurance and social assistance.

If we assume that the old-age security policy undergoes a natural evolution from the saving method in the first stage, to the pooling method by means of the insurance principle in the second stage, and then to the third stage of the method of transferring funds from active to retired populations, the Japanese system of old-age security may be considered to be in the second stage. The lack of family allowances may be another reason for the low level of redistribution of income achieved by social security devices.

At present, about half the beneficiaries of social assistance are at the same time engaged in gainful work with low wages. This might suggest that the lack of a family allowance scheme does make the role of social assistance greater than it might otherwise be. Recently, introduction of family allowances has been recommended by a number of public advisory groups to the government. Family allowances no doubt will serve to enhance income redistribution in favor of low income classes, although the main objectives of such recommendations are rather the potential remedial effects upon wage differences and on the existing age-centered system of wage calculation which bears little direct relationship to the nature and content of job, or possible effects upon birth rates in the face of the anticipated decrease of population in the near future. In any case, an effective family allowance scheme as well as a mature pension scheme will have to be realized before Japan can catch up with the prevailing level of social security in Western Europe.

Regarding the relationship of social security to the economic growth of Japan, there is no disagreement concerning its effective contribution. In the first place, it has had favorable effects on the maintenance and formation of healthy manpower due to advanced medical care. Second, social security has contributed to promoting workers' commitment to their particular enterprises, through its close ties with personnel management within companies. Third,

18. The following English language studies are available on the redistribution of income in Japan: Tomio Higuchi, "Income Redistribution and Social Security: Interpretation of a Japanese Survey," *International Labor Review*, 92, no. 3 (Sept. 1965); and Tadao Ishizaki, "The Income Distribution in Japan," *The Developing Economies*, 5, no. 2 (June 1967): 351–70.

it has played an important role as an instrument for accumulation of capital, particularly in the case of pension insurance schemes but also in the case of insurance schemes for unemployment and workmen's accident compensation.

The funding of pension insurance schemes has indeed been geared to state fiscal policy, through which a huge amount of capital has been invested in constructing the infrastructure, installing productive equipment, and creating new employment opportunities for a number of persons. It is not an exaggeration to state that pension insurance schemes, especially the general schemes, have themselves been converted into institutions for raising funds for economic and social development even though the vast amounts accumulated in the reserved funds have been eroded by increasing monetary depreciation. It must be added that, as the official interest rate for the capital invested from the reserve funds has remained at 5.5 percent a year, despite an average 10 percent annual increase in the general level of wages in the past decade, year after year the accumulated funds have been losing their capacity to finance benefit payments in real terms. This is a tragedy for the Japanese system of pension insurance in the context of rapid economic development. Moreover, the fact that these pension insurance schemes have become an indispensable and integral part of capital formation in state fiscal policy stands in the way of their achieving maturity. This point is the crux of the problem with the Japanese system of pension insurance. The system is operating at cross purposes: one purpose is old-age security, and the other is a fund-raising program for economic and social development. This ambivalent position of the pension insurance system cannot remain feasible for very long in the future.

In the final analysis, it may be stated that the Japanese pattern of social security has served the interests of the employed labor force. In this sense, if the dichotomy of consumption versus production is applied to the economic effects of social security in Japan, priority has apparently been given to the latter, up to the present.

Implications for the Japanese System of Industrial Relations

The trade union movement in Japan, which has been characterized by plural unionism at the national and industrial levels and by enterprise unionism at the plant and company levels, has more than a passing interest in social security, placing the subject next in importance to wage demands. Indeed, as has been mentioned, unions have succeeded occasionally in introducing and improving social security schemes. In particular, when the government has revealed its intention of imposing additional financial burdens on workers, as it has often done in an attempt to overcome financial difficulties in medical insurance, the unions have developed uncompromising resistance.

However, trade union membership in Japan has been as a rule confined to persons currently employed, excluding displaced or retired persons. Naturally, their immediate concern is centered around the defense of the interests of those in established employment, although the national centers have claimed to represent the interests of the working class as a whole. Moreover, the power of the trade union movement is dispersed both vertically and horizontally, and as a result its position in relation to the government and to employers as a whole has always been strategically weak in dealing with the policy issues in the field of social security. Thus, the unions have been obliged to play a passive role in social security policy making. In fact, the "balkanization" of employment markets, together with the compartmentalization of enterprise unions, has resulted in a lack of security for certain groups of underprivileged workers.

In this respect, it should be appreciated that representatives of the trade union movement have been given seats in certain governmental advisory bodies for social security. Together with other similar advisory groups on labor affairs, these bodies constitute an exception rather than the rule in the present political power structure of Japan. For example, the Council on Economic Planning, a central organ in its field whose members are drawn from among university professors and journalists, and from the "tech-nostructure" of big businesses, until 1969 did not include represen-tatives of the union movement except for a few experts recruited for subcommittee work.[19] Meanwhile, the economic plans pub-lished by the council, especially since 1955, have gradually placed emphasis on social aspects of economic development, although they have had little discernible influence on the actual evolution of social security policy because of their indicative planning nature.

It should be added that the union movement in Japan has devoted a lot of energy to the realization of Japan's ratification of ILO Convention No. 87 but has not paid much attention to ILO work in the field of social security such as the convention concern-ing minimum standards (No. 102, 1952). This is in marked con-trast to their attention to the work of the World Federation of Trade Unions and its Social Security Charter of 1961.

When we turn our attention to the administrative aspects of the social security system for workers, we find that administration and operation have been carried out, as a rule, by governmental bodies. Thus, the schemes for employment injury and unemploy-ment insurance have been operated, respectively, by the labor inspection services and PESO under the Ministry of Labor, and the general schemes for health and pension insurance by the Social Insurance Agency of the Ministry of Welfare. The same thing may be said of the administration of mutual aid associations, the social security institutions for public servants and public employees. In these cases the workers' and employers' organizations have been given only an advisory role in administration. Administration by the government itself is one of the features of the social security system for workers in Japan, in spite of the fact that their prototype was Bismarck's workers' insurance in Germany, which was based upon self-government by insured workers and their employers.

On the other hand, as already mentioned several times, em-ployers in large enterprises have been successful in gearing the machinery of social security to personnel management. Thus, the administration of a health insurance society and a welfare pension fund has been under the control of management, as is prescribed

19. See Koji Taira, "Participation by Workers' and Employers' Organizations in Economic Planning in Japan," *International Labor Review*, 94, no. 6 (Dec. 1966).

by the statutory provisions that the president of such a society or fund shall be the person representing the company concerned. Furthermore, in the case of health insurance societies, the post of secretary-general, which carries responsibility for administration, has been filled in most instances by former government officials who had worked in the field of public administration of social insurance. These health insurance societies have formed the National Federation of Health Insurance Societies and have been successful in bringing into their fold the trade union movement as well as employers' organizations. The federation has operated as a pressure group vis-à-vis the Japan Medical Association on issues of medical insurance.

The system of health insurance societies established within large enterprises as well as the mutual aid associations for public servants and employees, coupled with a system of automatic or compulsory retirement of member-employees around 55–57 years of age, has organically excluded the aged population from membership; thus it constituted a profitable insurance group of good risks. Such a practice is adverse to the medical needs of the elderly, who are more liable to incur chronic diseases. For this reason, the Japan Medical Association has been criticizing the system of health insurance societies as contrary to genuine health protection in the context of social security.[20]

It has been pointed out that in a representative Japanese undertaking there are at least three important elements on the basis of which personnel management policy is usually constructed: (1) the policy of lifetime commitment for permanent employees, (2) dominance of the seniority principle in the system of wage calculation, and (3) the use of a temporary work force and subsidiary or subcontract workshops. Thus, the system of establishing a health insurance society within each large enterprise has served to strengthen the lifetime commitment and the seniority wage system in the sense that these societies provide employees and their family members with a high level of medical care in kind and cash benefits as well as with advanced welfare facilities. This system has been made possible by high yields from contributions collected on the

20. Japan Medical Association, *Kokumin iryō nenkan*, 1966 [Yearbook on medical care for people], (Tokyo: Shunju sha, 1966) p. 18.

basis of the high level of average insurable wages and by the possible savings accrued from the pool of good risks within individual enterprises. Furthermore, the system of welfare pension fund will provide improved employee retirement provisions, through which workers may increase their expectations. Moreover, the employer may reduce his financial burden as he is exempted from paying that part of his contributions which corresponds to the income-related component of a pension under the general scheme of pension insurance.

As regards the relationship between a particular scheme established in a single enterprise and the general scheme of social security, as has been outlined above, a document recently published by a research institute established by financial and industrial circles in Japan stated: "The role of a scheme within an undertaking in relation to the general scheme has been evolved from its first stage as a forerunner of the latter, to its second stage as a substitute for the latter pending its full development, and finally to the stage of a supplement to the general scheme."[21] If such a statement is pertinent to the history of the Japanese system of social security, the existing system in large enterprises may be said to constitute the second stage of substitution for a general scheme.

However, it should be recognized that the existence of trade unions within large enterprises has improved the position of "the managed" in the sense that the social benefits and welfare facilities, which had been offered unilaterally by paternalistic employers in the prewar days, have come under the supervision of the trade union concerned or have been given as rights of employees instead of as a mere benevolence on the part of the employer. In any case, the role of the trade unions within enterprises is confined to a narrow range of action—at best, to increase the employer's share in the contributions to be paid by both parties, or to increase supplementary benefits.

As social security measures for employed persons have been tied

21. Nihon Keizai Chōsa Kyōgikai (*Japan Economic Research Council*), *Nihon no shakai hoshō seido no sai kentō* [Review of social security in Japan], Research Paper No. 67-5, mimeograph, 1967. This institute is organized and financed by the financial and industrial circles of Japan as an economic institute for Japanese businesses.

to a large extent to the employer's policy of personnel management, valid security legislation has not succeeded in eliminating the employers' paternalistic tendencies. Through these means large employers are in a position to display their influence over the operation of social security for their employees as well as to increase their political voice in determining state policy measures in these respects.

Under such circumstances, the principle of co-management of a social security institution has not been fully realized in Japan. According to Albert Thomas, the first director of the ILO, the management of insurance institutions constitutes for the working class an unrivaled school of democratic education, but in Japan this kind of education has not yet created in the working class willingness to share the responsibility for running a social security institution, though it has given them the capability of demanding the increase of benefits therefrom. This may be a reflection of the power relationships not only between workers and employers at the company level but also among the three partners in the overall system of industrial relations.

One cannot help but feel that the system of social security for workers has been developed in close relationship with the present system of industrial relations in Japan, the center of gravity of which has been the relationship at the company level between big employers and enterprise unions. Thus, the feature of compartmentalization in social security for workers may be, given the present power structure in Japan, a reflection more or less of compartmentalized industrial relations, which have been, in turn, a reflection of "balkanized" labor markets. One might assume readily that such a feature of compartmentalization of industrial relations and social security must be part of a syndrome of traditionalism in Japanese society. However, it is important, when interpreting such a feature, to take into account the fact that both the industrial relations and social security systems have been constituted at least to some extent by the legal framework legitimatized by the modern parliamentary system. Although organized workers have had the added complication of alienation from the political power structure, nonetheless, they have been enjoying the position of the "ins" in the economic system. The "ins" of the system have counterparts in the system of social security, disregarding the "outs" of both systems. In this sense it is difficult to state that social security has contributed to leveling work and living conditions in the context of the so-called dual structure of the economy.

Japan's recognized industrial development during the past dozen years and more has created profound changes in the labor aspect of the economy, exemplified by the fact that the proportion of paid employment to total employment exceeded 65 percent in 1970, and by the serious shortage of younger manpower. Such changes, coupled with the steady modification of the value system among the Japanese people, have gradually revealed the discrepancy between the present pattern of organizing social security and those requirements which will be adverse to further economic development as well as to social justice in "a welfare state." Symptoms are already discernible in the case of geographical health insurance schemes in the depressed areas.

In its *White Paper on Welfare for 1965*, the Ministry of Welfare pointed out the challenges facing the existing social security system in the decade from 1966 to 1975: a basic reorganization of medical security, maturing of pension schemes, and early introduction of a family allowance scheme. To this we must add still another challenge: meeting the consequences of the need for labor mobility in a changing economy. Employers and organized labor, two central factors in the system of industrial relations, will have to modify their attitudes in order to take "down-to-earth" approaches to these problems and to eliminate the backlog of differences in social protection.[22] Furthermore, a new dimension to this problem emerges as Japan assumes a greater role in aiding developing countries. This aid is likely to include policy suggestions regarding development of national systems of social security as an indispensable part of labor and manpower development.

22. Professor Takezawa points out that "at present a real challenge to business leaders seems to be in the question of what proportion of the national product can safely be invested in social security and other social development without causing economic retardation. Unless such programs are substantially improved, it will be difficult for business leaders to convince critical intellectuals of the superiority of the present system" (Shinichi Takezawa, "Socio-Cultural Aspects of Management in Japan: Historical Development and New Challenges," *International Labor Review*, 94, no. 2 [Aug. 1966]).

13. The Japanese Industrial Relations System: A Summary

The most salient characteristic of Japanese industrial relations is a stratification system based upon essentially nonoccupational criteria. Ranking by ascriptive position rather than occupational criteria related to achievement is deeply rooted in all aspects of Japanese life—in the family, in the community, in society, and in employment relations. Human relationships are defined and evaluated largely on the basis of social status and are in the main devoid of an occupational component. With the head of the family at the top, relationships between husband and wife, between parents and children, and among brothers and sisters have always been framed in terms of superior and subordinate rank, virtually without regard for merit or achievement elements. Indeed, the tradition suggests that vertical, that is, hierarchical, social relations rather than those based upon egalitarian norms represent the ideal.

In community life, the social ranking and status of warrior-farmer-artisan-merchant (*shi-nō-kō-shō*) established in the feudal era have continued to have great influence. In addition, there have been other kinds of rank, such as the old boss-control (*oyabun-kobun*) system, which still prevail in political, social, and even industrial and labor relations, as well as in business. In economic life, human relations centering around authoritarian control by the zaibatsu and monopolistic enterprises and ranking by social position in relationships between seniors and juniors were reinforced. Thus, social life in Japan as a whole can be ideally described as a complicated network of various status relationships largely determined without regard to occupational ability. Under this system based on rank, status, and length of service, industrial relations in prewar Japan acquired unique characteristics and stability.

However, there has always been a large gap between the "ideal" and the real. Industrial relations as a concept was based at first on the relationship of superior-inferior, at least through the Meiji and Taishō eras. In a lecture in an open seminar of the Japan Social Policy Research Association in 1907, the then influential Dr. Soeda stressed that the pattern of industrial relations that ought to obtain in Japan should be based on humane relations between master and servant (*shujū no jōgi*), this "unperishable vestige of the feudal system." Compassion and obedience based on paternalism were considered ideal and constituted the only norm applicable to labor relations in Japan. This was clearly a mode of human relations that rested on the ranking of ruler and ruled and was derived from premises quite contrary to the idea, espoused by Yukichi Fukuzawa in the early Meiji period, that all human beings were created equal. Apparently it was believed that industrial relations in Japan could be stabilized only by ordering human relations according to high and low rank. At the time the Factory Law was being discussed (it was adopted in 1911) the major point of discussion was how to avoid running the risk of upsetting the traditional order of labor control.

There was considerable interest in the question of what industrial relationships should be. Intellectuals in Japan thought that the labor movement then spreading through Europe and the resulting unstable industrial relations could be attributed entirely to the egalitarian ideas that were widely disseminated at that time. The whole of Japanese business society believed in guarding against the enforcement of the new Factory Law and in maintaining traditional human relations. There were two reasons for the strong campaign against the Factory Law within Japanese economic circles. One was the burden of increased labor and equipment costs required by the law. The second reason was the fear that enforcement of the law might bring about the rise of industrial relations based upon egalitarian ideas. In substance, these reasons were an expression of strong hopes for the advocacy of industrial relationships of a unique Japanese type, linked with traditional social relations, and for labor-management stability based on the continued subordination of a traditional servant class. However, the more intense this hope became, the more difficult it was for actual social relations in industry to be placed within the context of the traditional hierarchical rank, especially after the end of World War I.

The Origins of Lifetime Employment

As has been pointed out in Chapter 2, through the Meiji and Taishō eras, at least down to 1918, workers in Japan were highly mobile. The more skilled the worker, the more frequently he moved. Since at that time a worker's only chance to obtain higher wages and promotion to higher rank was to get a new job, whether old or young, skilled or unskilled, he moved if he had an opportunity. In effect, there were actually open, horizontal labor markets according to occupation. To move from one job to another was quite a natural and even respectable way of living, and those who would not move were regarded as unable and below average in skill. A worker was a worker in the Western sense of free labor insofar as he drifted and wandered. Undoubtedly, there were some differences in labor mobility, depending on whether the occupation was a traditional Japanese craft or a skill based on Western technology. However, it is clear that the rate of labor mobility was especially high, particularly among male workers.

Moreover, this mobility was closely associated in many ways with the life of workers. For each occupation, "horizontal" wage rates based on skill and experience existed in labor markets which were wider than an individual factory or enterprise. Older workers did not necessarily receive higher wages as they do under the present wage system. Rather, wage rates were determined by the ranking of an occupation or by the grade of skill within an occupation, without relationship to years of service in the same firm and without a necessary relationship to age. As a worker's years of service increased, he might be promoted, for example, from Class C to Class B in the skill classification of a specific occupation, and, with such a promotion, he might be paid a higher wage rate. But as long as he worked in the same occupation and his job remained in the same skill rank as that of his fellow workers, his wage was also the same as theirs and was not related to his years of service in the same rank. Thus, until the early 1920s, Japan's wage system closely resembled the Western model.

If there were differences in wage rates by enterprise for the same occupation, or if there were dissatisfactions within a skill group, the workers commonly moved. They suffered no disadvantages by moving because they were paid according to their ability or skill, wherever they might go. Mobility not only strengthened their sense of independence and self-respect, but it also resulted in the maintenance of wages at a reasonably high level. Average wages, except for female workers, were much higher than was the case after the mid-1920s. An indication of the prevailing wage level is found in the common expression, still heard, "you can live for a month on fifteen days of work" (*jūgo nichi hataraite hitotsuki kū*). Although wages then were clearly lower than in Western countries, they were high enough to allow a skilled worker to maintain a sizable family.

With mobility encouraging their spirit of independence and pride, workers believed that, wherever they might go, the sun and rice were waiting for them. In a sense, they enjoyed much more freedom than in later times, when the practice of lifelong service centering on new school graduates had developed in large enterprises. From an employer's point of view, the more skilled the worker, the more difficult he was to handle since mobility gave rise to greater independence. Related to the foregoing was the fact that many of the early labor unions were horizontal unions organized either by occupation or by region. The Engineering Workers' Union, or Tekkō Kumiai, and the Typographical Union, or Kappankō Kumiai, of the late 1890s, and the Yūaikai, which was founded in 1912 and later became the Sōdōmei, are good examples.

The system began to be replaced by "lifetime" employment

after World War I, and the latter became fully established through the rapid introduction of new production facilities in the name of "rationalization," centered in the large enterprises after World War I, and during the period of the post-World War I depression. New equipment and production processes were introduced with the objectives of escaping from the postwar recession, recapturing domestic markets, and recovering a share in world markets. Automatic machines, assembly-line mass production, and product standardization were the result. Rationalizing, by cutting costs, lowering prices, strengthening competitive power, and stimulating mass purchasing power, was considered the only way to weather the critical postwar situation.

As production processes in the large firms were divided into simplified jobs through the use of belt conveyors and assembly lines, the all-around skilled workers who had occupied key positions during the Meiji and the early Taishō eras became increasingly unnecessary. In their places trained workers were needed as production operatives. Since workers of this type were entirely different from the old type, large enterprises in Japan rapidly developed personnel policies centered on acquiring and training their own new labor forces. This was carried out with considerable success.

If the old-style skilled craftsmen were doomed for gradual extinction, the pressing need was for young operators trained in one-skill repetitive small operations. Moreover, these operators would require formal education in elementary, higher elementary, or junior high schools, and a record of good conduct. Thus, new school graduates replaced the older and more independent skilled craftsmen who had been characterized by high mobility, relatively high wages, and family responsibilities. The new young workers were employed as unskilled laborers immediately upon graduation rather than at some other time of the year, as jobs opened. Thus, the method of recruitment changed, with industry hiring only new school graduates through the schools at a specified time.

The recruits, upon completing their formal education (in most cases six years of compulsory education), were no longer trained under masters but were hired directly as production workers in the large factories. Factory management assumed the responsibility for their acquisition of skills. Training of operatives for the new equipment actually was beyond the ability of the skilled workers of the master-craftsman type, so each enterprise or factory established its own training facilities for new employees within the organization. Management then selected only those trainees who became proficient in skills, remained in good health, and were taken to have "sound" thoughts. Workers so selected gained the status of "regular" or "permanent" employees.

Since regular employees were trained intentionally as single-skill operatives for a particular type of equipment, that is, with largely nontransferable skills, needless to say they could no longer move from one work place to another at any time they wished. The status of a permanent employee was based on the tacit understanding that the new school graduates, after receiving skill training within a factory, would continue to work as employees at that factory or enterprise for an indefinite period of time. This was the beginning of the present-day system of permanent employment combined with the rule of retirement at the age of fifty-five. In turn, there developed the guarantee of lifetime employment for so-called permanent employees and the seniority wage system with automatic wage increases depending upon length of service which, because of uniform entry upon graduation from school, corresponded to age.

Although the permanent employment system based upon recruitment of new school graduates completely revamped previous employment practices, the guarantee of lifetime employment was achieved in practice only gradually. However, the high turnover previously experienced now ceased as older skilled workers were dismissed. Giving up mobility based upon skills, workers began to demand permanent employment in their work places. This was consistent with the emerging ideal of lifetime employment, especially in large firms. However, even today this ideal has been barely achieved among small and medium-sized enterprises, since the financial obligations involved are often considerably beyond the economic capabilities of such relatively small firms.

Employment security, which is relatively costly, was made economically feasible by the gradual introduction of the so-called seniority wage system. Before 1940, however, the practice of increasing wages in accordance with increasing age and length of service was not firmly established even in the large enterprises. Although in the case of white-collar workers wage increases based upon job rank were becoming the rule (following the practice in paying salaries of public employees), blue-collar workers had no system of periodic wage raises. However, as the permanent employment system began to be fixed, industry introduced a system of periodic wage increases to ensure security for the labor force. Wages began to be paid, not on the basis of job, occupation, or skill level, but according to years of service, an index consistent with the ascription status system characteristic of the society as a whole. Although the desirability of this kind of wage system will not be debated here, clearly it was the beginning of today's so-called seniority wage system.

Retirement allowances also were only gradually introduced for regular employees in the large enterprises. Finally, in order to secure the foundations of lifetime employment, seasonal and year-end bonuses, and various types of welfare facilities such as company housing, recreation, medical care, and educational activities financed by the employer were steadily developed by the large enterprises. These benefits were new, especially for male employees.

Thus, among the basic characteristics of the present industrial relations system, which were carried over from the prewar Taishō-Shōwa period, the so-called seniority wage system provides the economic support for lifetime employment. As mentioned above, the wages of skilled male workers had been relatively high during the Meiji and Taishō eras. Wages had to be high enough to maintain the average worker with an average size family. The high degree of labor mobility at that time made this possible. In contrast, the young recruits trained within the enterprise beginning in the late Taishō and early Shōwa eras were all single males, so that, as had been the case of the temporary migrant women workers during the Meiji and Taishō periods, they were paid barely enough money to maintain themselves as unmarried persons. Since the new workers were, for the most part, young, initially altogether untrained and then subsequently company-trained in skills largely untransferable, unmarried and without dependents, their starting wages were low. The "household" wage previously paid to a committed worker with family responsibilities gave way to a new "single wage," which would increase as the wage earner grew older and was assumed to have acquired new and additional social responsibilities. In addition to the social component of this wage system, periodic increases were given and various fringe benefits provided in order to encourage attachment of these workers to the enterprise and to further discourage turnover. As noted earlier, this wage system took root in the large enterprises. On the contrary, in the case of small and medium-sized enterprises, low wages in combination with poor welfare facilities and fringe benefits often forced workers to rely on home work by wives, children, and the aged, who earned small amounts of money to supplement the wages of the chief breadwinner, thereby making it possible for a whole family to achieve a subsistance level of income. This was the origin of the so-called multi-employee (ta-shūgyō shotai) household.

Since the end of World War II the lifetime employment rule has spread widely not only among large enterprises but also among small and medium-sized enterprises. Further, unlike the prewar period, the rule is now applied both to all sorts of white-collar and office employees and to blue-collar production workers as well.

The single exception is women employees. In the early Meiji era, as was explained in Chapter 2, female workers were girls from poor peasant families who were temporarily employed. After working for two or three years, most of them returned home, married, and never again appeared as factory workers. Their dream was to become the wife of a peasant farmer. As a result, from the beginning they had no interest in a lifetime employment system. It is notable that in the spinning, silk, and textile industries which through the formative period of Japan's industrialization formed the center of the industrial structure, 90 percent of the workers were girls from poor peasant families. Later, in the 1920s when women began to find work in offices of governmental agencies and private companies, their employment was again of very short duration. It was common practice for girls to work for a few years after graduation from elementary or junior high schools until they got married. Even though the average number of years of employment for females has increased considerably since the end of World War II, it still remains quite short compared with the figures in other countries. Consequently, as a rule, lifetime employment is still applicable only to male workers.

The Emergence of Labor Unions

As the nature of the Japanese work force changed in the late Taishō and early Shōwa eras, the large enterprises attempted to prevent young workers from joining labor unions. Immediately after World War I many large enterprises instituted joint labor-management conference systems (then called "factory committees" or "factory councils") as a policy designed to counter the attempts of labor unions to organize their employees. Judged from the results, the unions at that time were unable to "climb over the iron walls" of the large enterprises and get inside. Even though strikes or other disturbances occurred in various places, most were protest demonstrations against labor force reductions or dismissals of the old type of skilled male workers. Young workers newly recruited as permanent or regular workers into lifetime employment were not involved in union organization.

With the introduction of the lifetime employment system after World War I, there emerged a new type of "labor force" based on regular recruitment of new school graduates, training within industry, a permanent employment system, wages based on seniority and length of service, and welfare facilities provided by the big enterprises. As the new system developed among the large firms, workers ceased moving, and horizontal labor markets gradually disappeared except in the sector of small and medium-sized enterprises. As a consequence, horizontal labor unions also disappeared except among the small and medium-sized enterprises, where the lifetime employment system was not introduced because of financial reasons and where a high level of labor mobility still exists. After World War II enterprise labor unions became dominant, accounting for almost 90 percent of total union membership, and their development was conditioned by the lifetime employment and seniority wage system which took root between the two world wars.

In the pre-World War II period, labor unions became estranged from the large enterprises, especially since they did not acquire sufficient bargaining power through the formation of enterprise unions of the postwar type. Rather, most labor unions in the pre-war period were unions of highly mobile workers and accordingly were horizontally organized, centering their activities outside of the big concerns. Their members were primarily strikers, demon-strators, or the "flying columns" of proletarian political parties. An exception was the right-wing of Sōdōmei, which managed to get into large enterprises by adopting moderate and stable union policies aimed at concluding collective agreements, while the left-wing labor unions, confined to the sector of small and medium-sized enterprises, developed rather radical activities in many places under the control of professional union leaders and socialist agita-tors. These unions attracted the multiskilled workers dismissed by large enterprises and now without promising futures and secure statuses. An examination of the chronological development of the union movement in prewar Japan shows that most of the activities recorded are political demonstrations and disturbances led by these left-wing groups, while the labor-management agreements achieved by the right-wing unions, being less newsworthy, are less frequently recorded—a very important point often overlooked in studying the history of Japanese prewar unionism.

As skilled craftsmen were eliminated from the large enterprises, some found employment as labor relations staff people in their enterprises. Some, because of their all-around skills, found jobs in subcontracting factories. Still others became active local leaders or bosses of local labor union groups. The last-mentioned group dropped out of sight after the China-Japan Incident of 1937,[1] but in 1945 they often reemerged, sometimes as elder advisers to the

1. Japanese army units had been stationed in Manchuria since 1931. In July 1937, military extremists, without government knowledge or approval, provoked an incident near Peking. Quickly the Japanese army seized both that city and Tientsin, the other principal North China city. The Japanese civil government meekly supported the war brought on by the militarists. See Edwin O. Reischauer, *Japan Past and Present* (New York: Alfred A. Knopf, 1965).

new postwar labor movement or as Socialist Party members of the Diet.

With the lack of mobility between the large and the small and medium-sized firms, only within the latter sector did workers move from factory to factory. In fact, once a worker began a career in a small factory, he usually had to wander from one small firm to another for all of his working life, thus having a high rate of mobility. Young workers in small and medium-sized factories commonly did not settle down, faced as they were with low wages, few prospects for promotion and retirement benefits, and also no welfare facilities. They were constantly subject to manipulation by left-wing agitators or the militant union leaders, and many withdrew from the labor market, discouraged by the difficulties they faced daily in trying to earn a livelihood.

As shown by membership statistics, the postwar unions advanced by leaps and bounds. The union movement began from scratch in 1945. By 1949 the number of union members exceeded six million, and the number of unions reached 30,000. Several factors in combination explain this phenomenal growth. First, the Occupation adopted as one of its main objectives the protection and encouragement of "democratic" unionism. Under the cover of SCAP's power, the Japanese unions developed within the enterprise framework. This made it possible for the union movement to develop rapidly. Unions were not organized after a long bloody struggle but were formed "from above" as a result of the Occupation policies. Contrary to the prewar period, it was a safe movement for workers, after all.

While it is not clear why Occupation policy, under the control of the United States army, sought to protect and foster unions as an important factor in Japan's democratization, the policy proved highly effective for the growth of "democratic" labor unions in Japan. No doubt, the SCAP policymakers' image of a desirable labor movement at that time was patterned on the American Federation of Labor (AFL) or the Congress of Industrial Organizations (CIO). Certainly, they did not envision the all-inclusive unions organized by individual enterprise that actually did develop. One must conclude that the Occupation failed to understand the type of unionism that could emerge in an industrial relations

system based on a lifetime or permanent employment rule, like
that which prevailed among postwar Japanese enterprises, and an
age- and seniority-based wage system.

Second, following the February 26th Incident of 1936,[2] the
union movement in Japan went into a rapid decline, and when the
Shanghai Incident occurred in July 1937, labor unions were forced
to dissolve. In 1938, a totalitarian labor-management system was
forcibly set up by the military authority and secret police, under
the name of Sangyō Hōkoku Remmei (Alliance for Service to the
State through Industry), and in 1940 this was reorganized into the
Dainippon Sangyō Hōkokukai (Japan Association for Service to
the State through Industry). Various Sanpō, as these organizations came to be called, were established "from above" by factory
and by enterprise, with all employees, including managers, as
members. Thus, labor unions were crushed and no autonomous
unions existed in Japan for the seven years from 1938 to 1945.

During the vacuum of the wartime years, the Sanpō organizations had taken the place of unions. Even though the Sanpō were
in no sense labor unions (i.e., autonomous workers' organizations
for self-help), through these groups white- and blue-collar workers
during the war came to realize the importance of "organization,"
whatever the form. In other words, Sanpō, as a totalitarian movement, had spread throughout Japanese industry, including both
the large and the small and medium-sized enterprises. It is safe to
conclude that the idea of "organization" by enterprise was understood to have meaning for group discipline, apart from the original
purpose of the organization or its ideology. Thus, the rapid organization of enterprise unions soon after the war's end was an important development, as the Sanpō flag was replaced by the flag
of the labor union on the day of the war's end. This is not to say
that postwar enterprise unions are a continuation of the Sanpō.
However, if these totalitarian organizations imposed from above
had not been extended throughout the nation from 1938 to 1945,

2. Before dawn on February 26, a group of young officers from a Tokyo regiment,
leading fully armed enlisted men, went to the homes of several leading statesmen
and killed them. The conspirators had hoped to seize the government but were
persuaded to surrender. Though the revolt's ringleaders were punished, the incident
marked another important step along the road taken by the militarists toward their
goal of domination of the country.

enterprise unions probably would not have been organized as rapidly as they were after the end of the war.[3]

Third, the rampant postwar inflation and distress over the difficulties of living with soaring prices and terrible shortages made it necessary for most workers—including white collar—to organize unions if only to seek to raise their low wages and to reconstruct their idle production facilities. Their urgent sense of crisis in living made it quite rational to unify into a "combined" enterprise union, the objectives of which were to obtain a "living wage" and to reconstruct the production functions of "their" enterprise.

As has been explained in detail in the preceding chapters, since the onset of Japanese reconstruction following the close of the Pacific War, the renascent industrial relations system has been based upon essentially three structural characteristics: lifetime employment, a wage and general reward system based essentially upon the coincidence of age and length of employment, and the organization of workers into unions which, with few exceptions, are structurally coterminous with the enterprise in which the union members are employed. These three factors do not stand independently but are mutually related so as to constitute an integrated system. As we have seen, company level personnel practices, and indeed the economic and social basis for the formation of unions, are rooted in the custom of lifetime employment and an age-grade reward system, including wages. In its turn, the management system is strengthened and reinforced by the enterprise form of union organization and by the lifetime employment and special type of seniority systems.

Thus, in the large enterprises or large factories, enterprisewide unions organize only the permanent employees. Separate and distinctly small unions have been organized among employees in small enterprises and factories. Except for the All-Japan Seamen's

3. A rough parallel was the very rapid transformation of company unions into CIO affiliates in many American plants after the passage of the Wagner Act in 1935. The structures were there, complete with treasuries funded by the company. It was rather easy for organizers of CIO-affiliated unions to "capture" these company organizations and transform them into legitimate and legal unions whose members had already learned something of the strategies of organized and collective action. See Harry A. Millis and Royal E. Montgomery, *Organized Labor* (New York: McGraw-Hill, 1945), especially ch. 15; also, see Milton Derber and Edwin Young, ed., *Labor and the New Deal* (Madison: University of Wisconsin Press, 1957), especially ch. 3.

Union, or Kaiin, there are no cases of workers organized horizontally by industry, and thus no industrial unions in the strict sense of the word. At best, there are loose horizontal federations or joint councils; but fundamentally labor organization is characterized by the enterprise union organized solely by the regular or permanent employees of a particular enterprise or establishment.

The great majority of new employees are, as a rule, new graduates of middle schools, high schools, or colleges and universities. The labor market for new recruits is composed almost entirely of young men and women of the same age groups. Accordingly, age and starting wage have a very close correlation, while wages and salaries continue to be closely correlated with age and length of service to a given employer.

Thus, as we have seen, personnel administration in Japanese firms is geared primarily to supporting these elemental characteristics of the entire system. Though promotion to higher positions comes on the basis of experience and potential, the wage or salary continues to be a function of the basic factors of age, education, and length of service since initial entry. Because it is expected by both the employer and the worker that the worker as a rule will not be separated from the enterprise until he reaches the compulsory retirement age, and because the worker sees his employment as a career with the same employer, mobility tends to be restricted within the enterprise for the permanent or regular employee.

The distinction between regular or permanent workers as high-status key employees and the temporary workers who are initially employed some time after leaving school or midterm entrants who have previously worked for some time for another firm constitutes a status hierarchy and a basis for distributing jobs as well as rewards. The entire system is buttressed by an elaborate structure of intra-enterprise training which is geared to the peculiar and particular skill-mix needs of the separate firms. The more highly specialized the enterprise, the more isolated it is from other enterprises and the less likely that its employees will acquire those technical skills which are readily transferable from one firm to another and thus from one labor market to another. Thus, lifetime employment is neither an employment contract binding or otherwise limiting the freedom of workers nor an employment contract which legally prevents or prohibits the freedom of employers to discharge workers at their discretion.

The Reward System

As was discussed in Chapter 10, rewards in Japanese industry, particularly in the large-scale firms that constitute the most advanced segments of the economy, are distributed mainly on the basis of so-called seniority. This kind of seniority, however, has nothing to do with on-the-job seniority or occupational seniority as it is commonly understood in the United States. Rather, seniority in Japan, as noted earlier, is measured in accordance with total length of service to the firm regardless of the content of the job or occupation. Japanese labor-relations are based on the assumption that the longer one stays with the same enterprise, the higher one's position is likely to be and the more training is likely to be acquired. Wages or salary and other employment benefits reflect this very clearly. Indeed, age, length of service, skill wage, and prestige are all highly correlated and are taken as measures of the relative contribution of each individual to the firm.

Further, the presumption is made that age, wage level, length of service, and status in the organization are all very highly correlated with skill. Thus, one's total life experience in the enterprise is linked closely with the peculiarities of the technical system of that enterprise and is there intimately tied to that worker attribute which the employer most highly appreciates, namely skill. It is expected that there will be a high positive correlation between rate of increase in skill and length of service. While the rate of skill increase for various workers may differ and the rate at which a given worker increases his skill may vary over time, the correlation between skill and length of service will hold from the time of initial entry to the firm until the time of retirement.

Thus, the status order is based upon the idea of each worker having a career and not upon his holding a job or even performing work. Since these careers are expected to be predictable and are protected from the ordinary exigencies of labor market insecurities, the entire status order is the relevant norm which defines the duties and expectations of all parties.

Actually, there is no logical reason for distributing rewards on the basis of age, education, and length of service except to hold young regular employees in the enterprise by offering gradually increasing rewards. If in fact length of service is an accurate measure of the upgrading of skill or a high degree of experience, rewards and particularly wage increases based upon years of service may have some rationality. If it is not such an accurate measure, such an age-grade-based wage system is irrational, old skills and experience becoming obsolete with technological innovation. This issue is currently very much alive in Japan and is seen by many as the source of a fundamental contradiction in the existing system and a clear need for reorganizing a transformation of the whole wage system into an occupationally related structure. However, it is clear that this cannot be done without profoundly upsetting the other basic elements in the system—hiring practices, the employee status system, the enterprise union system, and all of the administrative structures that have been developed in conjunction with and in support of the main structural elements. In substance, the Japanese system of industrial relations, that is, the system by which men are managed in the industrial sector of Japanese society, must be seen as a set of structures, institutions, and practices highly integrated with the norms and the values of the entire society as well as with discrete elements of a subsystem of that society—and as an industrial relations system the elements of which are no less highly integrated.

Of course, high correlations between age, length of service, and earnings and between all of these and presumed skill are not peculiar to Japan. Commonly, employment protected by civil service norms in the United States would probably show a similar high correlation between these variables. Furthermore, while in European countries as a rule, wages are based on the market rate of a particular job as they are in the United States, in both the United States and European countries this market rate also varies in accordance with "skill," which is in turn correlated with age. "Skill" itself is a term that is highly variable in definition and usage such that it permits all sorts of social and other noneconomic elements to enter its determination and application to wages.[4]

In any case, it is clear that the income of the average American wage and salary earner who is head of a spending unit or a household peaks when the earner is in his early forties and falls thereafter. This appears to be true also in other Western countries. Furthermore, the peak-income age rises by education.[5] While the income profile for American male manufacturing workers peaks shortly after forty years of age, in Japan it peaks somewhat later (probably closer to the late forties) and falls thereafter.[6] Thus, though we have no direct comparative studies, there is prima facie grounds for the suspicion that age and skill, through the arrangements of seniority and other devices, tend to be correlated so that Japanese and non-Japanese income profiles over the lifetime of a worker look substantially the same. However, in Japan the noneconomic criteria operate far more explicitly than in Western countries. Distinctively more so than in other countries, in Japan it appears that the portion of the basic wage that corresponds to the market wage rate in other countries is a function of age and length of service and provides the basis for individual status rankings.

The Enterprise Union

Since employment in a specific firm, ideally, constitutes a career, membership in unions, insofar as that membership reflects employee status, is confined to that firm. Thus, as was discussed in Chapter 7, almost without exception unions in Japan are organized by enterprise. Further, since only the "regular" or "permanent" employees will have a career with a given enterprise, the union accepts as members only the regular employees. Though exceptions have been noted, existing enterprise unions are for the

4. See James G. Scoville, *The Job Content of the U.S. Economy,* 1940–1970 (New York: McGraw-Hill, 1969), p. 13.

5. See Harold Lydall, *The Structure of Earnings* (New York: Oxford University Press, 1968), pp. 112–25.

6. See Koji Taira, "The Dynamics of Japanese Wage Differentials, 1881–1959" (Ph. D. diss., Stanford University, 1961), p. 69.

most part independent and autonomous organizations. Higher-level affiliations hardly infringe upon this autonomy and independence.

As independent organizations, enterprise unions include white-collar as well as blue-collar workers and would normally be expected to do so since, as noted earlier, the *kind* of work one does is not the basis for distinguishing between and among workers. To be an employee of a given company is a principal basis of identification by both the worker and others in his community; the Japanese worker "belongs" to a given firm, rather than simply being employed by or in a specific enterprise. Thus, the status of permanent or regular worker coincides exactly with union membership and, ideally, the consciousness of union members is not distinguished from that of the worker's status as employee. Accordingly, the Japanese worker appears to be more sensitive to the prosperity of the enterprise than will typically be the case with his Western counterpart. Where loyalty to the enterprise is likely to be brought into conflict with considerations of union membership or union strategy, as is often the case with union leaders, the leaders will be separated from the enterprise and often become full-time union officials who then play almost no role in the relationship between the union and the firm from which they came.

The wide range of company activities suggests that enterprises are not only economic institutions pursuing profit but are also social security institutions caring for the life of each employee. This, of course, is consistent with the idea that, for the worker, employment in a given firm constitutes a career and promotes a sense of loyalty and belonging. In turn, the enterprise extends its concern for the worker to such areas as health, education, and his personal problems as well as those of his family. Far more than is the case in other advanced industrial countries, these concerns represent the basis of personnel administration and often the issues in negotiations between company and union.

Thus, one would expect that the enterprise-based union also functions as marriage counselor, travel agent, and recreation center. Japanese unions have made themselves ideologically responsible not only for the economic welfare of their members but even for the fate of their members as human beings. The typical enterprise union may be seen as an appendage of the firm to which its members belong. Formal bargaining is sometimes viewed as a ritual which does not really disrupt the mutual understandings and identifications that persist backstage.

The enterprise form of union organization has no exact counterpart in other industrialized countries. It is indeed one of the unique characteristics of Japanese industrial relations. However, very substantial elements of this form are to be found in the American case while practically none are seen in Europe. In 1970 approximately 150,000 separate union-management agreements were in effect in the United States and only 40 percent of the employees covered by contracts were involved in multi-employer negotiations. The great bulk of these are confined to single metropolitan areas. Thus, a majority of American union members work under contracts negotiated by their union with a single employer or for a single plant. In contrast, the great majority of European and Australian union members are covered by general agreements negotiated for large groups of employees on a multi-employer bases.

However, the similarity between American decentralized bargaining structures and Japanese ends with the structure itself. The roots of this form are vastly different in the two countries. While in Japan the development of localized bargaining stems essentially from the absence of social distinctions drawn from occupational differentiation, and from the relative particularisms that characterize Japanese life in general, in the United States the prevalence of plant and company negotiations may be seen as a natural outgrowth of the great size of the country, the highly competitive character of the economy, and the patterns of organization among employers and unions. National negotiations, as commonly found in Europe, are hardly feasible since in both Japan and the United States the upper-level national union and management organizations have much less authority over affiliates than the central union and employer confederations in most other industrial democracies, with the possible exception of Great Britian. Certainly, multi-employer bargaining associations are not unknown in the United States since they are quite common on the local level in big cities and in a few industries such as railroads and coal mining.

But just as there is no evidence that American employers are following the example of their European counterparts and forming national confederations with power to veto any important bargaining concession by a member firm, there is also no evidence that Japanese employers are doing this or are inclined to do so. Similarly, there is no evidence that either Japanese or American employers will follow the lead of employers in other countries, who have formed strong bargaining associations in virtually all major industries. Thus, it appears that in one important respect, collective bargaining structures, the Japanese and European situations are polar, with the American structure closer to the Japanese but not identical to it.[7]

Concluding Observations: A Look Ahead

Our examination of the development and components of contemporary industrial relations in Japan strongly supports the contention that the Japanese system, like those of the advanced industrialized nations of the West, has hardly remained static. Almost from the beginning of Japan's period of modern economic growth, Japanese industrial relations have undergone a series of innovative changes, which are still in the process of unfolding. The argument has been advanced that industrialization in Japan has been accompanied by, and has perhaps depended for its success upon, an immutable set of employer-employee relationships drawn from the Japanese cultural heritage; however, the evidence presented in the preceding chapters leads to the conclusion that Japan's industrial relations system has adjusted considerably to both tradition and change and, indeed, has experienced considerable tension over the reconciliation of these two forces. In this broad sense, Japan's industrial relations system is hardly unique. If, as is often claimed, there is a Japanese uniqueness, it appears to lie primarily in the combination of traditional

7. See Everett M. Kassalow, *Trade Unions and Industrial Relations: An International Comparison* (New York: Random House, 1969); and F. N. Bok and J. T. Dunlop, *Labor and the American Community* (New York: Simon and Schuster, 1970), pp. 208–09.

and modern elements comprising the system at any particular point or period in time rather than in the process of adjusting and changing the combination over time. The key question (see Chapter 1) to be answered is whether the direction of the adjustment and changes will inevitably "converge" upon the outcomes experienced or predicted in the advanced Western societies or will instead tend to remain apart on a distinctive and particularistic course. Our evidence is mixed in this regard, although surely there has been change and adjustment.

In Chapter 2, we began with the notion that social change had characterized Japanese society even before the onset of the modern period a century ago. The breakdown of "traditional" social relationships began even before the end of the Tokugawa era, and new forms and functions have been emerging ever since. This transformation has involved not only competing value systems derived from traditional society but also the superimposition of new values demanded by industrialization, urbanization, labor mobility, foreign influences, and the like. It is little wonder, therefore, that Japan's precipitous rush toward modern industrialism was characterized both by an economic and social "dualism" and by "imbalances" in income distribution and social welfare. The intriguing aspect of the transformation to industrialism is the degree to which the society achieved integration despite the conflicts and tensions that arose in its wake. As Chapter 2 suggests, this achievement at first was perhaps less the result of the imposition of traditional hierarchical controls over the society than of allowing the forces of the free market to structure the newly emerging relationships. Only after almost half a century of this process—by which time the educational level had risen considerably, the zaibatsu had become firmly established, and the government's military and bureaucratic oligarchies had fully formed—were the open market abandoned and compartmentalized and hierarchical social systems institutionalized in modern industry. These developments marked a major social innovation, which seemingly drew its strength from certain of the traditional social relationships but in actuality was first and foremost designed, consciously or unconsciously, to speed Japan on her way to increasing industrialization. It was a new "paternalism," perhaps not so much a continuation of Japan's traditional family system as a means of restructuring the labor force as the traditional family system began to crumble under the onslaught of industrialism. With the rise of militarism after 1931 and its dominance after 1938, even the "new" Japanese industrial paternalism, oriented and centered at the enterprise level, was rapidly giving way to centralized state control, oriented paradoxically to standardization and uniformity in treatment of the industrial work forces.

As discussed in Chapter 3, the reforms initiated by the Allied Occupation attempted to eradicate the elitist control that had characterized presurrender Japan; but the reforms were not so thoroughgoing as to revamp totally the existing social structures. Rather, the decade after 1945 was filled with confusion over competing goals for the nation, inevitably accompanied by conflicts and confrontations. In this context, a safe course was to retreat into the security of the enterprise, so that, once the challenge of radical labor organization was subdued—in part with the aid of the Allied Occupation—there appeared a reemergence of enterprise "paternalism," which again can be interpreted alternatively as still another adaptation to the changed conditions of the immediate postwar period. With the remarkable thrust of Japan's economic growth after 1955, the relationships finally established in the preceding decade of confusion began to be subjected to a whole new set of pressures that became increasingly apparent with the shortages of young workers after 1960. One would suspect that after more than fifteen years of these pressures, marked by the emergence of Spring Labor Offensive-oriented labor unionism, the Japanese industrial relations system must be growing increasingly ripe for still another wave of innovations.

As we have noted, public policy provides an overall framework for the rules and procedures in industrial relations. In tracing through the development of postwar Japan's public policy in these respects, Chapter 4 highlights the "excessive" legalism that has emerged: an enormous spate of legislation, administrative rulings, court orders, and the like, which become channels through which employers and unions attempt to structure their relationships rather than resorting to direct negotiations and collective bargaining. This heavy reliance on law, which originated in the

Meiji Constitution but rapidly accelerated after World War II, itself reflects a major innovation in the reshaping of industrial relations, especially in the tension generated by instituting the concept of contract to replace the tenacious hold of relative social status. In many respects, rights gained through law have been far in advance of actual practice. Despite the general abhorrence of relying upon judges, labor unions find the courts a major bulwark in protecting the rights they gained through the reforms of the Occupation. Employment security, too, has acquired considerable legal protection. In the light of these examples, "excessive" legalism has been signaling the breakdown of established patterns of industrial relations while awaiting the emergence of new forms of direct negotiations and bargaining.

The transformation is also being dramatically displayed in the labor markets themselves. Chapter 5 stresses the rapid erosion of the dual economy since 1955 and the consequent emergence of "wage consciousness" which existed only in a weak state so long as dualism persisted. The large rise in wage and salary employment, the precipitous drop in the agricultural labor force, the shift in labor demand toward heavy industry, the concentration of skilled workers in large firms, the alteration of the occupational structure and skill-mix, the drying up of "excess" labor supplies, and similar factors have been converting Japan into a single national labor market with increasingly uniform wage rates (at least for new school graduates) and an emphasis on worker versatility. These represent vast changes from the era of labor market "balkanization" and of particularistic work forces at the enterprise level whose members were compensated largely on the basis of education and length of service.

Nonetheless, organizational structures and social relationships have responded imperfectly to the long-run changes occurring in the course of Japan's industrialization. As Chapter 6 emphasized, the persistence of "vertical" hierarchies in Japanese enterprise has not been readily dispelled; and, while this "verticalism" should not be labeled "premodern" or necessarily "traditional," it has remained a unique quality affecting the entire system of Japanese industrial relations, unlikely to evolve as a result into a Western-type system.

Although one may argue that hierarchy based on social rankings also characterizes industrial relations in the West and that the difference compared to Japan is only a matter of degree, the "peculiar" emergence of Japanese "verticalism" and its persistence in the face of enormous economic, political, and technological change may be explained by an unusually strong set of historical forces peculiar to Japanese modernization and rooted in Japanese tradition. We have already noted that in the early decades of Japan's modern economic development, "horizontalism" was more typical of the industrializing sector than "verticalism." The latter, supported by political controls and a dual economic structure, represented a social innovation intended to cope effectively with increasing industrialization rather than a throwback to premodern patterns. The resultant structures such as the *nenkō* wage system, the practices of lifetime employment, the paternalistic welfare practices, the early retirement provision, and so forth were envisioned by the elitist leadership as means to a new future rather than to preservation of an old past (however much the rhetoric was phrased in terms of the latter). In this vision of the future based on surplus labor supplies and low wage levels, little room was allowed even for deliberative collective bargaining, let alone radical protest movements. Paradoxically, in the name of achieving equity and egalitarianism, the military seized on "verticalism" through the Sanpō movement to enhance Japan's war efforts.

Once fastened into the system, "verticalism" has proved difficult to eradicate, and it continues to blunt the emergence of class, craft, or occupational consciousness among workers, who see their immediate interests as tied to their places in their respective vertical hierarchies, buttressed by enterprise-based unionism and enterprise corporatism.

The various subject matter foci of Chapters 6 through 12 come to grips with the ebb and flow of tensions over the maintenance of "verticalism" in Japanese industrial relations since World War II. Management organization itself has undergone a professionalizing metamorphosis as the economy has grown and become increasingly dynamic. This has meant decentralization and autonomy in exercising managerial authority, in sharp contrast to the highly centralized structure of prewar zaibatsu management and control. It has meant also attempts to separate professional management interests from govenmental and political control. On the other hand, management has had its own internal conflicts, as for example, the difference in positions between Keizai Dōyūkai and Nikkeiren over basic philosophy, the wisdom of retaining the *nenkō* system, and the role of the enterprise union. With the advent of increasingly sophisticated technology and new concepts of rational organization, managements have become more and more functionally differentiated, thus requiring greater emphasis upon skills, knowledge, and performance rather than on status based on education level, length of service, and age.

Parallel dilemmas are found within the labor movement itself. The seeming divergence of the national centers and enterprise organizations reflects the disparate choices facing union membership as the economy has grown and further industrialized. The Spring Labor Offensive no doubt has been an exceedingly clever device used in the attempt to reconcile the horizontal ideology of the national centers with the vertical orientation of the enterprise unions in order to develop a new industrial unionism capable of combining the political goal of socialism and the economic goal of advancing worker living standards through effective collective bargaining. Again, disputes and splits even more severe than those within management circles rage among labor leaders over strategy and tactics and shades of philosophy. On the one hand, with economic prosperity, enterprise unionism has scored triumphs for its membership. But on the other hand, the triumphs have been achieved at the expense of tensions between younger and older members, white-collar and blue-collar, private industry and public employee unionism. While there are important signs that national unions may eventually predominate over enterprise unions, the situation at the moment remains highly fluid.

Collective bargaining as an institution for industrial rule-making has, within the above context, evolved rather slowly; but it has evolved and enlarged despite its lack of formal existence before 1945. As an "alien" practice, collective bargaining quickly exhibited its conflictual dimensions, and in the earlier postwar years it stood more for union-management confrontation than negotiation, especially as it was confined to the enterprise level. That collective bargaining was a form of engaging in disputes highlighted the tensions inherent in the vertical hierarchies of an enterprise work force subjected to the pressures of shortage of young labor, advancing technology, industrial concentration, and ideological appeals. When denied the alternative of out-and-out strike action, as in the case of public employee unions, it is readily shifted to the political arena. As a device for correcting "exploitation" in labor markets at the hands of monopolistic enterprises, collective bargaining, through the Spring Labor Offensive, has reinforced the standardization of "base-ups" and starting wages for new school graduates. It has yet to affect significantly the base of enterprise unionism: seniority wage payment systems, welfare programs, and so on. Changes in the latter may have to wait for further advances in technology and labor mobility, especially if governmental machinery, such as the autonomous Central Labor Relations Commission and the Public Corporation Labor Relations Commission, move in this direction.

Labor disputes have lessened in intensity since the epoch-making year of 1955, when the Sohyō leadership hit upon a strike formular that successfully launched nationwide wage struggles without destroying the enterprise union base of labor organization. This distinctive approach has been a hallmark of Japanese labor unionism, but its institutionalization may have reached the point where it generates further tension within the labor movement rather than serving as a means of conflict resolution between competing value systems. Certainly, the emergence of the strike weapon, even though its use has settled down into a set pattern, is a marked departure from the ideology of harmony preached by the prewar political and industrial leadership. Legitimation of the strike in Japanese industrial relations is another illustration of a major social innovation.

Less dramatic but probably more pervasive has been the incremental adjustment and transformation of the wage system. Analysis of the history of Japanese wage systems raises the question whether the *nenkō* system was ever anything more than an ideal form, rarely attained in practice. While education and length of service and, later, age have been used as proxies for skill level, this is not the same as saying that the *nenkō* wage system as practiced enshrined the values associated with the verticalism of the traditional family system. Rather, given the absence of occupational labor markets, the *nenkō* system was just as much a device for rationing skills and rewarding "merit." More interesting is the fact that the very structure of the *nenkō* system has been sufficiently flexible and adaptable to take account of a variety of factors other than length of service and level of education. The cultural elements could be used either way: to reinforce a vertical status hierarchy or to break it down in favor of skills and "merit." Since 1945, there have been pressures on the *nenkō* system in both directions. Initially, the radical union movement attempted to utilize the *nenkō* system as a means of achieving equity and enhancing egalitarianism. Subsequently, experiments with job evaluation attempted to stress skill and job content. Thus, the existence of pure *nenkō* systems has long been in doubt, although their conversion to market-determined rates was blocked by the slow development of labor markets throughout large sectors of the economy. The departure from pure *nenkō* systems was encouraged by the shortage of young workers and increased mobility, the development of minimum wage rate systems, and the influence of Shuntō-oriented collective bargaining. While the formalities of the *nenkō* system remain dominant, it is difficult to conclude that these wage systems are invariant and inflexible as labor market and technological factors change.

The flexibility of the *nenkō* system is further demonstrated by the entire system of personnel management at the enterprise and plant level. Again, there have been shifts in the conventional pattern of white-collar staff and blue-collar workers. Individual qualities have received special treatment within the enterprise collective. While the vertical hierarchy may serve as a general framework for advancement in status, job simplification, automation, continuous production processes, subcontracting, and special technical skills whittle away at the maintenance of rewards based on the vertical status hierarchy. True, this "dual" system creates tension, and a major innovation within Japanese management has been the development of specialized personnel staffs for the managing of these very tensions.

Finally, the Japanese industrial relations system has seen a slow and piecemeal development of social security aimed at shifting the burden of achieving one's place within his enterprise to the society at large. While Japan's social security system has been greatly elaborated since 1945, it is still largely oriented to protecting the workers who are the most secure already, and it lacks certain major ingredients, such as effective family allowance and old-age pensions, which are probably necessary to help bring about a more flexible and efficient use of human resources in a rapidly growing and diversifying economy. The framework for such a conversion is there, and, like other problems of institutional change in Japanese industrial relations, it can be utilized if the actors are able to shift their concerns from short-run to long-run considerations.

This brief review of the findings adds up to the notion that the Japanese industrial relations system has long been in a state of tension. Innovations have come at major turning points in economic and industrial development or in shifts in political control. There is little reason not to expect that innovations will continue to emerge (and after fifteen years of exceedingly rapid economic growth, the 1970s could see such changes). At work have been the differentiation of the industrial society under the impact of a dynamic technology, the demands of modern urbanization, the erosion of economic and social dualism, the gradual spread of popular participation in the political process, the clash of ideologies, and changing attitudes toward an open society—to mention the most prominent underlying forces.

None of this is to say that the outcome in terms of the industrial relations system must necessarily approximate more closely the outcomes in Western industrialized (or postindustrialized) societies. No doubt there will be features that resemble the West—as there have been in the past. Others will no doubt remain distinctively Japanese, though not necessarily traditional. In fact, by Western standards, Japanese innovations—by forging new combinations of traditional and modern elements—may present unheard-of advances in industrial relations that will need to be studied carefully by Western and non-Western nations alike.

Unions and Employers' Organizations

English Name	Japanese Name	Japanese Short Form
All-Japan Congress of Industrial Unions	Zen-Nihon Sangyōbetsu Rōdō-kumiai Kaigi	Sanbetsu
All-Japan Day Workers' Union	Zen-Nihon Jiyū Rōdō-kumiai	Zennichijirō
All-Japan Federation of Electric Machine Workers' Unions	Zen-Nihon Denkiki Rōdō-kumiai Rengōkai	Denkirōren
All-Japan Harbor Workers' Union	Zen-Nihon Kōwan Rōdō-kumiai	Zenkōwan
All-Japan Metal Mine Labor Unions	Zen-Nihon Kinzokukōzan Rōdō-kumiai Rengōkai	Zenkō
All-Japan Prefectural and Municipal Workers' Union	Zen-Nihon Jichidantai Rōdō-kumiai	Jichirō
All-Japan Property Insurance Labor Union	Zen-Nihon Songai Hoken Rōdō-kumiai	Zensonpo
All-Japan Seamen's Union	Zen-Nihon Kaiin Kumiai	Kaiin
All-Japan Telecommunication Workers' Union	Zenkoku Denki Tsūshin Rōdō-kumiai	Zendentsū
All-Japan Trade Union Council	Zen-Nihon Rōdō-kumiai Hyōgikai	
All-Monopoly Corporation Workers' Union	Zensenbai Rōdō-kumiai	Zensenbai
Committee for Economic Development	Keizai Dōyukai	
Engineering Workers' Union		Tekkō Kumiai
Federation of Economic Organizations	Nihon Keizai Dantai Rengōkai	Keidanren
Federation of Independent Unions	Chūritsu Rōdō-kumiai Renraku Kaigi	Chūritsu-rōren

General Council of Public Corporation and National Enterprise Workers' Unions	Kōkyō Kigyōtai Rōdō-kumiai Kyōgikai	Kōrōkyō
General Council of Trade Unions of Japan	Nihon Rōdō-kumiai Sōhyōgikai	Sōhyō
General Federation of Private Railway Workers' Unions of Japan	Nihon Shitetsu Rōdō-kumiai Sōrengō	Shitetsurōren
Japan Chamber of Commerce and Industry	Nihon Shōkō Kaigisho	Nissho
Japan Coal Miners' Union	Nihon Tankō Rōdō-kumiai	Tanrō
Japan Electric Power Workers' Union	Nihon Denki Sangyō Rōdō-kumiai	Densan
Japanese Confederation of Labor	Dōmei Zen-Nihon Rōdō-Sōdōmei	Dōmei
Japanese Federation of Chemical Industry Workers' Unions	Kagakusangyō Rōdō-kumiai Dōmei	Kagakudōmei
Japanese Federation of Iron and Steel Workers' Unions	Nihon Tekkōsangyō Rōdō-kumiai Rengōkai	Tekkōrōren
Japanese Federation of Synthetic Chemical Workers' Unions	Gōseikagaku Sangyō Rōdō-kumiai Rengō	Gōkarōren
Japanese Trade Union Congress	Zen-Nihon Rōdō-kumiai Kaigi	Zenrō Kaigi
Japan Federation of Economic Organizations	Nihon Keizai Renmei	
Japan Federation of Employers' Associations	Nihon Keieisha Dantai Renmei	Nikkeiren
Japan Federation of Textile Workers' Unions	Zenkoku Senisangyō Rōdō-kumiai Dōmei	Zensendōmei
Japan General Federation of Trade Unions	Nihon Rōdō-kumiai Sōdō-mei	Sōdōmei
Japan High School Teachers' Union	Nihon Kōtōgakkō Kyō-shokuin Kumiai	Nikkōkyō
Japan Industrial Training Association	Nihon Sangyō Kunren Kyōkai	
Japan Postal Workers' Union	Zenteishin Rōdō-kumiai	Zentei
Japan Teachers' Union	Nihon Kyōshokuin Kumiai	Nikkyōso
Japan Trade Union Council	Nihon Rōdō-kumiai Hyōgikai	
National Automobile Workers' Union	Zen-Jidōsha Sangyō Rōdō-kumiai	Zenji
National Enterprise and Public Corporation Labor Relations Commission	Kōkyō-Kigyōtai-tō Rōdō-iinkai	Kōrōi
National Federation of Industrial Labor Organizations	Zenkoku Sangyōbetsu Rōdō-kumiai Rengo	Shinsanbetsu
National Federation of Industrial Organizations	Zenkoku Sangyō Dantai Renmei	Zensanren

National Federation of Metal Industry Trade Unions	Zenkoku Kinzoku Sangyō Rōdō-kumiai	Zenkindōmei
National Federation of Paper and Pulp Industry Workers' Unions	Zenkoku Kamiparupu Sangyō Rōdō-kumiai Rengōkai	Kamiparōren
National Federation of Printing and Publishing Industry Workers' Unions	Zenkoku Insatsu-shuppan-sangyō Rōdō-kumiai Sōrengōkai	Zeninsōren
National Liaison Council of Labor Unions	Zenkoku Rōdō kumiai Renraku Kyōgikai	Zenrōren
National Railway Locomotive Engineers' Union	Kokutetsu Dōryokusha Rōdō-kumiai	Dōryokusha
National Railway Workers' Union	Kokutetsu Rōdō-kumiai	Kokurō
National Trade Union of Metal and Engineering Workers' Unions	Zenkoku Kinzoku Rōdō-kumiai	Zenkoku Kinzoku
National Union of Coal Mine Workers	Zenkoku Sekitankōgyō Rōdō-kumiai	Zentankō
Typographical Union		Kappanko Kumiai

Contributors

KAZUO OKOCHI

Born in Tokyo, Japan, in 1905. Graduated from the University of Tokyo, Faculty of Economics, in 1929. In 1945 he became a professor in the Faculty of Economics of the same university, lecturing in labor politics, and he served as president of the university from 1963 to 1968, when he retired. He is now a member of the Japan Academy, an emeritus professor of the University of Tokyo, and a councilor for the Japan Institute of Labor. Experience abroad: Visited institutes of industrial relations in America and labor unions in U.S.A. and England in 1954-55. Visited America again in 1960 and inspected employers' associations and arbitration organizations for industrial relations. Exchanged opinions with the leaders of representative American and European labor unions in 1961, Visited universities in West Germany, France, and England in 1966. Attended a seminar on Japanese-German Cultural Exchange at Bochum University, West Germany, in 1969. Publications: *Doitsu shakai seisaku shisōshi* [A History of German Socio-political Philosophy] (1936); *Shakai seisaku no kihon mondai* [The Fundamental Problems of Social policies] (1940); *Smith to List* (1943); *Shakai seisaku* [Social Policies] 2 vols. (1949, 1951); *Reimeiki no Nihon rōdō undō* [The First Stage of the Japanese Labor Movement] (1952); *Sengo Nihon no rōdō undō* [The Labor Movement in Postwar Japan] (1955); *Kurai Tanima no rōdō undō* [The Labor Movement in Taisho and Showa Period] (1970); and *Shakai seisaku 40 nen* [Forty Years of Study on Social Policies] (1970).

MIKIO SUMIYA

Born in Tokyo, Japan, in 1916. Graduated from the University of Tokyo, Faculty of Economics, in 1941, and later received a Ph.D. in economics. Member of the Public Corporation and National Enterprise Labor Relations Commission and chairman of the Commitee for Prices, Incomes, and Productivity (Income Policy Committee) in 1970-71. Experience abroad: Research scholar at the University of California, Berkeley, in 1956; attended the Chicago Conference on Cultural Change in 1960 and ILO Expert Meetings on Technological Change in 1964 and 1965. Publications: *Nihon chinrōdōshiron* [On the History of Wage Labor in Japan] (University of Tokyo Press, 1955); *Social Impact of Industrialization in Japan* (UNESCO, 1964); *Nihon rōdō undō shi* [History of the Japanese Labor Movement] (Yūshindo, 1966); *Nihon sekitan sangyō bunseki* [Historical Analysis of the Japanese Coal-Mining Industry] (Iwanami Shoten, 1968); and *Rōdō keizai ron* [Labor Economics] (Chikuma Shobō, 1969).

TAKESHI TAKAHASHI

Born in Tokyo, Japan, in 1915. Graduated from Tokyo College of Foreign Languages (Russian) in 1937 and received a Ph. D. in law in 1961 from Kyūshū University, Fukuoka. Now associated with the Tokyo office of an international institution, and a member of the Japanese Society of Labor Laws, and the Society of Social Policy, Japan. Experience abroad: Spent six months in Geneva in 1969 preparing a paper on certain aspects of industrial relations in Japan. Publications: *Kokusai shakai hoshō no kenkyū* [A Study of International Social Security Law] (Shiseido, 1968); *Shū itsukasei no jidai* [The Age of the Five-Day Work Week] (Nihon Keiei Shuppan Kai 1968); and *Furansu no shakai hoshō* [Social Security in France] (Ichirū Sha, 1955).

MASUMI TSUDA

Born, 1926; A.B. 1952, Faculty of Economics, University of Tokyo; Ph. D. 1962, University of Tokyo. Professor of Industrial Relations, Faculty of Sociology, Hitotsubashi University, since 1970. Member of the Minimum Wages Council and subcommittee chairman of the Industrial Homework Council, of the Tokyo Metropolitan Office of the Department of Labor; member of Board of Directors, Japan Academic Society of Social Policies. Publications: *Rōdō Mondai to Rōmu Kanri* [Labor Problems and Personnel Management] (Minerva Shobō, 1959); *Amerika Rōdō Kumiai no Kōzō* [The Structure of Labor Unions in the United States] (Nihon Hyōron Sha, 1967); *Nenko-teki Roshi Kankei* [The Seniority-based Industrial Relations Systems in Japan] (Minerva Shobo, 1968); *Rōshi Kankei no Kokusai Hikaku* [International Comparison of Industrial Relations in Thirty-five Countries] (The Japan Institute of Labor, 1969); *Amerika Rōdō Undōshi* [History of Labor Unions in the United States] (Sōgō Rōdō Kenkyūjo, 1972); "Japanese Wage Structure and Its Significance for International Comparisons," *British Journal of Industrial Relations*, London School of Economics, Vol. III (1965).

SEIJIRO UJIHARA

Born in Aichi Prefecture, Japan, in 1920. Graduated from the University of Tokyo, Faculty of Economics, in 1943. Presently professor in the Institute of Social Science, University of Tokyo, a member of the Advisory Council for the Public Service Personnel System, and a member of the Labor Standards Law Study Society. Experience abroad: Research scholar in England on a grant from the Japanese Ministry of Education, March 1971 to March 1972. Publications: *Nihon no roshi kankei* [Industrial Relations in Japan] (University of Tokyo Press, 1961); *Nihon rōdō mondai kenkyū* [A Study of Japanese Labor Problems] (University of Tokyo Press, 1966); *Sengo Nihon no rōdō chōsa* [A Labor Report on Postwar Japan] (Contributor; University of Tokyo Press, 1970); and *Nihon rōdō shijō bunseki* [An Analysis of the Japanese Labor Market] (University of Tokyo Press, 1971).

TORU ARIIZUMI

Born in Yamanashi Prefecture, Japan, in 1906. Graduated from the University of Tokyo, Faculty of Law, in 1932, and received a Ph.D. in law in 1960. Presently a professor at Sophia University and a professor emeritus of the University of Tokyo. Served as a member of the Central Labor Standards Council and is now a member of the Advisory Council for the Public Service Personnel System, a member of the Labor Standards Law Study Society, and chairman of the Social Insurance Council. Publications: *Rōdō sogiken no kenkyū* [A Study of Labor Dispute Rights] (Ochanomizu Shobo, 1957); and *Rōdō kijun ho* [The Labor Standards Law] (Ūhikaku, 1963).

WAKAO FUJITA

Born in Hokkaido, Japan, in 1912. Graduated from the University of Tokyo, Faculty of Law, in 1937. Presently a professor of labor law at the Institutute of Social Science, University of Tokyo. Publications: *Daini kumiai* [The Second Labor Union] (Nihon Hyōron Sha, 1955); *Nihon rōdō kyōyaku ron* [Collective Labor Agreements in Japan] (University of Tokyo Press, 1961); and *Rōdō kumiai undō no tenkan* [The Conversion of the Japanese Labor Movement] (Nihon Hyōron Sha, 1968).

NAOMICHI FUNAHASHI

Born in Yamagata City, Japan, in 1925. Graduated from the University of Tokyo, Faculty of Law, in 1947. Professor of law at Hosei University since 1959 and presently dean of the Law Department and chairman of the Ohara Institute for Social Research. He is also a member of the Central Minimum Wages Council, the Wages Council for Work Relief Projects, the Employment Deliberation Council, and the Special Committee for Labor Affairs, Economics Council. Publications: *Chingin no keizai gaku* [The Economics of Wages] (Hōsei University Press, 1950); *Nihon no chingin keitai* [The Japanese Wage System] (Ōtsuki Shoten, 1955); *Rōdō shijō to chingin keitai* [The Labor Market and Wage System] (Hōsei University Press, 1957); *Chingin riron kenkyū* [A Study of Wage Theory] (Jichōsha, 1958); *Shin chingin nyūmon* [A New Introduction to Wages] (Nihon Hyōron Sha, 1964); and *Tenkanki no chingin mondai* [Wage Problems at a Turning Point] (Nihon Hyōron Sha, 1971).

BERNARD KARSH

Born in 1921. M.A. in Sociology and Ph.D. in Sociology, University of Chicago. Member of the faculty of the University of Chicago from 1950 to 1952. Professor and head of the Department of Sociology, University of Illinois. Professor of sociology, Institute of Labor and Industrial Relations and coordinator of research, Center for Asian Studies, University of Illinois. Experience abroad: More than a dozen trips to Japan; has been affiliated with Keiō University and with the Japan Institute of Labor as a visiting scholar. Publications: Author and co-author of four books and more than forty articles on industrial relations and industrial sociology.

HISASHI KAWADA

Born in Ibaragi Prefecture, Japan, in 1905. Studied at Keiō University. M.A. in economics from the University of Pennsylvania in 1932. Professor at Keiō University from 1951 to 1971 and presently a lecturer at the University of Chiba. Publications: *Amerika rōdō undōshi* [A history of the American Labor Movement] (1955); "Industrialization and Educational Investment in the Meiji Era," in *Educational Investment in the Pacific Area* (1963); "Government Industrial Relations and Economic Development," in A. Ross, ed., *Industrial Relations and Economic Development* (1966); "Japan's International Technical Cooperation," *Keiō Economic Review* (1970); *Ajiajinteki shigenkaihatsu: Gijutsu kyōryoku to rōdōryoku kaihatsu* [Human Resource Development in Asia: Technical Cooperation and Manpower Development] (1969); *Ajia no rōdō jijō: Rōdōryoku kaihatsu to gijutsu kyōryoku* [The Condition of Asian Labor: Labor Force Development and Technical Cooperation in Japan] (1971); "Japan's International Technical Cooperation," *Keiō Economic Review* (1970).

SOLOMON B. LEVINE

Born in 1920 in Boston, Massachusetts. B.A. and M.A. from Harvard University in 1942 and 1943, respectively. Ph. D. from The Massachusetts Institute of Technology in 1951. Professor of economics and business at The University of Wisconsin,

Madison; chairman of The East Studies Program and faculty member of The Industrial Relations Reseach Institute, University of Wisconsin, Madison. Member of the faculty of The University of Illinois from 1949 to 1969. Experience abroad: A frequent visitor to Japan, served as visiting professor and research scholar at Keiō University, Hitotsubashi University, Tokyo University, and The Japan Institute of Labor. Publications: Include various books and articles in the labor and industrial relations field; *Industrial Relations in Postwar Japan* (University of Illinois Press, 1958); contributions to a number of professional journals and volumes on Japanese labor conditions.

HIDEAKI OKAMOTO

Born in Hiroshima Prefecture, Japan, in 1931. Graduated from Kyōto University, Faculty of Letters (Philosophy), in 1954. Presently professor in the Department of Business Administration, Hōsei University, and a research officer for the Japan Institute of Labor. Experience abroad: Studied at the University of Illinois on a Fulbright fellowship, 1954-56; visiting professor at the University of London in 1968. Publications: *Howaito karā* [White Collar: Modern Workers] (Kawade Shobō, 1964); *Kogyōka to genbakantoku sha* [Industrialization and the Field Overseer] (The Japan Labor Institute, 1965); and *Sangyō shakai gaku* [Industrial Sociology] (editor; Kawashima Shoten, 1968).

INDEX